A
History of the
Old Parish

of

HAWARDEN

T. W. Pritchard

First published in Wales in 2002
by
BRIDGE BOOKS
61 Park Avenue
Wrexham
LL12 7AW

A CIP entry for this book is available from the British Library

ISBN 1-872424-60-0

Typeset and printed by
Bridge Books, Wrexham

Cover illustrations
Front, clockwise from top left: The Broughton Wellington, Queensferry Munitions Workers, *Vanity Fair* cartoon of W. E. Gladstone, the main office block at John Summers & Sons, S.S. *Radstock*, Hawarden Castle, Lady Emma Hamilton, chain-making at Saltney, St Deiniol, Hawarden Bridge, Seal of the Peculiar Court of Hawarden.

Back cover: Poster advertising a voyage of the Royal Charter (Museums & Galleries on Merseyside)
Map of the Parish of Hawarden, taken from John Evans' Map of North Wales, 1795

Contents

Acknowledgments

My desire to write a history of the old parish of Hawarden is based mainly upon the curiosity I have always had to understand the background and landscape of the place where I live and in this case the place of my origin. I was baptised in Hawarden Parish Church but lived in Chester until the age of seventeen years and then came to Shotton until I was ordained. My father was born in Queensferry and my mother at Aston Bank whilst I spent my schooldays visiting an aunt in Mancot Royal. Having retired to live in Hawarden in 1998 and gradually becoming acquainted with the source material I decided to attempt to write a popular history of the old parish. This is the result and I apologise for the many subjects that have been omitted.

The debt I owe to people is enormous. I must have exhausted the patience of the staff of the Flintshire Record Office, Hawarden, with my endless applications for manuscripts. The generosity with which they made it possible to reproduce so many illustrations and allow them to be accessed is very apparent in the text. My gratitude and praise for their help is unbounded. Wherever possible, I have acknowledged in the text the use of all illustrations and my dependence on other local historians in the footnotes. This is my first attempt at using a PC and I must express my gratitude to Anthony Furse for encouraging me together with Bill Crease and his staff at Celtic Computers who guided my infant steps and Dave and Sylvia Roberts who supported me throughout. I am grateful to the Warden of St. Deiniol's Library, Hawarden, the Reverend Peter Francis, and his staff for their kindness. Geoffrey Veysey read the proof and answered my queries with his usual patience and expertise. Lord Jones of Deeside kindly read through the chapters on Shotton and Queensferry. Any errors remaining in the text are my own responsibility. Sir William Gladstone, Bart., K.G., has given me every encouragement and support. Alister Williams of Bridge Books has supported me with the benefit of his professionalism and his kindness as a friend.

T. W. Pritchard

Foreword

Anyone who picks up this splendid volume will at once realise how fortunate we are in Hawarden to have amongst us an historian of the skill, experience and industry of Archdeacon Bill Pritchard. He has unravelled and interpreted a huge variety of documents, and the story he reveals is full of interest.

Hawarden became a place of Christian worship many years, probably indeed centuries, before the Norman Conquest. That conquest brought in its wake the first authentic written facts, and Hawarden has been a place of more than local importance in the thousand years since then. First its church; then its castle; then its expanding agriculture; and later its mining and its industry, have made their mark. It has clay and coal in its mountain; iron and steel works; shipbuilding and maritime trade along its coast. Its ancient strategic position on the border of England and Wales, and on the main route to Conwy and thus to Ireland, has turned it into a crossroads between north and south, east and west.

This is the first general history of the area represented by the old parish of Hawarden. Richard Willett wrote a fine description 180 years ago, but like the remarkable William Bell Jones he was more an 'antiquary' than an historian. Besides, the Church to these authors was the Anglican Church, whereas the present work covers all denominations. There have been some distinguished specialised studies since those days, but Bill Pritchard has woven the whole tapestry; he has told the whole story, and has brought it vividly to life. He has however decided, in my opinion correctly, to omit Buckley, the most distinguished offspring of the old parish, because its history has already been recorded by talented writers beginning with Thomas Cropper's notable volume of 1923.

The art of the historian is to interpret: to create an edifice from a heap of jumbled stones; but Bill Pritchard has also shown us some of those individual stones, for he has enriched his book not only with drawings and photographs, but also with a selection of original documents, so that we can see exactly how the events he describes were recorded in their own times.

Sir William Gladstone, Bart., K.G.

1. Beginnings

Writing a local history may be compared to tackling a huge jigsaw puzzle. All the pieces are in a heap and we are faced with the task of completing the picture on the box. The picture is in a frame, which we vaguely call history. Local history is the picture we have of our own locality. It is our imaginary minds eye view of the past. Out of the heap of pieces we would expect to pick out prehistoric hunters, Roman soldiers trudging across the landscape, Welsh warriors fighting furiously with English knights, contented peasants tilling their fields, early colliers scratching coal from the surface, and fishermen in frail craft casting their nets for salmon: all these manual activities were the way life was lived until the modern age of machinery when tractors replaced horses, steam replaced sail, the petrol engine replaced the horse and carriage, and out of the sky appeared the aeroplane. Not only do people change, but the landscape also. Ancient forests have long disappeared to be replaced by open fields and built over by successive generations of houses. Ancient castles are despoiled and huge factories and industrial estates become the modern symbols of power.

The pieces of the jigsaw heaped together in a pile are what the local historian calls his sources; these are the pieces he must arrange to complete an accurate picture of his locality. It is generally the more detailed pieces representing recent events, which are completed first. Local people might recall these, or there will probably be a record of them available in the local archive. Photographs, newspaper accounts, buildings and artifax are available to give him an understanding of the last two hundred years or so. It is those pieces in the jigsaw picture which are more vague, the sea or the sky, that stretch as far as the horizon of our understanding, which are more difficult to fit together. For the local historian the vast expanse of 'sea and sky' is usually the fifteen hundred years dating from the birth of Jesus to the Union of England and Wales in 1536 (to choose an arbitrary point in time), which is the most difficult to understand and write about. In completing a jigsaw some familiarity with the subject is also necessary. The local historian needs to know as much as possible about each piece in the jigsaw in order to complete the overall picture. He must be prepared to accept that because of the scarcity of evidence some of the picture may be only viewed from a distance and drawn with the limitations imposed by the perspective of time.

In most cases someone else has attempted the task before and written about their locality. This is the case for the parish of Hawarden. In the nineteenth century Richard Willett, the village schoolmaster, in retirement, wrote an excellent history entitled *A memoir of Hawarden Parish, Flintshire, containing short introductory notices of the Princes of North Wales; so far as to Connect and Elucidate, Distant and Obscure Events*. In the twentieth century William Bell Jones, the postmaster of Hawarden, who filled many parochial offices — parish clerk, churchwarden, parish councillor — wrote an excellent history of the parish. Bell Jones made great use of the rich collection of parish records, printed national records, and the publications of many historical societies to write a detailed history of the parish and lordship of Hawarden. He limited his task to an account of the manor, lordship, and castles of Hawarden and Ewloe, the churches in the parish, and the life

Richard Willett, 1761–1829
[FRO PH PR/C/45]

9

William Bell Jones, 1868–1958
[FHS Vol.18]

of the parish as seen through the churchwardens and vestry accounts and minutes, and the records of the Rector's Peculiar Court which had the right to 'present people' who were in breach of church law.

This history attempts to tell the story of the parish of Hawarden more fully than Richard Willett , and in a simpler manner than Bell Jones. It is not meant to decry their efforts but to build on them. The story is continued until about the year 1950 through newspaper accounts, chiefly those of The *Chester Chronicle* and *The County Herald*, beginning about 1820. An attempt is made to illustrate the narrative with pictures and maps. The scope of the history is wider and covers the old parish and manor of Hawarden with the exception of modern Buckley, whose historians I rightly stand in awe of!

The history attempts to answer basic questions as fully as possible. I apologise in advance if I have failed to do this.

What area does this parish history cover? I have given the answer above as that of the old parish of Hawarden with the exception of modern Buckley. The parish has long been divided into townships, which eventually reached the number of sixteen. They are: Aston, Bannel, Bretton, Broadlane, Broughton, Hawarden, Mancot, Manor, Moor, Pentrobin, Saltney, Sealand, Shotton, Rake, Ewloe Town and Ewloe Wood.

When did people come to live in this area? This is difficult to answer, but there is no evidence of prehistoric or Roman settlement. The Romans did pass through Hawarden along the roads they made and there was probably a Roman settlement for fishermen and farmers on the border at Saltney. The first people to live in the area were the Welsh who practised their traditional farming in cleared areas of the extensive forest that covered the whole parish. A Celtic missionary saint Deiniol brought Christianity to Hawarden in the middle of the sixth century. The major influence on the parish was the immigration and colonization of settlers from the seventh century onwards.

Where did they come from? The area of the old parish of Hawarden lay eastwards behind the frontier lines of Wat's Dyke and Offa's Dyke that were built to contain the Welsh and prevent them occupying Chester. Anglo-Saxon peoples from Northumbria, Mercia, and especially Cheshire, moved in to displace the Welsh from the seventh century onwards. Their influence was considerable. A wooden castle was probably built at Hawarden and 'tun' settlements established by Mercian colonisers at Aston, Shotton, Bretton and Broughton. After the Norman Conquest towards the end of the eleventh century, a permanent manor and castle were established at Hawarden. From the eleventh to the end of the thirteenth century there was continuous warfare between the Welsh and the English across this borderland area. Some Welshmen settled in the western townships of Ewloe where Llywelyn ap Gruffydd built a castle in 1257. After the conquest of Wales in 1282 Ewloe became a manor under the control of the crown. The de Montalt family held the lordship of Hawarden as hereditary stewards of the Earl of Chester until they died out in 1329, when it passed to the crown until it was given to the Stanleys in the middle of the fifteenth century. This encouraged more English to move into the area and led to the expansion of the townships of Broadlane, Rake and Manor. Ewloe and Mancot townships attracted coal miners, whilst the upland plateau of Bannel and Pentrobin were the abode of Welsh cattle grazers.

What changes have taken place? There have been major changes in agricultural practices mainly as a result of the decay of communal farming, the emergence of private ownership and the enclosure of land particularly in the eighteenth century. Perhaps the greatest change came in the eighteenth century, when the river Dee was canalised by the 'New Cut' in 1737, and as a result thousands of acres of land were brought under cultivation in the township of Sealand. In 1781 a new township, Saltney, came into being as a result of the drainage and enclosure of common land. The major benefactor of the availability of this new land was the Glynne family, Lords of the Manor of Hawarden. As a result, new methods of farming were introduced throughout the parish, and mineral resources exploited by the improvement in the techniques of coal mining, brick making, and the development of other industries such as iron founding and shipbuilding. The reclaimed land has been used for the location of new industries, factories and airfields. Engineering skills have created bridges to carry new roads and railways across the parish, making it an important gateway into Wales.

What is the major theme of the history of Hawarden? The major theme of this story of Hawarden parish is the settlements that have been established over the centuries and the way in which they have provided for the religious, educational and social aspirations of the local population, who for centuries have laboured here to make a living, transforming both their own lives and the landscape which was part of the jigsaw of their being.

Settlers in Hawarden over the ages

When the place-name Hawarden is used in the text, it will refer to the whole parish not the township or village of that name, unless specifically mentioned. It will generally embrace the whole of the sixteen townships listed above. In 1839 it was estimated that the whole parish of Hawarden (including modern Buckley), contained 16,444 acres of land of which 9,009 acres were cultivated as arable land, 4,504 as meadow or pasture, and 600 acres of woodland. The remaining 2,331 acres were made-up land taken by roads, railways, pathways, streets, lanes, watercourses, industrial sites, coal mines, quarries, public and private buildings. These two thousand odd acres represent the land used by the community for communications, housing, and industrial activity over as many years. Most of the 16,000 acres would have been deep forest when the Romans came to Chester in about 70 A.D.

The Romans

Although the Romans did not settle in Hawarden they left their presence here by following the ancient route ways and establishing new ones. The legionary fortress at Chester (Deva) was built to control the auxiliary forts of Wales and the Pennines. The later boundary of Hawarden on the northeast was contingent with that of England and Wales at Saltney. Here, well outside the city walls, there were a couple of farming settlements and a small group of fishermen. The routes from Chester into Wales probably left the fortress from Handbridge, and

The position of Hawarden, from John Evans' Map of North Wales, 1795. Wat's Dyke can be seen bottom left-hand corner

in order to avoid the marshes of the Dee estuary, shared a common course for the first few miles along Lache Lane to Balderton. Here the road divided, one route continuing in a south-westerly direction through Ffrith and Corwen to the auxiliary fort at Caer Gai at the end of Lake Bala, and the other route turning west to Hawarden, through Broughton (where remains of the road have been discovered), on to Northop Hall, Northop, Halkyn and Pentre Halkyn to Holywell, following the higher ground. At Bretton, just east of Broughton, began the long straight road which followed the south-western shore of the estuary through Flint to St Asaph (?Varae), Caerhun (Kanovium), and on to Caernarfon (Segontium).

The Anglo Saxons

The small groups of Welsh tribesmen living in dispersed and semi-dispersed settlements and following their traditional farming methods, were disturbed and sometimes supplanted by the series of immigrations and conquests by the English which took place from the seventh century onwards. The Welsh tribesmen were members of the Deceangli who lived along the North Wales coastal area. There were two main frontier lines, which defined the inroads of the Saxon invaders. The first of these was Wat's Dyke; a linear earthwork that was made in the fifth century by the post-Roman kingdom of northern Cornovii to demarcate a political frontier between themselves and other Welsh tribes, the Deceangli and Silures further west. They were anxious to protect the western approaches along the Dee estuary to the Roman city of Deva and their territory eastwards (modern Shropshire), which included Wroxeter. The second frontier was made in the second half of the eighth century by the Mercian King Offa (757–96). It was a more substantial earthwork, which formed both a defensive line and a cultural frontier between the Welsh and the English. It ran from Treuddyn near Mold to Sedbury cliffs on the Severn estuary. The eighth century saw conflict between the Welsh Kingdom of Powys, which stretched as far north as Ystrad Alun near Mold, and the Kingdom of Mercia. In 924 Edward the elder suppressed the Welsh revolt. Fifty years later there was a long period of English domination, which was demonstrated by the submission of the British princes to King Edgar at Chester in 973, when the rulers of Gwynedd, Strathclyde, Scotland, Man and the Isles rowed him on the Dee. English Kings continued to dominate the area until the reign of Ethelred II (978–1016). The Welsh hit back and achieved success under Gruffydd ap Llywelyn until his downfall and murder by his own men in 1063. There was a brief interlude before William the Conqueror at the end of his campaign built a castle at Chester and installed Hugh of Avranches to defend the frontier in North Wales and consolidate the area, long ago colonised by the Mercians.

There are two things that demonstrate the extent of the English influence on Hawarden and its position as an English settlement on the border of the Welsh Kingdom of Gwynedd. These are the meaning of the place names for Hawarden and its entry in Domesday Book in 1086.

Place Names[1]

Hawarden/Penarlag. The English form of the name appears in the Domesday Book of 1086 as Haordine — heah + wording, 'high enclosure'. The Welsh name is earlier, *pennard + alafog*, which means, 'high ground' 'rich in cattle'. Owen proposes the following explanation.

Pennardlaawc was the name of a wide area which took its name from its caput on the eminence (pennard), a settlement which included a church and a fortification. The Mercian immigration and occupation gave the settlement itself a new name Haordine after the enclosure, which the Mercians captured or built. However the predominantly Welsh communities west and south of the town continued to use Pennardlaawc of lands and woods further west (*Koet pennardlaoc*) and they continued to call the town Pennardlaawc (*kastell penardlaoc*).[2]

The inference is that when the Mercians came there was a church in a protective enclosure near the castle and the English settlers used their translation of the Welsh place-name.

Aston. east + tun 'the eastern farm or estate.' The estate may refer to Llys Edwin in Northop. 'Tun' is old English for enclosure, farmstead, estate, village. In Domesday Book Aston appears as Estone.

Bannel. Welsh banadl, broom. Originally it was possibly the name of a farm.

Bretton. Probably Old Norse, Bretar, 'the Britons, the Welsh' + tun 'farm, estate.' In Domesday Book it appears as Edritone. Owen comments:

> The inference is that the inhabitants of Bretton were Welshmen or Britons who came with the Vikings. They could have been pressed into the Norwegian forces during some early sortie elsewhere. Perhaps they were

The townships of the Lordship of Hawarden and the Manor of Ewloe [based upon Hywel Owen The Place Names of East Flintshire] The township of Higher Kinnerton was part of the Lordship of Hawarden but not the Parish of Hawarden. The Township of Rake has been added

associated with the Irish Norwegian attack on Chester in 902 which failed but the 'Norsemen remained and settled in the district.[3]

Broadlane. The name first appears in 1532, brad + lane, 'broad lane', later it became the name of the township on either side of the lane, which included mostly the Hawarden Demesne Parks.[4]

Broughton. broc 'brook' + tun. 'brook farm'. The brook is the Broughton Brook, which forms the northwest boundary of the township. In Domesday Book, Brochetune.[5]

Mancot. An old English personal name, Mana + cot 'cottage, humble dwelling; shelter,' it usually referred to 'small insignificant places in areas of secondary settlement.' Lying scarcely a mile north of Hawarden the cot could have been for the storage of materials, a shelter for animals, a hut for herdsmen or simply a cottage.' It is first mentioned in 1284.[6]

Manor. The manor of the Hawarden Demesne. First mentioned in 1563.

Rake. A township in its own right at various periods, later incorporated into Manor, also associated with Broadlane. Rake means a 'path up a hill'. 'It forms the third path from the Saltney Marsh to Hawarden and the Chester–Ewloe road and corresponds to Rake Lane. There was another rake or path from Bretton which may have crossed Broughton and Moor to get to Saltney Marsh, and gave its name to the township of Rake. First mentioned in 1552.[7]

Moor. The low-lying area northeast of Hawarden. First mentioned *c*.1324. There was a house of some substance, which is mentioned in so many documents. In this township is Newtown, first mentioned in 1651. It is 'new' in contrast to the old Hawarden town and was built on land reclaimed with the improved drainage of

Saltney Marsh (before 1737), but for what purpose is not quite clear.[8]

Pentrobin. Welsh *pentre* 'village, hamlet' + personal name Hobyn (Robin). First mentioned in 1532.[9]

Saltney. Created a township at the time of its enclosure in 1781.

Sealand. This is reclaimed land north of the canalised channel of the river Dee which was completed in 1737. The name first occurs in 1726.

Shotton. Sceot 'a steep slope' + tun, 'farm on a steep slope'. The original Shotton was located where the present Higher Shotton is. It is first mentioned 1283–5.[10]

Ewloe Town. Together with Ewloe Wood part of the Lordship of Ewloe. Ewloe town is bounded on the east by Hawarden, on the west by Ewloe Wood, on the north by Aston and Shotton and on the southeast by Pentrobin.

Ewloe Wood. *Aewell* 'stream, source of stream' + *hlaw* 'mound, hill.' 'Just below Ewloe Castle (to the north), is the confluence of the Alltami Brook and the New Inn Brook (to form the Wepre Brook). In this township is Ewloe Castle built by Llywelyn ap Gruffydd in 1257.' In 1157 Henry II was ambushed here in 'koet pennardlaoc', 'the wood of Penarlag'. This township had a strong Welsh influence and the Manor of Ewloe belonged to Tegeingl under the Princes of Gwynedd.[11]

Domesday Book, 1086

You may have noticed that in the survey of townships given above the earliest four are mentioned in Domesday Book. William the Conqueror, meeting with his Council at Gloucester, in 1085, commanded a survey of all his lands in England. This was done on a county basis and the parish of Hawarden was included in the Cheshire returns in the hundred of Atiscros, which extended along the North Wales coast as far as Rhuddlan. These returns are the first records we have for the parish of Hawarden. The Domesday commissioners were given terms of reference for the information they were to gather. They were interested in the manor as the important unit of territorial administration. They wanted to know who held the manor in the reign of Edward the Confessor, the King who had promised the throne of England to William the Conqueror. Their enquiry centred around large estates; they were interested in arable land and ignored livestock, and asked for details on the number of acres ploughed, the number of plough-teams, what tax was paid, of whom the land was held, the number of workers bondmen or free, was there a church, what was the amount of woodland and other enquiries.

These are the returns which relate to the parish of Hawarden all of them in the Atiscros hundred.

> EARL HUGH holds HAORDINE (Hawarden) in demesne Earl Edwin held it. There are 3 hides that pay geld. The land is for 4^1/$_2$ ploughs. In demesne are 2 ploughs and 4 serfs. There is a church to which ^{1}/$_2$ carucate of land belongs, and there are 4 villeins and 6 bordars with 2 ploughs. There is ^{1}/$_2$ acre of meadow. Wood 2 leagues long and 1 wide. It is worth 40s. Two waste houses in the city (Chester) belong there.

What the Norman clerks are recording is that at the time of Edward the Confessor, probably after the defeat of the Welsh in 1063, Earl Edwin of Mercia, held the estate of Hawarden which is now in the hands of Earl Hugh of Avranches, the Earl entrusted by William the Conqueror to defend his lands including the coastlands of North Wales. There are three hides. A hide was originally the amount of land, which could be ploughed in a year using one plough with an eight-ox team. This could vary between 60 and 180 acres depending on the soil. This land was subject to geld. It was taxable. The land is for 4^1/$_2$ ploughs (a plough was equivalent to a hide). The demesne was the land retained by the lord of the manor upon which tenants gave free service according to the customs of the manor. The labourers were generally tied to the land; the bordar was given a cottage and some land for subsistence, and in return he was expected to work for the lord free or for a fixed sum; the villein was an unfree tenant who was tied to his lord. He had to ask permission of his lord if either he or his daughters wished to marry, and his heirs paid a fine to enter into his land. He had the right to graze a fixed number of cattle on the common pastures and to take hay from the common meadow. The serf was of the lowest status; he was virtually the slave of his master and could be sold to another person. The church at Hawarden is one of two recorded in Atiscros the other is Gresford. It was supported by ^{1}/$_2$ carucate of land (this was an alternative name for a hide). The wood at Hawarden was part of the great forest, which stretched across the parish as far as Flint and was to cause great difficulty to the English invaders. A league was generally 3 miles long. There was probably a motte and bailey castle here, which is not recorded.

> ROBERT OF RHUDDLAN holds of the earl BROCHETUNE (Broughton), Leofnoth held it and was a free man. There are 1^1/$_2$ virgates that pay geld. The land is for ^{1}/$_2$ plough, which is there with 1 villein. One and a half virgates

of meadow. It is worth 3s. and has a third part of a wood 1 league long and wide.

Robert of Rhuddlan was the cousin of Earl Hugh to whom he entrusted the military command of the borderlands. A virgate was generally about 30 acres. The same Robert holds there (at Broughton) 1 manor of $1/2$ hide that pays geld. The land is for $1/2$ plough. There 1 radman has this $1/2$ plough with 1 villein and 1 bordar. It is worth 3s.

HUGH FITZOSBERN holds BROCHETON (Broughton), Ravensward held it and was free. There are $11/2$ virgates of land that pay geld. The land is for $1/2$ plough. There 1 radman has this $1/2$ plough with1 villein and 2 bordars. Wood 1 league long and 1 wide. It is worth 5s.

HAMON holds ESTONE (Aston). Edwin and Thorth held it as 2 manors and were free. There is 1 hide that pays geld. The land is for 1 plough. This is there with 2 radman and 2 villeins and 3 bordars. There is wood 1 league long and as much wide. It is worth 10s. Of this land Ranulph holds 1 virgate.

RALPH THE HUNTER holds of the earl BROCHETUNE (Broughton). Wulfheah held it and was a free man. There is 1 virgate of land that pays geld. The land is for 1 plough. This is there in demesne with 2 serfs. There is 1 virgate of meadow. It is worth 5s.[12]

Domesday Book shows that Hawarden was more akin to Cheshire in social organisation and that centuries of immigration from England had given it that character. The place-names are of English origin rather than Welsh. Earl Hugh held the land in Hawarden; his successors in the twelfth century gave it to the hereditary stewards of Chester, the barons de Montalt. It was an important place for the Normans in their defence of the borderland and was to be the battleground between the Princes of Gwynedd and the English crown for the next two hundred years.

This was a formative period in the history of the parish, stretching from the end of the eleventh century to the conquest of Wales at the end of the thirteenth. One of the major tasks of the English crown was to defend its borders in both Wales and Scotland. In North Wales the Princes of Gwynedd refused to accept the over-lordship of the English and the boundaries imposed after the defeat of Llywelyn ap Gruffydd in 1063. The Norman Earls of Chester had the responsibility to defend the border, the March as it was called, and for this they gave land to their barons to hold in return for military service. These lands were called lordships, and the seat of the lord was usually in a motte and bailey castle in the manor of the lord. When the Welsh Princes became strong and threatened to overthrow the lordships and attack Chester then the Earl would need the assistance of his lord the king who would bring an army to campaign in Wales. Hawarden was the gateway to North Wales, and the Norman army assembled on the marsh at Saltney advanced into Wales either by the coastal route or, when the occasion demanded, cut their way through the thick forest. The Welsh soldiers were masters of guerrilla warfare and on at least two occasions demonstrated their power of surprise on their Norman adversary in Hawarden.

The castle was an important instrument of war in these days, serving many functions. It was principally a fortification used by fighting men as a base for attack or retreat, or an enclosure to which the civilian population could bring their cattle if necessary and seek shelter and protection from the wrath of an approaching enemy. If the king or his leading barons wished to confer or parley with their enemy, the castle was a useful rendezvous. The first market towns and boroughs in Wales were developed in the neighbourhood of the medieval castles, and the settlement in Hawarden falls into this category.

This is the backcloth to an understanding of the early history of Hawarden. Its major themes are these. The possession of the castle at Hawarden by the Earl of Chester from the time of the Conquest and its eventual occupation by his supporter and steward Robert de Montalt in the twelfth century, given to him with the lordships of Mold and Hawarden, to defend the borderland. The stewardship was hereditary and remained in the de Montalt family until 1329. Frequently in the period from 1140 to 1284 the lordship of Mold was in the hands of the Welsh, and de Montalt was forced to retreat to his lordship of Hawarden. At the western end of the parish of Hawarden is the manor of Ewloe. It belonged ecclesiastically but not politically to the parish, and was in the possession of the Princes of Gwynedd, as part of Tegeingl (Englefield). Whenever there was a dispute between the Welsh and Normans in the north, Hawarden would generally be part of the battleground, and castles were built at Hawarden and Ewloe to defend the territory of both adversaries.

It was said of Earl Hugh that he 'made castles and fortified places according to the custom of the French (Normans) and became lord of the land.'[13] In this way the Normans conquered, with their war bands terrorizing the countryside and bringing into subjection the native inhabitants. There is some doubt where the first castle in Hawarden was situated. CADW have suggested that Trueman's Hill in Hawarden was the site of a motte and bailey constructed in wood at the time of the Mercian invasion, and that a more substantial castle was constructed further east in the eleventh or early twelfth century by the Earl of Chester. The later site is larger, more impregnable and superbly placed. We will return to the castle when we discuss the events of the thirteenth century.

The first major event in the history of Hawarden after the Conquest was the visit of Henry II in 1157. The young Henry was exerting his authority following the anarchy of the previous reign of Stephen. He came into Wales to punish Owain Prince of Gwynedd who had taken advantage of the weakness of the crown. The Welsh chronicler gave a dramatic account of the event:

> Henry, king of England, led a mighty host to Chester, in order to subdue Gwynedd. And there he pitched camp: he was grandson to Henry the Great, son of William the Bastard. And Owain, prince of Gwynedd, after summoning to him his sons and his leading men, and gathering together a mighty host, encamped at Basingwerk. And he raised a ditch there to give battle to the king. And when the king heard that, he sent his host and many earls and barons beyond number, and with them a strong force fully equipped, along the shore and towards the place, which Owain was holding. And the king and an innumerable host, fearless and ready for battle, came through the wood, which was between them, which was called the wood of Hawarden. And there Cynan and Dafydd, sons of Owain, encountered him, and there they gave him a hard battle. And after many of his men had been slain, he escaped to the open country. And when Owain heard that the king was coming from the one side, and he saw the earls and a mighty host on the other side, he left that position.[14]

King Henry II had been ambushed and came close to losing his life in the extensive forest, ten leagues long and three leagues wide, noted in Domesday Book. The chronicler called the forest 'Koed Pennarddlaoc', the wood of Hawarden; another chronicler 'Coed Ewlo', the wood of Ewloe; whilst an English chronicler confuses matters by reporting the event as having taken place in the woods of Coleshill. Messham argues that the English chronicler meant the fighting beginning in Ewloe continued across the boundary into the commote of Coleshill, and that a more accurate name was that given by Gerald of Wales and the chronicler of St Werburgh's, the English name of Swerdewode. He points out that the boundary of the manor of Ewloe was wider than that of the later township. It was the boundary of Swerdewode on its eastern limits where it separated the manor from the lordship of Hawarden, and took in parts of the Hawarden townships of Killins, Shotton and Aston.

The Earl of Chester, Ranulph II, had created the Lordship of Hawarden sometime between 1147–53 and given it to Robert de Montalt I, as an incentive perhaps for the loss of the Lordship of Mold, and an inducement to defend his new lordship against the Welsh. He briefly held the manor of Ewloe (conveniently next to the Lordship of Hawarden), until Owain Gwynedd recovered it in 1165. The right to the manor of Ewloe was to become a matter of dispute in the distant future, but until 1282 the Welsh Princes of Gwynedd held it by right of conquest from the Earls of Chester, 'being but an extension of the earl's forest of Swerdewode', they regarded it as part of the commote of Coleshill and the cantref of Tegeingl.[15]

Relationships between the English Kings and the Welsh Princes were friendlier during the time of Llywelyn ap Iorwerth, Llywelyn the Great, in power from 1199–1240. He held both the Lordship of Mold and the Lordship and manor of Ewloe where in the latter it is said there was a Welsh township and a fortification of some kind. Llywelyn was succeeded in Gwynedd by his son Dafydd ap Llywelyn, whose brief time in power was blighted by opposition from King Henry III who drove him out of Mold and the four cantrefs including Tegeingl.

Roger de Montalt II was now in a position to fulfil his ambitions to reunite his lordships of Mold and Hawarden, and when the opportunity offered to increase his territory by annexing to it the manor of Ewloe. Roger II appears to have been a ruthless and ambitious baron who respected the power of no one. In 1249 the barons and community of Cheshire forwarded their complaints to Henry III, amongst which was that of an embankment raised by Roger in the common pasture at Saltney, which seems also to have been used as a meeting place and assembly point for military operations, and possibly also for tournaments. Henry ordered the embankment to be thrown down and the burgesses of Chester to be given their ancient seisin (possession), in the common pasture on the marsh of Saltney.[16] In 1258 Roger extorted from the Abbot and Monks of St Werburgh at Chester the manor of Bretton. Having seized Ewloe, Roger began to make a park of it by erecting fences, but in no time the new powerful Prince of Gwynedd Llywelyn ap Gruffydd, Llywelyn the Last, drove him out, and tore down the recently erected park fencing. Worse was to come for the Annals of Chester recorded that as a result of his misdeeds to the monks, Roger's eldest son died, and Roger II died in poverty in 1260, 'the common people being ignorant of the place of his burial.'

Ewloe Castle

Owain Gwynedd may have estab-lished a motte and bailey castle at Ewloe in the twelfth century. In 1257 Llywelyn ap Gruffydd fortified the manor and rebuilt and strengthened an older castle built in the corner of Ewloe Wood in 1210 by Llywelyn the Great. The castle is built in a strong defensive position on a promontory above the confluence of two streams. On the north side the ground falls away steeply whilst on the south the castle is overlooked by higher ground. There are defensive ditches on the east and the west. The main plan of the castle is simple, with an eastern upper ward and a western lower ward, the whole including the division between the wards enclosed by curtain walls. The entrance to the castle built in 1257 was by a timber bridge across the eastern ditch leading into the upper ward. The modern entrance is by a timber stair leading into the upper ward. In the upper ward is the Welsh Tower, which dominates the castle. It has a basement and first floor apartment, the entrance to which is at first floor level approached by an external staircase. Some of the accommodation for the Lord may have been in timber buildings in this ward. A West Tower built upon a rock is the sole building in the lower ward. It consisted of a single floor and basement entered by a trap door. In the lower ward were the domestic timber buildings to maintain the garrison — the hall, kitchen, buttery, *etc*.[17] Llywelyn appointed Ithel ap Bleddyn with the charge of the castle and manor of Ewloe. He managed to retain the confidence of Edward I and kept his tenancy until his death *c*.1295, when he was buried at Northop where there is an effigy of him in the church.

Llywelyn ap Gruffydd reached the height of his power in the years between 1255 and 1267. In 1255 he defeated

Ewloe Castle from the west
[FRO PH 18/38]

Ewloe Castle, the Welsh Tower from the east
[FRO PH 18/39]

his brothers Dafydd and Owain in battle and became the sole ruler of Gwynedd. He was soon to exercise his charismatic leadership over the whole of Wales gathering together all those with grievances against the English crown and appearing to them as a liberator. The time was advantageous because of the struggle in England between the king and his barons, and the imprisonment of King Henry and Prince Edward. Llywelyn's power was recognised when the leader of the English barons Simon de Montfort conferred with him at Hawarden Castle in 1264. Unfortunately this alliance was short-lived because of the death of de Montfort in August 1265, but this did not deter Llywelyn from striking a blow against the de Montalt inheritance by capturing Hawarden Castle and razing it to the ground in 1265. The Treaty of Montgomery made peace between Llywelyn and the English Crown in 1267, which recognised him as Prince of Wales and overlord of all the Welsh princes. The land between the estuary of the Dee was ceded to him. Llywelyn agreed that Hawarden be restored to Robert de Montalt, with the condition that no castle was to be built there for thirty years. All that Llywelyn wanted appeared to have been achieved.

In 1272 Henry III died, to be succeeded by his redoubtable son as Edward I, and this led to confrontation between two strong personalities. Llywelyn as a proud and ambitious Prince of Wales, and King Edward determined to be recognized as a feudal lord to whom homage was due. Llywelyn refused to do homage and was condemned as a rebel in November 1276; Edward entered Wales in the summer of 1277 and compelled him to submit by the Treaty of Conwy. Llywelyn was humiliated, losing his authority, land and dignity. Edward was determined to turn Wales into a garrison in order to subjugate the Welsh and began work on four major new castles at Flint, Rhuddlan, Aber and Builth, in the summer of 1277.

Hawarden Castle
In 1277 the de Montalt heir was a minor, but this did not prevent the family estates in England and Wales supplying a thousand archers and spearmen to the King's invasion forces. Between 1277 and 1280 the lordships

Hawarden Castle, a rather romanticised 18th century view by Samuel and Nathaniel Buck. Note the house built on top of the keep and the formal garden at Broad Lane in the foreground [FRO PR/740]

Hawarden Castle
[FRO PH 28/D/24]

of Mold and Hawarden reverted to the crown. Hawarden was granted first to Maurice de Craon, and when he sold it back to the king for £300, it was granted in January 1281, to Roger de Clifford. Roger III, heir to the lordship, married Juliana, the daughter of Clifford. On Palm Sunday, 1282, Llywelyn's brother Dafydd led an attack on Hawarden Castle, which marked the beginning of the final act before the conquest of Wales and its loss of independence. It is probable that Hawarden was chosen together with the other new castles that were being built to be a suitable target for the opening of the Welsh rebellion.

Edward I's reaction to this event is seen in a letter he wrote relating that:

> Certain Welsh malefactors went by night to the castle of Hawardyn with horses and arms, and assaulted Roger de Clifford and his familiaries dwelling with him in the same castle, and slew certain of them and burned the houses of the castle, and took Roger and carried him off and held him captive, and in addition their raiders went feloniously to the King's castle of Flynt and burned certain houses there as far as possible, and slew certain of the king's men there and committed robberies, homicides, and other enormities there … [18]

It was a wild night by any reckoning with violence taking place at Flint and Rhuddlan. When justice finally caught up with the rebels, it was alleged that Welshmen of Tegeingl committed over sixty offences at the outbreak of the rebellion with a number of people slain, including Fulk Trigald at Hawarden. On the night of Palm Sunday a gang of ten Welshmen came with force and arms to Madog's house at Broughton and 'stole and carried away his goods and chattels; sheep, oxen and other animals, corn and dishes and other goods to the value of £40.'[19]

It is probable that Hawarden Castle was part of Edward I's 1277 programme of castle building and was under construction in 1282. Arnold Taylor sees some connection architecturally with Caernarfon, designed and begun in 1283, and 'indications which link the design with others that are reasonably associated with James of St George.'[20]

This new castle replaced an older fortification on the same site. It was built of stone, probably using the main outlines of the previous castle. It was a motte and bailey castle with strong defensive earth works, the major feature being a large mound in a concentric enclosure formed on a steeply sloping side. Large ditches guarded the approach to the castle on the north and east sides. A circular two-storey keep crowned the westward facing motte, originally nearly forty feet high with walls fifteen feet thick at the base, which rise to thirteen feet. The upper storey had an octagonal interior, with mural chambers and wall passages similar to Caernarfon work of 1283, as is the wave moulding on the chapel doorway. The double corbelling in its upper floor is characteristic of a later stage at Caernarfon, and is also to be seen in the Whitley chancel of the parish church. The circular lower chamber was used as a storeroom and guardroom. A wall passage extends around the circumference giving magnificent views from the parts not protected by the ward. A portcullis defends the keep; the entrance gate is at the northern angle of the curtain walls, which enclose a ward of irregular plan. In the ward below the mound are living rooms and offices with the great hall abutting on the east side. At the foot of the motte outside the curtain wall extending northeast between the north and east outer ditches is the site of a barbican. Here is the entrance leading into the ward, and outwards a narrow staircase leads down between enclosing walls to where the drawbridge may have been sited, and from thence a stair rises to the barbican area.

There is strong evidence that the barbican was built in 1474 by Sir Thomas Stanley.

> Repairs done about the castle of Hawardyne … making a lime kiln together with breaking stones … the cartage of 50 loads of stone called limestone … breaking stones called asshelers (ashlar) … work of stone masons and other workmen hired by the day both for laying down the steps at the gate of the said hall … a new tower at the gate of the said hall … new axe and iron tools … 188 lbs of iron for making the windows and the doorsvand seven padlocks bought for divers gates of the castle.[21]

The castle fell again briefly in the revolt of Madog ap Llywelyn in 1294–5, and apart from an isolated incident reported in 1381, it remained impregnable until it was reduced in 1647.

The 1381 incident occurred in mid October. The reason for it is not known, although it appears to have been an unexpected action, which showed that with the element of surprise it was possible for a lightly armed force to get into the castle. William de Montagu, Earl of Salisbury petitioned the King and Parliament to report that:

> … as John de Mascy of Podyngtone came with men-at-arms and archers to the number of 100, *viz.* each arrayed with bacinet and habergeons … and the remainder with bows, arrows, spears and bucklers, on the Sunday next after the feast of St Luke … to make war at Hawardyn in the lordship of the Earl in Wales and to the castle of the Earl there … carrying two ladders with them and assaulting the ministers and servants of the Earl within the castle … and broke the house of one John, the son of Thomas, a tenant of the Earl in the town of Haywardyn , and made assault on one Richard Porter of the castle there, with their bows and arrows, against the peace of our Lord the king, to the great loss of the Earl; wherefore he prays remedy in this present Parliament.[22]

The conquest of Wales was achieved by 1284. It was the end of the conflict between the Welsh and the Anglo-Norman invaders, which had begun in the seventh century. The settlement, which Edward I imposed upon the vanquished was decisive. A string of royal castles were built to garrison the defeated Welsh and new towns established to receive English colonists, the shire counties were created to introduce administrative uniformity with England. Hawarden had its new castle, but it was not included in the new county of Flintshire, instead the ecclesiastical parish was coincident with the Lordship of Ewloe, now forfeit by the Princes of Gwynedd and annexed to the English Crown, and the Lordship of Hawarden, soon to fail in the male line and become subject to royal patronage. Peace brought greater opportunities for economic growth; trade with nearby Chester and the gradual change in land holding over the next two hundred years.

The Manor of Ewloe

One of the major effects on Hawarden parish of the conquest of 1284 was that the manor of Ewloe and its lordship was annexed to the English crown. This decision was for a time in dispute between the crown and the de Montalt family, now restored to their lordships of Mold and Hawarden, who wanted to add Ewloe to their possessions.

The manor of Ewloe comprised the two townships of Ewloe Town, and Ewloe Wood, with small portions of Pentrobin, Shotton, and Aston, with the western boundary, Wepre brook. The area of the manor was approximately 2,300 acres. It was rich in coal and wood and was regarded as a resource to the crown in its maintenance of the royal castle of Flint. After the conquest the Welsh manor of Ewloe was deliberately colonised by the English. As K. Lloyd Gruffydd states:

> According to a Lay Subsidy Roll of 1292 Ewloe was one of these *villata anglicana* as they were called. The manor was divided into an Englishry and Welshry. Twenty-four Englishmen and their families were settled on the better lands, amongst them some whose names survive in Buckley today, *e.g.* Duckworth, Fox, Ledsham, Messham and Whitley. Equally significant is the fact that the remaining twenty householders were of Welsh origin, which must be taken as evidence that the Cymry did not abandon their tribal lands after the conquest. It may originally have been the Crown's intention to create a borough at Ewloe.[23]

The value of the manor was revealed at an inquiry made in October 1295:

There are 480 acres of arable land in the demesne worth £14 a year. The two water mills are worth 60s; the agistment of the pasture (letting of grazing land) of Buckley, 10s; deadwood, 8s; an iron mine 6s. 8d; bailiwick of the forestry, 30s; pannage of the swine, 20s; (payment for the right to feed pigs in the wood); pleas and perquisites of the court, 21s. Total, £21 14s. [sic] Amongst the jurors were Simon de Eweloe, John the Miller, Alcok de Scotton (Shotton), and Madoc ap Rhys.[24]

The dispute between the crown and Roger de Montalt began in 1282. After the death of Llywelyn ap Gruffydd in 1282, Reginald de Grey, Justice of Chester, took the manor formerly held by the princes of Gwynedd, as forfeited to Edward I by right of conquest. This action brought a protest from Roger to the king who alleged that Reginald de Grey was withholding the manor from him, despoiling his woods, and making enclosures in the part of the woodland which had been cleared and converted into arable land by the dwellers in Aston, Shotton and Killins. In 1284, Roger's mother, Joan, when summoned to answer in the court at Flint why she should have dower in Ewloe failed to appear and her right was lost by default.[25] The king took action against her to return to him the vill of Killins at Aston with its 97 acres of land and 58 acres of land at Shotton. In 1290 Roger petitioned parliament alleging that an inquisition taken in 1267–8 confirmed that the lands at Ewloe belonged to his grandfather and they were delivered to Maurice de Croan as his guardian. This inquisition could not be found, and a further one held in 1294 rejected Roger's claims. The matter was finally settled at an inquisition held at Ewloe in 1311 when it was adjudged that the manor had belonged to Owain Gwynedd and descended through him to Llywelyn ap Iorwerth (died 1282), which he gave to Bleddyn ap Iorwerth to hold for him. Henry III had wrongly given it to Roger who attached the manor to his own neighbouring lands of Mold and Hawarden, to which it never belonged. Llywelyn had ousted Roger, and King Edward I took the manor in right of his conquest and defeat of the Welsh prince.

There are a few references to Ewloe in the fourteenth and fifteenth centuries apart from coalmining, which is dealt with in another chapter. The forest of Ewloe was used to supply timber to the royal castle at Flint. In 1304 when the castle at Flint was repaired, timber came from Ewloe Wood, to repair the wooden stockade with two hundred planks, and three hundred boards for a parapet, three beams for the outer bridge and one new bridge between the Great Tower and the inner bailey of the castle, and timber for making an engine to raise the new bridge. Branches were delivered for smelting lead on condition that the lord shall have every sixth foot of lead. It was common for the lord to express his generosity through the gift of timber. In 1357 Dafydd ap Bleddyn Vaughan was rewarded by the Black Prince with the gift of three oaks for good service, especially at the battle of Poitiers. The inhabitants of the borough of Flint enjoyed the favour of the prince when they were given three oaks to repair their church in 1357 and timber blown down by the wind in 1390. In 1346 lease was granted to Alan de Craven of the office of forester of Ewloe, also of the mills, coalmines and pasturage and perquisites of the court of the town of Ewloe for three years at £60 yearly.[26]

Castle mill and Lady's mill are mentioned in 1305–6 when John the miller paid 106s. 8d. for the two mills. In 1320 Richard Paynel and Richard Blunidel, farmers of the mill, were paid for repairing and strengthening the weirs according to an agreement made with the Chamberlain of Chester. In 1325–6 there is an account of the Lord's issues from his mills. The people of Ewloe were obliged to have their corn ground and for this service they paid in kind a due called multure: probably a sixteenth or twentieth. There were sales of corn, malt and flour, and wheat was sold for the provisions of the castle of Flint, together with oatmeal and best malt. In 1333, whilst still a minor, the eldest son of Edward III, the Black Prince, was made Earl of Chester. The revenues the prince received from the manor for the years 1301–28 and 1347–53 are to be found in his accounts. The sources of income are the same as those revealed in the Inquiry of 1295: the rent of the assize, the mills, the pasturage of Buckley, the mines of iron and coal, the pannage of pigs, and the court of the manor. Many of the customary payments occur in the accounts under their Welsh name: *amobr*, a payment made when a woman married; *ebediw*, a fine paid by a man for the privilege of entering upon his father's possessions; *twnc*, an annual payment extracted from the tenants for the lord's subsistence; *arianmedy*, a payment in lieu of field work in the lord's demesne; and *tolcester*, a fine paid for the privilege of brewing. We do not know the effect of the Black Death on the parish in 1349, but an indication that the pestilence caused great disruption may be surmised by the absence of accounts for that year and the suspension of the sheriff's courts between 1349–1352.

When the Black Prince died in 1376 the manor reverted to the crown. The English lords of the manor were notoriously rapacious and corrupt in their administration and at times the English settlers complained about the bailiff, particularly if he were Welsh. Such a complaint was made in 1391:

Aston Hall, watercolour by J. Boydell, 1761 [FRO PR/F/108]

Llywelyn who is Welsh, has been made bailiff by the steward of the manor and has inflicted from day to day many injuries, extortions and oppressions upon the English tenants there. Wherefore the community of the English tenants of the township wish for a remedy, and that Llywelyn be removed from his office, for no bailiff of Ewloe whilst in office may keep an ale house there, the wife of Llywelyn keeps an ale house and sells very weak ale by false measures and charges high prices. Llywelyn in breach of the peace took several horses and mares belonging to different men in a place called Buckley and marked them (cutting the ears, hairs of their tails, manes *etc.*), and sold them to various strangers.

In spite of this the English: Whitleys in Aston, Ravenscrofts in Shotton, Ledshams in Buckley, Messhams in Ewloe, began to acquire lands and lease mines. The manor changed hands twice at the end of the troubled reign of Richard II and after the execution of John de Montacute, Earl of Salisbury, Henry IV granted the manor for life to Sir William Clifford. Henry V leased the manor in 1413–4 to John Heleagh, together with sea coalmines there, excepting John de Ewloe tenant of the mines who was allowed to continue. In 1422 the manor was assigned to Queen Katherine the widow of Henry V, wife of Owen Tudor and grandmother of Henry VII. It is a mark of the prosperity of local gentlemen that they began to occupy prominent positions in the lordship. One of them, John Ledsham was bailiff of the lordship, and when he presented his account for 1435–6, he paid 30s. for the two watermills (Lady mill and Castle mill), which he promised to rebuild and give back in a competent state. He gave as the return for a mine of sea coals 26s. 8d, and for the pasturing of beasts within the Queen's woods, so leased to the community of the township for this year, fees for the feeding of pigs 2s. 4d., 2s. from the farm of getting clay for the making of clay pots, so leased to William the potter 12d. In 1437 the manor was leased to Richard de Whitley of Aston Hall, together with the coal mines, for seven years from the death of Queen Katherine. In 1444 a cadet branch of the Stanley family came into prominence in Ewloe and remained in possession of the manor for almost two hundred years. The grant of the lease of the manor by Henry VI to Peter Stanley, the second son of Sir William Stanley of Hooton, set them on their way. They are described as being of Ewloe Castle. The lease was renewed, and in April 1535 Pyers Stanley was granted Ewloe manor, 'with all mines of sea coal in the county of Flint, Flint Mill, fines and profits of the court with the tolls of markets and fairs; reserving all woods, quarries of stone, lead, coal, except sea coal, goods of felons &c. &c., paying annually £22. 10s and for the mill 4 marks.' In the seventeenth century the heiress Katherine married John Aldersey of Daniels Ash. By this time the 'Ewloe' Stanley property was widespread in the parish of Hawarden with estates in Ewloe, Hawarden, Broad Lane, Shotton, Manor, Newtown, Moor, Mancot, Broughton, Diglane *etc.* The lordship of Ewloe became the property of Sir John North in 1628, who sold it to Colonel Davies, who resold it to his nephew Robert Davies of Gwysaney. A rental of the town and lordship of Ewloe in the reign of James I *c*1620 gives a list of the tenants for agricultural purposes in two groups: on the English side twelve, and on the Welsh side fifty five. Amongst the chief landowners are the Whitleys of Aston, Ravenscrofts of Bretton, Ledshams of Wepre and Buckley, Messhams of Ewloe Hall, Dymocks, Turners, Rosingrave, Sparke, and Alexander Standish. All of these families were involved

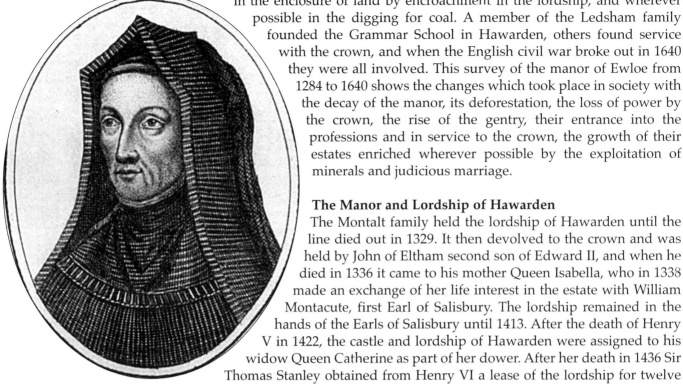

Lady Margaret Beaufort [FRO PR/C/24]

in the enclosure of land by encroachment in the lordship, and wherever possible in the digging for coal. A member of the Ledsham family founded the Grammar School in Hawarden, others found service with the crown, and when the English civil war broke out in 1640 they were all involved. This survey of the manor of Ewloe from 1284 to 1640 shows the changes which took place in society with the decay of the manor, its deforestation, the loss of power by the crown, the rise of the gentry, their entrance into the professions and in service to the crown, the growth of their estates enriched wherever possible by the exploitation of minerals and judicious marriage.

The Manor and Lordship of Hawarden

The Montalt family held the lordship of Hawarden until the line died out in 1329. It then devolved to the crown and was held by John of Eltham second son of Edward II, and when he died in 1336 it came to his mother Queen Isabella, who in 1338 made an exchange of her life interest in the estate with William Montacute, first Earl of Salisbury. The lordship remained in the hands of the Earls of Salisbury until 1413. After the death of Henry V in 1422, the castle and lordship of Hawarden were assigned to his widow Queen Catherine as part of her dower. After her death in 1436 Sir Thomas Stanley obtained from Henry VI a lease of the lordship for twelve years, and in October, 1443, Letters Patent to the lordships of Hawarden and Mold, which the family were to hold until the execution of James, 7th Earl of Derby in 1651. In 1455 he was created first Baron Stanley.

The Stanley family influence began in 1385 with the marriage of Sir John Stanley of Storeton to Isobel Latham, the sole heiress of Knowsley and Latham. Marriage, the seventh earl advised his son in the seventeenth century, 'is like a project in war, wherein a man can probably err but once. Let her (a wife) be not poor, how generous soever, for a man can buy nothing in a market with gentility'.[27] Lathams had as their crest the eagle and child. Isobel's father, Sir Thomas Latham, was illegitimate and legend has it that he was found as a mere babe, lying in the grass, below an eagle's eyrie. Service under Richard II and Henry IV brought advancement to Sir John Stanley who was rewarded for the suppression of the Percy Rebellion, by the grant of the lordship of Man in 1406.

Thomas, second Baron Stanley, married Eleanor Neville, daughter and heiress of Richard Neville, Earl Salisbury and when she died Margaret Beaufort, Countess of Richmond. She was the only daughter of John, first Duke of Somerset, a descendant of Edward III, being a grandson of John of Gaunt. As a child-bride in 1455, Margaret married Edmund Tudor son of Owain Tudor, and Catherine of Valois, widow of Henry V, and the mother of the boy king Henry VI. The marriage was brief: Edmund died of the plague at Carmarthen 1456, and their son Henry Tudor 2nd Earl of Richmond, was born posthumously. Margaret married for her second husband, in 1459, Henry Stafford, younger son, of the Lancastrian Duke of Buckingham. The triumph of the Yorkists in 1461 endangered the safety of any related to the throne, and the major concern of the Lady Margaret was for her son Henry Tudor. Margaret's second husband Henry Stafford died in 1482, and she married as her third husband Thomas Stanley. This brought her dangerously close to the Yorkist King Richard III who suspected Margaret as mother to the great rebel and traitor Henry Tudor, 'stirring him to come into the realm to make war'. Her new husband, Lord Stanley, was obliged by Richard to put her away: 'keeping her in some secret place at home, without having any servant or company', and her estates were transferred to Lord Stanley for life. When Henry Tudor landed at Milford Haven in August 1485, Thomas Stanley was forced by Richard III, to send his son George, Lord Strange, as a hostage for his loyalty. He took no part in the battle at Bosworth Field. However, it was his younger brother, Sir William Stanley, who late in the battle committed his three thousand men of Bromfield, on the side of Henry Tudor. Thomas Stanley is said to have placed the crown of England on the head of his stepson, Henry VII. Thomas Stanley was greatly rewarded being created Earl of Derby in 1485, and receiving a large number of estates. Unfortunately Sir William Stanley was executed as a traitor in 1495, accused of being implicated in the Perkin Warbeck plot. 'In this year', the Annals of Chester, records ' King Henry VII and the Queen and the king's mother came to this city of Chester. They rode to Harden on hunting the 28th day of July and the Earl of Derby and many more made great state with them'.[28]

Perhaps they visited some of the buildings in the locality which were receiving the patronage of Thomas Stanley and Margaret Beaufort, the most notable being St Winifred's well and chapel, Holywell, and Mold parish church. Both buildings are magnificent examples of perpendicular architecture, one of the major features being the profuseness of stone carving dealing with religious themes and displaying the arms of the donors. In Mold parish church the stone carving in the nave arcades represent, the emblems of the passion (the five wounds, the ladder, a spear, the Veronica on Holy cloth), the arms of the Stanley family (the eagle and child, the three legs of man, the stags head), and in the stained glass, heraldic remains of the arms of Henry VII. At St Winifred's well is carved the legend of the saint, the royal arms of Henry VII and Catherine of Aragon, and heads on corbels are said to represent those of Lady Margaret Beaufort and the Earl of Derby. Thomas Stanley died in 1504, and Margaret Beaufort in 1509. She was buried in Westminster Abbey in the magnificent chapel begun by Henry VII. Pietro Torrigiano, the Florentine artist, designed her monument and Erasmus composed her epitaph. Bishop John Fisher, her confessor said, 'all England for her death had cause of weeping'. Whatever additions were made to Hawarden parish church at this time no longer survive, although it was recorded that there was stained glass in the east window showing the arms of Stanley.

The Parish Church of St Deiniol, Hawarden

St. Deiniol, the sixth century founder

Most of the information we have of Deiniol, the founder of the church at Hawarden, is from a very late date. However he was highly regarded in Ireland in 800 A.D., his fame spreading throughout the Celtic church. Deiniol's reputation in Gwynedd led to the cathedral church at Bangor being named after him. His sanctity impressed his contemporaries of the sixth century, the age of the Welsh saints, and he was called abbot, bishop and confessor. According to the *Annales Cambriae*, Deiniol died in 584 and was buried on Bardsey Island

Only one copy of the *Life of St Deiniol* is known, which is in Latin and transcribed from an ancient manuscript by Sir Thomas Williams of Trefriw in 1602. A few extra details emerge from a poem written in 1527 by Sir David Trevor, parson of Llanallgo. The account of his life is typical of that of the Welsh saints, many of which were written in the eleventh and twelfth

St Deiniol, from the 15th century glass at Llandyrnog, Denbighshire

centuries. The attributes given to Deiniol were shared with his contemporary saints. He was of a royal house, his genealogy related him both to princes and saints, the churches dedicated to the saint trace his influence over a particular area, and miracles are attributed to him.

Deiniol was the son of Abbot Dunawd Fwr or Dinothus, son of Pabo Post Prydyn, by Dwywai, daughter of Llenog. He is often called Deiniol Wyn, the blessed. He was the brother of Saints Cynwyl and Gwarthan, and the father of Deiniolen. When Pabo and his family lost their territories in the kingdom that spanned the Solway Firth, they retired to Wales where they received the protection of Cyngen ap Cadell Dyrnllwyg, King of Powys, who granted them land and whose son and successor, Brochwel Ysgythrog, married Pabo's daughter Arddun. His son, Dunawd, embraced the religious life and founded the monastery at Bangor is y coed on the river Dee with the assistance of Cyngen and later Brochwel who generously provided for it, and it remained under the protection of the kin of Cadell for its brief existence. After his education at Illtud's school in the Vale of Glamorgan, Deiniol travelled through Pembrokeshire up to Tywyn and then along the Dee Valley. He founded churches at Bangor is y coed, Worthenbury and Marchwiel. Tradition has it that when Deiniol came to Hawarden he chose 'Daniel's Ash' (the site of the Gladstone memorial chapel), as the place to plant his preaching cross, prayed beneath the shade of the tree, and at sunrise, on the line cast by the shadow of his cross, built his simple church in the enclosure and set up a group of cells or huts; thus a Celtic monastery or clas was formed. Deiniol's great work lay ahead and he went onto Gwynedd, where he founded the monastery of Bangor, under the patronage of Maelgwyn Gwynedd who endowed it with lands and privileges, and later raised it to the rank of an episcopal see, coterminous with the kingdom of Gwynedd. Deiniol spent the remainder of his days here as Abbot and Bishop. During his time he attended the Synod of Brefi in c.545 with St Dyfrig and St David, when the churches penitential regulations were discussed.

The cult of St Deiniol is scattered throughout Wales, with a number of churches dedicated to him. Hawarden Church has two dedication festivals, one on St Deiniol's Day, 10 December, and the other on 14 September, the exaltation of the Holy Cross. The present calendar in the Church in Wales Prayer Book gives his feast day as 11 September, older Welsh calendars as 10 December.

The legend of the holy rood

Deiniol planted the Christian faith in Hawarden before the Mercian invasion from the seventh century onwards. The next notice we have of the church is of the tenth century, and is reputed by Richard Willett to have come from a lost Saxon manuscript. It is rather incredulous and may have been composed to discredit the church at Hawarden. The story relates that in the sixth year of the reign of Cynan king of Gwynedd, about 946 A.D., there was in the Christian Temple at a place called Hawarden a rood loft, in which was placed an image of the Virgin Mary, with a very large cross in the hands of the image, called Holy Rood. A very dry and hot summer burnt up the pasture and the inhabitants went to pray to the image that it would cause it to rain; but to no avail. Lady Trawst wife of the governor continued to pray earnestly and long, when the image, or Holy Rood, 'fell down upon her head and killed her; upon which a great uproar was raised, and it was concluded and resolved upon, to try the said image for the murder of Lady Trawst, and a Jury was summoned for this purpose'. Amongst the names of the local jurors were Leach, Span of Mancot, Corbin, Milling, Hewitt, Gill, and Pugh. The jury examined the evidence and declared Lady Trawst, to be wilfully murdered by the Holy Rood. The decision to carry out the sentence of hanging was opposed by Span, 'who, saying, they wanted rain, and it would be best to drown her — but was fiercely opposed by Corbin, who answered, as she was Holy Rood, they had no right to kill her, but he advised to lay her on the sands of the River, from whence they might see what became of her, which was accordingly done; soon after which, the tide of the sea came and carried the image to some low land (being an island) near the walls of the city called Caer Leon (supposed Chester), where it was found the next day, drowned and dead; upon which the inhabitants of Caer Leon buried it at the place where found, and erected a monument of stone over it, with this inscription:

> The Jews their God did crucify,
> The Hardeners theirs did drown;
> 'Cause with their wants she'd not comply,
> And lies under this cold stone.'

The place where this happened was named Rood Eye, or Rood Dee.[29]

After the Norman Conquest

Hawarden parish came under the jurisdiction of the Earl of Chester, and the lordship was eventually given to the Montalt family as hereditary stewards. The fortunes of the church were closely linked with this connexion. The advowson or nomination of the rector of the parish was in the hands of the lord of the manor, until the disestablishment of the Anglican Church in Wales in 1920.

Hawarden Church is mentioned in Domesday Book, compiled in 1086, when it had about 60 acres of land. In 1092 Hugh Earl of Chester gave the tithes of the manor of Hawarden and its holdings at Broughton and Wepre to the Benedictine Abbey of St Werburgh. In the thirteenth century the tithes of the parish of Hawarden were wrested from the monks of St Werburgh by Roger de Montalt, lord of the manor of Hawarden. In 1258 Roger restored to the Abbey lands in his possession in the Cheshire parishes of Lawton, Goostrey, Neston, Burera and Coddington. In return he received the manor of Bretton, the chapel and tenement of Spon, and the living of Hawarden. What was most important for the parish of Hawarden was that in this exchange the monks also surrendered the great tithes to the rectors thereof for ever. This arrangement was afterwards ratified by the Popes Honorius and Clement. This meant that the parishioners gave the rector a tenth part of the various products. Those that came from the ground, such as grain, timber, and fruit. Those nourished by the ground, such as calves, lambs, chickens, milk, cheese, and eggs. Personal tithes came from the net profits of labour and industry. In 1289 a most important concession was obtained for the parish of Hawarden, which eventually gave the rector and parishioners the rare privilege of being called a peculiar, exempt from the jurisdiction of the Bishop and Archdeacon. This gave the rector the right to set up his own ecclesiastical court. This will be discussed later. Roger, rector of Hawarden, obtained this privilege on 3 May in the church of Tarporley. The rector appeared before the Archdeacon of Chester, Robert Redeswell, arguing that:

> Whereas the access of the parishioners of Hawarden to the Consistory Court of Chester is excessively wearisome on account of the intervening water, hostilities and other reasons, the Archdeacon by his letters patent commissioned the Rector, in response to his urgent request, to act on his behalf in hearing cases between the Parishioners, and in corrections until Easter: reserving to the Archdeacon appeals, and corrections of the Rector himself. And because the Archdeacon was then engaged on his Visitation and was prevented from going personally to Hawarden, he gave the Rector authority on that occasion to visit the church there on his behalf. And the Rector swore faithfully to pay the Archdeacon 36s. for procurations, synodals, and perquisites up to Easter, half at the feast of St Michael and half at Easter.[30]

This was the thin end of the wedge as far as the Rector of Hawarden and the lord of the manor were concerned, and once this privilege was obtained it was never relinquished in spite of the pressure applied down the centuries by the Bishops of Lichfield, Chester, and St Asaph.

The architecture
There is no written evidence for the traditional date of 1272 usually given for the building of the church. This date was probably chosen because it coincided with the alleged date for the rebuilding of the castle. W. Bell Jones who was familiar with the church over a very long period came to these conclusions. He assumed that the Normans erected a church on the site between 1180 and 1280 and that the Montalts began building a replacement church at the end of the thirteenth century. Although many churches were destroyed in 1282, Hawarden was not amongst them. Maybe the security of the political settlement in 1284 gave more incentive for building a new structure. He estimated that the building of the church took place over a period of three hundred years. Its shape when completed at the end of the sixteenth century remained the same until the end of the nineteenth century, when a porch was placed over the chancel door in 1891, and vestries added in 1907. The plan, virtually the same as today, was a chancel, central tower, nave, north and south aisle or chapel, a south porch, west door, north door, and a priest's door in the south chapel. From the thirteenth century are the pointed arch and more slender pillars. Bell Jones cites the ground course, the first courses of stonework appearing above the foundations, and the buttresses. The windows of this period have all been destroyed but Rector Neville c1830 recorded an Early English style window on the north side of the chancel. Inside the church the nave arcade consists of octagonal piers with moulded capitals and pointed arches of late thirteenth and early fourteenth century work. The corbelling work in the Whitley chancel coincides with that in the old castle and probably shares the same date of the late thirteenth century. The two eastern piers are attached to the dividing wall between the chancel and the nave. The arches springing from these piers on the west, north and south sides are Perpendicular in style. Springing from the north and south of western piers supporting the tower, are two arches or flying buttresses reaching across the aisles, and this may have been the position of the western walls of two small transepts, which were later merged into the aisles. This Perpendicular work may well have been carried out under the patronage of the Stanleys. The tower is Perpendicular as are the south and west doorways.

Rectors of Hawarden 1180–1538[31]
The importance and wealth of the rectory of Hawarden in the medieval period is demonstrated by the fact that

it is often given to a relative of the lord of the manor. Below is a list of some of the outstanding rectors from 1180–1538.

1180 — William de Montalt. The son of Robert de Montalt and his wife Leucha. He was also Rector of Neston, which was his mother's dower.

1209 — Ralph de Montalt.

1216 — Hugh de Montalt.

1315 — William de Melton. 1307 Keeper of the Privy Seal and King's Clerk. 1317 consecrated Archbishop of York at Avignon by Pope John XXII. 1325 Treasurer of England. 'It was said of him that he was charitable and pious, parsimonious to himself, bountiful to the needy and religious'.

1423 — Marmaduke Lumley. Rector of Stepney, Treasurer of England, Bishop of Carlisle, translated to Lincoln.

1466 — James Stanley on the presentation of Sir Thomas Stanley his brother. He was also Archdeacon of Chester and Warden of the Collegiate Church, Manchester.

1487 — James Stanley (1435–1515), sixth son of Thomas Stanley, Earl of Derby. Became Bishop of Ely 1506, founded Jesus College, Cambridge. Excommunicated by the Pope for 'living with she who was not his sister.' He was over six foot eight inches in height. Fond of cock fighting. 'When too old and infirm himself to take to the field he sent 4,000 retainers, with an eagle's claw embroidered in gold on their breasts, under the command of his natural son, Sir John Stanley, to form the right wing of the English army at the battle against the Scots at Flodden Field in 1513'.

1505 — Ralph (or Randulph) Pool was presented to the living of Hawarden by Margaret Beaufort, wife of Thomas Stanley, Earl of Derby. He was on terms of great friendship with his predecessor James Stanley, who on his appointment as Bishop of Ely, resigned Hawarden. Pool was also sinecure Rector of Llandrillo in Ederynion, Prebendary of Hereford and of St John's Collegiate Church, Chester. He inherited the lordship of Pool and considerable property on the Wirral peninsula. The bench end which forms the end of the reading stall used by the rector in the parish church bears his arms, quartered with other Wirral families.

1538 — John Vaughan, LL.D., of Whitland in Carmarthenshire was appointed to Hawarden two years after he had completed his work as one of Thomas Cromwell's commissioners, together with Adam Becansaw, to investigate the abuses in religious houses which brought about the dissolution of the monasteries. In his will dated 27 January 1556, he desired to be buried in the church of Hawarden, bequeathed twenty nobles, (£6. 66p) to be distributed amongst the poor, a cup of silver and gilt with a cover to the Earl of Derby, and to Dafydd ap Rhys my scholar, all my books. He died in 1557.

2. The Seventeenth Century

The seventeenth century was to see many changes in the parish of Hawarden. One was the sale of the lordship of Hawarden by the 8th Earl of Derby to Sir John Glynne in 1653. Another was the coming into prominence of gentry families, and the interchange of estates. Local government was to change through the wider powers given to the parish vestry by poor law legislation enacted by the parliament of Elizabeth I. The great divide of the seventeenth century was the Civil War, which brought the conflict to Hawarden Castle on more than one occasion and involved the lives and fortunes of the gentry, whether or not they supported either the crown or parliament.

In Flintshire as in all Welsh counties, there was a gradual influx of English settlers after the Conquest. These families gained prominent positions in local society as officers of the lords of the manor, or in some instances fulfilling the role of mayor or sheriff of the city of Chester, after a successful business career. After the Act of Union in 1536, many Welsh gentry and particularly their younger sons, found a career at court or in the law which enabled them to accumulate wealth to spend on the purchase of land or at the end of their days to make charitable bequests. Examples of these trends may be found in the account of Hawarden families in the seventeenth century.

The first example is of the Ledsham family who settled in Ewloe. George and Richard Ledsham found fortune in the law, both of them being stewards of the Inner Temple. George was a man of wealth who had lands in the Wirral and elsewhere as well as in Ewloe, and expressed his desire to have a splendid burial service at St Paul's Cathedral.[1] He is remembered in Hawarden for the generosity of his endowment of £300 for the erection and maintenance of a free grammar school in the churchyard.

Another prominent family were the Whitleys who lived at Aston Hall for over five hundred years. They were involved on the royalist side in the Civil War. Thomas Whitley by his second marriage to Elizabeth Brereton had five sons: Roger, Richard, John, Ralph, and Peter. Thomas Whitley was fined £125 after the siege of Denbigh ended in 1646 'for delinquency in deserting his habitation and going into the garrison'. Captain Richard Whitley was killed in the defence of Hawarden Castle. The eldest son Roger, a royalist colonel was born in 1618 and educated at Gray's Inn. He commanded regiments of both horse and foot and was made governor of Aberystwyth, which he defended stubbornly until forced to surrender in April 1646. In 1648 he joined the royalist revolt, was captured at Beaumaris Castle and on his release went overseas. In the 1659 Rising he brought the King's commission to Sir George Booth and fortified Hawarden Castle before returning abroad to await the restoration of Charles II. This service and loyalty to the Stuart cause brought him riches, for he made a fortune farming the Post Office and bought Peel Hall, Cheshire, where he entertained William III on his way to Ireland. He devoted himself to politics, serving many years in Parliament as well as being four times mayor of Chester. He died in 1697 and was buried in Hawarden. The Whitleys lived at Aston Hall until the estate was sold in 1869 to W. E. Gladstone.[2]

The Ravenscroft family had branches in many parts of the country. A younger branch of the family came to the parish in the middle of the fifteenth century when Hugh de Ravenscroft was steward of the Stanley lordships of Hope, Hawarden and Mold. He married Isobel, daughter and co-heiress of Ralph Holland of Bretton. From this marriage are derived the Bretton and Hawarden branches of the family. A descendant of the Bretton line was George Ravenscroft (died 1592) who was Member of Parliament for Flintshire in 1563–7 and sheriff of the county in 1578–9. His wife Dorothy was the heiress of John Davies, constable of Hawarden castle and owner of Broad Lane, which came into the family. His sister Elizabeth married the Lord Chancellor Egerton, and his daughter Katherine married Robert Davies of Gwysaney, who came into possession of the manor of Ewloe. George Ravenscroft's second son, William, was trained for the law, became a bencher of Lincoln's Inn, 'Clerk of the Petty Bag' in the court of Chancery, and Member of Parliament for Flintshire in 1586–7 and 1601 and for Flint Boroughs in the 1620s, until his death in 1628. George Ravenscroft's grandson Thomas (the son of Roger, Rector of

Dodleston), was a distinguished musician born at Hawarden in 1592 and editor of *The Whole Book of Psalms* in 1621, and including forty-eight of his own settings. George's great grandson Colonel Thomas Ravenscroft, surrendered Hawarden Castle to the Parliamentarians in 1643, after which he went over to their side, and in May 1648 was appointed a member of the Parliamentary Committee, which supervised Flintshire. The colonel's grandson Thomas Ravenscroft (1670–98) of Broadlane, Sheriff in 1692 and Member of Parliament 1697–8, died leaving two heiresses, Honora and Catherine. In 1731 Sir John Glynne married Honora Conwy, Ravenscroft's granddaughter and almost doubled the extent of his estate.[3]

The Aldersey family began as merchants in Chester in the sixteenth century and married into a cadet branch of the Stanley family of Ewloe Hall. Anne Stanley married John Mostyn of Coed-onn. They had a daughter, Catherine Mostyn, who married John Aldersey of Daniel's Ash, and with her passed a large share of the old Stanley estates at Ewloe, Broadlane, Diglane and other parts of Hawarden. In 1643 Colonel John Aldersey supported Colonel Ravenscroft when Hawarden Castle was betrayed to Sir William Brereton.

The Civil War

The finest hour in the history of Hawarden old castle was its last. Its use to both sides during the war proved its strategic worth as a strong outpost of royalist Chester, and its position on the route from Ireland for royalist troops landing at Conwy or Mostyn. The war began in August 1642 when Charles I raised his standard at Nottingham. In October Charles was defeated at Edgehill and retreated to Oxford for the winter. In August 1643 Hawarden was garrisoned under its governor Colonel Thomas Ravenscroft. The parliamentarians gained the ascendancy strengthened by an alliance between Sir Thomas Myddelton and Sir William Brereton, which subdued Cheshire, although they failed to capture Chester, and in November crossed Holt Bridge. From Wrexham they advanced with a strong force made up of nine troops of horse and two small foot companies. By 11 November they were at the gates of Hawarden Castle, only to be surprised when they were opened for them by their royalist guardians. It was reported:

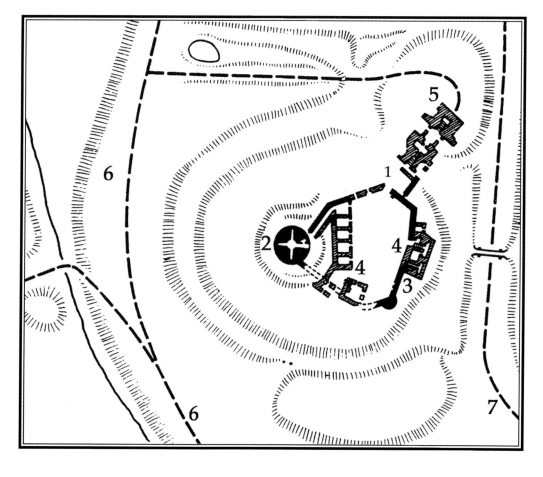

Plan of Hawarden Old Castle
[based upon E. W. Gladstone]

Key:
1. Entrance
2. Keep
3. Curtain Wall
4. Offices, living rooms, etc
5. Site of barbican
6. Present drive through park
7. 'Moat' old raod to Chester

Sir William Brereton, Parliamentary Major General.
[FHS Vol.6]

They came to Hawarden Castle which (was) by the faithless Col. Ravenscroft and Mr Aldersey, delivered to them without a gunshot; the delivery whereof was very discommodious to the city of Chester by stopping of corn, lyme, and all sorts of victuals which by ye Welsh was brought while that side was open'.[4] In the mean time the Archbishop of York and his fellow bishops from Bangor, Chester and St Asaph, retreated to Conway [sic] to await the arrival of royalist soldiers from Ireland. Their prayers were answered and the Irish troops were soon at Hawarden summoning the parliamentarians to surrender. The royalist generals Lord Arthur Capel and Lord John Byron visited the siege before going on to Chester, leaving Colonel Roger Mostyn and Colonel Thomas Davis in charge. It was reported by Orlando Bridgeman 'Hawarden Castle is now blocked up by 1,000 men, most of them of the country, and we are in hopes to starve them out.

Lord Capel wrote rough words to his adversaries threatening:

Not to starve you but to batter and storme you and then hang you all. I expect your speedy answer this Tuesday night at Broadlane where I am your near neighbour.[5]

There does not appear to have been much battering:

Sometimes they would at about 10 or 11 o'clock at night give us a volley of shot under the castle wall, but being answered 'they hasted home to their burrows or earthworks again'.[6]

The parliamentarians surrendered on 3 December, although contrary to the terms agreed the royalists abused some of them. The royalist Captain Byrch recorded the desecration of the parish church by the parliamentarians:

I myself, coming into the church of Hawarden the morning after they were there, found the Common Prayer-Book scattered up and down the chancel, and some well read man, without doubt, conceiving that the Common Prayers had been in the beginning of a poor innocent old church bible, tore out almost all Genesis for failing. It stood so dangerously, it was suspected to be malignant. In windows where there was oriental glass they broke in pieces only the faces; to be as frugal as they could, they left sometimes the whole bodies of painted bishops, though in their rochets. But if there was anything in the language of the beast, though it was but an *hoc fecit*, or at worst, *orate &c.* (and I but guess, for I could not read it when it was gone), which had stood many years, and might many more, without idolatry, that was dashed out. They had pulled the rails down about the table and very honestly reared them to the wall (it was well they were in a coal country where fuel was plentiful), and brought down the table to the midst of the church. Some of our soldiers came and swore it was not right … and set it close to the east wall again.[7]

The Civil War moved in favour of the parliamentarians In July 1644 the royalists were defeated at the battle of Marston Moor, Sir Thomas Myddelton met with success along the Welsh border and in February 1645 Brereton and Myddelton crossed the Dee with 2,000 men and besieged the castle at Hawarden, but fled because of the presence in the area of royalist troops. The parliamentarians

Sir Thomas Myddelton, 1586–1666, Parliamentary Major General for North Wales.
[FHS Vol. 6]

returned in April when Brereton crossed the Dee to intercept an ammunition convoy on its way from Anglesey to Chester. The convoy slipped into Hawarden castle to take refuge, and in the absence of the governor, Sir William Neale, away in Chester, his wife Lady Helen, supported by Captain Thomas Whitley as acting governor, withstood the siege conducted by Major James Lothian for Brereton. It was not an easy time and Lady Helen expressed her unease when she wrote:

> Our condition is very desperate for besides the approach of their mynes which is very neare ye great round tower they have brought over great peeces for five carriages we discovered, but whether they be all for Battery wee know not because ye worke they are making for one of them is conceived by ye captain for a mortar piece and that is making in the field above your seate.[8]

The siege was raised on 20 May when the royalist army came into Cheshire and the parliamentarians retired from Hawarden. Time was running out for Charles. Cromwell created the new Model Army, which showed its mettle at Naseby in June when the Ironsides annihilated the King's main army. On 24 September the King was in Chester when his forces were cut down at Rowton Heath. He left the city the next morning:

1645 Thursday Sept 25
   About 9 and 10 in the morning the King left Chester and went to Harding Castle, governed by Sir Wm Neale, stayed 3 hours, and that night to Denbigh Castle.[9]

At the beginning of 1646 Hawarden castle was again under siege. It came about that Lord St Paul slipped out of besieged Chester to meet with Sir John Owen at Conwy to organise relief for the city. He reached Flint Castle in safety and the governor of Hawarden was asked to light a fire on top of the keep to inform Chester that he had safely slipped through the enemy cordon. In reprisal for this action Major General Thomas Mytton, sent Colonel Massey and Lieutenant Colonel George Twistleton, to again besiege the castle.[10]

Sir William Neale was well prepared for another long siege with good stores of food and ammunition. The fate of Chester, surrendered by Lord Byron on February, made it most unlikely that Hawarden castle would ever be relieved. Neale refused to submit to the enemy without written permission from the King. This was granted and, on 16 March 1646, Neale marched out of the castle with his colours flying.

The fate of the castle was decided on 22 December 1646 when Parliament ordered that those royalist bastions of defence, which had so gallantly opposed them, should be slighted, and Hawarden shared the same fate as Flint, Holt, Rhuddlan and Ruthin.

Sir John Glynne (1603–66)

The last resistance of the royalists came on 3 September 1651 when Cromwell destroyed what was left of their forces at the battle of Worcester. Charles II escaped, but not so his loyal supporter James, seventh Earl of Derby,

Charles, 7th Earl of Derby, and his wife
Charlotte de la Tremouille and daughter, Lady Katherine
(after Van Dyke)
[FRO PR/C/20]

who was captured and executed at Bolton in October. The truculent Earl had refused to co-operate with the government committee responsible for extracting fines from their enemies. This was called the committee for compounding with delinquents. The Earl continued his opposition from the Isle of Man where Countess Charlotte threatened that if he would not go to England to join Charles II in 1651 she would take his place and 'bade him pull off the breeches and she would put them on, and then lead them on'.[11]

In July 1651 the Council of State, with the authority of three Acts of Parliament began to confiscate royalist estates and sell them. In order to salvage the Derby estates Charles the eighth Earl attempted to raise money to buy back his estates from the Commonwealth trustees. So desperate was he that in a complicated series of transactions he received money and signed documents and confirmed others in the ownership of confiscated Stanley estates. In 1652 George Twistleton the Governor of Denbigh, Humphrey Ellis, the governor of Hawarden, and Sir John Trevor of Trevalyn, acting as a syndicate, bought the three Flintshire lordships of Hope, Mold and Hawarden, from the Commonwealth trustees for £13,000 and agreed to sell the properties to Earl Charles when he could raise the money at the end of 1653. In the meantime the syndicate paid him £1,700 in return for which he legally recognised Twistleton's, Ellis's and Trevor's

Sir John Glynne, 1603–66, Lord Chief Justice.
[FRO 28/E/8]

joint tenures of the three lordships and subsequent conveyances of those estates made by the new owners. John Glynne decided to buy the manor and lordship of Hawarden from the syndicate, and for this he paid the Earl £1,700 with his agreement signed in Glynne's room in Lincoln's Inn and witnessed by him and Sir Orlando Bridgeman a former chief justice of Chester and a specialist in conveyance, he paid £9,000 to Trevor, Twistleton and Ellis by the Earl's particular direction.

Sir John Glynne was the second son of Sir William Glynne of Glynllifon in Caernarfonshire. The family were descended from Cilmin Droed-ddu, the founder of the fourth noble tribe of Gwynedd. John was educated at Westminster School, Hart College Oxford and Lincoln's Inn, and was called to the bar in 1628. By 1640 he was elected as Member of Parliament for Caernarfon and Westminster choosing the latter. He made his name almost immediately by his merciless summing up at the Impeachment of Strafford in 1641. He was made Recorder of London in 1643, but was accused of treason when he opposed the power of the army in 1647, pressing for its disbandment. For these views he was placed in the Tower from 8 September 1647 until 23 May 1648. Cromwell favoured him, and in 1654 he became sergeant-at-law, judge of assize and in the next year Lord Chief Justice. After the death of Oliver Cromwell, he resigned his judicial offices. He recovered his power at the Restoration of Charles II, who made him King's Sergeant, and gave him a knighthood and his eldest son William, a baronetcy. In 1661 Samuel Pepys wrote in his diary his impressions of the Coronation:

> Thus did the day end with joy everywhere; and, blessed be God, I have not heard of any mischance to anybody through it all, but only to Sergeant Glynne, whose horse fell upon him, and is like to kill him, which people do please themselves to see how just God is to punish the rogue at such a time as this; he being now one of the King's sergeants, and rode in the cavalcade with Maynard, to whom people do wish the same fortune.

The destruction of the crosses

Richard Willett said that there was in Hawarden an upper and lower cross both of which were demolished in 1641 by order of Parliament. On the site of the crosses, were planted trees, in 1742, by Thomas Fisher, the Parish Clerk. Hywel Wyn Owen[12] has identified the following:

Aston Cross, the Upper Cross — this is said to be on the site where now stands the Hawarden Fountain. Edward Lhwyd in 1699 records Aston Cross Well. It is here that the weekly market was held.

Lower Cross was situated near where now stands the House of Correction at the top of Crosstree Lane. Owen states that a 1733 map shows a 'recess' at the side of the road at this point.

The churchyard cross, mentioned in the 1663 Terrier, which Bell Jones locates: 'The Church stands, not in the centre of the enclosure, but rather to the north, the site of the ancient Churchyard Cross (now destroyed) being more nearly central. 'Apparently it was destroyed *c*.1643, leaving the base and part of the shaft (seen in a drawing of the church in 1745); this was replaced by a sundial in 1755 which in turn was replaced by a new cross on the old base'.[13]

An ordinance of Parliament passed on 28 August 1643 provided:

That before 1st November, 1643, all crosses in, or upon all and every the said churches, or other places of publique Prayer, Churchyards, or other places to any of the said churches. . . belonging, or in any other open place, shall before the said first day of November be taken away and defaced, and none of the like hereafter permitted in any such church. . . or other places aforesaid.

The ordinance was entitled, 'Monuments of Superstition or Idolatry to be demolished', and ten days later, the parliamentary soldiers took into their own hands to carry out this mischief in Hawarden Church and more likely to the other crosses mentioned above rather than in 1641.

Coningrene Cross was at the west boundary of Hawarden Township and situated in Ewloe. Bell Jones reported:

Rector Neville in his notes says that it was related by several old persons now living (c.1830), whose parents well remembered that the curate used to accompany the children from the free school in procession every Holy Thursday to the boundaries of the Hawarden Lordship. They proceeded first to the site of the Cross at Conings Grove at the western extremity of the town (where the manor of Ewloe commences and where the cross had been taken down by the Parliament) and there under a large tree, the Minister read a prayer and the children all knelt down. The latter carried white wands and those who had the longest received two cakes instead of one provided at the expense of the Parish.[14]

Crosses in churchyards were often the centres of the market place and in many parishes the place where labour was hired, hence the Welsh expression, *cyflog y groes*, and the wage of the cross and if a bargain made there was not kept it was called 'breaking the cross'. The cross sometime stood ten or eleven feet high and at the top there were usually niches with saints represented, and invariably the rood, with the virgin and St John.

One of the objectives of many of the parliamentarians was the abolition of bishops and the purging of Anglican clergymen who had royalist sympathies. This meant that many were dismissed and those ministers, sometimes Presbyterian, who were felt to be more suitable, were 'intruded' in their place. This is what happened in the parish of Hawarden. The patron of the living of Hawarden at the beginning of the civil war was the Earl of Derby. The rector at the beginning of the civil war was Christopher Pashley of the University of Cambridge. He had been chaplain to the Earl of Derby and was nominated to be a member of the Assembly of Divines. He was deprived of his living in 1643 and went to live in Shotton and enjoyed the friendship and benevolence of Sir Thomas Myddelton. Edward Bold succeeded Pashley in 1646 and combined the rectory with duties as a schoolmaster. He came to Hawarden with the approval of the Committee for Plundered Ministers whose brief it was to protect puritans, which they did by nominating them to vacant parishes. Bold died in 1655 and was interred in the chancel of the parish church. Laurence Fogg, his successor, was a Presbyterian but received episcopal ordination in Galloway in 1661. He was not ejected from Hawarden, where he had been among the first to restore the Prayer Book in 1660, but he resigned the living at the end of July 1662 because 'he scrupled the declaration against resistance to government required by the Act of Uniformity'. He spent three years in retirement and eventually became Prebendary and later Dean of Chester, 1692–1718. He was succeeded at Hawarden by his brother Orlando Fogg, who died at Hawarden in 1666.

Stability came with the appointment of John Price whose character and career is beautifully summed up in his epitaph inscribed on the palimpsest brass in the Whitley chancel. It was formerly on the north wall of the chancel by the door to the vestries:

> Here lie deposited the remains of John Price, Professor of Sacred Theology, the younger son of John Price of Rhiwlas Esquire, sometime Fellow of New College, Oxford and afterwards Prebendary of St Asaph, who eminently adorned the splendour of his lineage by unaffected piety towards God, sanctity of character, integrity and gentility. As a young man he led a troop under his brother William for Charles I. Thereafter he dedicated himself wholly to Christ and the Church, and, ordained into the priesthood, ruled this church for 18 years with the highest praise. He lived 63 years, 9 months, 11 days and died the 4th March, A.D. 1683.

The Church Court of the Parish of Hawarden

The Rector of Hawarden enjoys the privilege of issuing marriage licences under his own jurisdiction. No other incumbent in the diocese shares this privilege which is the sole function remaining of what was called an exempt jurisdiction. The Rector for nearly six hundred years enjoyed exemption from the control of the Bishop of the diocese. As we noticed

Rector Lawrence Fogg, DD, 1656–62
[B. Jones deposit, FRO D/DM/592]

above Roger, Rector of Hawarden in 1289, obtained the privilege of absenting himself and his parishioners from the Consistory Court of the Archdeacon of Chester because of difficulty of access '… on account of the intervening water, hostilities and other reasons'. This made the parish of Hawarden a Peculiar. To confirm this privilege the ratification by two Popes, Honorius III and Clement IV, was obtained. In 1830 the Ecclesiastical Courts Commissioners reported that there were nearly 300 Peculiars and recommended that they should be abolished. This was done in 1849 with the exception of causes Testamentary and the granting of marriage licences. Throughout the centuries, the Bishop of Chester attempted to recover his lost jurisdiction. In 1741 Sir John Glynne resisted the Bishop's attempt to wrest the privileges from the parish asserting the exclusive rights of the patron by appointing Hugh Thomas to officiate 'and no other person without my licence or consent to presume to officiate in ye same. I have caused ye seal of ye said church of Hawarden to be affixed. Dated from ye Castle of Hawarden 31 July 1741'.

The seal of the Peculiar is displayed in the parish church on three large tablets on the south wall, which list the rectors of the parish. The first known use of a seal was in 1391 when Roger Davenport attested a document with his seal, which was a representation of the Virgin and Child, which continued to be used until early in the seventeenth century. The seal of the Peculiar was made new at the Restoration by Rector Laurence Fogg. It represents Daniel in the lions den with the motto *Sigillum: Peculiaris: et exemptae: jurisdictionis: de: Hawarden* with arms of Fogg introduced on a small shield. Impressions in existence show that the device on the old seal in use in the years preceding the Commonwealth are practically the same, but without the arms of Fogg. Why was the old seal lost? Was it regarded with abhorrence because of so-called popish images? Why Daniel in the lions den? Was Daniel confused with Deiniol? Maybe the explanation is that Puritan enthusiasts regarded the church courts as 'dens of lions, and mountains of leopards. . . the cages of uncleanness'?

The Hawarden Court met in the consistorial court, a room screened off at the east end of the Whitley chancel. The Annual Visitation of the parish usually conducted in other parishes by the Bishop or Archdeacon was in Hawarden under the jurisdiction of the Rector and was held in May, usually on the Tuesday preceding Holy Thursday. In the period from the Reformation until the middle of the eighteenth century, the court would meet for business at least once a fortnight. Its officials each wearing their own particular judicial garments and wigs attended the court.

The chief officials of the court were the Commissary, Surrogate, and Registrar. The names of the Commissary

Seal of the 'Peculiar and Exempt Jurisdiction' of Hawarden [FHS, Vol. 4]

between 1563–1663 are known. Three of them held the degree of Bachelor of Law. After this date no Commissary seems to have been appointed, the chair of the court being either taken by the Ordinary (the Rector) in person or by a Surrogate appointed by him. There is a list of surrogates from 1573 to 1814, and Registrars from 1562 to 1828.[15] The surrogate appointed was often the curate of Hawarden or a neighbouring incumbent. The Registrar was the key figure in the court an essential officer to every ecclesiastical court, qualified as a notary public and thoroughly conversant with church law.

Another important officer of the court was the Apparitor, or Summoner, so called because it was his job to 'summon' persons to 'appear' as the court required. He was the court's messenger, delivering citations to those parishioners presented by the churchwardens. He attended all the court sessions and acted as Beadle. His role has been sympathetically described by E. R. C. Brinkworth:

Generally of humble status, the Apparitor had to be literate … the job was an arduous, and often dangerous, one; it involved constant tramping through the parish, and no one was pleased to see him, because not only did his official activities generate considerable hostility — abuse and assault, even — but it was felt that he was all the time acting as the eyes and ears of the ecclesiastical authorities, always snooping, picking up gossip, and monitoring the daily (and nocturnal) activities of his fellow parishioners 'as a kind of ecclesiastical gestapo', then passing on the names of those who were offending — or suspected of offending — against church law so that the churchwardens could include them in their presentments.[16]

The church exercised a dominant influence on the lives of the people. The principles established by the Church of England at the Reformation were that everyone in the nation should attend church — this what was meant by Uniformity — and the monarch was the head of the Church, the Supreme Governor — this meant the Church was established by law made in Parliament where the rules or canons enacted by the church became law. The enforcement of the rules of the church was through the church courts.

The records of the Hawarden Court survive from the years 1554–1858 and include the act books of the peculiar, 1667–1858, and wills, administrations, inventories, and some other consistory court papers.[17]

In the process of calling the court the citation was published by the registrar summoning the accused 'to answer personally certain articles concerning their souls health and reformation of their manners especially concerning crimes and misdemeanours as mentioned opposite their names'. The churchwardens and their assistants the sidesmen, played a leading role in maintaining everything relating to the church building and acting as guardians of the community's morals and general behaviour as the canons of the church directed. There were 30 sidesmen to bring the guilty to justice, two from each township in the parish of Hawarden. They were generally regarded as informers. Any neglect of the fabric of the church, neglect of duty by church officers — including the churchwardens, the parson, the schoolmaster, and others was presented to the court in what was called a presentment.

Who were the people who could be presented in the church court at Hawarden? Canon 109 of 1603 reads:

Whitley Chancel Peculiar Court [B. Jones deposit, FRO D/DM/592]

Notorious crimes and scandals to be certified into ecclesiastical courts by presentment.
If any offend their brethren, either by adultery, whoredom, incest, or drunkenness, or by swearing, ribaldry, usury and any other uncleanness, and wickedness of life, the churchwardens or questmen, and sidesmen in their next presentments to their ordinaries, shall faithfully present all and every of the said offenders to the intent that they, and every one of them, may be punished by the severity of the laws, according to their deserts, and such notorious offenders shall not be admitted to the holy communion till they be reformed.

Amongst other groups of people who could be presented were schismatic, disturbers of divine service, non-communicants at Easter.
Canon 85 of 1603 —

Churches to be kept in sufficient reparations
The churchwardens or questmen shall take care and provide that the churches be well and sufficiently repaired, and so from time to time kept and maintained that the windows be well glazed, and that the floors be kept paved, plain and even, and all things there in such an orderly and decent sort, without dust, or anything that may be either noisome or unseemly, as best becometh the House of God, and is prescribed in an homily to that effect. The like care they shall take, that the churchyards be well and sufficiently repaired, fenced, and maintained with walls, rails or pales, as have been in each place accustomed. . . but especially they shall see that in every meeting of the congregation peace be well kept; and that all persons excommunicated and so denounced, be kept out of the church.

The defendants summoned to the court and having been presented could either plead guilty or innocent. If the accused party maintained their innocence then they were required to 'purge' themselves by returning to the court at a later session with a certified number of friends and neighbours to testify to their belief that the defendant was telling the truth in denying the charge. These witnesses were called 'compurgators' and the defendant met their expenses. Compurgation was brought to an end by statute in 1660.

Here is a list of the variety of reasons given for the summoning of parishioners to face the rector of Hawarden or his surrogate in the court held in the Whitley chancel.

The first category concerns offences against sexual morality, what the Prayer Book called 'notorious evil-living', incontinence, or breaches of the marriage vows. Here are a few examples of what was the commonest category of offences presented.

John Myers for not dwelling with his wife. 1571.
Richard Pulford and Ann his wife for living a disorderly life in scolding, brawling, and disturbing their neighbour. 1592.
David Griffith and Elizabeth Foxe for fornication. 1634.
John Knight and Elizabeth Foxe for the like and failed to send his servant maid away with child and to keep company with three besides his wife and for harbouring his daughter in childbed. 1634.
John Meredith of Shotton for fornication with Mary Shone Spinster. 1663.
Robert Okell of Broadlane gent. for fornication with Dorothy Connah spinster. 1724.
Catherine Barnes for fornication and bastardy. 1763.
John Evans of Hawarden 'peruke' (wig) maker for adultery with Alice Bevan widow. n.d. 18th. Century.
Complaint of Catherine Weigh against Ann Millington for calling her a whore and 'an old hairy witch' and accusing Thomas Weigh her husband of stealing a thrave of Mr Whitley's (tithe) wheat. n.d. 17th century.
The second category concerns absence from church and the profaning of the Sabbath.
Mr. Whitley of Aston for taking the parson's wife into a (stall) where he had no right to come, and by means whereof Divine service was disturbed. 1571.
Ellen the wife of Robert Jones and Elisabeth Tathem for misbehaviour in time of service. 1637
Elisabeth Jenkins of Hawarden widow for repairing to a charmer at Chester. 1637.
Peter Maurice of Hawarden for wandering out of Church at the time of Divine Service. 1637.
Thomas Fox and others of Broadlane for sleeping usually during Divine Service. 1637.
William Adams of Broadlane for going out of the church at several times and loitering in the churchyard. 1638.
William Walworth and John Meredith of Shotton for lying along in the churchyard; and neglecting the church in the time of Divine Service; also William Rowley of Ewloe for selling in the churchyard at the time of sermon and refusing to come into church when he was spoken to by one of the Sidesmen; item Ralph Kelly for suffering Robert Davies of Broadlane to stay in his house at the time of evening prayer with a stranger. 1638.

Alexander Parry of the Manor and Margaret his wife for not partaking of the sacrament at the feast of Easter and other festival days as any charitable Christian ought to do, and they are delinquents by the space of two years last past to the great reproach of the parishioners. 1636.

Thomas Jones of Pentrobin for labouring in his garden and baking bread on the Sabbath day. 1637.

Several persons for selling ale to extravagant persons at the time of Divine Service. 1637.

Edward Perkins of Broadlane for retaining disorderly persons to play at unlawful games in his barn on the Sabbath day. 1637.

Richard Ridgate of Broadlane for employing two servants to carry water for brewing on the Sabbath day. 1637.

Alice Roger, widow, for making her servant to delve in her garden on a Sunday. 1638.

John Foxe of Mancot-ye-lesse for standing with his hat on his head and talking to ye disturbance of the Congregation at ye administration of ye Sacrament of Baptism. William Adams for not kneeling in ye time of prayers, and John Thomas for sitting with his hat on in the time of Divine Service. 1640. (These were probably Puritans).

We present William Brandreth of Hawarden for not sending his children to be catechised, John Siddall and others for not sending their children and servants to be catechised. 1640.

We present Jane Combach of Broughton and the wife of Richard Evans of Hawarden who are Popish recusants (Roman Catholics). 1640.

Robert Robinson for keeping his family and his servants to work on 5 November and for not coming to church. 1661.

Robert Ravenscroft of Broadlane for weaving on Christmas Day last past.

The regulations of the church with regard to marriage were strictly enforced. Persons wishing to marry were required to have their banns published or obtain a licence. Sometimes these regulations were evaded and clergy could always be found to officiate without regard to them. These were regarded as 'clandestine marriages' and couples going through such ceremonies when discovered were brought before the church court to explain such an irregularity.

Randle Whitley and Dorothy his wife for marrying without banns asking. 1592.

William the sailor to prove his marriage. 1640

Lewis Bryan and Ann Edwards to prove their marriage. They confessed in court that they had been married in a house in the Parish of Mold without licence or banns asked, by the ministering of Mr Powell curate there. 1670.

Francis Gill and Elizabeth Wynne his wife for clandestinely marrying. The said Francis confessed in court that he was married upon the 2nd day of Feb. 1700 to Elizabeth Wynne in the Castle of Chester about three of the clock in the afternoon, by one Richard Woodward, a minister and in Holy Orders, as he was informed: which said Woodward is now and then was in Gaol in Chester Castle. There was then by and present at his said marriage the Turnkey of the Keeper or Gaoler of the Castle, and a woman who drew drink in the said Castle, but their Christian names he doth not know. 1701.

Another category of offences concerned the shortcomings of the incumbent and churchwardens and the abuse the officials of the court suffered.

John Whitley for because that he do not bring forth the chalice that he hath in his keeping. 1563.

Robert Garrett and William Clerke Church Wardens for letting down the walls about the Churchyard. 1568.

Master Parson for because that he gave no proclamation in the church within the great aisle; also the said Parson for because he do not keep resident here, and because he do not keep a bull and a goose for the parishioners. 1567. This was Thomas Jackson who had been given the living by the Earl of Derby at the age of eleven years in 1561–2. Bringing these matters before the court was one way in which the parish could show their displeasure.

The churchwardens for not providing the books of Homilies and the first and second Tome. 1591.

John Hewitt of Bannel, George Miers of Ewloe and Edward Mitchel of Rake, sidesmen chosen by the Parish, for refusing to come and make presentments and neglecting their office and not discharging their duties. 1636.

Catherine Shone for threatening to throw scalding water upon the officers of the Church, if they should come into her house to execute their office.

Catherine the wife of Richard Shone, for giving railing speeches to one of the officers for doing his duty. 1637.

The court also exercised a supervisory role to prevent malpractice and false teaching by making licences obligatory for physicians, midwives, and schoolmasters.

Catherine Price of Ewloe for practising Midwifery without license. 1674.

The Court was responsible for controlling seats in church. Where people sat in church was a sign of their social standing in the parish. Seats became part of the property of the family and were passed on from one generation to another.

Persons having title to a vacant place in the church to show cause why they should not be confirmed to William Corbin of Broadlane gent. And his successors as appurtenances to his mansion house in Broadlane. 29 October 1735.

The church was well regulated in the eighteenth century. This is shown, for example, in:

The presentment of the churchwardens of the Parish and Parish Church of Hawarden given at the Consistorial Court of the Reverend Richard Williams Rector and Judge of the said parish and Court held in the said Parish Church on Friday 21st day of May 1742.

We ye Churchwardens of ye said Parish Church aforesaid having considered the articles of enquiry to present as followeth:—

As to the Parish Church of Hawarden (excepting a chancel belonging to Thomas Whitley Esq.) the churchyard and walls, and the repairs of the Font, Communion Table, Linen, Communion Vessels *viz*: A large dish, two flagons, two large cups, two salvers, all gilt with gold (being the noble gift of the Honble. Sir John Glynne Bart. and his worthy Lady Honora Glynne), Reading Desk and pulpit, Churchwardens seat, Bible and Common Prayer Book, Register Book, Surplices, Chest and Alms box and other Church furniture.

We have nothing to present as to the Rector and Curate, their legal institution and induction, the due discharge of their sacred office, reading the full divine service, preaching, catechising, residence, loyalty, conformity, celebrating the Lords Supper, Baptising, visiting the sick, Marrying, Burying, Registering, Perambulations, Exemplary Lives, and Sound Doctrine. We have nothing to present concerning the Parishioners in general (excepting Thomas Whitley Esq., who never was at Divine Service in our time of office but once, and then concerned in liquor) their conversation and devotion at Divine Service, their observation of the Lords Day and Sacraments, Marrying and Burying. We have nothing to present concerning our Church officers and their due election. Schoolmaster, Parish Clerk, Physician, Midwife, late Churchwardens, and their just account, provision, Commission and execution of their office.

We have nothing to present (except ye Schoolmaster). We present Thomas Whitley Esq. for not keeping his chancel in repair likewise for refusing to pay his church leys and absenting himself from the Parish church.

We present Thomas Crachley for not paying his church leys.

We present the Schoolmaster for neglecting his duty in the Free School.

Jo: Boydell, Robert Jones. Churchwardens.

The other business the Court dealt with was the proving of wills, issuing a Probate Act to authorise the executors to carry out the provisions of the will in cases of intestacy, and granting Letters of Administration.

Being called before the Court and found guilty must have been forbidding because of the nature of punishment meted out to the miserable sinner. The guilty could be either dismissed by the Judge with a warning or be ordered to do penance. Fornication and adultery were considered serious enough to demand a full public penance whilst less serious offences such as swearing, drunkenness, and absence from church could be made in the rector's house in the presence of the churchwardens. The performance of public penance could be both terrifying and uncomfortable. The penitent appeared on the appointed Sunday morning bare legged, bare footed and bare headed with a white sheet around the shoulders and carrying a white wand stood in the church porch and when the service began was escorted by the Apparitor up the church into the chancel and knelt before the reading desk until the prayers were finished. The minister delivered an exhortation and the penitent repeated after him a public confession, expressing contrition for the particular sin committed, and then leading the congregation in the Lord's Prayer reconciliation with the community was complete. Excommunication was more serious and meant that the guilty was cast out of the communion of the church being deprived of the sacraments and attendance at church. There were other disabilities: the excommunicate was not given Christian burial, could not make a will, could not bring an action, give evidence in court, act as an executor or be named as a beneficiary under a will. Forty days after the sentence was published, the bishop of the diocese could certify the excommunication. To be reconciled to the church the excommunicate 'humbly petitioned benefit of absolution'.

In the Hawarden Church court most penances were required for the sin of fornication although they were imposed for other reasons.

John Hibbert of the Moor for clandestine marriage with Mary Browne. 5 August 1636.
William Porter of Shotton for suffering ale to be sold in his house on the Lord's Day. 5 August 1636.
Hugh Richardson of Broadlane for baking bread. 5 August 1636.
Ellen wife of Robert Molineux for scolding with her neighbours. 8 March 1640.

The major reason for excommunication in the Hawarden Church Court was for contumacy, that is, refusal to obey the order of the court, in most cases being the failure to either turn up to the court, or, failure to pay costs or fines imposed.

The records of the Hawarden Church Court show the way behaviour was controlled in a close-knit community. The offences brought before the court were breaches of Christian discipline which were regarded as being harmful to the souls health of the accused and contrary to the peace and well being of the community. In this respect they were necessary although in many instances perhaps a little petty, and giving plenty of opportunity of causing further mischief by the way the information of the offence was obtained.

The Township
The Act of Union in 1536 brought the parish of Hawarden into Flintshire and transferred administrative power to the county rather than to the local lordship. In the reign of Elizabeth I (1558–1603), the government began to use the parish as an organ to implement legislation for the care of the poor. This was a policy, which was virtually in use until 1929. One of the major officers appointed by the various acts of parliament was that of the overseer of the poor who was responsible for distributing relief. To meet their obligations, the freeholders of the parish met together at a vestry meeting, usually held in church, to raise a rate. In a big parish like Hawarden the vestry, the governing body of the parish, would include representatives from all the townships in the parish. Out of this body the officers would be chosen to collect the rate, serve as overseer of the poor, and act as surveyor of the highway.

By the sixteenth century, the townships of Hawarden were Aston, Bannel, Bretton, Broadlane, Broughton, Ewloe Wood, Ewloe Town, Hawarden, Mancot, Manor, Moor, Pentrobin, Shotton, and Rake. Sealand became a township later than the sixteenth century, and Saltney was created a township in 1778 by the enclosure act. All of these townships were distinctive in character and have continued to be so, as this study will reveal. The character of these townships was shaped by the geography of the parish and the settlers who colonised them. Examples in Hawarden parish in the sixteenth century were the scattered communities of Aston and Shotton; the Ewloe townships, formerly in dense forest, but by then almost cleared with waste and common land to the south; the estuarine townships of Sealand and Rake and Moor; the street nucleation of Bretton; and Hawarden itself with its strong manorial foundation.

The township arose all over Britain not later than the Early Iron Age (the sixth century B.C.), and from it was descended the Welsh tref. A thousand years later the Anglo-Saxons settled in the Hawarden area and renamed their townships from the tun, (meaning a farmstead, estate, village) — Aston, Bretton, Broughton, Shotton — and introduced their own type of settlement. These first settlers, both Celtic and Anglo-Saxon, lived off the land, they established rural communities which were agriculturally independent, they were a social and kinship group with a territorial ring round them, chiefly the township, but extending for some purposes into the parish as a whole. As an agricultural and self-subsistent unit they settled in areas which would provide them with ploughland for their grain crops, meadowland to grow fodder, rough pasture to graze their cattle, woodland for fuel, housing, ploughs and other tools and implements. If there was fishing nearby it would be a further incentive to settle. The community in the township was interdependent. This was reflected in the large arable field cultivated in common and available for common grazing after the harvest. The common meadow grazed in common, except before the hay harvest, and the open common pasture or waste. The woodlands, later absorbed into demesne land held by the lord, were rich in timber, fruits, berries, small animals and pannage for pigs.

The Domesday Book entries for the parish of Hawarden reminded us that it was held by Earl Edwin of Mercia as demesne land before the Norman Conquest and afterwards by the Earl of Chester who granted the lordship to the de Montalt family. Hawarden had thus been held as an estate or manor for a long time. The lord of the manor of Hawarden and the lord of the manor of Ewloe between them exercised their influences across the whole of the parish, particularly in the period from 1284–1536. The manor was a legal and administrative unit and a unit of agricultural organisation. It was also a unit which attracted colonisation, more people to meet the needs of the lord, and in this way the townships of Broadlane and Manor came into existence. The estate workers, a miller, a

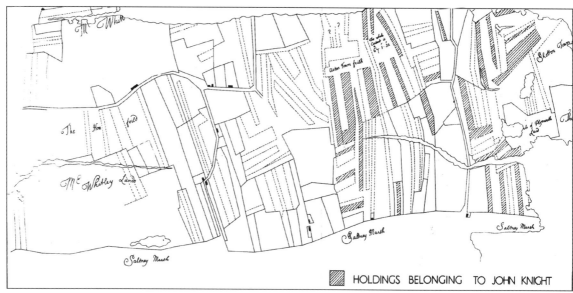

Town fields in Aston and Shotton, c.1651
[Dorothy Sylvester, FHS Vol.15, p.16]

huntsman, a forester, a bailiff, were clustered in cottages in the vicinity of the castle. The lord of the manor retained part of the land, called the demesne, for his own use, while the rest was tenanted or else used for common waste. The manor was beneficial to the whole of the parish and its township because of the advance of cultivation and pastoralism. It was very much a unit of control because of its feudal nature.

The lord farmed the demesne himself, usually by paying wages, and by labour services. The villein, or unfree tenant, held his land by agricultural services. He was obliged to work so many days a week for the lord and also to do boon work, a duty to do such seasonal work as ploughing and harvesting. It was a full day's work by one man from one family to be performed on a number of days in a week and the way he paid his rent for his land by fulfilling various tasks such as hoeing, mowing, carting, sheep shearing, *etc.* Freemen paid a fixed money rent.

The manor became an organisation for regulating the seasonal routine of farming. The extensive use of common pastures and open field cultivation was based on co-operation and benefited from direction by the manorial court. The court determined when the open fields should be thrown open for grazing on the stubble, the time for ploughing, the number of beasts each farmer should put on the common land (his stint).

The commons and wastes were important to all the inhabitants of the township and the manorial tenants. Their common rights were those of pasture for cattle, sheep and horses; turbary — to collect peat; stoves — to gather wood; and, piscary the right to fish in the pools of the manor.

The open fields of the manor of Hawarden were usually below the 200ft. contour line 'on the fertile and easily ploughed plains and low platforms flanking the Dee estuary in Ewloe, Aston, Shotton, Hawarden, Broad Lane, Mancot, Moor, Manor and Rake'.[18] The agricultural land of a township was farmed in large fields divided into strips, long enough so that a plough team of oxen did not have to be turned too often, and narrow because that was all that could be ploughed in a day's work. Parts of the open field could be converted temporarily into leys — grass. The township usually had two large fields that could be used for cropping. It has been suggested that the regularity of the layout of the fields is a result of the regulation by the manorial court. They were laid out in long parallel lands often over 1,000 yards long and divided into furlongs which had a number of strips. Some of these large fields may have stretched over township boundaries. In Broadlane the following common-field names occur: Shawfield, Springwell Field, Mill Hill Field, Broad Lane Field, later Broad Lane Town Field. In Hawarden: Wigdale, the Greet, the Lower Greet and the Higher Greet, the Higher Springwell Field and Springwell Field, suggesting that the Springwell and Shawfields were partly in Hawarden and partly in Broadlane.[19] In Hawarden in the fifteenth century the open fields were Town field (east of the castle in the vicinity of Rake lane), and Higher Great field (by the railway station).

Common meadow was also to be found in the township. In the fifteenth century the manor of Hawarden had 'lot meadows' beyond the arable fields, land divided and allotted annually and in the care of a hayward. 'In the seventeenth century, the Hawarden deeds testify to the existence of common meadow also in Broad Lane, Aston, Broughton, Rake, Manor, and Mancot. There was a meadow in Broad Lane near Springwell Field called the Sich, and one of the same name in Aston, the Reede Meadow in Broughton, Knights New Hay and New Crofte in Broughton Manor. It is evident that the organization and plan of these river and brookside meadows was similar to that of the open arable fields'.[20]

There is some evidence of the nature of the manor of Hawarden in 1464 and 1474–7 in two documents from the Moore Deeds. Moore was an official of the Stanley family involved with the administration of their estates.[21] The 1464 document is a rental of Thomas Lord Stanley and shows that he is receiving rent from his tenants for 584 selions (strips in the open fields). The second document is a compotus roll or a financial account of the manor, which supplies some interesting information. It gives an insight into the way the manor was run. The affairs of the manor are taken care of by the receiver, accountant, and auditor during the absence of the lord and his lady. Their arrival with their guests is always met with great preparation and ceremony. The wages of those who work on the demesne land are given: the swineherd, the hayward, and the shepherd. It is apparent, that personal service for centuries the custom of meeting the duties to the lord, has been commuted for a money payment. Only one person is mentioned as rendering a specific service and that is Jankyn Lech for guarding the castle gate for three nights.

Quotations from the compotus roll of 1474 give some indication of the working of the manor:

And in allowance of a meadow called Tremellmede charged above at 10s. per annum in rent at the lord's will in Broughton because it is mowed for the stock of the lord himself and for the stable at the manor there for the beasts of the lord himself for the aforesaid time — 10s.

And in allowance of rent of a close lying in Pyngfeld containing 24 acres and 15 perches of land lying in the manor charged above at 66s. 8d. per annum because they lie in the hand of the lord himself and are sown with grain of the same lord for the household at the grange of the lord at the manor this year — 66s. 8d

And the expenses of lord and lady, William Stanley Knight, James Stanley, John Stanley my lord's brothers, William Haryngton Knight, John Mallevere Knight and John Ryseley, and their servants staying at Hawardyne in the month of September this year for four days, as in bread, wine, ale, wax, beef flesh, mutton, fresh fish, poultry, spices and other victuals and necessary expenses, together with provender for their horses for the same time … £18 11s. 10d. with 401 white loaves delivered at Lathom and a carcass of beef and three carcasses of mutton.

And the cost of ploughing and harrowing the manor heys this year sown with oats … 23s. 4d.

And paid for ploughing land there, both of fallow and arable, for sowing barley in the same and manuring and harrowing the same … 25s. 11d.

And paid for leading one cart-load of ash-trees cut down this year in the park there and carted to the said manor for making ploughs therewith … 12d.

And paid to John Browne shepherd for buying ointment for the sheep there 2 1/2d., and for leading rushes from Saltney for strewing the sheepfold 2d., and for mending divers defects and the walls of the same house 20d. And paid for washing and shearing 176 lambs this year in all 2s. 6d.[22]

There is a longer account of the expenses and work of John Browne in 1477, which gives a detailed report on the year's profits and losses, with an account of sheep butchered for the lord's household at Hawarden, wool-tax payments and totals of fleeces and sheep.[23]

These are some of the entries:

Sheep killed for the boon-workers of the manor — 7.
Sheep killed at the lord's guest chamber at Hawardyn in November 1477 — 7
And those killed by foxes this year at the time of lambing 20 and those dead 34.
And for 20 stones of wool from 273 shorn fleeces remaining from the last account.
And for 26 stones of wool, each stone containing 16 lbs, from 280 shorn fleeces obtained from all the sheep.
Total 46 stones. And there remain in the keeping at Hawarden 20 stones and at Chester with Huxley 26 stones.

What becomes clear from these Stanley accounts is that he was allowing holdings to fall out of tenancy and he himself to farm the land, and increase his stock of sheep. There was also a tendency to extend the area of arable cultivation by recovering new land from the waste, not by converting it into strips, but by turning into an enclosed holding. In 1235 the Statute of Merton recognised the lord's right to enclose on condition that he left sufficient grazing land for his free tenants. No doubt the reason that the Stanleys 'copped out' hundreds of acres on Saltney was to increase their flocks of sheep.

By the end of the Middle Ages there is a steady growth in land held in severalty, that is, in separate enclosed fields. This was done in various ways. By the clearance and drainage of new land which was never shared out in strips. By the consolidation of existing strips by exchange or purchase into compact blocks under a single ownership. And by the sub-division of common or wasteland. An example of this was at Ewloe in the seventeenth century when a number of local landlords — Robert Stanley, Ann Mostyn (widow), Thomas Whitley, Ann Griffiths, Thomas Ravenscroft, Thomas Ledsham and Thomas Sparke — were accused as 'covetous persons, of the whole castle town and lordship', of procuring leases and dividing the demesne lands among themselves, claiming to be freeholders paying a quit rent. They had removed meres (boundaries), bounds, erected enclosures, felled and taken away timber, taken away the stone and lead from the castle, concealing land and dug coal pits. These accusations were answered by arguing that the lordship of Ewloe extends into the townships of Shotton and Aston, 'but the lordship of Hawarden also extends into the townships of Shotton and Aston and comprehends the larger portion of them and the meres and bounds are not certain'.[24]

By the beginning of the eighteenth century the full communal phase of agriculture was at an end as is evident by the number of leases and grants of individual strips in the townships of Aston, Shotton, Manor, Moor, and Rake. From the 1730s onwards there was a general hastening of the movement to enclose some of the common fields of the Hawarden townships. There are details of the division of Broadlane Township in 1734, the division of the Town Field of Aston in 1736 and Shotton in 1759, as well as an undated general exchange of lands in Mancot where it made it more convenient and economical to mine for coal. The eighteenth century was to change the landscape of the parish entirely, and field and settlement patterns that had endured for centuries were swept away.

Some names of common fields

Aston: Aston Meadow, Aston Town Field, Home Field Town Field.

Shotton: 1651 'Hom Field' in Aston and 'Towne Field' in Shotton. They are highly quilleted areas occupying the greater part of the two townships.

Mancot: evidence of extensive medieval field strips, Mancot Fields (1611), a common field shared with Aston. Meadow Field (1550).

Broughton: Common Meadow, The Hay Field, Big Town Field, Broughton Town Field, The Reed Meadow. Crooked Lounds — strips of arable land in a common field that are crooked.

Manor and Rake: Lord's Meadow, The Rake Hey, The Great Rake Hey.

Bretton: in 1549 the whole district of Bretton is described as 'a forest'.

Bretton Cops, probably part of the '600 acres copped out aforetime' by the Stanley family. (Willett 1822).

'A large place call'd ye Cop was taken in out of Saltney by ye E. of Derby. This may be two miles in circumference and is excellent Land'. E. Lhuyd.

'a parcel of land in a close called Nine Ridges'. (Hawarden Deed 116, 1580).

Edward Lhuyd, Parochialia 1699.
The Townships
1. Hawarden
2. Br. Lane
3. Rake & Manner
4. Bretton
5. Broughton
6. Pentrobyn (Pentre Hobyn y Saeson) and Baunel.
7. Ewlo. 8. Aston & Shotton.
9. Gr. & Little Mancott. 10. Moor.
The Houses of Note
1. Bretton to ye Late Tho: Ravenscrt. Esq. Member of Parlt. who has left 3 daughters.
2. Aston Hall: Thomas Whitley Esqr.
3. Broughton Hall Geo. Hope Esqr.
4. Diglan belonging to ye Evans and now to Mr Wm. Critchley.

5. Shotton farm: Mr Ravensct. but now Mr Lloyd a merchant.

6. Ibidm. Mr Whitley. (note this is probably Aston Hall).

7. The old Hall in Ewlo belong'd formerly to ye Mostyn's, but now to Mr Critchley of Daniel's Ash. This is thought to have been the oldest house in the Parish.

8. Daniel's Ash. Mr Tho: Critchley. Here's a Barrow or Artificiall mount call'd Trueman's Hill near ye Town. And another called Konna's Hey in Broad Lane.

Here were formerly two Parks

1. The Old Park in sr. Wm. Glyn's Ldship, which belong'd to ye E. of Derby.

2 The little Park wherein ye Castle Idm.

Ewlo wood tho so called, is now all inhabited, and no wood at all remaining.

3. The Eighteenth Century

The period from 1688, the year of the Glorious Revolution, to 1815, the year of the battle of Waterloo, is often referred to by historians as the long eighteenth century. It was an era that transformed Britain. In these years it became the United Kingdom following political union with Scotland in 1707, and with Ireland in 1800. Although America gained her Independence in 1776, this loss was overshadowed by victories at Quebec and Plassey in the 1750s , and the extension of Empire to Australasia. The population in Hawarden at the beginning of the eighteenth century was estimated at 3,150, living together in one of the largest parishes in the country, being roughly twelve miles long and eight miles wide. This area was to be subject to such changes as were undreamed of in 1688. The landscape was changed by the canalisation of the River Dee in the 1730s, and the enclosure and drainage of thousands of acres in less than a hundred years. In 1760 the complaint was made to the High Sheriff on the difficulties encountered travelling to Chester:

> If you turn your eyes on Saltney Marsh, you will there see carriages (or at least as much of them as the horses have been obliged to leave behind), with their load, standing immovable for days together, and the eleventh of this month is remarkable for a horse being swallowed up upon the New Road and afterwards drawn out by a rope, quite dead.[1]

The parish registers contained numerous instances of persons buried, who had met with violent death on the marshes between Hawarden and Chester. One 'found with his throat cut', another with 'his head gashed', another 'drowned in the water-ways'. At the end of the century the area was drained and enclosed and traversed with a new road system, an enterprise greatly encouraged by the growing coal industry. On the banks of the New Cut, as the canalised river was called, warehouses began to appear, linked to the coal and clay industries by wooden tramways. The town of Hawarden began to grow, and attract a multitude of craftsmen who were able to pursue their trades from home and sell their wares in the newly established market, and at the periodic fairs held there. These were cordwainers, weavers, peruke-makers, chairmen, flax spinners, whitesmith, wheelwright, cooper, malster, thatcher, and a variety of estate workers. Its growth attracted job seekers from outside the parish. If any of these strangers fell sick they would not be qualified to receive relief, unless they had received a settlement certificate, otherwise they would be removed back to the parish from whence they came. Caring for the sick and poor became the major burden on the parish in the eighteenth century. In order to do this the parish raised a ley (levy or rate), to meet the cost. The benefit agency was the parish governed by its rector, churchwardens, overseers of the poor and other freeholders, in a vestry representative of all the townships. The parish was a hierarchical society with the squire at the top, other gentry together with the parson, and a number of professional men — attorney, surveyor or land agent, architect, and doctor below. In the next tier were yeomen and tenant farmers, below them colliers and labourers, and at the very bottom of the pile the indigenous poor.

We have two small glimpses of the parish of Hawarden at the turn of the eighteenth century. The first is from *The Journeys of Celia Fiennes* who passed through Hawarden in 1698 and took the opportunity to visit her cousin Ann Fiennes, the wife of the Rector, Dr Beaumont Percival. She recounts crossing the river by a bridge into Flintshire:

> … and so crossed over the marshes, which is hazardous to strangers, therefore Mr William Allen (the Mayor of Chester), order'd his son and another gentleman to ride with me to direct to Harding which was 5 mile.
>
> Att Harding, where was my Relation, Dr Percivalls wife, who was Minister of that place; his parish was 8 miles in extent and 2 lordships in it and the ruines of two great Castles in it remaines, its good rich land here much enclosures and woods; in a tarresse (terrace) walke in my Relations garden I could very plainly see Chester and the River Dee with all its washes over the marsh ground which look'd very finely; here are sands which makes it very difficult for strangers to pass without a guide … [2]

Sir William Glynne, 2nd Bt, 1662–1721
[FRO 28/E/3]

Dr. Percival was rector from 1685–1714, and had been given the living of Hawarden by Sir William Glynne, 2nd. Bart. who resided at Henley Park in Oxfordshire. The living was vacant for thirteen months before an appointment was made because William, Earl of Derby, claimed to present the vacancy, but Sir William brought an action against the Earl and obtained judgement.

Joseph Taylor of the Inner Temple gave the next account in 1705 in his account of *A Journey to Edinburgh in Scotland*:

> We crossed the Roodee to Harden the first town we came to in Wales where we saw the ruins of an old castle. There was a wake at Harden, which was very diverting to us. The country lasses were dancing in the middle of the town & seeing them so merry for a frolic we got off our horses & danced with them 2 or 3 of the Northern Volunteers. Kissed them all round with which they were very well pleased. We went afterwards to a Gentleman's house to drink some Welsh ale & found it very strong.[3]

Sir John Glynne, sixth baronet (1712–77), was the epitome of an eighteenth century squire and a person who dominated the parish of Hawarden by the range of his achievements and power of his personality. He was the eighth child and fourth son of Sir Stephen Glynne, third baronet. On his succession to the family estates in 1721, Sir Stephen sold off the family estate of Henley Park, at Bicester in Oxfordshire, and came to live in Hawarden in 1723. The old castle was uninhabitable having been slighted during the Civil War and plundered for its stone by the first baronet. Thomas Ravenscroft the owner of Broad Lane Hall, situated near the old castle, had died in 1698, leaving no male heir, and it was his daughter and heiress Honora Conwy, who leased the mansion house to Sir Stephen. Both Sir Stephen and his successor (also Stephen), died in 1729, and the next heir William, died of the smallpox whilst staying at Aix-la-Chapelle, in 1730. The succession then passed to Sir John Glynne, who the next year at the age of nineteen years, married Honora Conwy, fourteen year old daughter of Honora and Henry Conwy, Esq., of Bodrhyddan, Flintshire, and granddaughter and co-heiress of Thomas Ravenscroft of Broadlane. This marriage was to last until 1769, and produce fourteen children. On the death of his wife Sir John wrote a moving tribute:

Sir John Glynne, 6th Bt., 1712–77, with his wife Honora, Lady Glynne (née Conway), c.1752
[FRO 28/E/6]

> Thus died one to the world unknown who though greatly descended. When she came into the world found no father, never knew a mother without brother sister or friend, a world which she was born a prey to but however lived to despise it, under all the disadvantages of Temporal Acquisition, Heaven furnished her with every Ingredient or Eternal Felicity, for from thence she learned never to speak ill to any, she never spoke but from the sincerity of her heart, without vanity, without folly, without envy, without so much as a wish to gratify any worldly passion. She had a Pride, but nowhere so much as in the Cleanliness and neatness of her person and attire and in the decency and becoming gravity of her manner and conversation. What time she allowed herself from the Service of God (which was her greater pleasure) she bestowed chiefly on needlework of the most exquisite sort. Her amusements were the most innocent, all of them of the domestic kind, and she had no peculiar attachment to any of these.

Notwithstanding all the injuries and wrong she met with from her guardians, and of those to whom the care of their estate was committed, who defrauded her at least of Ten thousand pounds she brought a fair inheritance into the family into which she married, and left it, for she wasted not her own or her husband's substance during the 37 years she was a wife …[4]

The combined and increasing incomes from the Glynne and Ravenscroft estates in the parishes of Hawarden, Dodleston, Kinnerton, and Hope, over a period of nearly fifty years and then for another twenty years during the minority of the eighth baronet (1780–1801), laid the foundation of a substantial estate. Sir John in his lifetime added to the estate by the purchase in 1749 of the Diglane estate for £513 from the Cratchleys and George Hope, and in 1764 the Daniels Ash estate from the Crachleys.

The income of Hawarden when he came of age in 1732 was £792, which he raised to £1,390 by 1760. On top of this was Lady Honora's estate in Hope Parish of £652, and in Hawarden £521. An inscribed stone put up by the baronet expresses his feelings on the times in which he lived during his forty-seven years as Squire of Hawarden.

> Trust in God for Bread, and to the King for Justice,
> Protection and Peace. This Mill was built AD 1767
> By Sir John Glynne Bart. Lord of this Mannor:
> Charles Howard, Millwright. Wheat was at this year
> 9s. and Barley 5s. 6d. a Bushel. Luxury was
> at a great height, and Charity extensive; but
> the poor were starving riotous and hanged.

Sir John Glynne lived in the reign of Queen Anne (d.1714), George I (d.1727), George II (d.1760), and George III (1760–1820). During his lifetime the political life of the nation was disturbed by two Jacobite rebellions, which sought to put the Stuarts back on the British throne. The country was steadied for over twenty years by the rule of Sir Robert Walpole, a Whig, the friend and supporter of the new Hanoverian dynasty. Sir John Glynne was a member of the Tory party, and with his contemporaries and fellow squires and landed gentry in north-east Wales a staunch Jacobite and a member of the Cycle of the White Rose, which met every three weeks on a cycle or roster basis to toast the health of the young Pretender, dream about his return, and to plan opposition to the government. The leader of the Jacobites in Wales was Sir Watkin Williams Wynn (1693–1749), who was said to be in correspondence with the Stuart court. As early as 1734, at the age of twenty-two years, Sir John was pitched into an electoral contest to fight the seat of Flint Boroughs against Sir George Wynne of Leeswood, a candidate supported by Sir Robert Walpole. Sir George Wynne made a fortune from a lead mine at Halkyn which is said to have given him £330,000 in twenty years. Sir John triumphed in the poll by 270 votes to 258; however, the bailiffs disallowed 24 votes, and declared Wynne elected, a decision later upheld by the Commons.[5] It was long believed that Glynne's expenses were £35,000 and Wynne's more, and that the cost of this election crippled the Hawarden Squire for a long time. In fact the expenses were much less: £4,033 14s shared between Sir John Glynne and Thomas Mostyn. Sir John Glynne was returned unopposed for the County seat in 1741 and five times between 1753 and his death in 1777 for Flint Boroughs. It was noted that in 1768 he bought four voters 'a pint of ale apiece' and, including the cost of bell-ringing, spent under £2 altogether.[6]

In 1745 his Jacobite loyalty got the better of him as Whittaker reported:

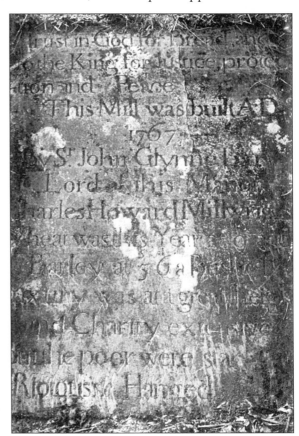

The inscription on the Hawarden millstone
[FRO 28/H/9]

It appears that, in company with the Rector Williams of Hawarden, he drank the Pretender's health kneeling on the bowling green of the Stag's Head Inn, Hawarden. They probably thought their act passed unnoticed; but a certain Madam Hatrell was watching them. She saw the interesting sight of the two most respectable gentlemen in the parish on their bare knees drinking to Prince Charlie. Thinking others might possibly be interested, she conveyed information to the authorities; and the unfortunate servants of the White Rose were speedily removed to London. After the obliging customs of the day, they were left in prison for three dreary months probably forgotten, until one day they appeared before the Privy Council. In the absence of proof, they received pardons for all they might have done. One reason for the absence of evidence was that the Hawarden people had taken strong measures to show their disapproval of Madam Hatrell's action. They smashed her furniture and windows, and hinted that they would be pleased to do the same to her if they had the chance. She, not unwisely, disappeared, and consequently was not available as a witness.[7]

It is said that when the Prince Charles heard such stories as this replied; 'I will do as much for my Welsh friends as they have done for me; I will drink their healths'.

Although allies in drinking the health of Bonnie Prince Charlie, Sir John Glynne and Rector Richard Williams never got on together. When appointed, Richard Williams was the curate of Hope and was offered the living of Hawarden, first because he was a kinsman through his wife's family to Dame Honora Glynne, and second he gave the assurance that he would vacate the living in the event of Sir John having a son who fulfilled the necessary qualifications. Sir John had reason to think that the Rector went back on his word. In his diary Sir John Glynne records 'I spoke to the Rector about Stephen going into Orders', and he later wrote to the Rector asking him to resign and the day following 'received the Rector's answer'. It appears that the Rector refused. A further diary entry reads, '1770 3rd January. On Wednesday at noon died Richard Williams Rector of Harden, a man I tied myself to by presenting him to the living. Twenty-eight years we lived in disagreeable harmony. He died a dishonest man'. Stephen Glynne was ordained deacon in 1769 and priest two weeks later, and instituted to the living of Hawarden on 31 March 1770. He was to succeed his father as seventh baronet in 1777. The patron and his successors learnt an important lesson, and the living of Hawarden was kept within the family until 1929, apart from the appointment of F. S. M. Bennett (1910–20).

Sir John Glynne was an improving landowner and had the scope to do so on the large acreage, which was united by the Glynne and Ravenscroft inheritances. Capital could also be obtained when the occasion arose, to acquire neighbouring small estates such as Daniel's Ash and Diglane to increase his holding.

Close by in Manor Township lived Josiah and Mary Boydell. In 1743 they received a lease of 109 acres of land in the vicinity for a rent of £20 a year, a goose at Christmas and the customary renders and services, with consideration for the 'faithful services of Josiah Boydell and the careful nursing and bringing up by Mary Boydell of five of the children of Sir John Glynne and Dame Honora his wife'. Josiah Boydell gave to the estate what his wife had given to the family, 'careful nursing'. The gratitude and affection continued unto the end when Sir John noted on 5 January, 1758: 'Be it remembered that Mr Josiah Boydell My Agent came into my Service the beginning of the year 1734 & continued therein till remov'd by Death which happened on Friday the 16 Day of Dec. 1757.' Josiah was succeeded by his son Thomas who served the estate with distinction, especially during the minority of the eighth baronet. Another son was the famous London engraver John Boydell, who later took his nephew another Josiah as apprentice. The family established themselves as agents and surveyors of the Hawarden estate for over the next hundred years, and their name appears on many plans and deeds. In 1762 they lived in the house now known as Kentigern in Rectory Drive. The coal

John Boydell, Alderman of London, the engraver
[FRO PR/C/27]

Hawarden Castle and Park. A line engraving by William Henry Toms after Thomas Badeslade, 1740. Note the ruins of the Old Castle and the Ravenscroft Broadlane House bottom right.

Broad Lane House before castellation. A watercolour by Moses Griffith
[FRO PR/F/115]

mining and enclosure activities of Sir John Glynne are treated in another chapter.

Slowly Sir John began to improve his demesne land. Cautiously he began to plant trees. 'In 1732', he noted, 'I commenced planting in Broadlane'. These were probably the nineteen lime trees planted in a circle at the northwest corner of the modern castle known as Sir John Glynne's dressing room. '1734 the limes surrounding the base of the old castle were planted'. '1738 the little park adjoining the old castle was planted and stocked with 100 head of Deer'. '1747 the Booberry hill was planted with forest trees of my own raising in the castle orchard'. This was part of an on-going scheme to restock the estate with timber, which had been sold off for £5,000 in the 1660s. Over six hundred acres were planted. In 1749 Sir John planted 13,300 oak, 3,000 ash, 1,000 beech, 1,780 fir, 720 elm, and 410 hornbeam, some 21,000 trees in all and in 1766 six hundred and forty evergreens and shrubs were added. Outside the demesne land Sir John was prepared to use the trees on the estate to further his industrial purposes when he noted in his diary in 1760 that 386 trees were felled at the Bannel and 100 of them went to the pits and the remainder to the river, possibly to be used either for tramways or wharfing facilities.[8]

Patiently Sir John had been accumulating money to build a new mansion house with more accommodation to replace the old Ravenscroft house with a new Broadlane House.

Sir John strove to build it out of what he called the Fund Account. This 'took its rise and name from several sorts of money that did not immediately arise out of the old rents on the Rent Roll, but whenever in those years their was any Tenement that dropt out of the lease, those improved Rents went to this Fund Account which together with diverse Cole Rents, & other incidental acquisitions were thrown together and called the Fund & from thence it was proposed to build Broadlane'.[9]

The new house replaced the one shown on Badeslade's line engraving of 1740, which occupied a position about a hundred yards south of the present castle. This old Ravenscroft mansion was of wood and plaster construction with two gables projecting with each wing extending eastwards. It was a 'sizeable house and according to a valuation of 1729, it had 45 sash windows, 16 transom windows and 25 windows partly glazed'. The old house was taken down and replaced with a square plain brick building with stables and other offices on each side of the entrance court. The builder of the new house was Samuel Turner of Whitchurch, who was thanked by his patron 'for his inspection and honest calling, for he was a very honest man'. He was assisted by his nephew Joseph Turner who lived in Hawarden for awhile before moving to Chester. The three-storey Palladian brick house was begun in 1750 and finished about 1757 at a total cost of £2,624 10s. A further £517 was spent on the outbuildings, and on a house called Diglane (now known as Broadlane), which still exists as a mid-Georgian building about 20 yards to the east of the new castle'.[10] In spite of the loss of the main building accounts, the names of some of the principal craftsmen employed on the house survive. The carver was named Phillips, the plasterer Oliver, the marble work in the chimneypieces was provided by Mr Sefton, and the ironwork by Tillson.

Small works in addition to the planting were undertaken in the Park. At the time of the failed harvest in 1740 when disease and famine stalked the neighbourhood, Sir John provided the unemployed with work when he had them construct an amphitheatre, made of turf, surrounded by several platforms rising one above the other.[11] He built the stone bridge over the road between the garden and the castle in 1771. The kitchen garden north west of the house probably dates from this period. In the southwest corner of the park is a gateway flanked by rusticated stone piers, side gates and ruined twin stone lodges, formerly called Sir John's Lodge. After the death of Sir John, his successor his son Stephen received a plan addressed to him dated 1777 and described as a plan 'of the Intended Park at Broad Lane. . . with some Alterations By William Emes' which 'shows sweeping carriage drives, the public road removed to the north, a large lake to the south of the castle, and planting belts and clumps. This plan was almost certainly not carried out.'[12]

After his wife died in 1769, he was very lonely and in March 1772 he married Miss Augusta Beaumont, governess to his daughters. Sir John died quite suddenly on 1 June 1777, mourned by the whole parish.

'On the evening previous to the burial, his body was removed to the church, where it was placed in state in the vestry-room; which being hung with black and lighted up, was open all night to the public. There were torches dispersed about the church, and at the porch'.[13]

It was Sir John's grandson, Sir Stephen Richard Glynne, eighth baronet, who encased and castellated Broadlane. He inherited his title on the day of his birth 19 May 1780 (for his father had died tragically whilst hunting on 1 April). During his long minority his trustees managed the estate with efficiency, and his mother

The castellation of Broad Lane House by Thomas Cundy, 1809–10
[FRO PR/F/114]

Mary Bennet of Farmcott in Staffordshire was an astute woman and capable of driving a hard bargain. The value of the estate increased, as did his income and capital, and there was money available for building works. The young boy loved the ruins of the old castle and must have played there, imagining himself as a doughty defender of the royalist cause. A poem of his written when a schoolboy in 1793 shows his romanticism and love of antiquity, which his son too was to inherit.

> A castle is here, the delight of its owners,
> High bosom'd in trees so romantic, and spruce;
> Montalto's old Barons possess'd once its honours
> To curb the assaults of the Welsh was its use.[14]

This vein of romanticism never left him, and when he married Mary Neville, the daughter of Lord Braybrooke, related to five Prime Ministers, it must have increased in him the desire to create a home worthy of such a heritage. The young bridegroom first approached John Nash, adept in the castellated style. He produced a scheme dated July 1807 costing £8,378. Eventually the work was given to Thomas Cundy, senior, who completed his scheme for the enlargement and castellation of Broadlane in 1809–10. Further additions were made in 1830 when the main entrance was moved from the south side to the north, which eventually received a porch built in 1889 by Douglas & Fordham, a gift from the family to commemorate Mr and Mrs Gladstone's golden wedding. In the 1860s George Shaw of Saddleworth constructed an addition in the northwest corner of the castle, which contained Gladstone's study, the Temple of Peace.[15]

Deiniol's Ash

The first mention of the house is in 1478 when Roger Machilde and Alice his wife are described in a deed of '*St. Danialis de Hawarden*'. In the sixteenth century it was the home of the Aldersey family and in the seventeenth century it came into the hand of the Crachley family who had influence in the area as Parliamentary Sequestrators. It had attached to it 'a chapel in the Church of St Deiniol's' as it is described in the marriage settlement of Thomas Crachley in 1681. It probably had the same status as the Whitley chancel, which was attached to Aston Hall until voluntarily surrendered by Admiral Dundas in the nineteenth century. When the house and estate was bought by Sir John Glynne in 1764, the rights in the church for seating and burial were alienated to the Glynne family, and the chapel on the north side of the chancel was thus used for the Gladstone memorial chapel in the twentieth century.

Above: Deiniol's Ash Farm
[B. Jones deposit, FRO D/DM/592]

Right: Deiniol's Ash as it is today
[courtesy of Mr & Mrs David Connah]

Diglane, 1896
[Robert Bankes]

Probably the early core of the house was built by William Aldersey, who was mayor of Chester in 1560, as a timber-framed storeyed hall. 'Considerable additions were made in the early seventeenth century, including a storeyed porch and a new parlour wing, all of brick'. There is a former Great Chamber with a moulded stone fireplace with a high quality contemporary wall painting on the lintel depicting the scenes from the life of St Deiniol which rank amongst the very best in Britain at their early seventeenth century date.[16]

Diglane now called Broadlane

Originally part of the Stanleys of Ewloe estate, which passed into the hands of the Aldersey family on the marriage of Catherine Mostyn heiress of Ann Stanley and John Mostyn of Coed On. It came into the hands of the Minshull family. William Minshull of Diglane whose will is dated 1619, left money to buy a Communion Book and a carpet (cover) for the Communion Table. The house was later vested in the Evans family. John Evans of Diglane died in 1659, and his son alienated the property to Robert Shone, a chandler in Chester and sheriff there in 1676. In 1679 it was purchased by Mr William Crachley, tenant of Manor Farm, a younger son of Thomas Crachley esq., of Daniels Ash. It was mortgaged by a Crachley to his kinsman, George Hope of Broughton, who sold it to Sir John Glynne in 1749.[17] The house was include in Sir John Glynne's building scheme for Broadlane and was largely rebuilt in 1757 and 'given a show-piece façade to be seen from the new house which was built opposite'.[18] George Neville in his manuscript history of *c*.1830 remarked 'Diglane Hall is at present in bad repair, its removal altogether, would widen the present access to the Castle, lay open much of its eastern elevation, & thereby from many points of view, greatly improve the general effect.' This was not carried out, and for over forty years Diglane was used as an orphanage by Catherine Gladstone, and in two World Wars by the armed forces. The house is now called Broadlane and has retained much seventeenth century timber with a fine dogleg stair.

Parish Government

Parish records provide more information about the ordinary people who lived in the community — the peasant, the cottager, the craftsman, and the farmer *etc.* — than any other source in Wales. Some of these records have been better preserved than others. They used to be found in the parish chest usually kept in church, but over the last sixty years many have been deposited in the National Library of Wales at Aberystwyth, or since 1976 in the local County Record Office. Family historians rely on parish registers of baptisms, marriages and burials to give them some information in tracing their family history. Parish registers were ordered to be kept in 1538 when Thomas Cromwell appointed the incumbents (the rector or vicar), as registrars. They still hold this office today, alongside the compulsory state system, which was introduced in 1837. In mediaeval times lay people who resided in a parish were appointed churchwardens as 'the proper guardians or keepers of the parish church'. In 1571 Canon 89 provided that:

> All Churchwardens or Questmen in every parish shall be chosen by the joint consent of the Minister and the Parishioners, but if they cannot agree. . . then the Minister shall choose one, and the Parishioners another.

One of the responsibilities of churchwardens was to be responsible for paying the bills for the running of the church and meeting such expenses as derived from his office either by order of the church vestry, archdeacon, bishop, or act of parliament. The principal method of raising money to meet these expenses was by levying a church rate. There were no collections in church, as we know them to day; they are of recent origin. By the custom of the country, the common law, it was generally regarded as an obligation that every parishioner was bound to repair the church according to the portion of land he possessed in the parish, this was assessed in the parish meeting, and a levy or rate authorised sometimes once a quarter to be collected by the church officers. The accounts of the churchwarden were presented to the vestry annually at the time of their expiry of office, which was usually on the Monday after Easter.

Amongst the church records deposited at the Flintshire Record Office Hawarden are parish registers from 1586, churchwarden's accounts from 1656, and minutes of vestry, select vestry and Easter vestry from 1654.

Here are some examples of churchwarden's accounts:

The accounts of John Marhelt and John Millington Churchwardens in the year 1674.
The Disbursements of the Churchwardens.
Pd for bread and wine to the Communion at Whitsunday 0 6 1
It is the churchwarden's responsibility to supply the bread and wine.
Pd for ringinge the 29th of May 0 8 0 The date celebrating the restoration of Charles II
Pd for ringinge the fifth of November 0 8 6
The date of the gunpowder plot 1605 when the Catholic plot to destroy the Houses of Parliament was discovered.

pd to Edward Millington for one fox head 0 1 0
foxes were regarded as predators
pd for mowinge the Church Rushes 0 3 0
rushes were put on the church floor to make it safe and convenient to walk upon because of the unevenness caused by intra mural burial.
pd for mendinge the first bell Irons & Drawing it up 0 3 0
pd for Bossinge the great bell capper and other Iron works 0 8 1
pd for Glassinge the church windows 0 14 8
pd for Glassinge the Schoole windows 0 1 0

1740 The accounts of George Knight Church Warden, and of his
Sidesman John Moss ye younger in the year 1740
To the amount of four church leys rec'd £ s d
from Bretton 2 4 0
from Broughton 3 8 0
from Pentrobin & Bannel 2 4 0
from Hawarden 2 16 0
from Broadlane 2 4 0
from Manor & Rake 2 4 0
The Accounts of William Read Churchwarden & of his Sidesman William Fox for ye year 1740
The charge from Ewloe and Ewloe Wood 3 0 0
To do. recd from Aston & Shotton 3 12 0
To do. Recd from Mancott 2 4 0
To do. Recd from Moore 2 4 0
Tot: recd 11 —
Discharge as per Disbursements
By expenses at ye procession in riding the Boundaryes of ye Parish 0 15 0
By cash paid for a coat and waistcoat for Thos Saladine an old & Decay'd parishioner 0 12 0
By cash pd Samuel Taylor & others for killing 5 young cub foxes at 1s. each 0 5 0
By do. For destroying two wild Catts this year 0 6 8
By do. For 3 1/2 Gallons of wine agst the monthly Sacraments 1 1 0
By expenses (vizt. 3 journeys to Chester to fetch the sd. wine 0 4 8
By Cash pd Mary ffox widow for cleaning the Church & churchyard agst Whitsuntide 0 10 0

In 1776 it was ordered:

That on account of the great number of sparrows in the Countrey to the damage and loss of the several farmers of this Parish it would be of service towards the defraying of them to allow a certain sum for every dozen that shall be brought to the churchwardens two pence be paid.' Twenty years later the vestry was more cautious when it ruled, 'that the churchwardens do not in future pay any money for sparrow heads & eggs, it appearing that persecution increases rather than diminishes them & care is to be taken that what Foxes & Urchins are paid for should be really caught in this Parish.

There are some entries in the accounts relating to Hawarden Free School (the Grammar School)

1749 By the Repair of Hawarden Free School the same being in a very decayed & ruinous condition, & inspected by proper artificers, who reported it to be very dangerous for the Master & Scholars to resort to £19. 9s. 9^1/2.

1749 It was represented unto us that the Free School is in a very decayed & ruinous condition, & ought to be forthwith inspected and repaired by proper workmen to be chosen for yt purpose … .
We do hereby order & direct, that Isaac Newell and Edward Nanngreave, the present churchwardens, do take care that the necessary Repairs of the said Schoolhouse be done in the cheapest, speediest and most effectual manner they possibly can. The expense thereof be defrayed by the Parish as heretofore has been accepted for time immemorial.

1755 September 28. It was ordered that the upper-room in the schoolhouse should be properly fitted up at the charge & expense of the parish for keeping the publick records thereto belonging.

The Parish was likely to be summoned to appear at the Quarter Sessions to answer for any neglect in the repairs to the Highway. The responsibility for the roads rested with the parish and each township repaired its own roads with stone from the common quarry under the supervision of surveyors of the highway appointed to serve for a limited period by the vestry. In 1727 the inhabitants of Ewloe Township had to shift 'above sixty loads of stones' to repair their road. Bryn Ellis reported:

In 1770 a defence was prepared for Sir John Glynne against a prosecution for not repairing Daniel's Ash Lane, claiming that it had always been a horse way or bridleway. Both Aston and Shotton were presented in 1773 for not repairing Allinders Lane to Hawarden, it being a road to church. Much work was done in the parish in 1799 as certificates of repair were submitted for Leicester's Lane in Broughton, Kinnerton Road in Broughton and Pentrobyn, Hope Road and Penyffordd Road in Pentrobyn and Bannel.[19]

The same writer also draws to our attention the criminal record of William Ithel of Hawarden who made regular appearance at the Quarter Sessions. He first appeared in April 1750 when he was bound over to keep the peace. Four years later he was found guilty of sheep stealing in Hawarden and Broughton and being involved in an assault. In January 1756 he was involved with others in stealing coal in Ewloe. Ten years later he was arrested with John Stubbs for destroying rabbits on the Warren at Broughton. He was also charged on three occasions with assault. The vestry elected the constables involved in bringing these criminals to book.

The Magistrates sitting in Quarter Sessions could order the guilty to be punished in their own community as on 29 April 1756 they ordered that Anne Cheshire, found guilty of a felony, 'be stripped down to the waist and whipped at Hawarden from the Upper Cross to the Lower Cross on Saturday, May 3, between the hours of ten and twelve'.[20]

Transportation to New South Wales in Australia or the other penal colony Van Dieman's Land in Tasmania was a punishment that began to be meted out towards the end of the eighteenth century. This is what happened to Anne Catherall, the wife of John Catherall of Wood Lane, and Elizabeth Huxley widow of Shotton Lane End, who were sentenced to be transported for seven years at the Court of Great Sessions in Flintshire in 1796. Both women were charged with others of stealing and carrying away twelve linen sacks and twenty-one hobbets of oats from the cart of William Roberts near the Boar's Head. Both women were found in possession of a sack of the oats, and although they pleaded their innocence the jurors came up with a sentence, which proved them guilty.[21]

For the town drunk or other nuisance the stocks and the House of Correction were a lesser punishment. This building was originally situated on what was known as the football field, a piece of land adjoining the churchyard, upon which is built St Deiniol's Library. A new House of Correction was designed by the architect Joseph Turner towards the end of the eighteenth century and stands on the site of the former whipping post and stocks at the end of Cross Tree Lane.

We noticed in the churchwarden's account quoted above, the expenses incurred for the boundary procession. This originally took place in May during Rogation tide, the week after the fifth Sunday after Trinity, according to

The House of Correction photographed c.1910
[FRO 28/N/11]

an instruction dating from the reign of Queen Elizabeth I. The parson wearing his surplice and accompanied by the old men of the parish, young boys and others, were to go in procession round the bounds of the parish pausing to say prayers at the meer or boundary stones. At these boundary markers the young boys would have their ears tweaked to help them remember where they were. It was important to ascertain their location for on the knowledge of the boundaries depended the collection of the tithe for the parson's stipend, the rate assessment, eligibility for poor relief, and the right of marriage and burial in the parish church. An entry of 1727 gives the 'expences in riding the Procession & for ale & cakes to the School boys 20s. 1739 was a special year after the recent opening of the River Dee after its canalisation.

By cash pd an Extraordinary Expense attending the riding ye Bounds of ye Parish on ye Procession Tuesday (*viz*) for Drink at ye upper flat amongst a select number of ye Parishioners who went over the Navigation Cutt in order to ascertain ye Limitts of ye parish 3s.

There was always trouble with the Chester parishes which shared a common boundary St Mary's at Saltney and Trinity at Sealand:

1748 By my Journey and Expenses down to the Sands and for assistance there to break down and demolish certain Mear stones within this Parish, which were Erected by the Inhabitants of Trinity Parish in Chester. 4s.

It was recorded in the Vestry Book in 1807 that the Rector of Hawarden and the Rector of Trinity Chester agreed to the boundary which was perambulated on Ascension Day —

… from the line of the boundary between their respective parishes from Blacon Point to the stones in the Garden by the River Side opposite to the bank of the enclosure made on Saltney. It takes its course from the said stones in the said garden, according to the stones set down thereby by the Parish of Hawarden in 1762, at the back or each side of which, the Corporation of Chester set down stones in 1765, to meet the line of the stones set down by the River Dee Company in the boundary between Cheshire and Flintshire.

From to time the parish needed to update their information with regard to its exact extent and the ownership of land. This was very necessary towards the end of the eighteenth century when new land had been enclosed and the expense of keeping the poor was rising. In October 1784 Mr John Earl of Overton in Cheshire was requested by the vestry, 'to make a survey of the whole of the Parish and specify every field in it with its quantity and value which he will transcribe into a book and make an assessment thereon after the rate of sixpence in the pound'. He was further instructed in December 'to survey the lands upon Sealand for their better information to lay a tax upon those lands towards the maintenance of the poor of this parish at large'. In September 1785 an assessment of three pence in the pound was made according to the new survey and this received the approbation of the Justices, for the use and relief of the poor in the parish of Hawarden. The 1785 Survey was one of the very informative documents made at this time, as was the one in 1815 after the death of Sir Stephen Richard Glynne, but this was made for estate purposes and not for the use of the vestry.

In order to honour the dead and make funerals both respectable and reverent, parishes usually went to the expense of supplying their own hearse and this was the case at Hawarden in 1808. To meet the expense of sixty guineas for a new hearse and harness from Joseph Cooper, coach maker of Wrexham, the cost of erecting a hearse house, and the purchase of two new surplices, the vestry ordered that a rate be levied not exceeding four pence in the pound.

In 1740 on the birth of a son and heir to Sir John Glynne, the ringers, Willett recounts, in their expression of joy, cracked some of the bells, the recasting of which cost £150.[22] What really happened was that the parish bought six new bells from Abel Rudhall, Bell Founder, in Gloucester, and sold the five old bells to him reducing the cost to £103 19s. 6d. with carriage and hanging of the bells, bringing the total charge to £130 10s. 6d.

The interest in the proper singing of the Psalms in the eighteenth century was an object dear to the hearts of the Hawarden parishioners. In September 1761 the vestry passed a resolution:

> … that the church wardens do wait upon the Rector of Hawarden to acquaint him that it is the desire of the parishioners that encouragement may be given to good Psalmody in the Parish church of Hawarden in such manner as he shall please to approve.
>
> Order'd that Mr Symons teacher of Church Musick be paid the sum of forty two pounds for the teaching & instructing sixty voices in the art of psalmody for a whole year … and the said Mr John Symons is to give due attendance every week during the whole year for the instructing of them.

There was probably an amateur band or orchestra to accompany them for there is reference to 'repairing the pitch pipe' and the purchase of a new bassoon.

The other major concern of the parishioners was that the church be kept in a good state of repair. We have seen that this was primarily the concern of the rector and churchwardens. The rector was responsible for the repair of the chancel, Thomas Whitley responsible for the chancel named after the family, and the owners of the Crachley chapel for its repair. If these parish officers neglected their duty, they would be reminded at the Peculiar Court or by the Glynne family. Thomas Whitley of Aston Hall, living there in the middle of the eighteenth century, seems to have been a most disagreeable person, often drunk, always absent from worship, and refusing to repair his chancel. There were occasions in most centuries when urgent work was necessary to the church fabric. In the seventeenth century in the 1630s and 1660s, in the eighteenth the turn came in the 1760s, and the work done is recorded in the vestry minutes. As happens when churches are repaired, once the work is started it becomes increasingly apparent that more is needed.

In September 1760 the vestry were presented with a new plan of seating in the church when it was proposed 'that on the north and south sides, next ye walk (by the aisles), 'to be common sittings'. It was also proposed to make a new pulpit and desk. To pay for the work it was decided by the vestry to grant twenty-four church leys. Possibly this meant that the work was to be spread over six years with a church rate being collected quarterly? In

Hawarden Parish Church, 1742, by John Boydell. Note the base of the churchyard cross, left foreground
[FRO PR/F/120]

June 1761 it was decided that four new windows be made, two on the north side and two on the south side, according to the committees recommendation. The committee included the Rector Richard Williams, Sir John Glynne, Ralph Whitley Esq., the churchwardens and the architect, Joseph Turner. To prevent interference and vandalism whilst the work was being carried out it was ordered 'that a person be immediately employed to look after the churchyard & to keep all children &c from coming near the church on account of keeping the windows from being broken & that the said person be allowed four pence per week for doing the same till Easter next'. When the work was reviewed in March 1762 the committee 'approved of the new seating & altering the church'. Presumably this included the four new windows. After the disturbance caused to the fabric they decided to tidy things up by directing:

> … that the inside of the church be plaistered, the walls & pillars to be finished off with white stoko (stucco), The north and south roof, ceil'd betwixt the principal timbers, the centre roof to be rendered betwixt the spars, and the ringing (chamber) be ceil'd; and the timber that appears to sight, after the ceilings & renderings are done to be painted; and that the west window be repaired, & glazed, with Bristol glass in the manner the windows are already done, and that the centre isles of the church be flagg'd, and that a large seat be erected for the convenience of christenings, and that a marble font be provided for the same, and that the south door already done & not provided for, be paid for, and that the alterations of the ringing floors and stone stair case be provided for, and the sum necessary according to the estimate brought in by Mr Joseph Turner to compleat the same amounts to one hundred & seven pounds one shilling and ten pence — which sum we order to be rais'd by the parish for the purpose.

Three months later, in June 1762, it was discovered that the roof of the north aisle 'is very much decay'd that it cannot be effectually repaired without uncovering the whole aisle'. By this time they were running short of money and they instructed that 'Mr Turner shall support and repair in the best manner he can the present roof without uncovering the same'. Thus leaving the problem for future generations to solve and pay for. But there was more to be done and the vestry used hyperbole to justify the work both to themselves and others.

> We have also laid before us further intended alterations proposed in Mr Turner's Design and his estimate of the expence thereof, and are of opinion that it is perfectly consistent with the honour due to the house of God, and the credit of this Parish and as such do recommend it, to the Gentlemen, who are the Trustees for the publick money of this lordship as a proper subject for their consideration.

They were appealing to the Hawarden Embankment Trustees for financial assistance towards the repair work from the annual £200 received from the River Dee Company. The further repair work recommended by the architect was 'the state of Mr Crachley (of Daniel's Ash), chancel'. They recommended that it should be taken down, rebuilt and made uniform with the other part of the church. Before this could take place they required the consent of Mr Crachley. To obtain his permission they offered to compensate him with the provision of 'a proper pew or pews' and if he didn't agree with this then he would be asked to reimburse the parish for their expenditure on the work spent in the repair of his chancel. Mr Crachley was in financial difficulties and there is no doubt that he acceded to the request of the vestry.

When the repairs took place in 1764 a gallery in the west end was removed. In 1706 it had been agreed by the vestry that seats should be placed there for the principal freeholders in the parish church, including Sir William Glynne and his heirs, and William Crachley and his heirs, and others. The rearrangement of the seating in 1761 was to make provision for the removal of the seats in the gallery. In 1765 some of the newly erected seats were sold off to pay for the cost of alterations. This was the largest programme of repairs and alterations undertaken in the eighteenth century. Mr Joseph Turner died in 1807, by this time he was living in Chester where he had been raised to the dignity of an alderman. He lived for a while at the Elms next to the House of Correction he had built. There is a tablet in the church which pays tribute to him stating that: 'The many splendid and public works on which he was engaged in the counties of Flint and Denbigh and Chester will be a lasting memorial of his taste and ability as an Architect'.

Caring for the poor

The great Poor Law Act of 1601 made the parish the unit of administration to care for the sick, the poor, to provide the opportunity for binding young people as apprentices, and to compel the sturdy beggar and vagabond to work. The Act also provided that the parish vestry appoint a special officer to carry out these responsibilities. He was called the overseer. Another Act of 1662 gave the direction that 'any stranger settling in the parish may be removed forthwith by the justices unless he rents a tenement of £10 or finds security to discharge the parish of his adoption from all the expense it may incur upon his behalf'. These regulations were the law of settlement and removal.

For over two centuries generations of overseers administered the Poor Law. The only training they received from the vestry was from those who had experience of the work. In 1749 the list of the duties of the overseers were set down in the vestry minute book. It was recorded that it was the custom on the appointment of overseers of the poor to have their duties explained to them verbally by the vestry clerk. The minutes explained that it was unfortunate that the overseers have not observed the directions given to them 'pretending either forgetfulness or ignorance to palliate such neglect or omission of duty, from whence no small inconveniences, as well as unnecessary charges have arisen. For remedy whereof it is ordered that in future every overseer of the poor shall upon the commencement of his office have a written paper delivered to him by the vestry clerk which shall contain some of the most essential parts of his said duty.

1. To enquire about strangers & their families who come to reside and request certificates or testimonials of their legal settlement and if not enter into a bond of indemnity with sufficient sureties.
2. Overseers not to receive leys (rates), from persons whose names are not on the assessment but to receive directions from the vestry clerk.
3. Overseers not to make contract or agreement with surgeons for the cure of paupers who shall meet with accident or misfortune. But *n.b.* in case of sickness, or families thereby or otherwise reduced to poverty or actual want, overseers have a discretional power to relieve them &c but then, they must not do it upon hearsay, but upon personal view, and inspection of the premises from whence the complaint arises & then to acquaint the said vestry clerk therewith.
4. Overseers to meet in vestry the first Sunday in every month immediately after the evening service & sermon are ended. If he does not he will thereby incur the penalty of twenty shillings to be levied on his goods & chattels &c.
5. That every overseer for the time being do acquaint all such persons living within their respective divisions, who lodge or entertain any vagabond — people, such as gypsies, or any such like kind of foot travellers that they are not, at their perils to lodge or entertain them above one night or two at the most.
6. Overseers to collect their assessments as soon as possible.

A few examples of the overseers work in the eighteenth century will give some idea of the way in which they tried to cope with so many different cases and circumstances. The following selection shows the direction given to the overseer after a discussion in vestry.

If possible the vestry gave relief to enable the supplicant to earn his living. It was ordered in 1750 'that Saml. Wolfe do buy a couple of Hob asses to employ Thomas Lightfoot a poor young consumptive parishioner in order to get him a competent livelihood, he not being in a condition to do any servile laborious work. In 1760 Matthew Cacklonn was allowed three shillings a week 'he being very much burned in a Coal Work & his wife ill of a fever'. Edward Ankers was allowed a sum of money in 1764 'sufficient to purchase a viol, in order to support, maintain & keep himself from being burdensome or troublesome to the parish. Two women were allowed horses. Catherine Mesham of Ewloe in 1758 was given 20s. 'towards buying her a horse wherewith she is to struggle for a livelihood', and widow Morris of Bannel, a year later, 30s. 'in order to carry coals to support her family'.

In exceptional cases of sickness the vestry would often contract with a 'specialist' local healer in an attempt to find a cure. In 1734 the overseer was asked to strike a bargain 'as cheap and easy a rate as he can with Mrs Davies (formerly Vincent) for the cure of Mary Turners sore legs'. Mrs Hyde of Chester was paid the sum of one pound fourteen shillings, for the cure in 1749 of John Davies of Ewloe in the state of lunacy, he the said Davies having already paid as far as his circumstances would provide. Mr Wilbraham, a Chester surgeon, was asked if he would agree to cure Catherine Messams lameness on condition that he was paid '10 guineas, if she is cured, or nothing if he fails'. In 1765 it was 'ordered that Abraham Thomas's boy is to agree for lodging for Elias Kenrick at Wepre on account of his illness, in order to bathe in the salt water & likewise to allow him a reasonable subsistence till further order. When Chester Infirmary was opened in 1755, parishes, if they subscribed, were entitled to send patients there. Hawarden vestry began to do this in 1781.

The vestry were responsible for clothing the poor and the recipients were often forced to wear a badge, with the initials of the parish sown on. This is seen when in 1726 the vestry bought cloth and flannel at Flint Fair and asked the overseer to 'discretionally dispose of it to such poor as have occasion for clothes & will wear the badge'. John Robinson, curate of Hawarden in the mid-seventeenth century, left money for clothing ten poor persons of the parish yearly forever, which yielded £3 a year. In 1740 the vestry ordered John Jenkyn tailor to 'be forthwith employed to buy as much coloured flannel as will be sufficient to make gowns for ten poor women of this our parish, with such other trimming as shall be found necessary for making the same and distribute them to the ten poor widows under mentioned, they being by us adjudged (without favour or affection), to be real objects of charity'. The interpretation of Robinson's bequest was the occasion of an assault by Thomas Fisher, a former vestry clerk, on his successor Edward Thomas, in January 1746. It appears that Fisher and his wife were friendly with Mrs Hatrell, the person who reported seeing Sir John Glynne and the Rector on their knees on the bowling green, drinking the health of the Pretender.[23]

The Act of 1601 gave authority to churchwardens to bind out poor children apprentices. In order to place out the great number of children available to reluctant takers, it became the common practice to ballot for them. In many case they were ill-treated and shared the fate of Oliver Twist. In 1738 it was ordered 'that Mary Parry (a poor girl) lately placed out as an apprentice to and with Thomas Huntington of Ewloe Green, who lately ran away from her sd. apprenticeship be forthwith remanded back to her service, being allowed a petticoat & a new pair of stockings'. Any children who were sent to the poor house were bound apprentice as soon as they were eligible.

Illegitimacy increased in the eighteenth century. Any single woman discovered bearing a child was taken before the magistrates and examined in order to determine the father, and the parish to which she belonged. When the father was discovered he was forced to enter into a bond to support the child, and if the woman belonged to another parish she was moved back there to prevent the child becoming eligible for support. In 1778 it was ordered 'that the overseers of the poor be directed to make use of every lawful means to relieve the parish from the maintenance of the several illegitimate children with which it is now supporting and unnecessarily charged'.

There were other occasions when parishes were forced to maintain children whose responsibility belonged elsewhere. The major culprits were absconding fathers. An example occurred in Hawarden in January 1745 when the vestry minute stated:

> Information was made to us that one George Wright Tailor & Parishioner had lately enlisted himself into the King's Service as a foot soldier in the Guards & was marched off towards London, having left a wife & two small children behind him, which sd. wife this day appeared in vestry, & set forth her poverty & inability to convey herself & children to London to her sd. husband & therefore craved a proper allowance from the parish for that purpose.

The parish were prepared to help her get to London on condition that she gave proper security that the children would not be returned to Hawarden and become a burden to the parish.

In time of war every county was required to raise a specified quota of men to serve under the Crown. Each parish contributed, deciding by lot which men were to serve the three years required. If they were reluctant they were to provide £10 for a substitute. This is seen in the vestry minutes at the time of the Napoleonic war when on 30 November 1796 it was ordered that the overseers 'do as soon as possible engage five men volunteers upon the best terms they can to serve in his Majesty's Army before the 12th of December ensuing & produce them to the Regulating Officer & do such things as necessary according to the above act'.

Parish vestries and overseers were often accused of cruelty and callousness in their treatment of the poor. The following examples from the Hawarden minutes show humanity rather than harshness on the part of the parish officers:

The case of Elizabeth Pickering

1740 November 4th. That upon the representation of George Knight of Bretton & John Lache of the same setting forth the miserable condition of Elizabeth Pickering of Bretton wife of Wm. Pickering labourer, who since her lying in, is grievously afflicted with a certain tumour or swelling in her breast & side, that has perfectly reduced her to a state of inability & weakness, and her said husband (tho' a very industrious labourer) is not of ability to pay a surgeon to inspect her present condition in order to effect a cure. We order Geo. Knight do support Elizabeth Pickering as far as ten shillings will extend and that John Dias Surgeon in Chester be forthwith sent for to take care & inspect the condition of the sd. Elizabeth Pickering & apply what is necessary in her present case.

1740 December 2nd. That Geo Knight one of the present Wardens do pay Mary Boden the person who tended

Elizabeth Pickering the sum of one shilling a week for a month past & for so long as she shall be employed in her sd. Service & the said Eliz. Pickering shall continue in her state of weakness & disorder.

The case of the Cowley family

1740 November 4th. Peter Cowley of Ewloe Collier is admitted to the Poor House upon the following condition *vizt*. That all the profits arising from his labour & work be secured towards the support & maintenance of his three children (William, Margt. & Alice) and paid into the hands of one of the overseers of this parish by the respective Reeve of such Coal pit where Peter Cowley shall work, and that Peter Cowley before his admittance bring along with him such bed or beds he has, with all other his household goods.

Five days later Margaret Cowley was apprenticed to Edward Nangreave of Aston and her brother William was bound to Robert Thornton of Pentrehobyn. A month later on 2 December Peter Cowley was discharged from the Poor House taking his old bed with him. The family had survived and readjusted to circumstances.

The case of the Roberts family

The case of the Roberts family of Broughton is chronicled over three years. It begins in December 1749 when John Roberts of Broughton appeared before the vestry to plead the cause of 'the necessitous and deplorable condition of three of the fatherless and motherless children of the late Thomas & Mary Roberts. How that they are in actual want, and most grievously afflicted with scald heads, and very unfit either to be brought to the poor house or to be set out apprentice or to any service'. The vestry were well disposed to do all they could to help the orphans by medical and financial assistance. The youngest child aged four months was sent to a wet nurse in Lower Kinnerton at a yearly rate of £3 5s. 'removable upon any miscarriage or just occasion'. In February two children were provided with linen caps and the youngest little boy was given a flannel petticoat. In 1752 one of the children William, was put in the care of his uncle John, and the parish were still paying for his treatment. By the end of the year the vestry ordered that he 'be cloathed from top to toe with all things necessary for him, and when he is fit he must be forthwith apprenticed'.

The case of Thomas Bartington

In April 1743 the vestry had strong words to say about the character of Thomas Bartington declaring:

> … that he is in a condition to acquire a livelihood by his labour and ought not to be encouraged in idleness as heretofore, he being a stubborn, insolent and dangerous person, having this day publicly declared that if any person in the poor house would assist he would soon demolish and pull down the poor house or words to that effect; so that we adjudge him fitter for a House of Correction than the Poor House, & there put to hard labour to prevent any further damage that he might otherwise commit and therefore think it proper to apply to a magistrate for his commitment.

Eventually the law caught up with him when Sir John Glynne sent him to Flint gaol, echoing the words of the vestry and describing him as 'an idle stubborn & incorrigible Rogue of Strength & Ability to work, & will not'.[24]

However, when winter came two years later, on 1 November it was recorded: 'This day Thomas Bartington an old incorrigible pauper was ordered to be admitted into the poor house tomorrow morning and to continue therein during his good behaviour and no longer'.

The Poor House

> There children dwell who know no parents' care;
> Parents, who know no childrens, love, dwell there!
> Heartbroken matrons on their joyless bed,
> Forsaken wives, and mothers never wed;
> Dejected widows with unheeded tears,
> And crippled age with more than childhood fears;
> The lame, the blind, and far more happiest they!
> The moping idiot and the madman gay.[25]

Thus wrote the poet Crabbe about the eighteenth-century poor house. We can only see it through the eyes of those who administered the Hawarden poor house during its twenty-two years of existence between 1736–68. Willett say it was established in 1736 at a cost of £114. In January 1737 Samuel Weld the master was paid 1s. 3d.

per week to maintain each pauper in the poor house. In May 1740 a Select Vestry was appointed 'for the good management, proper support and good maintenance ' of the poor house. The members were John Crachley of Ewloe, gent., John Mousdale of Shotton, gent, Josiah Boydell & Wm. Corbin of Broadlane gent, Edward Dewes of Broughton gent, Peter Millington of Pentrobin gent, Thomas Fox, Joseph Fisher, Richard Brown and William Bartington of Hawarden, yeomen, together with the churchwardens & overseers of the poor.

In November the previous year the vestry had drawn up a memorandum governing the running of the poor house. No one was to be admitted into the poor house without the special direction of one or more of the committee. On Sundays, Holy Days and other proper days, the poor were to report to church constantly, accompanied by the master or his wife, and at the end of Divine service they were to decently repair home. The poor under no pretence were to wander abroad to any distant place or village without the special direction of the master, neither were they to bring anyone into the poor house as guests without the consent of the master and mistress. Breakfast was between seven and eight in the morning, dinner between twelve and one, and supper between six and seven. They were to receive clean linen weekly, and the beds were to be clean sheeted every month. If any of the inmates at any time profanely swore they were to be deprived of their meal, and for a third offence the master was to report them to a magistrate. If children offended, the master was to 'give such severe corporal correction as may deter and frighten them to offend in the like manner in future'.

In May 1741 the minutes reported:

That since the building of a poor house and fixing their management under the direction of a select vestry the parish has found great benefit and advantage thereby and the large expense which heretofore attended the supporting of the poor has been considerably reduced notwithstanding the scarcity and dearness of all sorts of grain & other eatables during the whole course of the said year which we must attribute to good economy and the well governing of the poor house.

They added that they were determined to protect their method of supporting the poor and keep 'the whole inviolable'. The select vestry also expected that those who could work should do so. In January 1741 they ordered:

That one of the overseers provide forthwith some few materials such as awls, lasts, knives &c. and employ Samuel Davies a poor lame youth in the poor house in the business of a cobbler, and that whatever he gains by his labour shall be paid into the hands of Thomas Anker Master of the Poor House for and towards his maintenance.

It was further ordered:

The Poor House, 1736
[B. Jones deposit,
FRO D/DM/592]

That the poor in the poor house be constantly employed in such labour as they respectively qualified for, & that upon neglect or refusal, the master shall give immediate information to the parish officers.

Nearly twenty years later new regulations were issued by the vestry for the conduct of the poor house. These regulations fell into five main areas. The first concerned work and followed the national trend of the poor house becoming a workhouse. The hours of work were to be from 7*a.m.* till 11*a.m.* in the summer, and from 8*a.m.* till eleven in the winter, with afternoon work from 1*p.m.* till 4*p.m.* all the year round. If they 'proved refractory and refused to work, due complaint be made upon oath before a magistrate, and the said pauper be discharged from the poor house and punished as an incorrigible rogue'. The second regulation concerned the education of the children in the poor house. A mistress was provided to teach the children to read and sew. She was paid twelve pence a week for her victuals, and a shilling a quarter for each child. The children were to be instructed from 11*a.m.* to 12 noon and from 4*p.m.* to 5*p.m.*, 'and that they be employed all the other hours the same as for the elder people'. Attendance at church was governed by the third regulation. 'That the elder people shall be admonished to go every Wednesday and Friday to church and obliged to go there every Sabbath day morning and evening. And that the children go to church every Sunday and be brought by their mistress to say their catechism there every Friday during Lent'. Clothing the poor was the fourth regulation. Every child was to have one suit of clothes yearly with two shirts (or shifts), three pair of stockings, & shoes *&c.* in proportion. The aged paupers were to have one suit of clothes, with shirts, shifts, stockings and shoes *&c.* every year at Michaelmas. The Mistress of the poor house was required to repair and mend their clothes. The final regulation stipulated that no child was to be admitted into the poor house under two years of age. If they were under two years they were to have proper nurses provided for them.

By the year 1767 the vestry were tired of the effort and expense it required to maintain the poor house and they decided to make a contract with the guardians of the House of Industry at Great Boughton in Chester. The poors field was leased to Sir John Glynne and the overseers auctioned the goods and furniture in the poor house. The transfer of the inmates to Chester was conducted on a trial basis, which eventually became permanent in the 1770s. Thus ended the life of the poor house in Hawarden. It was not until 1853 that the boundaries of the workhouse Union of Great Boughton were altered and 12 townships detached and added to the one newly established at Broughton.

Lady Hamilton

Lady Hamilton was born Amy Lyon in 1765 at Denhall in the parish of Neston where her father Henry Lyon was a blacksmith. He died seven weeks after her birth. Her mother was Mary Lyon (née Kidd) who was born in Shotton in 1743. The Kidds had arrived in Hawarden parish from Madeley in Staffordshire and settled in Shotton

Mrs Kidd's cottage, demolished c.1890 (now the site of the chemist's shop
[FRO 28/L/66]

Right: Lady Emma Hamilton by George Romney
[FRO PR/C/16]

Township near the Killins coal workings. Her grandfather Thomas Kidd worked for Walter Stubbs under George Berks as a collier. When he died in 1761 his wife Sarah came to live in Hawarden in a thatched cottage, which once stood between the Fox and Grapes and the chemist shop. The cottage was of a cruck construction with red sandstone steps. Across the road, where the HSBC Bank now stands, was the house of Honoratus Leigh Thomas, a hardworking surgeon, who was married to a member of the Boydell family. It was probably owing to the influence of her grandmother that the pretty precocious girl was engaged as housemaid to the Thomas family. Here Amy Lyon spent a couple of happy years in the bosom of the Thomas family and close to her grandmother. This was the prelude to the adventurous life of Amy Lyon who went to London at the age of thirteen. Arriving in the capital with her aunt Sarah she later met the Hon. Charles Greville and was painted by George Romney. By this time she had changed her name to Emma Hart. Her beauty opened doors, and eventually she met and married Sir William Hamilton the British Government's representative at the Court of Naples. After the Battle of the Nile in 1798, Admiral Nelson brought his fleet into port at Naples and so began a tempestuous relationship, which ended in the death of the nation's hero at Trafalgar and Emma Hamilton's rejection, poverty and death, at Calais in 1815.

4. Coal Mining and Iron Founding

The Middle Ages[1]

There is evidence of coalmining activity in the parish of Hawarden from the beginning of the fourteenth century. This coincides with the conquest of North Wales and creation of the county of Flint by Edward I in 1284. After 1301 the mineral rights within the manor of Ewloe belonged to the Earl of Chester and in order to dig for coal a licence was necessary. Here there were outcrops of Main and Hollin coal near the surface. Bleddyn ab Ithel Annwyl, the Forester of Ewloe, was granted such a licence and may have taken advantage of his position by exploiting new mine workings within the wood. From 1322 various pits in the manor were leased to Bleddyn. In 1331 a group of Cheshire men took over the 'farm' of coal for three years at an annual rent of £8, but by 1341 Bleddyn was again the sole lessee, a position he retained until he perished in the Black Death. His son Ithel took his place and paid £5 6s. 8d. for the leases. In 1394 Bleddyn's grandsons were still operating in the manor. Other pits in the manor were held from 1365–87 by David de Ewloe, Collector of the Customs at the Port of Chester and Mayor of Chester in 1381. William de Meysham and Robert Launcelyn, a former sheriff of Chester, followed him. In 1395 the lease of the sea-coals passed to John de Ewloe, Mayor of Chester 1404–10; he acquired a further licence which he held until 1418 to sell coal from his own holdings and from certain other lands rented direct from the Lord at 8d.

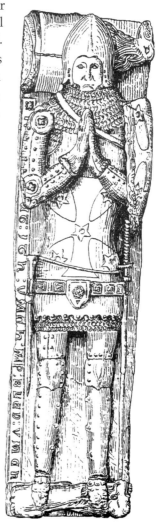

an acre. The revolt of Owain Glyndŵr in 1400 interrupted trade until 1408. There is evidence of a lease of some open workings in Ewloe in 1408, and the existence of a 'mine' of sea coal in Hawarden in 1426. Richard Whitley took the lease of 'the Lordship, together with the coalmines' in 1437 for a period of seven years but did not renew it. A deed of 1452 nullified a mortgage held by Whitley on David Costantyne's lands in the townships of Aston and Shotton on condition that if Whitley acquired any coal out of the said property Costantyne would be entitled to a moiety of such coal. For the next fourteen years, members of the More and De Poole families worked the mines. In 1461 the lease of the coalmines of the manor of Ewloe came into the possession of the Stanleys of Hawarden who held it until the death of Edward Stanley of Ewloe Castle in 1572. The lease for coal was taken over by Henry Kingswell in 1575 who relinquished it before it expired in 1594. At the beginning of the seventeenth century, coalmining permits were held by the local gentry, the Whitleys and the Ravenscrofts for their own domestic purposes.

At the end of the sixteenth century the surface coal in the manor of Ewloe appeared to have been worked out, and in 1606 it was said 'the Cole mynes are and have been longe wholli decayed and yeld no profits at all to his Majestie.' In early mining coal was taken from the surface by digging to a depth of no more than ten feet, and once the pit was exhausted, a new one was dug along the line of the seam. In medieval times the coal was taken to the local castle to be used for the iron forges or in the burning of lime for building. Later it became more used for domestic purposes and by craftsmen. Unfortunately there is not the same evidence for coalmining activity in the manor of Hawarden because the documents for the lordship are lost. However, it is known that there was a mine of sea-coal at Mancot in 1426 and coal was being extracted at the appropriately named Diglane in Hawarden in 1445–5.

Effigy of Ithel ab Bleddyn, c.1395.
[Colin A. Gresham, Medieval Stone Carving in North Wales, *p.199]*

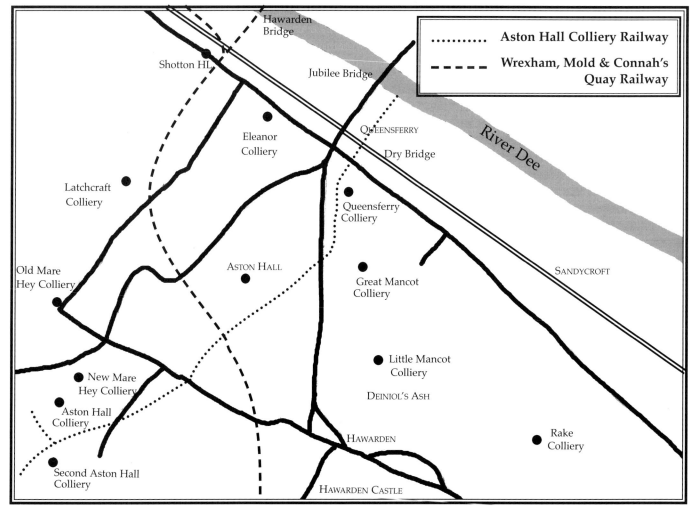

Collieries in the Hawarden area

The Seventeenth Century

In the sixteenth and seventeenth centuries coal was beginning to be worked in the neighbouring manor of Hawarden. In 1547 William Kettel, servant to the Earl of Richmond, was digging coal at Great Mancot, and to assist he called upon 'expert men', a team of colliers from Ewloe, Richard Ledsham and John Fox, under the direction of John Duckworth. In 1555–6 Thomas Salisbury of Flint had coalmines in the township of Shotton next to Wepre Brook. By 1620 'Colepitt Hills' were recorded on the lands of Robert Griffith in the township of Aston. In 1677 Captain Yarranton refers to the importance to Chester of the Aston mines in his advocacy of improvements to the river Dee, and drew a little sketch of them on his map of the area.

Chester was an important centre for the sale of Hawarden coal. Sometimes it was shipped from Wepre Creek but more often carried across Saltney marsh by pack mules to Handbridge, to be sold at the Maypole there, some of it being sent to Dublin where there was as great a demand for it; for example a total of 7,709 chaldrons was shipped across the Irish Sea in the year 1638–9. A chaldron was equal to two tons in weight of coal. Both places suffered from a shortage of supply during the Civil War. The Act of Parliament for the Canalisation of the River Dee in 1733 gave to property owners of adjoining lands the right of 'using and enjoying convenient ways of carrying and conveying the said Coales and Minerals for banking or stacking in the same.' The completion of the canalisation of the river Dee in 1737, the New Cut as it was called, brought the river channel nearer to the townships in Hawarden Parish where coal was waiting to be exploited.

The Eighteenth Century

The major problems facing the development of the coal industry in the eighteenth century were those, which needed technical improvement in ventilation, drainage, and transport. The first problem to be solved was the

A water-powered pumping engine for drainage of coal pits. Sir Roger Mostyn's engine from Thomas Dineley's Account of the Official Progress of the Duke of Beaufort thro' Wales in 1684.

means of the extraction of coal from deeper workings. Pits had to be safely dug, shored up, and the workforce protected from accident and injury. In the eighteenth century the steam engine, or the 'fire engine', as it was commonly called, made it possible to pump water from greater depths. Thomas Savery patented his engine in 1698, Thomas Newcomen his in 1709, and James Watt produced the definitive invention in 1769. Wooden railways for horse-drawn wagons came early to the coalfields in the seventeenth century and were gradually replaced by iron rails and steam drawn locomotives. The distance between Buckley, the furthest point to the Dee, was about five miles with the gradient for the loaded wagon running down hill, other coal producing areas were nearer, and all developed rail roads to the river wharves. With the exhaustion of surface coal more capital was needed to exploit the deeper coal and this resulted in the partnership between the local landlord and those with entrepreneurial skills, usually, in this case immigrant coal masters.

Sir John Glynne[2]

We see this in the exploitation of coal on the Hawarden Estate by Sir John Glynne (1712–77), sixth baronet. The Glynnes sold up their Oxfordshire estate at Bicester and came to live in Hawarden in 1723. By the early death of his brothers, John the fifth son succeeded to the estate and added to it by marrying Honora Conway, the Ravenscrofts heiress of Broadlane. The most important mining activities in Hawarden Parish were carried out under the lands of the lordship. Evidence for these activities is found in the Hawarden Deeds. In 1714 coal under the estate of Thomas Crachley of Daniel's Ash was leased to gentlemen from Flintshire and Staffordshire. In 1738, Madam Haytrel, the widow of George Haytrel of Staffordshire, worked coal with the aid of a 'fire engine ', in a pit near the Boar's Head, Ewloe, probably on the site of the Mare Hey workings

George Sparrow, an ironmaster with other Staffordshire partners, worked coal in the townships of Ewloe Wood and Shotton from 1700 onwards. Latchcraft colliery in the township of Shotton was situated between Killins farm and Wepre woods. It closed after awhile, but was reopened in 1740 by George Hope who built a wooden truck-way from the colliery to the river Dee. The colliery is said to have been abandoned in 1801 although the site was connected by a later tramway. In *c.*1730 John Salt worked the Castle Hill colliery in Shotton township.

In 1743 Sir John Glynne leased the coal under his wastes and other lands in the townships of Great and Little Mancot to George Hope of Chester

Latchcroft Colliery spoil banks
[FRO 62/27]

Killins Farm, Higher Shotton, the site of an early colliery
[FRO 62/24]

for twenty-one years. In 1748 a new lease was made to Hope for thirty-one years for the coal in the Mancot and Aston townships. The annual farm-rent was one eighth of the Main Coal and one seventh of all other coal raised, or its cash value, together with forty tons for the use of Sir John.[3] In Mancot in 1748 there were probably five pits; the depth of coal varied between 120 and 225 feet.

In 1750 Sir John leased his coal in the townships of Pentrobin and Bannell for thirty years to Mr Walter Stubbs, of Beckbury, Shropshire, an attorney at law, who according to Willett, had 'about the year 1747 obtained from Mr James Gartside, all his interest in the lease of Mr Lloyd's coals, in the Lloyd's Hills and raised the same by means of a Fire Engine.'[4] The farm-rent was a tenth of the coal raised which was anticipated to be more than £60 a year. The amount varied; in 1753 it was £2, in 1755 it was more than £2,000. The mine operated by Stubbs was known as Sandycroft Colliery, (it is often confused with Sandycroft on the river). The output of Sandycroft Colliery in 1778 was 12,000 tons. Coal was supplied after 1776 to the Hawarden Foundry of W. & J. Rigby and some to the Pentrobin lead smelting-works of Richardson, a Chester silversmith. The main local markets were Chester, Flint and Holywell. In 1751 Stubbs was granted the right 'to level the ground and lay rails from any coal pits in that part of the lessor's lordship.' The contemplated tram road was to run from Sandycroft old colliery near Lloyd's Hills, Buckley' past the lead smelting works at Pentrobin northwards along Moor Lane, Hawarden, to the river at Sandycroft Mark.

George Hope and Walter Stubbs met with success because they leased lands where Main Coal crops out and was not too deep from the surface to be effectively drained by the 'fire engine.' One of the difficulties George Hope faced in the Mancot townships was the old division of the land into arable strips. This was overcome in 1748, when Sir John's lands were brought together, to make a larger area. But this was still not effective enough to make mining economic. This could only be achieved by the acquisition of the mining rights of the land.' In 1789, Lady Mary Glynne, guardian of the infant lord of the manor, Sir Stephen Richard Glynne, anticipated the termination of Hope's lease by acquiring the mining rights of the land of six neighbouring owners (Thomas Nangrieve, John Wilcox, Charles Linsey, Thomas Bennett, H. Leigh Thomas, and Mrs Wardle), and those of the glebe lands of Hawarden Rectory, for forty years; the farm-rent was a tenth of the value of the coal raised in each case.'[5]

Sir John Glynne died in 1777. His heir Sir Stephen Glynne, Rector of Hawarden, married Mary, daughter of Richard Bennett, of Farmcott in Shropshire. Sir Stephen died on 1 April 1780, and a son was born posthumously on 19 May. Lady Mary Glynne was an astute guardian, as we have seen above in connection with the land in Mancot township. In 1790 taking advantage of the termination of George Hope's lease and the increased value of the coal works in Mancot, Lady Glynne leased all the coal lands under her guardianship within the several townships of Mancot, Pentrobin, Bannel and Hawarden, to Thomas Botfield of Dawley, for a return of one-eighth of the value of the coal raised, and forty tons annually for private use. In the words of Rawson, Botfield became the great coal master of the whole district, and in the lease of Mancot Colliery in 1790, undertook to 'sink so many pits as will be necessary to carry on the works in an effectual manner', and within three years 'to erect a fire-engine and a canal (drainage level) of sufficient power effectually to drain the mines.' Enough workmen were to be employed at Mancot to raise sixty tons of coal daily in order 'to supply the sea and Chester sale of coal to as great an extent as the same can possibly be carried to.'[6] Botfield increased production at Mancot but unfortunately he died in 1801 and his executors surrendered the lease. The successors of Botfield were William and John Rigby, iron founders in Hawarden *c.*1776, and later shipbuilders in Sandycroft, and William Hancock, brick and tile maker, whose family came to reside at Aston Bank.

Transport for the merchandising of the coal was provided by the building of railways to the bank of the newly canalised river Dee to what was referred to on the maps as the Mark. Thomas Pennant defined the Mark as the place ' where the vessels lie to receive or discharge their lading.'[7] They were variously known as Moor Mark, Sandycroft Mark and Mancot Mark.

Mancot Old Railway[8]

This was a wooden railway built about 1740 to link Big Mancot with the river at Mancot Mark as a result of a lease to George Hope to mine coal in the township. The railway passed from Great Mancot Colliery along the west edge of Mancot Lane via Pentre to cross the marsh to Mancot Mark This was replaced about 1793 by the Mancot New Railway.[9]

Mancot New Railway

Boyd argues convincingly that 'an iron plateway replaced the wooden line at Mancot on the same course as the Old Railway and was used by successive lessees throughout the varying fortunes of the colliery.' Lewis said that Beriah Botfield of Old Park Furnaces near Coalbrookdale, Shropshire, built a line at Mancot in 1793 from Little Mancot to the Dee.

The Nineteenth Century

Coal mining activity reaches its height in the parish of Hawarden in the nineteenth century. For this account the mines in Buckley are not included in the discussion, but the tramways and railways, which cross Hawarden parish, are. The pattern of activity, which emerges in the second half of the eighteenth century, is continued in a more sophisticated manner in the nineteenth. Pits become deeper, more men are employed in a closely regulated industry, both the investment needed and the rewards expected are higher, as well as the risks. Coal is in more demand as the industrial revolution is fuelled by steam to drive its mills and factories, power its ships, and locomotives to transport goods all over the world. The local coalfields in the parish are clustered in the townships and the names given to the various collieries relate more to the area than to a particular mine.

In the first half of the nineteenth century the parish may be divided into two. In the eastern and northern part the Hawarden estate is dominant leasing its collieries in Mancot, Pentrobin, and Buckley. In the southern and western parts the Dundas family, heirs, to the Whitleys, lease their collieries in Ewloe, Aston and Queensferry.

The industrial advance in Hawarden parish is seen in the report of Richard Willett in 1822:

> About the time of Mr Botfield's retirement (*c*.1800), a Company under the firm of Leach and Co. engaged Sir George Prescott's, and other coals, and they also formed an iron railway through the Aston Estate, down to the River for the discharge of their Collieries, and these works generally employed four hundred and fifty men, and raised annually 72,000 tons of coals, by means of twelve Steam Engines, from seven horse power, to sixty horse power.[10]

The firm of Leach and Co. arrived in the parish in 1799. It was made up of partners from the Oswestry area, the parish of Hawarden, and Chester. They were concerned with the exploitation of coal and clay. For this purpose they leased land from the Aston Hall estate to build their brickworks, sink their coal pits, and make 'an iron plate way' of about a mile and a quarter in length to convey their products to the Dundas wharf at Queensferry. The heiress to the manor of Aston, Ann Whitley, married in 1782 Charles Dundas of Barton Court, Berkshire. The manor comprising land in the townships of Aston, Ewloe and Shotton, was rich in coal and clay, and ripe for further development. The estate owned a large wharf at Queensferry, which for a period of over fifty years provided the Dundas family with a monopoly for the shipment of coal, tiles and bricks from the locality. Leach & Co. built a tram road to link their enterprises with the wharf. One of their pits was the Aston Colliery, later called Queensferry Colliery. They were the original owners of the old Knowl lane brickworks, to be followed by other proprietors, amongst whom were Richard Ashton (1841–67), and afterwards the Prince brothers.

More permanent as clients of the Dundas family were the dynasties of Rigby and Hancock who went into partnership in 1792. The Rigbys were principally iron founders. John Rigby I (1742–93) built his foundry *c*.1776 at the east end of Glynne Way, where now stands the Institute. His son William Rigby II (1768–1842) succeeded to the foundry and became the partner of William Hancock II. Other Rigbys were John Rigby III (1794–1852), iron founder, engineer, maker of steam engines, and ship builder. Honoratus Leigh Rigby (1795–1851), manager of the

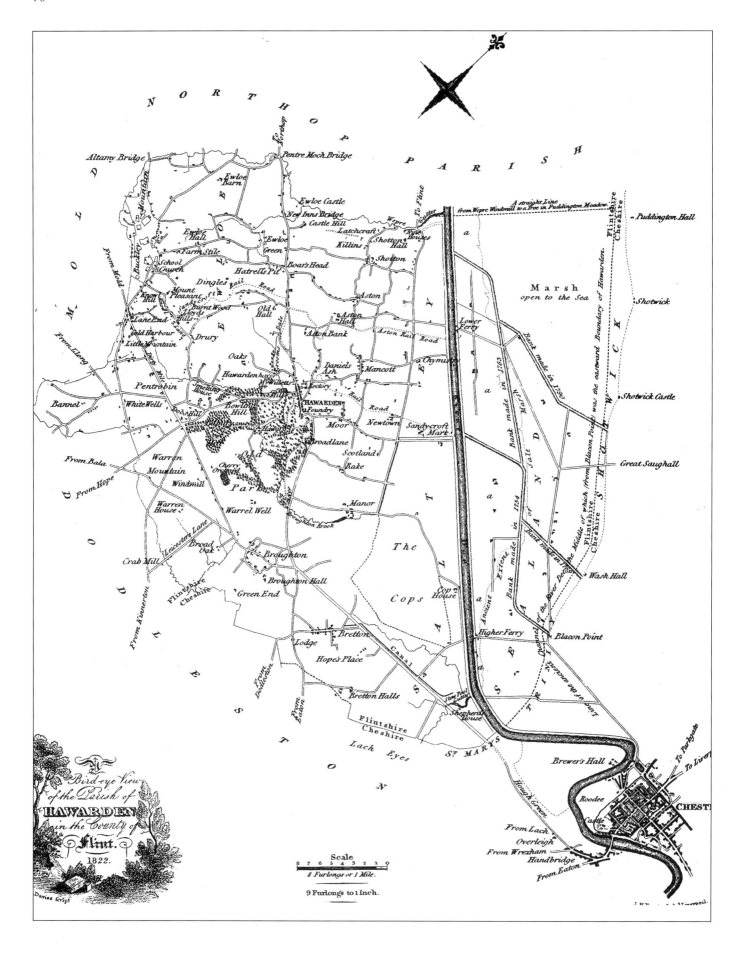

Bird-eye View
of the Parish of
HAWARDEN
in the County of
Flint.
1822.

Davies Script

Scale
8 7 6 5 4 3 2 1 0
8 Furlongs or 1 Mile.

9 Furlongs to 1 Inch.

Chymistry at Pentre and his brother John Rigby (d.1866), the last of the family to partner the Hancocks. William Hancock I of Ewloe and Pentrobin established a brickworks in 1792. It was his son William Hancock II (1762–1833) who partnered William Rigby II. They built a tram road to give access to the river. The Hancocks were coalmasters, brick and tile manufacturers, and ship owners. Their principal works and colliery was at Lane End, Buckley. William Hancock III (1799–1865) was a shrewd businessman and by 1860 his firm were shipping over 30,000 tons a year of their products by means of the local railways and the river Dee. By the time of William Hancock IV, the Rigby and Dundas families were no longer involved in the local industrial scene. The Hancock family resided at Aston Bank, and Frederick Leigh Hancock (b. 1851) lived at Wold House, Hawarden.

In 1806 Charles Dundas conveyed cottages in Mancot to William Hancock. Coal was leased in 1807 at Green Ends in Ewloe, and Main coal under 3 acres on the west side of Gorsty Field and Rushy Meadow in Ewloe. The partnership received a lease in 1815 of 'all main coal under 3 fields called Jenk Riddings, the Sparrow Field and the Lower Field in the parish of Hawarden, with liberty to sink pits therein, and all the main coal under adjoining lands northward as far as the Great Fault, for £350 per acre. In 1824 they were granted the lease of coal under land in the townships of Ewloe and Aston. A lease of 1837 by James Whitley Deans Dundas (1785–1862, later an Admiral in the British navy), gave mines of coal in Aston, Shotton and Ewloe for a term of 31 years, a rent of £300 every two years, and £150 per acre of Hollin, Yard, Main or Brassey coal of a thickness of seven foot, plus another annual rent of £300. One of the named collieries was Mare Hey near the Boar's Head, which was reopened in 1809.

The ace, which Dundas held in his hand and was never afraid to use, was his monopoly over the means of reaching the river with coal and manufactured clay products. For example in 1844 the Rigby-Hancock partnership was granted the exclusive use of the Dundas railway through Ewloe, Aston and Shotton to his wharf on the River Dee. Boyd has described and defined the Aston Tramroad:

> The system extended from Pentrobin Colliery, near Lane End Brickworks, Buckley, to the south bank of the river at Lower or King's Ferry as then known. As completed the system was made up of two sections: the southern end was built by Rigby and Hancock after they went into partnership in 1792. It was to carry their products — coal, tiles, pottery, bricks, and drainpipes *etc.* — from Lane End brickworks and was about one and three quarters miles long. The southern portion traversed the lands of the Glynnes of Hawarden, and the northern that of Dundas of Aston Hall. The northern section itself consisted of parts of three earlier tramroads.[11]

The first part was built by Leach & Co. around the year 1799 to carry their products a mile and a quarter to the river. The Hawarden Estate Plan of 1815 shows 'there existed a continuous tramroad from Queensferry to Higgin's Croft, entirely on Dundas lands, constructed between 1809–15.'

The Tithe Map of 1839 shows a new line altogether, making a junction with the original Leach line northeast of Aston Hall and making a detour of the Hall to the west; it rejoins the 1809–15 line a little to the north of the Northop-Hawarden road. From this new piece, westwards-stretching branches served Latchcraft Colliery (clearly still productive), whilst a second branch ran to Old Mare Hey Colliery (confusingly known at times as Hawarden Colliery), alongside the road west of Ewloe. This line features on 1869 edition maps and was the ultimate form. By the late 1860s it only carried the traffic of those who refused to patronise the new Buckley Railway.[12]

The cost of transport and wharfage at Queensferry became an issue of great importance in the 1850s. Admiral Dundas was intent on using his monopoly to extract the highest rates for carriage on his tram road. The Buckley brick and coal masters decided to boycott the Dundas tramway and build their own railway to Connah's Quay. This alternative transport system was constructed in two stages. First came the Buckley Railway, opened on 7 June 1862, an event that went unreported in the press but received a telling notice and publicity in an advertisement from Messrs. Charles Davison & Co. Firebrick and Tile Manufacturers, Buckley Mountain. Charles Davison had quarrelled with Dundas in 1857. As Surveyor of Highways to Saltney Township, Davison took Dundas to court to force him to raise the height of a swing bridge, which he alleged was causing an obstruction. Announcing the virtues of the new Buckley & Connah's Quay Railway, Davison pointed out that their works were now in direct communication with the LNWR which renders loading and unloading from carts and tram-wagons unnecessary, Connah's Quay is three miles nearer than Dundas' Sidings, and in future Connah's Quay

Facing page: Richard Willett's Map of Hawarden Parish, 1822, engraved for his Memoir of Hawarden Parish. *This is the first 'modern' detailed map of the parish which shows the coal workings, the foundry, the railways, the two ferries and Sir John Glynne's canal.*

will be used as a shipping port instead of Queensferry — its superiority over other places on the Dee is well known and needs no comment.[13]

The railway ran from Buckley following a route, which connected it with the principal collieries, and brick works at Ewloe, Northop Hall, and Connah's Quay, with a link to the LNWR. From 1 May 1866 the Buckley Railway was worked by the Wrexham, Mold & Connah's Quay Railway, both for passengers and freight.

In the meantime Dundas assigned a new lease of coal on the Aston estate to William Thompson, and for them to use the existing Aston tram road to the river at Queensferry. In its final form the tram road had been cut back to terminate at the Aston Hall Colliery, and adjacent brickmaking premises. In May 1865 Messrs Fenton & others took a lease of the estate's mines and minerals. Hancocks continued to use the Aston tram road between his Lane End tram way. Admiral Dundas died in 1862. The Aston Estate was verging on bankruptcy when W. E. Gladstone bought it in 1869 for £57,000, and in the same year compensation was paid by WM&CQR to the parties interested in the Aston Tram Way in respect of the section of the line known as the Buckley & Aston Tramway Co. The Tram Road ceased work in 1869 and was replaced by the Aston Hall Colliery Railway.

The Hawarden Estate Coal and Railway Interest

The Hawarden Castle Coalfield

We have seen above that the Glynne mining activities at the end of the eighteenth century were in the townships of Mancot, Pentrobin, and Bannel. These continued after the death of Thomas Botfield, when his leases went to Rigby and Hancock. They were responsible for building the Sandycroft Rail Road, which was about four and a half miles in length, from near Lane End, Buckley in the north down to the riverside at Sandycroft Wharf. This railroad serviced the Buckley collieries in the south and Little Mancot Colliery in the north. About 1840 the Sandycroft line was abandoned between Buckley and Little Mancot Colliery.

The story of Sir Stephen Glynnes disastrous industrial and mining adventure at Oak Farm, in Staffordshire, in the 1840s is told later. It brought him to the verge of ruin, and saddled the Hawarden Estate with a massive debt, which was not cleared until the end of the First World War. In spite of this Sir Stephen together with his brother-in-law, W. E. Gladstone, were always looking for a means of recouping the loss to the estate. In the light of this, great hopes were pinned on a scheme for finding coal on the Hawarden Estate close to the Mancot coalfield nearby at Rake Lane Farm.

The entries in Gladstone's Diary from 1856 to 1864 record the quest for coal. There was optimism at the beginning and Gladstone was a regular visitor to the pits and borings. The scale of the operation was reported in December 1856:

> 700 acres of the Hawarden Castle Coalfield the property of Sir Stephen Richard Glynne, Bart. has lately been the subject of agreement with gentlemen eminent in the coal trade, Messrs Robertson and Darby of Brymbo, and Mr Darlington of Ince, who are now engaged in skilful and extensive operations for the development of seams of coal. Four of these seams, through previous trials, are proved to have an aggregate thickness of thirty-two feet.[14]

In December 1856 at the Castle they 'burned a fire with Hawarden coal'. In July 1862 there were favourable boring operations at Mancot, but two years later it was decided to abandon the scheme at the Rake in August 1864. In the meantime, in 1862, a standard gauge railway was built from the LNWR, across the road, southwards to Rake Lane and westwards to the Little Mancot colliery. At the War Compensation Court in 1921 the information was given that the average tonnage over the Hawarden Castle Railway, 1909–13, when the collieries and pit works were working, was 13,271. The trustees of the Hawarden Castle estate claimed £3,526 compensation, for the removal of 2,810 yards of their private four mile long railway by the Ministry of Munitions in March 1921. The Great Mancot Colliery, which had been working intermittently since 1850, was closed in 1885. The Mancot Colliery was leased to Messrs Plant, Rose and Plant in 1862, who held it until 1865.

A report on Mancot Bank Colliery for 1865 gives the information that the surface area was 173 statute acres, the colliery plant was well arranged, effective and substantial, and that five cottages were let at 2/6d per week. 'A branch railway is laid up to the pits from the main line from the Chester and Holyhead Railway. Provisions are also made for forming a connexion with the Wrexham & Connah's Quay Railway.'[15]

Another report was given in September 1878 by Henry Beckett of Wolverhampton, on the coalfield adjoining Mancot Colliery, which was bounded in the north by Mancot colliery, the west by the road from Queensferry to Hawarden, and on the south by Cross Tree lane. The upper coals near the outcrop had been extensively worked by the 'old men' many years ago and worked over an area of 30 acres by Messrs Botfield. Ribs and pillars of coal remained to be won over a considerable area. At Mancot colliery the hollin, brassey, and main coals were partially worked out and the shafts in a very bad state of repair. The main coal was supposed to be intact under the piece of land purchased by W. E. Gladstone from Sir George Prescott. The upper coals in the estate should not be worked . 'The lower seams lying beneath the Main coal, of whose presence under the whole of the estate there is no question, in fact they have actually been proved in the rector's meadow and in Daniel's Ash, are so far is known in a virgin state, consequently future colliery operations would be based principally on these valuable coals. The position of the estate for colliery purposes could scarcely be more favourable especially as regards land sale, and a short branch line might easily be made to form a junction with the Aston Hall Colliery railway to facilitate foreign transit.'[16]

The Eleanor Colliery

The Eleanor Colliery was on the Queensferry to Shotton Road near to Hurlbutt's Drive. There were three shafts, two of them for drawing. The colliery opened in 1868 and closed ten years later. Coal seams were worked under the river Dee towards Sealand at a depth of 300 to 500 feet. Mr Isaac Davies who was associated with the colliery built Eleanor Terrace eight cottages, dated 1877.

The Colliery Company was owned by Earl Spencer and Sir Richard Glynne and leased to the Prestatyn Colliery Company. The press reported on the colliery on the opening of a branch line to connect with the LNWR. It was nearly a mile in length from the colliery to a double siding affording accommodation for about 800 tons of coal most of it to be sent by ship to Dublin. The account of the opening throws light on the reaction of the miners to this event:

> About two o'clock a number of proprietors and other gentlemen assembled at the Eleanor Colliery, and after the works had been inspected, a wagon containing ten tons of coal was drawn along the new branch line, followed by a band of music, whose excellent playing considerably enlivened the proceedings. The wagon was decorated with flags, and bunting was also exhibited from several houses and prominent places in the locality.
>
> The line having been formally opened an adjournment took place to the Hawarden Castle Hotel Queensferry and after dinner the guests met the men in a large tent erected in a field fronting the Hotel. Here the workpeople employed at the colliery were regaled with an abundant dinner in celebration of the event. The men and the boys numbering about 150 all respectably attired, and some wearing rosettes, walked to the tent in procession headed by the band of music. An interesting circumstance occurred in the proceedings, when one of the colliers, a fine young fellow, asked permission to address the meeting which was readily granted, and stepping forward, he called upon all present to join him in offering up their thanks to God for his gracious protection of them hitherto in their dangerous avocations, and to implore his gracious protection hereafter. The assembly immediately and with greatest reverence knelt down, and an extempore prayer was offered with great zeal and earnestness. The remainder of the day was spent in innocent amusements, and in the evening, on leaving the hotel to take the train for their various destinations the promoters were accompanied to the station by the band, and hearty cheers were given by the work people for the Prestatyn Colliery Company.[17]

The difficulties attached to the sinking of the colliery were described. In sinking the first shaft very little difficulty was encountered, but in sinking the second shaft an immense bed of quick sand was met with, and to penetrate it cast-iron cylinders had to be brought into operation. The 'set' or 'take' consisted of 500 acres and there were four seams of coal: one of 9 feet, two of 4 feet each and one of 3 feet. The Company spent £20,000 opening out the colliery which produced first class coal both for domestic and steam purposes. The daily output was no less than 500 tons of coal.

Aston Hall Colliery

In October 1869 W. E. Gladstone offered £57,000 for the Aston Hall Estate belonging to the Dundas family. He wrote in his Diary on that occasion; 'If I have any ambition, it is to make an Estate for my children.'[18] With the purchase came the Aston Hall, Mare Hey and Queensferry Collieries. Gladstone's financial instinct for a shrewd investment was correct. The Aston Hall estate nicely complimented that of the Hawarden Estate, which had been settled on his eldest son, W. H. Gladstone. If there had been disappointment over the search for coal at Mancot and the Rake, the Aston Hall Colliery would more than make up for it. When the Aston Hall Colliery closed in 1909 it was noted; 'This colliery with Mare Hey Colliery, under the management and partnership of Horace Mayhew, contributed about £100,000 profits and royalties to the estate.'[19] Of Mayhew it was recorded, 'he was the first to make the estate minerals pay, and from 1888 to about 1902 coal profits paid off most of the old debts on the Hawarden Estate.'[20] W. E. Gladstone enjoyed being the landlord, if only for a short time, and went on a tour of the newly acquired estate, visiting the coalmine and brickworks. In January 1871 he gave a dinner at the Queensferry hotel to the Aston Tenantry 'some 70 large & chiefly small & addressed them on the proper conditions of the important relations established between us. They were most hearty.' In September he 'went with Catherine and Stephen to the Aston Works to see the Vases made there.'

The Aston Hall Colliery was the rich centre of what was known as the Great Ewloe Coalfield in the area of which were many small pits worked over the years. Aston Hall Colliery in 1865 had two main shafts, named the Main Coal Pit and the Rough Coal Pit. Plans of the Colliery indicate premier, brassey, way, beach hollin and rough coal.[21] The *Mining Journal* summed up the situation there in December 1871:

At the Aston Hall Colliery, near Hawarden, of which Mr Gladstone is the lessor of the land and minerals, prospects are now more healthy than they have yet been. And the mine and works connected with it will soon be in a position to make handsome returns to the proprietors, gentlemen principally resident in Yorkshire, all who have sunk a large sum in opening out and in making extensions. A line of railway is being made from the colliery at Queensferry where the Holyhead branch of the London and North Western passes. The men are now getting the five feet and three feet seams, both excellent coal, a good deal of the steam qualities being sent for the use of the Holyhead steam vessels. The line of railway, the first sod of which was turned by Sir Stephen Glynne, Bart. last month will be about three miles long, Messrs Jardine and Son being the contractors. The brick and tile works in connection with the colliery are also being profitably worked, the clay being got in connection with the coal and being of excellent quality.[22]

Aston Hall Colliery
[FRO 28/N/117]

Old Aston Hall Colliery office,
watercolour
[FRO PR/F/1541]

The Aston Hall Colliery Company Railway was opened on 16 August 1872. A single line railway it connected the Colliery with the Chester and Holyhead portion of the LNWR. The route of the railway was described:

The new line, which is about three miles in length, commences from that siding a little below Queensferry station, continues for a distance on an embankment as far as Queensferry colliery, to which there is a branch from the left, and the proprietors of that colliery pay for the running powers over it; then there is an incline of 1 in 100, and after passing through two cuttings of sand and gravel, one of them being a rather deep one, there is another incline of 1 in 50, and then Aston Bank is reached, and the line declines gently to the colliery. There are only two sharp curves, one just below the junction with Queensferry siding, and the other near to where the water tank is fixed, and from which point it is intended to carry on the line down to the river, for the shipment of coal by water. The importance of the new line, therefore, can hardly be over-estimated, and it is not improbable that the output at the colliery, at present 200 tons per day, will be so far increased by these additional facilities for traffic, that the colliery will become one of the most extensive in North Wales.[23]

Boyd gives the following account of the route of the railway from the interchange sidings made with the Hawarden Loop Line in 1890:

From these sidings the Colliery Railway ran straight as an arrow downhill, the panorama of Deeside spreading out like a cloth below it, due northeast in a straight line to the Queensferry Colliery. There, taking up a short link line, it turned to a northerly direction for a short distance to gain the elderly embankment earthworks of the Aston Tram road which it used — suitably widened for the purpose — as it made a bee-line for Lower Ferry.

The precipitous descent of the railway from colliery to riverside put it firmly into Mineral Railway category! The function of the locomotive would be simply to act as a brake to restrain the loaded wagons as they came down the hill. . . the Company must have been an excellent customer to some foundry which cast renewable brake blocks.[24]

There is an account of an Aston Hall Colliery dinner held in February 1874 under the auspices of the men's Sick and Accident Club, which was funded from surplus funds:

The dinner was entrusted to Mr Mason of the Glynne Arms, Hawarden, who catered in good English style, roast beef and other joints, succeeded by plum pudding. They started from the works at noon, and marched four deep, preceded by the Hawarden Brass Band, and arrived at the Green, where the dinner was provided in a large tent, to which 350 men sat down. The repast being finished the first toast was proposed by Mr Gregory, of Little Mountain Colliery, 'health and prosperity to the Aston Hall Colliery Co.'. In response Mr Newton, underground manager spoke of the difficulties the company had to contend with in the past, the large amount of capital they had expended, and, as large employers of labour, that they ought to have the respect and support of the men.[25]

The respect and support of the men was put to the test a few months later when in June they were in dispute

with the management over a 15% wage deduction. Four non-unionists refused to join the striking miners. Hanson the colliery manager asked Gladstone to evict strikers from estate cottages. Gladstone, accompanied by his son Stephen, met the miners and addressed them. He defended the right of the four to accept lower wages adding, 'It is my duty to give every reasonable support that is in my power to Mr Hanson', and under the implied threat of eviction the miners accepted a 10% wage reduction.[26]

In 1883 Horace Mayhew, an Essex man, became associated with the Hawarden estate. He had considerable experience as a mining agent and coal proprietor in Wigan, and became in turn manager at Aston Hall Colliery, mineral and estate agent and partner in 1901 with Henry, Herbert and Gertrude Gladstone, in the Aston Hall Brick and Coal Co. From the time of his arrival, the coal production at Aston Hall for the next few years was 30–40,000 tons a year. The colliery was troubled by water in 1894 but this was soon remedied.

> The Aston Hall Colliery, which has suspended work in consequence of water in the pit, has commenced working again. Very powerful pumping machinery has been erected, driven by electricity. The Aston Hall Brick works has also been fitted with a complete installation of electric lights. The work under these new and favourable conditions is going on both day and night. We are glad these works, which give employment to so many men, are again in full and robust working order.[27]

In 1907, the Aston Hall Colliery and Brick Co. Ltd., then nearing the end of its life, employed over a thousand men and boys. The colliery closed in 1909, as it was found impossible to work the wall and bench seam at a profit. In February there was an extensive sale of the colliery and brick works plant and machinery. The auctioneer expressed the regret of all at the breaking up of the colliery, which for such a number of years had given employment to so many. The pits, rails, plates, scrap, iron sheds, staging and timber, found ready buyers at very high prices.[28] In 1912 the colliery offices were converted into two houses. In 1916 there were a number of railway wagons belonging to the partnership valued at £4,500, and in March 1917 the Ministry of Munitions took up the Aston Hall Railway paying compensation of £10 per ton.

Mare Hey Colliery

There are two collieries of this name. The first may be the one worked by Madam Haytrel in 1738 which was situated near the Boar's Head on the junction of the Hawarden Northop Road and the lane leading to Higher Shotton. Willett says that she erected the first fire engine in the district. The area was in the estate of the Dundas family in the early nineteenth century, who leased the coal intermittently to the Rigby and Hancock partnership. The new Mare Hey Colliery was situated a short distance in a northwesterly direction from the Aston Hall Collieries and was later linked to their railway. It was part of the Aston Estate bought by Gladstone in 1869. The colliery was reopened in 1885 to exploit main coal. In 1892 'after an exceedingly intricate & prolonged negotiation conducted for the estate by Mr H. N. Gladstone there was an amalgamation of the Aston Hall and Mare Hey collieries.' The Mare Hey Colliery was worked out towards the end of 1894.

Queensferry Colliery

The Queensferry Colliery was leased to members of the Thompson family between 1856–68 by the Dundas Estate. It was on the route of the Aston Hall Colliery Railway. It was situated near the present caravan site on the east side of the Queensferry to Hawarden road. In 1873 it was acquired by the Aston Hall Brick and Coal Co. from Mr Alexander Ward. It was closed sometime later and re-opened in 1903. In October 1906 the *Chester Chronicle* optimistically reported that, 'a correspondent informs us that the Queensferry Colliery Co. have recently struck several seams of coal, and that this will likely mean the giving of additional employment to a larger number of men in the district.'[29]

This was not to be, and the colliery failed in 1909, the principal loss falling upon Horace Mayhew, and Henry and Herbert Gladstone. One of the reasons for the re-opening of the colliery was to establish the right of the Hawarden Estate as Lords of the Manor to the minerals on the Sealand side of the river. This had been disputed by F. Potts of Chester and in a lawsuit taken as far as the House of Lords the Judges found in favour of the Estate. 'But the supreme calamity was the absence of main coal under Sealand, an exceptionally lengthy tunnel had been driven to realise the coal.'

The Hawarden Loop Line
W. E. Gladstone enjoyed the world of industry and the company of successful entrepreneurs. His apprenticeship in government at the Treasury and the Board of Trade in the 1840s gave him an understanding of the railways and their regulation. Towards the end of his life industrialists lionised him. One of them was the Salford born, Sir Edward Watkin, who was an advocate of the channel tunnel and under his direction excavations began in 1881, but he was better known as a Railway King. After a successful career in Greece and Canada he became chairman of the Manchester, Sheffield and Lincolnshire Railway. It was his ambition to see the practical union of the Welsh railway system from Cardiff to Liverpool. The railway crossing of the Dee in Hawarden parish, linking up with the M. S. & L. was an integral part of this scheme, to which W. E. Gladstone gave his wholehearted support. Sir Edward Watkin responded by inviting William and Catherine Gladstone to take part in the ceremony of laying the first cylinder of the railway crossing of the Dee, the Hawarden Bridge in 1887, and its opening two years later. Both Gladstone and Sir Edward Watkin enjoyed a public spectacle more so if they were at the centre of it.[30] This happened on 4 September 1888 when they were both invited to speak at the Welsh Eisteddfod in Wrexham. Watkin used the occasion to publicise the Hawarden Loop Line nearing completion. Gladstone left Hawarden from a temporary station to join Sir Edward up line at Hawarden Junction on the train recently exhibited at Manchester. They arrived at Wrexham in triumph and it is not surprising that the report of the Eisteddfod was to some extent overshadowed by railway news. One of the press reports forecast:

> In the future there are vast possibilities before the new line or rather lines, because the scheme includes not only a line between Chester, Connah's Quay and Hawarden, but what is far more important a direct route from North Wales to Liverpool … there is expected to be much traffic between the coal mining districts of Wales and the salt district of Cheshire … and Connah's Quay may draw some of the traffic from the Weaver and the Mersey if the dues compare favourably. The Hawarden branch or loop will doubtless afford most acceptable accommodation to the great brick, tile, and drain manufacturers of the Buckley district, which will thus gain a direct outlet to the Manchester and Liverpool markets. Mr Gladstone has for many years advocated the establishment of a more direct route from the mineral districts of North Wales to the manufacturing centres of Lancashire and Yorkshire.

Sir Edward Watkin in his Presidential address stated that 'What those, who wanted to see Welsh resources developed dreamt of, was the Welsh railways, as far as possible, worked in union, for the benefit of Welsh interests.'[31]

Sir Edward Watkin and W. E. Gladstone were together again on 21 October 1892 when the Premier cut the first sod of the new Wirral Rail near the golf club and the place where John Summers and Sons were a few years later to develop as offices. Once again Gladstone was called upon to occupy the centre stage for the benefit of the chairman of the Manchester, Sheffield and Lincolnshire Railway Company, a situation which the following newspaper report well understood:

> The first sod of the Wirral Railway which is to give Wales direct communications over the Dee with Liverpool, and which will form a new route between Chester and Birkenhead was cut today by the Premier in the presence of a large concourse of railway magnates, ship owners, coal owners and others. The spot which the ceremony took place is near, and in fact covers a small part of the golf ground which adjoins the Chester and Hawarden Railway as the latter runs on to Dee Bridge. The line when made, will form a curve skirting the golf ground, and just at the point where the line gets into the straight, a junction will be made with the existing line from Chester forming a

The first train from Hawarden Station to Liverpool Central Station via Hawarden Bridge and the Mersey Tunnel, 1896 [FRO 28/N/126]

triangle, as do the lines running from Manchester into Liverpool Road Station and into the Northgate Station, with the line from one station to the other. As is customary with M.S. & L. on these occasions 'money no object' was the motto in regard to the preparations for the ceremony. For three weeks a large band of workers were busily engaged putting up the pavilion in which the luncheon was held today attended by 250 guests. Just outside the building a structure closely resembling a pulpit was erected for the accommodation of Mr Gladstone who was the central figure in the day's ceremony, and who has taken so keen and long sustained an interest in the development of railways in the district.

The Premier and party entered Sir Edward Watkins special train at Hawarden and reached the scene of the ceremony at 1.40 *p.m.* The main object of the proposed line is to obtain a connection between the Manchester, Sheffield and Lincolnshire Company's system beyond the Dee Bridge and the Birkenhead docks for mineral and goods traffic. For that purpose therefore a main line will be constructed from the Dee Bridge and will join the Seacombe, Hoylake, and Deeside line at a point near the Birkenhead Docks Station …[32]

Friendly Societies

The Friendly Societies were founded in the eighteenth and nineteenth centuries to provide financial assistance to the workingman and his family in the time of sickness and death. The alternative source of assistance for the poor and destitute, a place of last resort, was the workhouse where conditions were harsh and intolerable. The Friendly Societies on the other hand fulfilled many functions for the workingman. They encouraged self-help and thrift, they provided an opportunity for comradeship and a relief from the tedium of long hours and unsatisfactory working conditions, they gave the workers a sense of dignity and purpose, which could be demonstrated publicly without arousing the suspicions of their employers and magistrates. For many it was the first and only experience of holding responsible office in a voluntary organisation. The ritualism of their meetings and funerals bound them together in life and death. Their solidarity and loyalty to Church and State was displayed in annual processions usually held on public holidays when the men went out of their way to show respect to their employers and landlords, and it was an opportunity to say thank you for his services to the benefit club Doctor. They were licensed by the state from 1793 onwards to disassociate them as agents for political change from the Trade Union Movement. They were influenced more by paternalism than socialism, although for many it was their first experience of organised self-government. They were usually affiliated to national organisations, which bore such mysterious names as the Independent Order of Oddfellows, the Loyal Order of Ancient Shepherds, the United Order of Druids and other like sounding names.

The oldest known Friendly Society in Hawarden was the Union Society instituted on 3 May 1819 and known as the 'Old Club'. The anniversary of the foundation of Friendly Societies was usually celebrated on Whit

Monday. There is an account of a joint celebration of their anniversaries by the Union Society and the Loyal Order of Ancient Shepherds in Hawarden in 1873:

> About 10 *a.m.* the members of the Loyal Order of Ancient Shepherds assembled at the Glynne Arms Hotel and headed by the Sandycroft band in their new uniform, and a splendid new banner marched to Ewloe. In the meantime members of the Old Club had also assembled and paraded the street. Headed by their banner and the band of the 2nd Flintshire Hawarden Volunteers, and accompanied by Sir S. R. Glynne, Bart. and the Revs S. E. Gladstone, F. T. Chamberlain, and the Hon. and Rev. A. V. Lyttelton they marched to the church, passing under the crooks of the Shepherds, who had previously arranged themselves in the road leading to the church. The members of the two societies presented a striking contrast, the Shepherds being chiefly young men, while the members of the Old Club were all aged, but hale and hearty looking men, evidently possessing strong constitutions. When the service at the church was ended the procession was reformed, the members of the Old Club proceeding to the Fox Inn, where a capital dinner had been provided. The Shepherds returned to the Glynne Arms Hotel, the dinner being served in Mr Mason's usual style in a commodious tent on the bowling green. After the meal the usual loyal and patriotic toasts were drunk and duly honoured with enthusiasm, including the 'health of the surgeon of the society Dr O'Kelly. Dancing was shortly commenced and was kept up with spirit to the strains of the Sandycroft band till nine o'clock.[33]

In 1863 the Shepherds celebrated their first anniversary with a service in the Methodist New Connexion chapel where an appropriate sermon was preached by the Rev. J. White 'who afterwards walked at the head of the procession with Dr O'Kelly, and dined with the club. The men were expected to attend church to hear a sermon there and the bell actually began to ring; but they preferred chapel for once, because their application to the clergy for a sermon had in the first instance been refused.'[34]

At the quarterly meeting of the Shepherds in May 1888 made up of twenty-five delegates from the Hawarden District, the total number of members was reported as 1670, with the sick and funeral fund standing at £6,495. On Whit Monday 1890 the Shepherds accompanied by the band of the Denbighshire Hussars and the Druids by the Crewe Steam Shed band marched to church for a service after which the Shepherds proceeded to Sandycroft and returned to the Boy's Schoolroom, Hawarden, for a meal. The Druids marched to Ewloe and then returned to Hawarden visiting the homes of their employers, and finally calling at the Rectory where Mr Gladstone was spending the day.

> Selections having been played by the band the ex-Premier stepped out and said, 'we all admire your band, and I hope you will have a fine day and enjoy yourselves'. A visit was then paid to the Girl's School-room, where a cold collation, served in excellent style by Mr and Mrs Temple of the Coffee House, soon succumbed to the vigorous attack of the 150 assembled Druids.[35]

The Friendly Societies are still in existence but their purpose of providing essential benefits was removed by the welfare legislation introduced by Lloyd George before the First World War and the Welfare State after the Second World War.

Hawarden parish was not immune from industrial action notably in the coal strikes before the First World War, the great Shotton Steelworks strike of 1910, and the General Strike of 1926. Henry Gladstone, Lord Lieutenant of Flintshire, noted:

> 1926. General Strike. 25 special constables enrolled at Hawarden. Flint was quiet though the Motor Bus Service was interfered with at Buckley. During the Strike a 'Service' Voluntary Office was opened in a room at the Estate Office with an official representative from Mold.[36]

The Nine Hours Movement

One of the demands of skilled workers in Britain in the nineteenth century was for legislation to regulate the length of the working day. The ideal was an eight-hour working day. This was not achieved until the twentieth century when the bargaining powers of the trade union movement became stronger. The general aim in the 1870s was for a nine-hour day. This was conceded by the employers at the Sandycroft Foundry and Ratcliffe's Engineering Works in Hawarden in the new year of 1872, when the celebrations of the men were reported in the local press:

> The village of Hawarden was enlivened in a very unusual way, by the sound of music and the gay appearance of

Friendly Societies walking through Hawarden village, Whit Monday, 1908 [FRO 28/P/37]

a large banner upon which was inscribed in large letters 'success to the Sandycroft Works and the Nine Hours System.' This was headed by the band of the works and followed by a large number of the employees of Messrs Taylor and Co. who had met together to show their hearty appreciation of the boon, which had been granted to them, unsolicited. About two o'clock a procession was formed at the works, and marched thence to Hawarden the band playing some lively tunes and after parading the principal streets, about 130 of the men assembled at the Glynne Arms, where an excellent dinner had been provided for them. At the invitation of the men the officers of the company were present. The local manager Mr Tregellas took the chair and in referring to the nine-hours he said. 'The system would give them an additional five hours a week for study and improvement. Sandycroft would not only maintain its present character for the quality of the work it turned out, but he hoped would be a continual benefit to the locality and a source of profit to the shareholders.

On the same day a similar demonstration was made by the employees of Messrs Ratcliffe's and Sons of the Hawarden iron works who assembled at the foundry early in the afternoon, each wearing a rosette, and headed by a large banner bearing the motto 'Peace and Plenty, and the band of the 1st Flintshire (Buckley) Engineers. The most novel feature in the procession, which marched through the village, was a wagon in which the operation of riveting was performed by a set of men in first-rate style. At the lower end of the village the procession was met by the employees from Sandycroft. After parading the streets the employees of Messrs Ratcliffe and Sons adjourned to the Fox Inn where about seventy of them sat down to an excellent dinner. Mr James Ratcliffe presided and said 'It was a pleasure to know that good feeling existed between employers and employed, and he was happy to be able to say that strikes and disputes between masters and men were in that neighbourhood at least, things almost unheard of. He trusted that the introduction of the nine-hours system would be an incentive to the men to greater efforts and more honest work and he hoped that many of them would become members of the Hawarden Institute and spend their evenings there.[37]

In the same month the men at the G.W.R. Carriage Works in Saltney had their working hours reduced from 57$\frac{1}{2}$ to 54 hours a week and celebrated the news with a public dinner at the Brewer's Arms Saltney. There were other industries where the employers were not prepared to make concessions to reduce the length of the working day. In the spring of 1872 one hundred and fifty farm labourers mostly from the parish of Hawarden met at the Wellington Hotel Rooms, Saltney, determined to assist in the formation of an agricultural labourers union 'throughout the kingdom.' The colliers and brick maker's preferred a show of strength as was seen in their May demonstration at Buckley in 1873.

On Saturday last the colliers and brickmakers of Buckley and district mustered to the number of about 2,000 for the purpose of showing that union is strength, and to induce others to join the United Miner's Association. About nine o'clock in the morning the men and boys formed in procession and marched to Mold. During the afternoon they returned to Buckley, headed by the Longton flag of the association, the Buckley brass band, which came next, playing 'Put me in my little bed.' The band of the Hawarden Volunteers came soon afterwards playing 'The Red, White and Blue ' being preceded at some distance by a flag, 'The Rhosllaneruchog [sic] and North Wales district.' It was remarked by many who witnessed the procession that the youthful colliers appeared to enjoy better health than the brick makers. In the evening the procession was reformed and proceeded to a piece of ground known as the 'mountain', where the men were addressed on the object of their meeting together. No provision had been made for the speaker who mounted a heap of building materials for which Buckley is so famous, bricks.

The Rigby Family Iron Founders

We have noticed above the family firm of Rigby, Iron Founders, Hawarden. The foundry was set up John Rigby I (1741–93), at the east end of Glynne Way in about 1776. His son William Rigby II (1768–1842), was in partnership with William Hancock II as coal masters and brick makers, and John Rigby III (1794–1852) worked the Hawarden Foundry and opened a branch in Sandycroft in the 1830s, where he specialised in building iron steamships, making use of his knowledge of steam engines and his engineering skills.[38] In 1776 John Rigby I was in communication with Boulton and Watt concerning a newly patented reciprocating engine, and in the early part of the nineteenth century the foundry was well known for its skill in casting and boring cannon, making cylinders, and the fabrication of small cast-iron bridges, steam engines and boilers for locomotives and steamships. Richard Willet in 1822 stated:

> In the Town of Hawarden also, is an Iron Foundry and a Smithy, with a Boring Mill, all on a large scale. There is an Old Establishment, of great and deserved note and where articles are fabricated from the great Fire-engine (steam pump), of sixty horse-power, to the smallest kitchen utensil; and this work affords employment and support, to about one hundred persons.

The *Mining Journal* of 15 February 1845 reported a destructive fire at the Hawarden foundry and iron works. As well as confirming that the foundry was still working in Hawarden it gives other information.

> On Thursday a very disastrous fire broke out in Mr J. Rigby's establishment at Hawarden, by which considerable property has been destroyed. Smoke was first observed issuing from the second floor of the pattern warehouse, which is in all three stories high. Unfortunately, no engines being on the spot, much time was lost before those from Chester had arrived, by which time the roof and floors had fallen in, and every effort to save any portion of the patterns proved unsuccessful. Fortunately, the fire was confined to this one building — for the foundry, being separated from the pattern warehouse by a stable and row of cottages, the former was speedily torn down, and the cottages well played on by the engines, and thus further destruction stayed. The injury done to the works is estimated at £3,500, the whole of which is covered by insurance in the Alliance Office. We are authorised to state, that the fire will not impede the execution of any contract in which the concern is engaged.

In 1852 the first Literary and Scientific Institution in Hawarden commenced in two cottages on the site of the old foundry.

The Ratcliffe Iron Works

Daniel Ratcliffe appears in *Slater's Trade Directory* of 1856 as a boilermaker. Later in his career he asserts his firm was established in 1846. Bradley says that Ratcliffe came to the 'Hawarden Iron Works' on buying the former Rigby premises advertised in the *Railway Times* on 10 July 1847. At some time or other the premises of Ratcliffe moved to a site just west of the existing railway bridge. In 1874 the firm describe themselves as 'Iron & Brass Founders, Engineers & Boilermakers.' The firm expanded and obtained further premises near the railway stations at Broughton Hall, Saltney and Padeswood. Daniel Ratcliffe's advertisement in the *Chester Chronicle* in April 1865 gives the scope

Ratcliffe's Iron Foundry, Hawarden, 1846–1920, c.1856   [FRO 28/N/69]

Certificate of the Steam Engine Makers'
Society, Hawarden Branch, 1854
[C. J. Williams, Industry in Clwyd]

of his business activities as, 'Engineer, Boiler Maker, Iron and Brass Founders, Mail and General Factor.' Ratcliffe informed his customers 'that in addition to the articles of his own manufacture, he keeps for the convenience of his customers, a large assortment of spades, shovels, chains, riddles, India rubber, machine made bolts and nuts &c.' By 1887 the Ratcliffes had moved away from being a wholesale ironmonger to retailing reconditioned goods. His advertisement describes the firm as 'Mechanical & Consulting Engineers, valuers of plant and machinery, and agents for the sale or purchase of all kinds of new and second hand engines, boiler and general machinery, iron and steel, rails, bars, forging &c.'[39] 'The ledger of John Fletcher, 1876–85, in account with Edward Ratcliffe, boiler maker Hawarden', shows that Fletcher was in partnership with Edward (d.1897), son of Daniel. Edward Ratcliffe was described in *Slater's Directory*, 1895, as an 'engineer and machine merchant'. The ledger shows that he operated from Broughton Hall and probably Padeswood, buying up engines, boilers, steam pipes &c from the Lancashire coalfield, repairing and reconditioning them, and selling them on at a profit to customers in North Wales.[40]

In August 1890 the local press recorded the opening of a boiler stores at Hawarden new station and Edward Ratcliffe's intention of enlarging the store yard and bringing in more boilers similar to those in the large stores which he kept at Broughton Hall and Padeswood stations.[42]

The relationship with the work force was good. In 1866, Daniel Ratcliffe's workmen with their wives had their annual Christmas supper in the boiler makers club-room at the Fox Inn when dancing interspersed with songs and recitations was kept up with spirit till midnight. When the Hawarden branch of the Steam Engine Makers Society celebrated the Jubilee of the Society in 1874, thirty members of the local branch met for their dinner at the Fox Inn. The Hawarden Branch had been formed in 1828. To celebrate Queen Victoria's Jubilee in 1887 Edward Ratcliffe (described this time as machinery broker Hawarden), gave a feast of 'a monster 'Tato' pie to the children at Broughton.

On Friday October 28 a large table was splendidly laid out in the magistrates room at the Glynne Arms Broughton Hall, around which table were seated about sixty poor children. A few minutes having been passed in silence, a monster potato pie was carried in made by the landlady of the hotel, Mrs Cannell, and nicely baked by Mr Edward Prince. It consisted of pork and potatoes and weighed 1cwt. 1 qr. 14 lbs. (154 lbs.).' After the meal they all proceeded to an adjoining field, where all kinds of games were resorted to under the leadership of Mr Thomas Bailey of Hawarden. Nuts, sweets and toys were freely disposed of by Mr and Mrs Ratcliffe to the children.[42]

In the next generation, after the First World War, the firm could not withstand the depression in trade which began to appear in the 1920s. In December 1922 F. J. Ratcliffe was faced with bankruptcy because 'he was unable to place a number of boilers he had bought for customers who were unable to take them and he had to put them into stock.' To avert a disaster he branched out into the motor trade and catered for passengers and haulage. He appeared in *Bennett's Directory*, 1936, as a machinery merchant so Ratcliffe's survived for a few more years

5. Hawarden Village

The history of nineteenth century Hawarden reflects in some ways that of the nation. It is a story of industrial enterprise seen in the exploitation of coal and clay, the growth of new settlements occasioned by the opportunities for trade and new industries, a growing expertise in agriculture with new reclaimed acres to plant, and improved breeds of cattle to pasture. It is a unique history in many ways because W. E. Gladstone, four times Prime Minister, was its most famous resident for nearly half a century. The presence of Gladstone gave the village and its inhabitants a sense of pride, self-confidence and well being all, of which were reflected in its institutions and buildings, as the community was transformed by Victorian high endeavour. Hawarden village and castle became a place of pilgrimage as thousands came to see the People's William with his sleeves rolled up, felling trees!

Nineteenth century Hawarden is best understood in terms of the fruits of the union between Catherine, the daughter of the patrician Glynne family, and William, the brilliant politician son of a rich Liverpool merchant. This union made a lasting contribution to all spheres of village life. The Glynne/Gladstone partnership provided a family leadership for the enrichment and improvement of the population of Hawarden.

Sir Stephen Richard Glynne, 8th Bt., 1780–1815
[FRO 28/E/5]

We begin the survey in 1815 with the death at Nice in April of Sir Stephen Glynne, the eighth Baronet. He succumbed to tuberculosis at the age of thirty-five years, leaving a widow and four young children. The first part of the story is concerned with the influence on the Glynne family of George Neville, brother of the young widow, Lady Mary Glynne. They were the children of Lord and Lady Braybrooke of Audley End, Essex. George Neville was appointed rector of Hawarden, by Sir Stephen in 1813, who on his death bed, said to his wife, 'I had hoped, in fixing him at Hawarden to have ensured us all much comfort and happiness, but now I thank God that I have lived long enough to raise you up such a firm supporter there.'[1] The Reverend George Neville with his wife Lady Charlotte more than fulfilled the confidence placed in them by their late brother-in-law as they exercised their trust from the rectory in Hawarden.

Lady Mary Glynne was a devoted mother anxious to provide the very best for her children by protecting their health, encouraging their education and strengthening their characters, which development she carefully recorded. All four children were to have a lifetime's connexion with Hawarden, and a close bond with one another.

Sir Stephen Richard Glynne, born 22 September 1807, was the eldest son, and became ninth baronet and succeeded to the Hawarden estate on the death of his father. Stephen was handsome, precociously clever, had an astonishing retentive memory, but disliked games, preferred his own company, developed a passion for church architecture, and a dislike of any form of estate management. He never married. Henry Glynne, 1810–72, the second son, became member of Parliament for Flint Boroughs, 1831–2, and rector of Hawarden on the resignation of his uncle George Neville in 1834. Of an equable temperament, Henry Glynne enjoyed country life and was a faithful rector with a ministry of the same pattern as his predecessor. Henry and Stephen Glynne were known as' the gentle brethren'. Henry Glynne married Lavinia Lyttelton. His eldest sister, Catherine Glynne (1812–1900), married W. E. Gladstone in 1839, at a double wedding, with her younger sister Mary (1813–57), the bride of George Lyttelton, 5th Baron. The Glynnes, Lytteltons, and Gladstones became an extended family, with many ties with Hawarden. The two sisters became known as the beautiful Miss Glynnes. It is interesting to note that their mother, Lady Mary Glynne (d.1854), was related to five Prime Ministers: George Grenville, grandfather; Lord Chatham, great uncle; William Pitt, first cousin; Lord Grenville, great uncle; and W. E. Gladstone, son-in-law, not counting that he was Prime Minister four times.

George Neville added the name of Grenville in 1825. For convenience we shall call him Rector Neville. Rector Neville (1789–1854) was a pluralist, holding the living of Hawarden as well as being Master of Magdalene College Cambridge. At Hawarden he enjoyed tithes worth over £3,000 a year, and made alterations to the rectory in keeping with his income. He was held in great respect by his parishioners, and had what Richard Willett described as 'a laudable and unremitting zeal for our Church Establishment, and to extend and render permanent its effective influence throughout his jurisdiction.'[2] Rector Neville imposed a pattern of ministry in Hawarden which was to serve as an example to his successors and make an enormous difference to parochial life. He closed a number of public houses, successfully reduced drunkenness, and was concerned in the reformation of the life-style of his parishioners. In pursuit of moral improvement in the parish there was maintained a close connexion between the castle and the rectory. There was a dedication to providing education for all classes. He showed a zeal for the provision of church buildings and the maintenance of the parish church. He made the rectory and its curtilage comfortably and orderly.

Hon. Mary, Lady Glynne, (née Neville) 1784–1854
[Hawarden Castle]

The Glynne children at Audley End, Stephen, Henry, Catherine and Mary. By Henry Edridge, 1816
[Hawarden Castle]

Elementary Education

An example of the closeness between the rectory and the castle is seen in the beginnings of education in the parish for the general population. It was decided soon after Neville's arrival in 1813 that an elementary school should be set up in Hawarden under the patronage of himself and his sister, Lady Mary Glynne. There existed at the time three Dames schools, two on the old terrace near the Wynt and one in the Wynt, and an infants school kept in old thatched cottages in Rectory Lane. In 1814, the new elementary school was established in the old Tithe Barn. The large long room was divided into two: one room was used for schooling 160 boys, and the other, 140 girls. The school was run on the method advocated by Andrew Bell an Anglican clergyman, whose ideas were adopted by the National Society for Promoting the Education of the Poor in the Principles of the Established Church set up in 1811. The basic principle of Bell's method was that the older children taught the younger. The Tithe Barn was ideally suited as the school

premise, because much of the teaching was done with the children standing up. When they sat down for some of their lessons, the benches were arranged in hollow squares reminiscent of a military formation.[3]

Neville established other schools along the same lines in the parish at Buckley in 1820, and Broughton in 1822. Regulations were drawn up for the well being of the school children and the advice of their parents described as, 'Rules to be observed by parents whose children are admitted into Lady Glynne and Mr Neville's Schools in the parish of Hawarden, which are recommended to be pasted up in some conspicuous place in each Parent's House.' There were ten rules, the chief of which instructed parents to send their children at 8.30*a.m.* and 1.30*p.m.* on

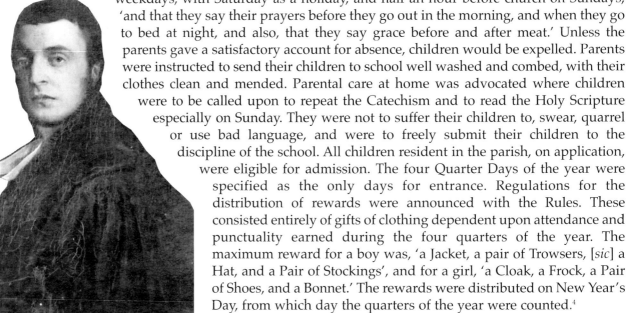

weekdays, with Saturday as a holiday, and half an hour before church on Sundays, 'and that they say their prayers before they go out in the morning, and when they go to bed at night, and also, that they say grace before and after meat.' Unless the parents gave a satisfactory account for absence, children would be expelled. Parents were instructed to send their children to school well washed and combed, with their clothes clean and mended. Parental care at home was advocated where children were to be called upon to repeat the Catechism and to read the Holy Scripture especially on Sunday. They were not to suffer their children to, swear, quarrel or use bad language, and were to freely submit their children to the discipline of the school. All children resident in the parish, on application, were eligible for admission. The four Quarter Days of the year were specified as the only days for entrance. Regulations for the distribution of rewards were announced with the Rules. These consisted entirely of gifts of clothing dependent upon attendance and punctuality earned during the four quarters of the year. The maximum reward for a boy was, 'a Jacket, a pair of Trowsers, [*sic*] a Hat, and a Pair of Stockings', and for a girl, 'a Cloak, a Frock, a Pair of Shoes, and a Bonnet.' The rewards were distributed on New Year's Day, from which day the quarters of the year were counted.[4]

Rev. George Neville Grenville, 1789–1854
[B. Jones deposit, FRO D/DM/592]

When the parish church was restored (1816–7), care was taken over the seating of the children of the National School, and their religious instruction. Rector Neville was an antiquarian and scholarly in his pursuits. He was instrumental as Master of Magdalene College, Cambridge in having the diary of Samuel Pepys edited and published by his brother the 3rd Lord Braybrooke in 1825. Rector Neville was also interested in the history of Hawarden parish and amongst his notes there is a detailed account of the restoration of the church in 1816–7.[5]

Church restoration 1816–7

The restoration work consisted mainly in the repair of roofs, outside walls, flooring, the insertion of new windows, new pews, a gallery and the reordering of church furnishings. The total cost of the work was £1,416 8s. 2d., divided as follows.

The East Chancel belonging to Sir Stephen Glynne, Bart. The whole of the East end and part of the North side walls were taken down and rebuilt with a large new Gothic window and one door the roof and also North

Windows were thoroughly repaired and whole inside ceiled & plaistered, new pews erected and half the aisle adjoining floored.

This work cost £471 4s. 6d. The bill includes payment to the architect, Benjamin Gummow 'for plans and estimates.'[6]

Neville comments on some of this work.

The large east window was put up in 1817, & in badness of taste fully accords with those in the nave: the arms of Glynne are introduced impaling Neville

Seating of school children in the chancel of Hawarden Church
[B. Jones deposit, FRO D/DM/592]

on a lozenge: & of Neville impaling Legge, on a shield. The windows removed in 1817 were in a very dilapidated state: it contained some fragments of painted glass on which a part of the arms of Man (the arms of the earl of Derby the previous Lord of the Manor) could still be seen: these relics are now placed in the centre part of the new window.

The Altar Table is a fair specimen of carved oak about the age of James 1 (1603–25). The floor on which it stands is raised 4 steps, & is brought forward 14 feet from the east window; the intermediate space is appropriated for a pew for the national schools.[7]

The responsibility for the work and the payment of the cost was divided between the Rector, the Parish and Charles Dundas.

The Rector of Hawarden — 'the old Rectory pews were taken down and 5 new ones erected, and a new pavement was laid on half the aisles adjoining.'[8]

The Parish of Hawarden — 'a new roof was put upon the Vestry room, the outside of which was repaired and cemented and the inside repaired and newly fitted up — a Gallery for school children was made behind the Communion Table — the table and rails were repaired — the cushions &c stuffed and covered and a new floor and steps laid — a stove & flues made to warm the Church — a new reading desk, the pulpit altered and re-fixed and both covered with Crimson — all the new wood work painted as also some of the old, a great part of the inside of the Church was coloured, the roof of the Hearse house altered, curtains were placed on the organ gallery & along the aisles, 4 new rain water pipes.' The cost was £441 6s. 6d.'[9]

Charles Dundas — 'the South Chancel belongs to Charles Dundas Esq., but being in a dilapidated state, he gave it up to the parish with a donation of one Hundred pounds towards repairing it; upon which under the direction of the Honble & Revd. G. Neville the south wall was taken down and rebuilt with 2 new Gothic windows and a double door, a new roof was put on, and the inside was ceiled plaistered (except the Rectory pews' part), and floored and fitted up with pews entirely new.' The cost of this work was £452 3s 9d. and was paid for by Mr Dundas' gift of £100, the sale of pews to Mr Hancock, Mr Willett, Earl Grosvenor, Mr Rigby, Miss Jones (Weppra). The three-decker pulpit was removed from the pier of the south side of the tower opposite to that of the north. The remains of the Rood Screen were removed. As Rector Neville explained — 'The stairs which led up to the Rood Loft over the Screen was outside the building, & very probably in the same site with that which goes up to the Belfry.'[10]

The font was removed from the place it occupied near the west door and a baptistery made for it at the northeast end of the chancel. On the south side of the chancel in 1770 a vestry room was made when a space, 'was parted off from the east end of the Whitley Chancel. This chamber is furnished with presses in which wills & other documents connected with the Peculiar are deposited. The Ordinary's chair is placed in a niche in the centre of the room.'[11]

In 1825 the organ gallery at the west end was extended the whole breadth of the Church. Neville also mentions that, 'except four Hatchments, there are no memorials to the Glynne family, although for above a century they have all been interred in this Church within a vault near the Reading Desk, or in that under the Altar inherited from the Ravenscrofts. There is also a vault belonging to the Rectors, & one under the Whitley Chancel which is attached to Aston Hall.'[12]

Buckley Church

Rector Neville began a policy, which was followed by his successors of building district churches, schools and parsonages. The first place to receive this group of buildings was Buckley. The Parliamentary Commissioners granted a sum of £4,000 for building St Matthew's Church, 1821–22. The architect was John Oates. A further sum of £2,000 was raised by subscription. This endeavour is an illustration of Neville's vigour and social connections. Subscriptions were solicited from all over the country and at the head of the list was the Prince Regent, followed by his son-in-law, Prince Leopold. Neville himself gave £100 and Lady Glynne £20. The laying of the foundation stone by his nephew Sir Stephen Glynne, was an unforgettable scene for the people of Buckley. Four hundred school children witnessed the procession from Hawarden to Buckley Mountain of the Hawarden Yeomanry Cavalry, their Band of Music, and a trumpeter led by the church officials and agents of the estate, followed by the carriages of the families at the Rectory and the castle escorted by detachments of cavalry and other carriages.[13] Two years later the township of Broughton was provided with a church, school and parsonage with the same ceremony and enthusiasm.[14]

Above: Hawarden Church and Rectory, south prospect.
Watercolour by Thomas Boydell, 1756
[FRO PR/F/123]

Above: Hawarden Rectory. Watercolour by M. Parker, 1825
[FRO PR/F/125]

Right: Hawarden Rectory garden. Watercolour
by Charlotte Neville, 1822
[FRO PR/F/127]

The Rectory

Neville came to a substantial parsonage in 1813, and to this he added a *port cochère* on the west side and the main staircase. Hubbard describes it as 'stark, sparse and amateurish', suggesting that Neville may have been his own architect.[15] But whatever the design the rectory was a happy place with delightful grounds, which Neville describes:

> A paved terrace of 124 feet extends the whole length of the east front and terminates at one end by steps leading up to a green house which faces the south. A glebe field of two acres has been taken into the garden on the north side of the house and made into plantations and shrubberies. The home scene is greatly improved by lowering a deep hollow lane at the eastern extremity of the old enclosure. The gardens comprehend nearly six acres and are surrounded by a deep stonewall, which from their varied and elevated position is completely concealed. There are two formal parterres of flowers within the enclosure and few places can boast of so much varied scenery and within so small a space of ground.[16]

Royal Visits

Hawarden was graced by two royal visits during Neville's incumbency. The first by Prince Leopold in 1819. He was the ill-fated husband of Princess Charlotte, daughter of the Prince Regent, later King George IV. The second was by Princess Victoria, with her mother the Duchess of Kent, as they passed through on their tour to north Wales in 1833. Neville noted that:

> This occasion called forth all the loyalty of the Inhabitants who manifested it by decorating their windows with laurels, and hanging across the street festoons of flowers and evergreens under which the royal carriages passed. A relay of horses met them in the centre of the garden front of the Castle. The injunctions of the absent owner were strictly enforced, and every mark of respect shewn to the future sovereign. 500 National School children ranged on the top of the wall, which separated the garden from the park, and the yeomanry and populace at the base produced a very striking effect.[17]

Rector Neville left Hawarden in September 1834 to make room for his nephew. Henry Glynne had come of age, taken orders, and now it was time for his brother to present him to the family living. 'The gentle brethren', as squire and parson, would run the parish in tandem. But it was not without affection that the parishioners marked the departure of Rector Neville and his wife Lady Charlotte. They were presented with a massive silver candelabrum weighing 600 ozs. The parishioners expressed their feelings in the inscription. To 'their Rector on his retirement from the scene of his active services as a memorial of their respect and esteem. Respect for the fidelity with which he has discharged, during 20 years, the duties of an arduous cure; gratitude for the munificence with which he has promoted the spiritual and temporal welfare of his flock.'

The marriage of W. E. Gladstone to Catherine Glynne, 1839

And now there emerged another on the scene who was eventually to have care of the welfare of a nation and empire and influence the lives of many in the Victorian age. William Ewart Gladstone was an Eton and Christ Church, Oxford, acquaintance of Sir Stephen Glynne. William romantically proposed to the beautiful Catherine Glynne in the moonlight in the Coliseum at Rome. Catherine Glynne was a member of the aristocracy and through her mother related to the great political families. The Hawarden estate gave the Glynne's a leading place among the county families. Her brother Sir Stephen was a Member of Parliament and Lord-lieutenant of Flintshire. Catherine was high spirited, amusing, unpunctual, disorganised, but with a tremendous zest for life, a sense of fun, a love of family and with a great compassion for the unfortunate. William came from a rich Liverpool Scottish mercantile family. He was a rising politician; serious minded with a pietistic religious disposition and increasing high church views. He combined a high sense of purpose and responsibility with great physical and emotional energy. Catherine and William complemented one another's characters and developed a great love and dependence upon one another, which was to last throughout their lives. They were married on 25 July 1839 in Hawarden Parish Church. It was a double wedding: Catherine married William Ewart Gladstone and her sister Mary, George Lyttelton. George Neville (now Grenville) performed the ceremony. Stephen gave Catherine away, and Henry, Mary. Gladstone recounted the occasion in his Diary:

> Soon after 10 Sir Watkin (Williams Wynn) arrived & we set off in about 12 carriages over the grass, round the

Left: The young William Ewart Gladstone (1809–98) in 1838. Oil painting by William Bradley

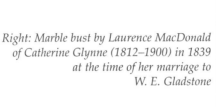

Right: Marble bust by Laurence MacDonald of Catherine Glynne (1812–1900) in 1839 at the time of her marriage to W. E. Gladstone

old Castle, & into & through the village. Oh, what a scene! Till 12 when we started I fought almost in vain against such a gush of delight, as I had not yet experienced. Such an outpouring of pure human affection on these beloved girls, combined with so solemn a mystery of religion! Every house was as a bower, the road arched & festooned, flowers & joined hands amid the green; & the deepest of interest on every face: a band & procession of Societies at the head. The mass thickened as we came nearer to the Church. From the highroad all the way to the door was carpeted: the Churchyard portion strown with flowers & dear little girls with the baskets: the order perfect. George came with my father & me after the brides. The Church was full: & as we walked up the aisle the organ & a hymn began & took away what little power of resistance I had left. At the Altar I found my beloved: we went towards the left: & were joined first: but the same opening & conclusion served. Uncle George performed the service with dignity & great feeling, & entire — Stephen gave C. & Henry M. My beloved bore up pretty well: her soul is as high & strong as it is tender. There were many tears. George gave way in the vestry a little: where we signed.[18]

The Oak Farm Crisis

Within ten years the Hawarden estate was facing extinction and Sir Stephen Glynne bankruptcy. This crisis was the reason why William and Catherine Gladstone came to live at Hawarden Castle. Lord Lyttelton and W. E. Gladstone each took a one tenth share in the industrial adventure of their brother-in-law Sir Stephen at the 94-acre Oak Farm, Stourbridge. Sir Stephen sold land for £55,000 to finance the scheme. The partners had an unlimited liability and as manager James Boydell, who was totally reckless. The crash came in 1847. Sir Stephen gave his own account of this disaster:

In 1840 operations were commenced for developing the mineral resources of the Oak Farm Estate in the parish of Kingswinford in Staffordshire & these were carried on for some time on a very extensive scale. The working of coal & iron was practised in a very ambitious manner & the works were extracted by the erection of forges, furnaces &c so as to rival the largest in the district.

There was certainly a large promise of success & excessive income, & if & no doubt if, proper prudence had been observed, & the works let on royalty to some experienced party, they would have turned out profitable. But owing to the sanguine temperament of the Manager all this was disregarded. Representations were made to the owner which induced him to allow an enormous outlay for extending the operations to an amount quite unjustified as it afterwards proved, according to the usual principles of trading & the result was that such vast liabilities were incurred by the owners, without receiving profit from the undertaking, as to cause very serious anxiety & embarrassment for several years.

The consequence was of course the Bankruptcy of the Oak Farm & Sir Stephen Glynne, though not included in the Bankruptcy, was obliged to meet the heavy liabilities he had incurred. In order to pay these off great sacrifices had to be made, expenses of every kind to be reduced & a large portion of land not only in Hope & Kinnerton but also within Hawarden Parish was sold.

Hawarden Castle
[FRO 28/C/24]

This led to an altered state of things from 1847 to 1853 when the house was in a great measure shut up & Sir Stephen Glynne passed much time with his brother at the Rectory. In the year 1853 an arrangement was made by which Mr & Mrs Gladstone with their family settled to make their home at Hawarden Castle from after the close of the London Parliamentary season, bringing their establishment with them & sharing the household expenses with Sir Stephen Glynne.[19]

Rather than break up the Hawarden estate, because it was the birthplace of Catherine and Stephen, Gladstone took on the burden of paying off the debt of about £330,000 to which he contributed £267,000. The Hawarden Estate was formally cleared of debt in June 1919. Veysey described the rescue operation:

An immediate decision was taken to sell land to the value of £200,000. Lands in Broughton were sold for £80,000, while the London and North Western Railway purchased property to the value of £15,000 for the new Chester–Holyhead Railway. Earl Spencer bought land at Queen's Ferry for £25,000. Gladstone himself, with his father's help, purchased a total of 1,559 acres including the Shordley estate (three farms and two cottages), and the Chester Block (lands in Broughton, Manor, Bretton and Saltney) for £72,330 between 1849 and 1852.[20]

Sir Stephen remained the head of the household, with an income of £700 *pa*. He was happy to share the castle with Catherine and William and their family. The Gladstones he referred to as the Great People, and he enjoyed the company they attracted. The Gladstones, Lytteltons, and Glynnes were a large extended family with Hawarden bases at the castle and rectory. There were twelve young Lytteltons, eight Gladstones and four Glynnes.

Henry Glynne, Rector

Henry Glynne with an incumbency of thirty-eight years was the longest serving rector of Hawarden in the nineteenth century. From 1851 he was also Rural Dean of Mold and Canon of St Asaph from 1855. His brother Stephen, was a member of the St Asaph Diocesan Committee for the building of churches, and chairman of the committee for the restoration of the cathedral in the 1860s.

Henry Glynne's first act as rector was to build a substantial boys' school to the north west of the church on what is now Gladstone Way. The elegant building of mellow sandstone was bought by the local Freemasons in 1913 and is used as a Masonic Hall. Later with the support of his mother and brother, Henry Glynne built the church, school and parsonage at Pentrobin in 1843. He was responsible for the church and school at Lache-cum-Saltney, 1853–55, and co-operated with the River Dee Company in the building of Sealand Church in 1867. Robert Phillimore spoke highly of him. 'It is not too much to say that more has been done by the Church in fulfilment of her great mission, during the period of his incumbency than during the two centuries which preceded it.'[21]

Henry Glynne married in 1843, Lavinia, the sister of George 4th Baron Lyttelton. It was a loving but short, tragic marriage. A son was born in 1848 '& all Hawarden was alive with joy on the birth of the heir. Between five & six it died.'[22] Lavinia died in October 1850. Gladstone recorded in his Diary, 'Lavinia was a soul singularly pure and sweet though quite mature: she was infancy and womanhood together. It is well with her: Earth has lost, and Paradise has gained.'[23] Two daughters were to follow their mother in the 1850s: Catherine in 1854 and Honora 1859.

Rector Henry Glynne, 1813–72
[B. Jones deposit, FRO D/DM/592]

Hawarden Church — Restoration, Fire and Rebuilding

In the 1850s Henry Glynne was involved in the restoration of Hawarden Parish Church. No doubt influenced by his brother Stephen, Henry was determined that St Deiniol's should become more ecclesiologically correct. To this end he engaged James Harrison, the leading Chester architect of his day, who had done work for him at Saltney. Extensive improvements were carried out. These included the replacement of the pews in the nave by solid oak stalls, the introduction of stained glass into several of the windows, and reseating in the main and south chancels.

All this work was in vain, for in the early hours of the morning of 29 October 1857 an arsonist caused considerable damage to the church. Gladstone's niece Lucy Lyttelton gave the best account of the destruction:

The much-loved, time-honoured old mother church was set on fire between three and four in the morning, and before the afternoon was destroyed with the exception of the walls, tower, and chancel windows and stalls. The whole of the nave and aisle roofs fell in, and the chancel one will have to come down. The W. window, stonework and all, is destroyed; the tracery of the others still stands; all the glass shivered, except in the chancel. Miss S. awoke me at about 1/2 past 5 to tell me, news having been sent to the Castle of it. We scrambled on to the leads of the house, and from thence saw the red glow beating high in to the sky above the trees. Before 7 1/2 we went to see. The flames were then being subdued, but the whole floor of the body of the church was a mass of burning beams and red-hot ashes: the columns blackened and stripped of their plaster (a good thing, by the way), the last of the nave rafters burning away in its place across the top of the chancel, and the broken mullions of the W. window alone remaining, the font a shapeless ruin, the roof of the chancel, which still stood, smouldering and occasionally breaking out into flame, the fire-engine fizzing, roaring, rushing, spouting, drenching, a line of schoolboys passing buckets, rather enjoying the fun, an excited crowd all round; the beautiful Memorial windows looking down upon the wreck serene and unmoved in the morning light, and the old clock melodiously chiming the quarters as if nothing had happened.[24]

Gladstone, with the experience behind him as Chancellor of the Exchequer, became treasurer of the restoration fund. Once again the family of Glynne-Gladstone came to the rescue contributing most of the cost of restoration on condition that the parish raised £1,000 by levying a rate. Sir George Gilbert Scott was appointed architect, entrusting the execution of the work to Mr Howe of Stafford Cottage, Hawarden. Howe had recently restored Lord Lyttelton's church at Hagley.

The church was re-opened on 14 July 1859 in the presence of the Bishops of St Asaph and Oxford. The Dean of Chichester, Dr Hook, preached on the Sunday in the morning, and the Reverend W. F. Neville, son of Rector Neville in the evening. The celebrations were marred by the death on 18 July of Honora Glynne, daughter of the Rector

Sir Stephen Glynne viewed the restoration as being complete and very successful. He recorded in the Hawarden Castle Event Book a list of the chief features of the work. They are of great interest for they explain the present re-ordering of the church and its main features both inside and out.

1. New roofs to every part of the Church. The South Chancel where the damage by fire was comparatively small, had an ugly modern roof, that it was thought necessary to replace it.
2. The former windows of the nave replaced by some of Edwardian character (thirteenth century), and two small windows at the west end of the aisle long walled up were opened and restored.
3. The pillars of the nave being much shattered by the action of the fire were rebuilt exactly as they were originally & while the work of rebuilding was proceeding the original arches were supported.
4. The North-eastern pier of the tower, being found rather insecure was underpinned.
5. The nave was fitted with open benches of oak with well-carved ends.

6. The chancel stalls were made good, as far as they had been damaged by fire.

7. The arcade on the South of the Chancel was wholly rebuilt because, though not injured by the fire, the work was found to be so indifferent, & so much tampered with in the repairs of 1816.

8. A chamber was built out on the N.W. of the chancel to receive the organ.

9. A new screen was placed in the South chancel so as to partition off the east end of it for a vestry & a new window was opened in the East wall, afterwards filled with stained glass in memory of Captain Whitley Dundas.

10. A new Altar of oak — a new pulpit of Painswick stone with shafts of Devonshire Marble — A new Font of the same material.

11. A short spire of timber covered with lead was added to the tower, covering the whole square of the tower — rather more like some French or Belgian Specimen than those found in England. This was a great improvement as the tower was rather short & heavy & would have appeared so much more so after the raising of the roof of the nave & chancel.

12. The north wall of the nave was rebuilt, being found unsound & thoroughly badly built, though not damaged by fire. All pillars of decayed stone masonry about the church were made good; the South porch reconstructed & the Southern & Western doorways restored.

13. The whole of the interior walls are of the bare stone, except in the South or Whitley Chancel, where in consequence of the new work in 1816 the plaster was necessarily retained.

Some of the monuments were so much injured by fire that they could not easily be replaced. Those of the Ravenscrofts were not very materially damaged & were re-erected in the Chancel.

The First Literary & Scientific Institution, 1854

Elementary education, the growth of industry and the increasing availability of newspapers and magazines led to the establishment of public reading rooms and popular lectures. This was a national movement inspired by the leadership of Dr Birbeck and Lord Brougham, which came to Hawarden in 1854. The Reverend Waldegrave Brewster, the energetic curate of Hawarden, was instrumental in founding a Literary & Scientific Institution. Its first home was on the site of the present Institute. It met in a building, which was two cottages knocked together where Rigby's iron foundry once stood. The first librarian recorded is John Wright whose name appears in the census of 1861. In the 1891 census he is replaced by his single daughter Ann aged 34 years. A newspaper report of 1856 gives an account of the first two years of the Institute's existence.

Sir Stephen Richard Glynne,
9th and last Bt., 1807–74
FRO 28/B/21

It commenced with a library of 750 volumes which now contains 900 volumes. Sir S. R. Glynne is president of the society; and when at Hawarden, he regularly attends the council meetings, and takes much interest in all its proceedings. That it is successful we may judge from the fact that there were 2,300 readers last year, and 1,200 volumes were issued, which are a large number for a place so circumscribed. During the winter months, discourses on historical and literary subjects are given by the Revd. W. Brewster; Dr Moffatt gives a course of lectures and demonstrations on physical science; and Mr de Troy conducts classes in mathematical sciences and the higher branches of arithmetic. Visitors also give occasional lectures. The members and friends of the institution held their anniversary on Thursday last week. In the early part of the afternoon 900 people partook of tea in the National School room, the Revd. H. Glynne in the chair. They afterwards repaired to the beautiful pleasure grounds of Hawarden Castle, which, through the kindness of Sir Stephen Glynne were thrown open for the enjoyment of the party.[25]

The Hawarden Succession

The decision for Catherine and William Gladstone and their family to live in the Castle with Sir Stephen Glynne was made in the 1850s. Sir Stephen settled the estate on the Gladstones eldest son, Willy, in 1852. In 1867 W. E. Gladstone paid Sir Stephen £57,000 for the full reversion of the estate to his eldest son, after the lives of Stephen and Henry Glynne.

In the 1860s W. E. Gladstone's political career was reaching its height. He held the highest offices of state, as Chancellor of the Exchequer, 1859–66, and Prime Minister, 1868–74, and Hawarden came into national prominence. Henry Glynne busied himself with his clerical duties as Rector and Rural Dean. His brother Stephen spent time with him at the rectory and busied himself with his church tours and architectural notes. It was evident that the Glynne brothers would not provide a male heir. The two brothers died within two years of each other. Rector Henry Glynne died in 1872 from the shock caused by lightning, after being caught in a July thunderstorm. Robert Phillimore paid tribute. 'If ever man was attached to the Parish he was — his home was there, his happiness, in spite of many sorrows, was bound up with it. His heart was in his work. He loved his people, from whom he was rarely absent, and they loved him.'[26] His memorial is the alabaster reredos in St Deiniol's Church, which represents the institution of the Sacrament of the Lord's Supper. After the funeral Sir Stephen Glynne, patron of the living offered it to his nephew, the Reverend Stephen Gladstone, who was rector of Hawarden, from 1872–1904.

Sir Stephen Glynne, the ninth and last Baronet, too, died suddenly as his successor W. H. Gladstone recorded in the Events Book:

On the 17th of this month (June) died Sir Stephen R. Glynne the owner of Hawarden Castle. He was seized with a sudden affection of the heart in Shoreditch, just outside the Railway Station, on his way from the Eastern Counties to Wellington College, and expired in full consciousness and without pain in about half an hour.

The loss of one endowed with such rare gifts of mind, such innocence of heart and gentleness of disposition, creates a void, which to those who knew him, time will scarcely fill up, but will rather deepen and magnify. Hawarden can never again be the same to those who remember and cherish the calm sunshine of his presence in their midst. Such at least is the feeling of his successor in the possession of the Hawarden Castle Estats, Mr W. H. Gladstone, after the lapse of one year from his uncle's death.[27]

The two Gladstone nephews now followed their Glynne uncles as squire and parson, albeit under the shadow of their formidable parents. Catherine and William Gladstone by their brilliance, energy and good-will had begun to impose their presence on Hawarden. Sir Stephen's death came near the end of his brother-in-law's first turn as Prime Minister in 1874. By this time the Gladstones had lived in the castle for twenty-one years and turned it into a family home for themselves and their seven surviving children. In the mid 1860s Gladstone engaged the architect George Shaw of Saddleworth to make additions to the northwest corner of the Castle. This included his study the Temple of Peace.

The Orphanage and Home of Rest

Catherine and William were concerned with the needs of the poor and destitute. W. E. Gladstone gave a generous portion of his income to charity, and both Catherine and William always responded to any crisis in a practical way. When the supply of cotton from the United States failed during the Civil War, William Gladstone provided work for six men from the Lancashire cotton towns to make new walks in the Castle grounds. Catherine turned Diglane, a house in the grounds, into an industrial home for the training of Lancashire girls for service.

When cholera broke out in London in 1866, Catherine Gladstone was involved with Catherine Tait and Catherine Marsh in caring for children whose parents had died in the epidemic. She opened a home at Clapton for victims recovering from the cholera and when this was transferred to Woodford Hall the boys were brought to Hawarden in 1868. The census return for 1871 recorded that there was an orphanage for infants, which housed nine boys between the ages of 5 and 9 years. Close by was a second building which housed 25 orphans, 23 of whom were from London. In 1881 there were 26 boys and 2 girls. By 1891 the number of children was reduced to 15, from a widely scattered area. It was estimated that between 1868 and 1892 one hundred and thirty boys had gone out from the home into various branches of work. Boys were admitted between the ages of four and ten years, and some stayed for ten years.[28]

Some letters from the boys of the orphanage survive. There is a long letter of February 1875 when Henry

Scharpe wrote to Harry Gladstone, who had just arrived in India. Scharpe wrote with respect and affection, giving him all the news of Hawarden: the dogs Tip, Dandy and Alp, the progress of the pony, the exploits of his father and brother in lopping trees in the Pleasure Grounds, and 'the large snow house the Gentry and Ladies made. Mr Herbert called us and let us go in one or two at a time and Miss Helen came in with us.' His most important item of news was the job he had been given in the Estate Office, Hawarden, at five shillings a week, together with a suit of clothes and a pair of shoes a year.

Another boy William Lloyd, who left the Orphanage in 1871, wrote to the Matron Mrs Hills, requesting a certificate of vaccination from Dr Moffatt. He reports that he is living near Portland Place in London, and that the clergy of St Andrew's Well Street, where he was lately a chorister, 'have got me a situation as a clerk in the West Indian Docks, having passed first in the examination for the appointment.' William concludes, 'I was confirmed in 1874, which may be interesting to Mrs Gladstone to know, and I should be glad if you could tell her how grateful I am to her for her kindness to me in giving me such a start in life.'

The Orphanage was still in existence when Catherine Gladstone died in June 1900 when a description was given:

> Mrs Gladstone's Orphanage is more considerately spoken of as 'The Home'. It is entirely without any paraphernalia, which brands the inmates as recipients of charity. There is no attempt at anything like a uniform and anyone meeting one of the home boys passing through the streets would simply see a neatly attired lad who might have come from one of the better class cottages of the village. Every morning and afternoon a group of healthy looking boys from the Home make their way down to the village school where they receive their training side by side with the other lads of the locality, and join in their sports. Mrs Gladstone took a real interest in her young charges. The Home boys were Sunday by Sunday to be seen in their places immediately in front of the pew occupied by the venerable couple. The choir, too, has among its members several of the Home boys. The present number of inmates is 30, and the cost of maintenance is about £500 per annum. When the lads have passed through the various standards at the National School situations are found for them, and there are many of them now holding positions of responsibility and trust. When the first Armenian refugees came to Hawarden, and had an interview with Mr Gladstone, there were Mrs Gladstone's lads waiting to see them depart, and one of the refugees, on being told through an interpreter who they were, made them a short speech in his native tongue, which being translated for them told of the terrible sufferings of the Armenian people. The result was that unknown to the authorities, the lads made up among themselves from their pocket money, a small sum, which was sent for the relief of the sufferers.[29]

After the death of the founder there was a change of policy. It was announced in 1905 that, 'the Hawarden Orphanage is not intended for the most destitute class of child, but for those whose homes are more refined, if not less poor. The charge is £15 a year and at present we have four vacancies.'[30] The Orphanage was allowed to lapse, 'about this time, having fulfilled its mission'.

Catherine Gladstone also maintained a small Home of Rest for Women for a number of years in the buildings at Hawarden Castle.

Hawarden Town

In 1828 Hawarden is described as 'a respectable thriving little town. The principal street is spacious and well paved. The market-day is Saturday, and fairs are held on the 1 October and the 24 December, for cattle.'[31] Changes had taken place in the eighteenth century when the

A group of boys from the Orphanage, 1905
[FRO 28/M/75]

Catherine Gladstone's Home of Rest for Women in the grounds of Hawarden Castle [FRO 28/C/32]

Glynne family took up residence in Broadlane House named after the township in which it was situated. Broadlane township at this time was one of the most populous districts in the parish. Sir Stephen Glynne, the eighth baronet, continuing the work of his predecessors had great designs to lay out the gardens and parkland of his demesne. He went further in 1809 and turned Broadlane mansion house into Hawarden Castle. This scheme included the diversion of the road from Chester to Holyhead, which at that time passed through the grounds between the old castle and Broadlane House. This was done in 1804 when the present roadway was made. At the same time the people living within the castle grounds were moved out. Rector Neville remarked c.1830, 'within the last century every house not connected with the Castle and its appendages has been taken down, some of which stood within the precincts of the ancient Castle, and several in the immediate vicinity of Broadlane Hall.'[32] This movement of tenants coincided with the building of terraced houses on the south side of the main street which is now known as Glynne Way. There are two blocks of buildings distinguished by their building materials. At the east end, Brick Row and at the west end, Stone Row. On the opposite side of the road at the east end was Rigby's foundry and a row of cottages named after the proprietor. As we will notice the main street in Hawarden stretching westwards into the Highway changed considerably in the nineteenth and twentieth centuries with, generally speaking, dwelling houses on the south side and public buildings on the north side. Tradesmen and small shopkeepers occupied many of the dwelling houses on the south side. 'A List of all the Inhabitants of the Town of Hawarden was taken on the 5th day of July 1816', this was probably related to the detailed survey made of the whole parish the previous year. The list covers 161 households with the numbers in each, the total 743, and in addition 30 in the poor house. This list probably includes inhabitants in other rows of cottages built along the highway or set back from it. The occupations were those of colliers, foundry workers, agricultural labourers, tradesmen, shopkeepers, schoolteachers, publicans, surgeons, and ministers of religion. A number of inns or beer houses were interspersed along the road: the Horseshoe opposite Ratcliffe's Foundry, the Stag's Head Inn at the end of Stone Row, the Castle Inn at the junction of the Highway and Gladstone Way, the Blue Bell next to the Glynne Arms, and the Fox and Grapes.

The Rural District Council named the streets and the lanes of Hawarden village in the 1920s. The Wynt or Wint, means path, way, and is where the old post road used to pass through the Wint between the old and new castle, until it was re-routed in 1804.[33] The Glynne Way identifies the village with the family of that name. Church Lane is comparatively modern, being made about 1780 when the old entrance in the churchyard, near the rectory was closed. Rectory Lane was known in the sixteenth century as Priest's Lane, in the 1663 terrier as Church Street, in 1718 as Parson's Street, 'the Rectour lets leases for 21 years of 15 house with some land belonging to each. The houses lye together in a street called Parson's Street.'[34] Crosstree Lane, was cut in 1794 to make it easier to cart coal from Mancot by avoiding the Hollow Lane. At the junction with Glynne Way is an old lime tree, planted by Thomas Fisher, the parish clerk, in 1742 to commemorate the site of the Lower Cross destroyed in the Civil War.

Hawarden High Street at the beginning of the 19th century
[FRO PR/F/130]

Nearby is the House of Correction. Hollow Lane went from the Upper Cross or the Aston Cross (destroyed in the Civil War), near the fountain, down to where it forked, west to Daniel's Ash and south to Little Mancot. It now passes besides the Glynne Arms and east of the rectory Gardens to come out opposite to where Beefsteak Row stood near the Rector Drew School. The Highway was called by this name in a fourteenth century document. Highfield and Truman's Way were first developed for housing at the end of the nineteenth century at the time of the gold rush to north-west Canada, and because of the high price obtained they were known as 'Klondike' and 'Dawson City.' Near to Truman's Way is the boundary between Hawarden and Ewloe manors. Nearby on the Ewloe side where the road bridges the railway line was Cuningreave Cross pulled down in the 1640s, and a tree erected on the site by Thomas Fisher in 1742.

Hawarden village, 1896
[Robert Banks]

The old thatched cottages gradually disappeared. In 1877 the estate built a block of three cottages opposite Church Lane at a cost of £570. Brick and slate were becoming the chief building materials. Mrs W. H. Gladstone took a leading part in the movement to eradicate drunkenness and was responsible for opening the Welcome Coffee House at 15, The Highway, in January 1881. The purpose of the building was set out in the local press:

> Soup, will be provided every week-day from 12 to 4p.m., and will also be sold within these hours for use at home at one and a half-pence per pint. Children attending the National Schools may have the basin of soup at one pence. The eating-room is on the ground floor, and is open to all. Upstairs there is a commodious room for men only, with good fires, where games, draughts, chess and dominoes will be found, with daily and weekly newspapers. On Sundays from 2 till 6p.m. this room will be open as a reading room only, with periodicals, papers, &c. During the day of the opening a brisk trade was done, and the rooms have been largely used every day since. Mr and Mrs Braham Taylor have been appointed to the management of the rooms, which it is hoped, will be a great convenience to the neighbourhood.[35]

A new court house was opened in July 1887, and the Petty Sessions were held there for the first time.

The supply of water to the growing number of households in the village was becoming difficult. There were village pumps at each end of the main street but at times they were inadequate. In 1884 it was reported, 'great scarcity of water in the village-none of the village pumps available. Mrs Fairbrothers' tap failed to-day, Oct. 17.' In order to remedy crises such as these the Hawarden & District Waterworks Company was incorporated in 1883 to supply a large area, which included Hawarden parish, Mold, Buckley and Leeswood. Eventually reservoirs were established at Cilcain and other places, and in 1908 one was opened on Truman's Hill. 'The new reservoir is a well-finished work, and does credit to the firm entrusted with its construction. It has a capacity for 25,000 gallons, and is enclosed by a bank, while a footpath runs round its sides. The object of the building is to supply the district between Hawarden and Queen's Ferry, where several new buildings are being completed, and it will be found a boon to this poorly supplied area.'[36] Gas was supplied by the Gas & Coke Company Ltd. Hawarden, of which William Thom of Springfield was the chairman.

The railway came comparatively late to the village of Hawarden. Other parts of the parish experienced the advantages of good communications from the use of the Chester & Holyhead Railway from 1848, and the Mold & Denbigh Railway in the 1850s and 1860s. In August 1888 Mr Gladstone travelled from Hawarden to attend the Wrexham Eisteddfod. It was announced that 'the Right Honble. gentleman will travel over the new Hawarden Loop Line and it is stated that Sir Edward Watkin will drive the engine.'[37] The Hawarden Bridge which carried the Manchester, Sheffield & Lincolnshire over the Dee at Shotton was formally opened by Mrs Catherine Gladstone on 3 August 1897. The opening of the completed Hawarden Loop Line took place on 31 May 1890, and the first train from Hawarden to Liverpool Central via Hawarden Bridge and the Mersey Tunnel was in 1896. In the 1880s large numbers of navvies, railwaymen and mechanics had been engaged on the work of opening up these new lines. It was reported in April 1888 that,

Operations are being busily pushed forward in the construction of the Hawarden loop line which it is expected will be completed this summer. Nearly 400 men are daily employed, the work being very heavy, the first cutting being over a mile long, whilst over some of the dingles an embankment sixty feet high has been raised. Mr Wooley, the contractor, has also commenced operations at Shotton, so that soon all the work will be in progress between Buckley and the Dee Bridge.[38]

Hawarden. The competitive decoration of Stone Row cottages for the 1896 fete.
[Robert Banks]

The rector of Hawarden was much concerned for the men's welfare and engaged the services of a trained evangelist and arranged concerts for them. He hoped that the coming of the railway would bring 'fresh blood and larger ideas to the area.' In 1896 he expressed his concern to his brother Herbert on the consequences of cheap and convenient travel from Liverpool to Hawarden and its impact on the village, 'You may expect the railway to do its utmost to advertise; & consequently perhaps hundreds, or even thousands on Good Friday, Easter Monday &c. They will I fear greatly demoralize the village and its surroundings if they come habitually in numbers.' The rector's fears were confirmed when Hawarden was suddenly invaded by 15,000 passengers who arrived on August Bank Holiday Monday and completely overwhelmed the resources of the line.

Mr Gladstone speaks in Hawarden

Mr Gladstone's long period in government, as Chancellor of the Exchequer, Prime Minister, or Leader of the Opposition, put him in the forefront of British politics for nearly forty years. Hawarden became a popular and essential place for newspaper correspondents. In many ways Gladstone enjoyed being a media figure. As a wily politician and a great statesman, he appreciated that there were many ways in which he could present his views to the general public through being reported in the press. Gladstone's main political stage was the House of Commons, but of all nineteenth century British statesmen he was supreme in promoting his ideas on a wider stage. He became the master of a nationwide political campaign, the 'whistle stop tour'. He never wasted an opportunity to get a message across. Of course Mr Gladstone was more than a politician, he was a great Christian statesman earnestly intent on fulfilling God's purpose for him and the nation at large. Living in Hawarden for over half the year, provided him with opportunities to speak at annual village events, the Horticultural Show, the Institute Fete, the Hawarden Estate Rent Audit dinner, and other occasions. People visited him from all over the world. In the summer Hawarden was full of trippers hoping to catch a glimpse of him either in church or in the Castle grounds. Four occasions in the 1870s are chosen to illustrate the way in which Mr Gladstone used these opportunities to speak to either visitors or the people of Hawarden.

The first occasion was the speech of Mr Gladstone on the twenty-first anniversary of the Hawarden Literary and Scientific Institution held in September 1875. His address was on the subject of Labour and Mental Culture. Gladstone spoke about the changes in living conditions since 1800, the higher educational standards in Scotland, the availability in the Institute of journals in both the Welsh and English languages, Translations of biblical commentaries, editions of Shakespeare and the major poets and history books.

'Though the institution has come of age, yet I trust in another sense it is in its infancy, and that it will grow beyond its present dimensions and embrace various parties other than those to whom it has hitherto addressed itself. It depends upon you whether it shall thrive or not. It requires no large efforts, no great sacrifices. It addresses itself to you, with the benefits it confers, far beyond anything it asks in return. Its fate depends upon you to answer the question we put to you, whether you will support it?'

He said that the British were an indolent people as regards mental cultivation, and advocated the value of industry in exercising and training the mind.[39]

The second occasion took place in a more informal way in August 1877. 1,400 excursionists from Bolton arrived in Hawarden Park by permission, and arranged for a mid-day meal and tea to be provided there by Mrs Rowland of the Glynne Arms. Mr Gladstone was aware of this arrangement and used it to its full advantage in order to captivate his visitors:

'Well in the afternoon he was seen to issue forth, accompanied by his wife and son. Both father and son carried heavy axes and were attired in loose suits, and as they walked off in the direction of the woods they were followed by a large number of the excursionists, who loudly cheered him, and many pressed forward to obtain a hand shake, which favour Mr Gladstone granted to the ladies, but inexorably refused the sterner sex. Stepping in front of a large ash tree, Mr Gladstone, amid the renewed cheering of his admirers, proceeded to divest himself of his straw hat, light coat, necktie, and vest; and then slipping his braces over his shoulders, and unbuttoning his shirt collar and wrist bands, he seized the axe and at once commenced to cut at the tree assisted by his son.' And, 'on Mr Gladstone resting for awhile from his work the choir of the Baptist Chapel at Bolton who had accompanied the excursionists stepped into the open and chanted the 23rd Psalm. It was excellently rendered, and at its close Mrs Gladstone, who had been seated on a fallen trunk, rose and very earnestly thanked the choir, at the same time expressing a desire for a hymn. At the termination of the hymn Mr Gladstone resumed his occupation, and as the chips flew about, a rush for their possession was made every few minutes by the more

W. H. Gladstone (right) and the family tree-felling at HAwarden in the 1880s. [St Deiniol's Library]

enthusiastic admirers of the Right Hon. gentleman.'

The Gladstones, father and son, continued with their task, the choir sang on and afterwards votes of thanks were expressed by the visitors and they got what they hoped for, words from their hero. Mr Gladstone said 'We are very pleased that you should have the fresh air and the opportunities which railways now give.' He deplored the conditions under which they lived. 'There are three things which tend to make large towns disagreeable; one is, the disagreeable smells; another is the want of pure water; and the third is, the enormous abundance of smoke.' They pressed him to speak about the Eastern Question but he refused, continuing, 'I want you — those of you who have houses and votes — think of these things I have been speaking, because you have a good deal of power in your hands that you may employ usefully in getting these nuisances abated. It is a very shocking thing. God made this world to be pleasant to dwell in — I don't say to make a town as good as the country with respect to beauty, but I think it is a very rational thing of us to do what we can to see that it is less defaced and less deformed than it has been.'[40]

The next month, September 1877, Gladstone spoke at the Hawarden Grammar School when he was called upon to distribute the prizes. This was the kind of occasion he enjoyed. He was speaking at an educational institution to teachers, parents and pupils, in terms of duties, responsibility, and vocation, set within a Christian community. These are some of the remarks he made to the pupils:

I know from practical experience that the first beginning of effort and the reward of effort is a most important event of life.' He told them that it was not easy to be a teacher, 'You are testimonies to your Head Master Mr Webb, and I entreat you, to do by your own efforts everything that is in your power to lighten his labours.' He spoke to them about their parents. 'Parents likewise make great sacrifices to get their boys to school. They have a deep impression and conviction that they are giving to their children something that is very valuable, something that is altogether indispensable, something that will be highly fruitful of results, something that will help them on the road to happiness and virtue.' He spoke about learning. 'I do not say that knowledge is the only thing for which man lives in the world. Man lives in the world in order that he may be made better before he goes out of it, and for the general training and formation of his character. Knowledge is an indispensable portion of that training and development. Knowledge of all kinds, knowledge of God and of your duty is the great knowledge.' His final exhortation to the scholars was given in words, which were to be placed on his memorial in Hawarden Church. 'The nature of man is capable of sinking to the most deplorable depths of corruption, debasement, cruelty and all things else that are bad, but if rightly handled, if we employ in a proper manner the means which Providence has placed in our hands, the nature of man is a work so noble that we can hardly conceive, almost, how creative power itself can go beyond it. Be inspired with the belief that life is a great and noble calling; not a mean and grovelling thing, which we are to shuffle through as we can, but an elevated and lofty destiny.[41]

The final example of Mr Gladstone speaking at Hawarden is altogether informal and should be regarded as remarks, which he made at an event, which happened in the village. The newspaper gave it the headlines, 'Mr. Gladstone on Cookery'. Gladstone had gone along to support his wife Catherine in one of her good works. She had arranged for a series of cookery lessons to be given by Miss Mary Vincent of the South Kensington School of Cookery, in the Girls' School on a Wednesday afternoon. The local newspaper made a story out of it, which shows the curiosity of Mr Gladstone and his ability to enjoy himself, and to extract an important lesson out of the most ordinary event.

Miss Vincent who was assisted by a kitchen maid, gave an admirable descriptive lecture. Mr Gladstone, who was preceded by Mrs Gladstone, arrived at the school and watched Miss Vincent make up a number of dishes with the greatest of interest. He asked questions about the ingredients of each of the dishes, and in the course of the lesson tasted the items like the rest of the audience, and pronounced them excellent. He marvelled at the way things were made up, and was particularly struck at the care taken to prevent waste, and the way in which was commonly consigned to the slop tub as useless was made serviceable.[42]

Gladstone then asked Miss Vincent a number of questions: the price of sugar, the making of Vienna flour and the batter for rhubarb tart. He tasted 'some artisan cakes' and greatly praised them. At this point he made a speech, addressed to Miss Vincent, again stressing' the duty of everybody to be economical and to avoid waste', and illustrated this with a story of Americans coming to Britain during the War of Independence and teaching the English people how to make soup from ox-tails' He concluded by praising Miss Vincent for her excellent demonstration and observing, 'but still in principle I am sure what you have been kindly showing is applicable to all classes of the community'.

In the 1880s Gladstone bore tremendous political burdens mostly concerned with the Irish Question. The family gave him the utmost support, particularly his daughters Mary and Helen, who acted as his secretary for some purposes. His eldest son Willy was proving an excellent landlord, and was married with a young family. Henry returned from India at the end of the decade and became the business adviser to his father. Gladstone respected and supported Stephen as rector of the Parish and looked to him for spiritual guidance. Herbert was the most successful politician of his sons. William and Catherine Gladstone played a leading part in the community. No event was too insignificant for them to attend. Everyone in the village was their friend. Margaret Hughes, 'Lady Margaret', the 'old Hawarden and Chester Carrier' who lived in Wigdale was the recipient of Mr Gladstone's Inverness capes and they often exchanged words of friendship and advice. When she died in 1894, members of the Castle family attended her funeral. To the people of Hawarden they were a large united family. A special bond existed between the Castle and the village, which was willingly transferred from the Glynnes to the Gladstones. This mutual loyalty between members of the family and the local community was expressed in a number of ways during the last decade of the presence of William and Catherine amongst them.

The Golden Wedding, 1889

Catherine and William Gladstone celebrated their fiftieth wedding anniversary in London. Lord and Lady Aberdeen put on a special golden wedding breakfast at Dollis Hill, when a Millais portrait of Gladstone and his grandson Will, was unveiled. In the evening a reception was held for them at the National Liberal Club. They received a telegram from the Queen and a letter from the Prince of Wales. Gladstone entered in his Diary:

Holy Communion at the near Church 8*a.m.*
Our 50th anniversary or golden wedding. For me it should have been a day of retreat & recollection, of mingled thankfulness & shame. But was one (after the service) of incessant calls outwards of every kind. Most loving visits, greetings, gifts, correspondence, business in its inevitable increasing round so that I am whirling round & round instead of being deeply still. I am indeed overwhelmed with undeserved kindnesses.

The celebrations at Hawarden were reserved for 3 August, a hectic special day for the parish. The Gladstones set off from London at nine. 'Special train, & feast on board by Sheffield to Chester & Dee Bridge. Spoke at Grantham & twice at the Bridge. A very striking scene. Then on to Hawarden: we were received with much affection & all possible display. Spoke as well as I could; but it was very ill'.

Before coming up the hill to Hawarden, Catherine Gladstone made the official opening of the Hawarden Railway swing bridge over the Dee which linked North Wales with Merseyside.[43] They reached Hawarden at 6*p.m.*, two hours late, the church bells were ringing and the bands of the Denbighshire Hussars and the 1st Volunteer Battalion Royal Welsh Fusiliers played to the waiting crowds. All the houses were decorated with flowers and greetings. At the principal entrance to the park a floral arch had been erected upon which was displayed a simple 'Welcome Home' At the entrance to the village the horses had been removed from the carriage, which was now drawn by 30 workmen from the Hawarden estate and proceeded to the Castle where the Gladstone's children and grandchildren awaited them. Here Mr Gladstone received a warm greeting from Petz his faithful dog. Formal congratulatory addresses were presented by Mr F. L. Hancock of Wold House, and Alderman W. Johnson of Broughton Hall, and Mr Gladstone in thanking them told the gathering that

'everywhere where we have been, there have flowed forth upon us in extraordinary abundance the tokens of the goodwill, the sympathy, the indulgent judgment, and the large affection of our fellow-countrymen of all ranks and all stations We rejoice to think that it is in the heartfelt union of local communities in this country where lies the secret of the national strength, and we do earnestly and humbly believe that we, the people of Hawarden, are in common degree a united community.'[44] The gift of the parishioners was a public drinking fountain designed and executed by Mr Edward Griffith of Chester, which was unveiled on Gladstone's birthday on 29 December 1890.

Mr & Mrs W. E. Gladstone & Mr & Mrs W. H. Gladstone all drove in an open carriage to the site of the fountain at one o'clock. Loud cheering heralding their progress and arrival. They were escorted by a procession formed of the band of the Denbighshire Hussars, the Sandycroft Volunteer Fire Brigade and the Manchester Boy Soldiers. After Mrs Johnson of Broughton Hall had unveiled the Fountain, Mr Gladstone said, 'I thank you profoundly for this remarkable memorial which is an ornament to the village of Hawarden'.

In the same year the family gave their parents a stone built north porch with windows on each side to replace the wooden structure, which was affectionately known as the bathing machine. The new porch became a favourite place to pose for photographs with visiting dignitatories.

The Hawarden Institute and the Gymnasium

One of the strongest of local societies in the 1880s was the Hawarden Young Men's Society under the patronage of Mr & Mrs W. E. Gladstone. Strong support came from their youngest son Herbert, who had the energy and organisational ability of his father. He masterminded the building of the Gymnasium in 1891, and the rebuilding of the Institute two years later. Herbert Gladstone had the support of the schoolmaster secretaries of the Institute, J. H. Adkins and Fred Green. The Gymnasium was built to encourage a flourishing group of gymnasts who emerged from the Young Men's Society, which generally met in one of the local schools. Their activities were reported in May 1888 when they gave a demonstration in the Boy's School.

The first item on the programme was a running match, in which all the members of the Young Men's Society, in costume, took part with great credit. They went through a series of light dumbbell exercises. They have already established a reputation for their parallel bar performance among the athletic world of Cheshire. In June they were addressed by Professor Stuart on 'Manliness', and held an end of season celebration, in the Hawarden Infant's School, when the founder of the Society, the Revd. Harry Drew, presided, afterwards there was dancing in the Girl's School.[45]

W. T. Bailey built the gymnasium for £850, and the institute for £1,175 17s. 4d. In order to raise this money the Committee with the encouragement of the Gladstone family decided to exploit the place which Hawarden enjoyed in the affection of the nation by advertising over a period of three years an annual Fete and Flower Show held in the Park and Castle Grounds. For the first of these gigantic occasions 117,000 bills and posters were sent all over the country, and 325 special trains arrived at Hawarden every day.

Mary Drew described the first Fête in her diary.

HAWARDEN, Tuesday and Wed. Aug. 23 and 24. — All went off quite perfectly, heavenly weather, as many thousands as the railways could bring, the people orderly and happy beyond description, the place in its most radiant looks, the P. M. meek as a lamb led out into flower garden whenever Herbert ordered it. Elected on Wed. M.P. for the 26th time. The Golden Wedding presents on view, an overwhelming success; over 6,000 people saw

The Hawarden Institute and Gymnasium, 1896
[Robert Banks]

them, in at oak door, out by porch. The selling was a great grind. Mrs. Toller and I made £80 between us the 2 days; altogether about £1,8000 taken, of wh. £600 must go in the heavy expenses. The music tiptop, but we were too busy to hear it. Was in the tent from 8 *a.m.* to 9.30 *p.m.* on the Wed.[46]

The building of the Institute went ahead and at the last moment W. E. Gladstone consented to perform the opening ceremony on Whit Monday, 22 May 1893. In his speech he went back to familiar themes, stressing the importance of community unity and making good use of opportunities for improvement. The Institute he saw as being there to promote 'a sense of unity, brotherhood and common interest in the community, and the cultivation of social intercourse among all classes, especially labourers of this parish, many of them highly intelligent men who would use the Institute on a footing not only of moral, but social equality.'[47]

The newspaper gave a full description of the new building with its caretaker's quarters, and the varied facilities of the Institute: billiard room, reading rooms games room, a special room for junior members, the library, and a committee room.' Adjoining the institute provision is made for an armoury to contain the militia store of the district, with a sergeants' room. The style of the exterior is plain and quiet, being a simple adaptation of Elizabethan renaissance to village purposes, with mullioned and transomed windows filled in with lead lights. The buildings have been substantially carried out by Messrs Bailey of Hawarden, under the direction of the architects Messrs T. M. Lockwood & Sons of Chester.'

Gladstone's speech was widely reported, and attracted another positive gesture from Sir Isaac Pitman, who sent 'a further consignment of books, making his noble gift of books up to the number of 2,000. The collection includes all the principal standard works, many of them beautifully bound, and will form the foundation of a reference library. Messrs Ward Lock & Co. have also promised some volumes of their publications to the library.'[48] By 1896 the Library was catalogued as having over 4,000 volumes of which Mr Gladstone had presented 82.

Further evidence of the high regard for the Institute and its patron came in May 1897 when it benefited from a substantial bequest of property made by a Hawarden old boy, W. Jones of Herne Hill, Kent. When W. E. Gladstone died in May 1898, the Institute was draped in violet and white trimming.

In the last hundred years the Institute has had a varied life. Its patron W. G. C. Gladstone was killed in action in 1915, Viscount (Herbert) Gladstone died in 1930, and in 1934 his brother Henry Gladstone on behalf of the trustees offered the freehold of the building to the Institute. In the First World War it provided hospitality for soldiers in charge of the anti-aircraft gun, who were granted free use of its facilities. In the 1920s tennis courts were added. Institute dances proved to be popular. During the Second World War a voluntary aided canteen was set up. For the duration of the war, the Vickers Armstrong factory at Broughton through the Ministry of Aircraft Production, requisitioned and rented the institute.[49]

Mr Gladstone's Legacy — St Deiniol's Library

Mr Gladstone began to keep his diary when he was a schoolboy at Eton. The last entry was made when he was losing his sight in the 1890s. The diary is a marvellous work, which has been printed in its entirety in fourteen volumes. One of the things that Gladstone faithfully recorded was the books he read, and it has been estimated that the number was at least twenty one thousand. He enjoyed not only reading them but was expert at arranging them. He invented his own way of arranging bookshelves, the method of which he pressed on all librarians he

The entrance to the old St Deiniol's Library, 1896
[Robert Banks]

met, including those of the Bodelian Oxford and Lord Derby's at Knowsley. He first used this method of arranging his books at Hawarden Castle in the library he created there, which he called the Temple of Peace. The man who made his bookshelves for him was the local carpenter, William Bailey who was also to make his coffin when he died.

There were many reasons why Gladstone collected books. First of all he was a scholar who read and wrote throughout his long life, not only in Greek and Latin but also in Italian, French, and German. He published books on Homer, Bishop Butler the eighteenth century theologian, and when he visited Pope Pius IX, he spoke to him in Italian and quoted St Augustine. The Italian poet Dante he regarded as one of his masters as he did the Greek philosopher, Aristotle. He wrote often in the national journals and in pamphlets on the place of the Church of England in contemporary society . He was sympathetic to the Greek Orthodox Church and critical of the Church of Rome at the time of the First Vatican Council. Second, he was a politician who was always thoroughly prepared to be the master in debate, and his library was full of contemporary books, pamphlets and Government Reports. Third, he was a traveller, not only throughout the British Isles, but also in Europe, and he was curious about topography and his own Scottish heritage. Fourth, he enjoyed reading novels and poetry, and was a great friend of Ruskin, Tennyson, and other writers. Fifth, and here we must stop, although the subject is by no means exhausted, he was a countryman, who took a great interest in horticulture, and the keeping of poultry. Books relating to all these area of knowledge are to be found in St Deiniol's Library.

The idea of creating and endowing a library came to Gladstone in 1882 when he attended the funeral of Dr Edward Pusey, one of the leaders of Oxford Movement. Afterwards it was decided to found an institution at Oxford to his memory, which should take the form of 'a College of Clergy in Oxford, to be a centre of religious faith, theological learning, and personal faith.' This was the seed sown deep in Gladstone's mind. By 1889 he began to realise his idea. There was no time to be lost for Gladstone was then in his eightieth year. He ordered two large corrugated iron buildings lined with wood. This idea I think he obtained from his friend, Sir Edward Watkin the Railway Magnate, who had a chalet of this kind in Snowdonia. The two buildings were planned to house Humanity and Divinity Rooms, with seven smaller rooms, five of which were arranged as studies and two as bedrooms. The Library was fitted with the system of shelving devised by Gladstone to house the 29,000 volumes brought from the Castle. The laborious task of carting the books from the Castle and arranging them on the shelves of the new library became a substitute exercise for Gladstone who was no longer able to swing an axe. The Library was to be a residential institution, and the Hostel was provided by the fortuitous resignation of the headmaster of Hawarden Grammar School in 1893 when Gladstone was enabled to take over the building. Eventually he decided to call the Library St Deiniol's, the Celtic saint after whom the church is dedicated. It received its first residents on 2 February 1894.

On 6 November 1895, Gladstone wrote in his diary: 'I have this day constituted my Trust at St Deiniol's. The cost of the work has been I think £41,000 to £42,000 . . . May God of His mercy prosper it.'(Today's equivalent would be £2 million not counting the value of the books). The main purpose of the library was to be a place of Divine learning to be used 'for the purposes of research, literature, education, and instruction with the view of the promotion of religion and sound learning.' The Foundation Deed established a permanent institution under the governance of Trustees. Gladstone appointed the first Warden, G. C. Joyce, in 1896. Gladstone died in May 1898 and a National Memorial Committee was set up and the chairman the Duke of Westminster asked the family if they approved of the idea 'of a permanent and handsome building for the books.' They agreed, and John

The visit of H.M. King Edward VII in May 1908
[FRO 28/F/51]

Douglas the architect was charged by the Memorial Committee to give the Library its proper dignity, and in its design to allow for the convenient addition of a future hostel. On 18 September 18 1899, Catherine Gladstone performed her last public act by moving the first sod, and the Duke of Westminster laid the foundation stone on 5 October. Earl Spencer, who had succeeded the Duke as Chairman of the National Memorial Committee, opened the Library on 14 October 1902. The foundation stone reads; 'In this building erected to his memory by a grateful nation is preserved the Library of William Ewart Gladstone who, eminent no less as a Theologian than as a Statesman, established this Foundation for the advancement of Divine learning.' Almost immediately the Gladstone family came forward with the offer to contribute £8,000 for the cost of erecting a Residence. This was completed in June 1906, and a Chapel established in the Residence in 1910. Extensions have taken place over the years. A bookstore was added in 1924, and twelve new bedrooms were added to the Residence in 1934. Further extensions took place between 1981–85 with the enlargement of the east wing. Between 1978 and 1991 an extensive rebinding and conservation programme was undertaken. A new bindery was opened in May 1988, named after David Mclean whose company constructed the building, which was converted into living accommodation in 1992.

The number of books in the Library has grown from Gladstone's original donation of 30,000 to 250,000. When

St. Deiniol's Library and Residence, John Douglas architect, completed in 1906
[St Deiniol's Library]

the Residence was built in 1906, a muniments room was installed to store the Gladstone Papers. These were removed in June 1930 when as it was recorded they 'were packed in a pantechnican supplied by Browns of Chester drawn by horses (to avoid any risk of fire) and placed at the General Station in a truck, and were delivered at the British Museum on the afternoon of 1 July'.

The first hundred years of the Library's existence has been characterised by the loyal devotion of successive Wardens of the Library and the way they have worked closely with the Trustee body to be faithful to the ideals of their founder. For many years the Library trained men and women for ordination in the Anglican Church. Candidates are no longer sponsored by various dioceses as in the past to train for the ordained ministry at St Deiniol's, but the opportunity for theological education is still pursued, and the Library is used by various churches of the United Kingdom for clerical and lay training, reading weeks, retreats and other purposes. The Library has become a popular centre for sabbaticals and scholars taking up residence to enjoy the various scholarships offered by the Library to promote Divine learning. These are open to students from all over the world. This helps to promote the ethos, which was the founder's intention, that of sound learning and an ecumenical understanding, as well as enabling people to find rest and refreshment. The Library has received two Royal Visits, by Edward VII In May 1908, and Queen Elizabeth II in the centenary year of Gladstone's death in 1998. Two Prime Ministers have visited the Library, Lloyd George in 1923 and Harold Wilson as a Gladstone Scholar, 1936–7, and when he spoke at Founder's Day in 1986. The Founder' Day Lectures were initiated by Henry Neville Gladstone in 1931. 'We have aimed ', he wrote, 'at selecting as lecturer one who had personal acquaintance with my father.' These lectures are still continued. The general public have access to view the Gladstone Exhibition, see the interior of the Library, and use the refreshment facilities.

The Death and Funeral of W. E. Gladstone

In June 1897 Gladstone opened the Jubilee Road Bridge at Queensferry.[50] He was in fine form and made an amusing speech, but by November he began to suffer great pain from cancer of the palate, a condition of which he was not informed until the following March. He returned to Hawarden to die, surrounded by his family. His daughter Mary played for him on the piano, and his granddaughter Dossie sang his favourite hymns, 'Rock of Ages' and 'Praise to the Highest in the Height.'(Gladstone preferred 'highest' although Cardinal Newman's lines are more usually known as 'holiest in the height.')[51] He died on 19 May 1898, Ascension Day, just before five o'clock in the morning, 'in 'the clock room', formerly occupied by Sir Stephen Richard Glynne. The partition wall dividing it from Mrs Gladstone, the dressing room had been removed in January. The foot of the bed was against the north wall. Over the bed on that wall hung the text, 'The Lord lift up his countenance upon thee, and give thee Peace.' Over the text hung the engraving of Millais's portrait of Newman. Mrs Gladstone & all the grown up members of the family were present at the end.'[52]

When the news of his death was made public the press besieged Hawarden, and twenty-two extra postmen and women were drafted in to deal with the messages. The London illustrated papers devoted their issues to the life and death of W. E. Gladstone. One them, the *Black and White*, produced sketches of Mr W. B. Jones, Postmaster, the Telegraph Messenger, Tolling the Bell at St Deiniol's Church, and preparing Mr Gladstone's Coffin — the scene in the carpenter's shop. Both Houses of Parliament adjourned after voting that Mr Gladstone be given a State Funeral and interred in Westminster Abbey. The State Funeral was arranged to take place on 28 May, and from thence until the body was taken to London on the 25 May. Hawarden was the centre of the news.

On 24 May Gladstone's body was laid in the Temple of Peace robed in his Oxford gown, and some three thousand people filed through. Early next morning the body was placed in the coffin made by William Bailey and taken on a wheeled bier to church with the family walking behind for a service of the Holy Communion. The church was opened at eleven o'clock for the public to pay their last respects, thousands of people poured into the village, and many more had joined them by evening when the coffin began its long journey to Westminster Hall for the Lying in State.

At the end of Evening Prayer the solemn procession left the church pausing as it did so to sing the hymn 'Days and moments quickly flying.' The procession was led by a clergyman carrying the cross so recently given as a memorial to Archbishop Benson who had died in the church two years previously; behind followed the coffin on a bier covered with the same pall which had covered Benson's coffin. They emerged into Church Street kept clear for the boys and girls of the village to say farewell. Here the single note of a cornet announced the hymn, 'Hark my soul it is the Lord', which was quickly taken up by the treble voices. Emerging from Church Street the

The funeral of W. E. Gladstone; the cortege passes through Parliament Square en route from Westminster Hall (centre background) to Westminster Abbey, 28 May 1898
[FRO 28/A/53]

procession was joined by the carriages of the mourners as it made its way to the Memorial Fountain. Here the crowds in their mourning best were flanked by the men of the Second Battalion of the Royal Welsh Fusiliers in their scarlet uniforms and the dark dress of the Liverpool Mounted Police. The procession crossed by the Memorial Fountain and paused at the Leopold Gate then into the Park to sing the hymn 'Rock of Ages cleft for me, let me hide myself in Thee'. The bier was borne in turn by four parties of bearers, relieving one another: colliers, estate workmen, tenants, and labourers. Lovingly and gently they resumed their journey through the park and as they reached the Castle in sight of the room in which Mr Gladstone died, they stayed to sing the hymn 'Forever with the Lord.'

Thenceforward the way led through scenes of changing beauty and semi-solitude. The crowds had fallen away; there were only a few stragglers waiting in the darkened pathway of the wood. The rabbits scuttled away, the cows looked up with slow wonderment from the brook, and lowed at the unaccustomed intrusion. At last Broughton Lodge came into sight, more than an hour after the bier had left the Church; and here the procession halted for the very last time. Here Mr Gladstone's hymn of trial and parting was sung, 'Praise to the holiest in the height.' There was a mile of road to be traversed, and in the hedges there was not a vacant spot whence the procession could be seen. The old pauper men and women came out of the workhouse to see; people had even climbed the telegraph poles and the porch of Broughton Church, where the minute bell was tolling. At Broughton Hall Station, where the railway line cuts the road, the throng reached the height of its size with the neighbouring fields full of mourners. The train named after the great man thirty-two years before had been long waiting at the station. The van, which was to carry the coffin to London, was hung with violet and silk.[53]

London was reached after midnight and the coffin taken to Westminster Hall where the Duke of Norfolk received it for the Lying-in-State. Early next morning the first of thousands of mourners came to pay their respects and throughout the day people filed passed the catafalque. At 10.30 next morning members of both Houses of Parliament processed to Westminster Hall to pay their respects to the man who had been a giant amongst them.

The statue of W. E. Gladstone in Westminster Abbey
[FRO 28/A/47]

At eleven the cortege slowly passed to the Abbey entering through an escort of boys from Eton College.

Mary Drew wrote of the dignity and sorrow of her mother:

As she entered the great west door of the Abbey, the vast concourse of people, seated tier above tier on each side of the nave, spontaneously rose as she walked slowly up the centre. 'She went in like a widow, she came out like a bride' — so did the whole ceremony uplift and inspire her. The scene at the grave was indeed memorable. As the last solemn strains of the Dead March were dying away — Mrs Gladstone, a noble and pathetic figure, by the open grave, gazing down upon the coffin of her husband — the Prince of Wales, afterwards King Edward VII, was seen to approach. Bending down, he reverently kissed her hand; his example was followed by the other pall-bearers, Prince George (later King George V), Lord Salisbury, Lord Rosebery, Mr Balfour, the Duke of Rutland, Lord Spencer, Lord Kimberley, Sir William Harcourt, Lord Rendel, Mr Armistead, and Lord Pembroke (who represented Queen Victoria). To each one of them, as they bent down, she spoke some appropriate word, showing far more self-control than any of these deeply moved friends.[54]

Catherine Gladstone survived her husband for just over two years. She was able to attend the dedication of the stained glass window by Sir Edward Burne-Jones commissioned by the children of Catherine and William as a thanksgiving 'for the long and blessed lives of their parents by their sons and daughters'. In September 1899 she cut the first sod for St Deiniol's Library. Lovingly cared for she gradually fell into decline and died peacefully on 14 June 1900. Four days later she was interred with her husband in Westminster Abbey. A memorial-fund in her memory was set up which raised £11,000 for the Catherine Gladstone Convalescent Home at Ravensbury House at Mitcham in Surrey. After the First World War, Henry, her third son, bought the former Munitions Factory Hospital at Mancot and dedicated it to his mother who throughout her life had shown so much compassion to the orphan and the needy. She was the last of the Glynnes of Hawarden Castle. A remarkable woman who was married to the greatest man of his age. This union of Glynne and Gladstone is commemorated in Hawarden Parish Church.

The Parish Church of Hawarden

It would be easy to see the Parish Church of Hawarden as merely a mausoleum to the memory of the Glynne/Gladstone family. In one way it is, for they lovingly restored the church after its destruction by fire in 1857 and beautified it, filling the empty windows with the finest stained glass of the age in a tribute to their loved ones. Likewise with the awe-inspiring luxuriant monument to Catherine and William in a memorial chapel created for the purpose. But we miss the point if we fail to recognize these adornments as dedicated to the glory of God as were the lives of those whom they commemorate. We will look at this more closely below.

Stephen Gladstone, second son of William and Catherine, was rector of Hawarden from 1872 — 1904, and was followed in the same office by his brother-in-law, Harry Drew, the husband of Mary Gladstone, from 1904–1910. The family saw the office of rector as one of great responsibility, which was to be exercised with devotion and excellence of purpose, to be carried out thoroughly and prayerfully with a sense of vocation. When Stephen was ordained deacon in December 1868, Gladstone wrote in his diary: 'It has been a special joy of this December that our son Stephen is given to the Church: 'whose shoe's latchet I am not unworthy to unloose'. Stephen received the greatest support from his parents who were regular worshippers, but never interfered in the running of the large parish. During the last half of the nineteenth century most of the parish became industrialized with collieries, brickworks, ironworks, and shipbuilding. Churches and schools were built in several districts, and assistant clergy employed, their stipends being paid by the rector out of his salary. If there was a religious ethos it was Tractarian, with its emphasis on the regular celebration of the Holy Communion, Penance, the Daily Offices, ceremony in worship, with a good musical tradition. All this was established in Hawarden Parish. But there was more. The Gladstone daughters followed their mother in doing good works, helping with the Orphanage, training the women to be good housewives, caring for the children in their Day and Sunday schools, introducing children's services, and playing their part as District Visitors. In 1895 Stephen Gladstone claimed that there were 311 laypersons involved in the mission of the church in the Parish. The list included church officials, choir members, Sunday school teachers, District Visitors &c. The Gladstone sons played cricket in the local team, took an interest in the Gymnasium, organised the great fetes to raise funds for the Institute which they emphasised should be for the leisure and improvement of the working class. This close co-operation between the Castle and the church has continued.

The Thanksgiving Window

The west window in Hawarden Church is the last work of Sir Edward Burne-Jones, and was dedicated days after the death of W. E. Gladstone in the presence of Catherine and her family, and at the time of the death of the artist.[55] The inscription on the window reads: 'For the long and blessed lives of their parents by their sons and daughters.' It was Mary Drew who suggested that Burne-Jones should be commissioned. He was a friend of the family, and made sketches of both herself and her daughter Dossie. As an old lady Dorothy Drew still remembered the mice scampering around the water pipes in the artist's studio. Fitzgerald speaks highly of this window:

> The problem of four lights is solved by a majestic Nativity which goes across them all. With the strange spiky forms of Burne-Jones's latest work and clear cold blue colouring, there is a concentration of all the lines on the Mother and Child, the last thing visible in Hawarden Church today as the evening light fades. The old pattern-maker could still make a pattern.[56]

Mary Drew felt: 'the sunset glory that transfigures this window is touchingly appropriate.' The subject of the Nativity, 'embodying the great doctrine of the Incarnation. Were Hawarden Church without any other attractions it would be well worth visiting for this window alone.[57]

The Gladstone Memorial Chapel

The memorial chapel stands on the north side of the main chancel and the inscription on the north wall of the chapel reads: 'To the glory of God and in reverent and loving memory of William Ewart Gladstone and Catherine, his wife, this shrine has been built, and this monument placed, within the church where they worshipped, in the home that they loved, by their son, Henry Neville Gladstone, July 28 1906.' It was dedicated in July 1906 to mark the wedding anniversary of William and Catherine Gladstone, and on the day, which marked the coming of age of their grandson William Glynne Charles Gladstone, the heir to the estate. John Douglas built the chapel, and Sir William Blake Richmond made the monument. Edward Hubbard describes the monument as being 'of luxuriant Arts and Crafts character, with the variations in materials typical of the 'New Sculpture' of the turn of the century.[58] The central panel on the south side of the monument quotes some words of the great man.' 'All I write and all I think, and all I hope is based upon the divinity of our Lord. The one central hope of our poor wayward race. [W. E. G. 1893] Be inspired with the belief that life is a great and noble calling, not a mean and grovelling thing that we are to shuffle through as best we can but an elevated and lofty destiny. [W. E. G. 1877] The central panel on the north side pays tribute to Catherine Gladstone. 'Strength and honour are her clothing. She openeth her mouth with wisdom. In her tongue is the law of kindness. Let her own works praise her in the gates. [Proverbs xxxi] It would not be possible to unfold in words the value, which the Bounty of Providence has conferred upon me through her'. [W. E. G. 1898]

Richmond wrote a description of the monument which gave an explanation of its symbolism:

> The figures of Mr and Mrs Gladstone lie in the boat of life. There are two prows; the boat proceeds ploughing its way through the sea of life. The prows are winged; the winged ships alluded to by Homer. The owl is typical of Wisdom, and also bears relation to the owl of Athenia and the wisdom of the great statesman. The Cross lies on the head of Wisdom; Sacrifice leaning on Wisdom. The hand rests calmly on the Cross; symbolising their united faith. The figure of the Saviour is typical of Peace; sleep more than death. At the four ends of the Cross are the emblems of the Evangelists. The Angel is Victory over Death, not dead, but sleeping. The whole group is intended to suggest

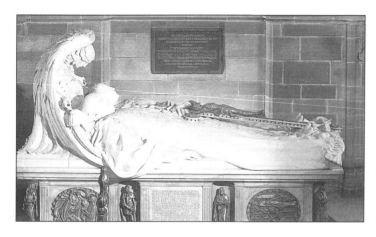

eternal peaceful movement on through eternal ages.

Richmond continues with this description, which is totally related to a summary of Gladstone's intellectual and spiritual life. At the four corners of the Monument are niches which epitomise Gladstone's master spirits: Danté, poet and patriot; Homer, epic poet; Aristotle, the subjective philosopher; and David, poet, statesman and king. The four patron saints of the United Kingdom refer to Gladstone's Christian statesmanship. On the north side of the monument, reliefs illustrate the motherhood of Mrs Gladstone, her motherhood not only to her own children, but to all the poor and those in need of kindness. The stained glass windows in the background, Ezekiel, Jeremiah, Isaiah, are a reminder of the prophetic nature of Gladstone's statesmanship. St Elizabeth of Hungary and St Catherine of Sienna are significant types of good women whose example was followed by Mrs Gladstone.

Another memory of Gladstone is his Latin translation of the hymn 'Rock of Ages' set on a marble tablet and place on the wall near the pulpit by his grandchildren.

William Henry Gladstone (1840–91)

William Henry Gladstone, the eldest son of William and Catherine Gladstone succeeded his uncle Sir Stephen Glynne, Bart. to the Hawarden Estate in 1874. He married in 1875 the Honourable Gertrude Stuart youngest daughter of Lord Blantyre. A Burne-Jones stained glass window of two lights placed in the north chancel of the Church in 1908, commemorates them both. The window with its pre-Raphaelite figures and colours depicts angels of paradise with their musical instruments. W. H. Gladstone was often compared with his uncle Sir Stephen Glynne as resembling him in his great refinement, and in a peculiar charm of manner and in some of his tastes, but he was also very different, being an active sportsman. He played football and fives at Eton, and became a noted alpine mountaineer. He followed his father to Eton, and to Christ Church Oxford. He was chosen to be a travelling companion of the Prince of Wales and then entered Parliament in 1865 representing Chester, 1865–8; Whitby, 1868–80; and the Eastern Division of Worcestershire, 1880 and 1885. He was a Junior Whip, 1869–74. But his heart was in music rather than politics He was a great lover and student of ecclesiastical music, and close friends with many leading musicians. Mr Walter Parrott organist of St George's Windsor, said of him, 'you will remember that Mr Gladstone compiled a hymnbook. It is the only one I know in which there are no bad tunes.' He played the organ at the parish church and formed a choral society, which met in the Castle outbuildings. There were three children: William Glynne Charles, born 1885; Evelyn Catherine, born 1882; Constance Gertrude, born 1883. He became the much-respected Squire of Hawarden during the agricultural depression, and where necessary made rent reductions. The family built the Red House at Wigdale in 1883, and occupied it until his father's death in 1898, when they returned to the Castle. In the summer of 1888 he began to exhibit signs of giddiness and seizures due to a brain tumour He died in July 1891 after an unsuccessful operation, greatly mourned, leaving as his heir, William Glynne Charles Gladstone.

William Glynne Charles Gladstone (1885–1915)

When Gladstone died in 1898, the hopes for the future of the Hawarden Estate rested upon his grandson. The inheritance so preciously guarded since the Oak Farm disaster and the upbringing of the heir, was put in the hands of faithful trustees, his mother and two uncles, Henry and Herbert Gladstone, who exercised their charge with sagacity and love. Will as he was affectionately known to distinguish him from his father and grandfather, was born on the 14 July 1885. He attended Eton from 1899, entered New College Oxford in 1904, and was President of the Union in 1907. He became respected for his openness of character, independence of mind, and a loving and sympathetic nature, which endeared him to all who knew him. Added to this was a determination to

do what was right for his tenants and later his constituents. Added to his pureness of heart there was charm and resolution.

The Coming of Age Festivities was held at the end of July 1906 when landlord and tenantry mingled together at a Great Fete in Hawarden Park. Twelve hundred residents and tenants on the estate came together to greet the Young Squire and wish him well, and went away impressed by his modesty and determination to follow the family traditions. At the same time he was playing in a cricket match for Hawarden Park, and was presented by his fellow members with a silver inkstand and illuminated address. His ambition was to enter Parliament, and he prepared for this by foreign travel to the Far East, and a spell as Honorary Attaché to Lord Bryce the British Ambassador to Washington. The Hawarden Estate was not neglected for:

> He inaugurated a system of farm competitions for prizes which he gave, and started ploughing competitions. He did all he could to make the Small Holdings Act operate, and in the erection or improvement of farm buildings and cottages he strained the limited resources of the estate. He gave to the Parish Council a public recreation ground. But his most important operations were the foundation and work of the Hawarden and District Farmers Association.[59]

In 1911 he was appointed Lord-lieutenant of Flintshire, and attended the investiture of Edward as Prince of Wales at Caernarfon. The same year he was elected as Liberal Member of Parliament for Kilmarnock Boroughs, and in 1912 was invited by Prime Minister Asquith to second the Address at the opening session of 1912, which was his maiden speech. He made his mark in the House by his speeches on the Welsh Disestablishment Bill. When war came he regarded it as his sense of duty to volunteer. He was commissioned as a 2nd Lieutenant in the 3rd Battalion of the Royal Welsh Fusiliers in 1914. On 15 March 1915 he was ordered to join the 1st Battalion at the Front. Whilst he was there he wrote to his mother on 4 April, 'Please let the Orphanage soldiers know that they can wander over the Park Woods and Old Castle'. They were members of the R.W.F. Whilst in the lines at Laventie he was struck in the forehead by a rifle bullet on 13 April, and died painlessly after being unconscious for two hours. His Uncle Harry brought his body back to Hawarden on 22 April, where it was placed in the Temple of Peace and laid to rest in the churchyard. Many tributes were paid to his memory including this one from Mr H. H. Millar of Shotton:

> When the late strikes were on [1912 Coal Strike], and even after the war had started, I received a letter from the deceased gentleman, asking me if there were any cases of distress in Shotton, or any children shoeless, and if so would I let him know. He was a man who never wanted the many people he helped to know where the money

Lieutenant W. G. C. Gladstone, killed in action, 1915
[FRO 28/B/6]

came from. Whilst at Wrexham, Mr Gladstone was a general favourite with the men. Before he arrived at the Barracks the men had very few games, *etc.* to amuse themselves, but upon his arrival he purchased all that was necessary for the men to pass a happy time.[60]

In memory of Will his mother and sisters erected a Rood Cross in Hawarden Church, the work of Sir Giles Scott, and it was dedicated on 13 April 1916, the first anniversary of his death. A mural tablet records:

> The Holy Rood above this Chancel Arch was restored by his mother and sisters, while by his tenants and many friends from far and near the Gladstone Wards of the Chester Royal Infirmary were dedicated to the memory of the young Squire of Hawarden, who wrote in words and wrought in deeds in the trenches in France hid life's own best motto: It is not the length of existence that counts, but what is achieved during that existence, however short. Less than thirty years — but crowned with the love than which no man hath greater, he laid down his life for his friends near Laventie, April 13, 1915.

Mary Gladstone and Harry Drew

Mary Gladstone (b.1847) was the fifth child and third daughter of the Gladstones. Like all the children, particularly the daughters, she was very close to her parents. She once remarked, 'so few people have lived their whole life with their father as the centre of history.' She had no formal education, which caused her great concern. She was rescued from this by her own intelligence and friendships. After 1879 she began to share in her father's political work, and acted as his unpaid secretary and political hostess. Mary Gladstone also had a great deal to do with the management of Hawarden Castle and the organization of her parent's lives. This was in some ways compensated by the close friendships she made with distinguished people such as John Ruskin and Edward Burne-Jones. It was to Lord Acton she owed the greatest debt for intellectual stimulus, and he it was who guided her reading. At the age thirty-nine years, she fell in love with Harry Drew her brother's curate in Hawarden and they were married in 1886. She shared the care of her aged parents with her sister Helen, but still finding time for motherhood and to share her husband's pastoral work. One daughter Dorothy Mary Catherine Drew was born in 1890, and became a great consolation to her grandparents, being affectionately known as 'Dossie'.

Harry Drew (b.1856) was a Devonshire man. He studied at Keble College, Oxford. After intending to study for the Bar he felt the vocation to be ordained and was influenced by Charles Gore to come to Hawarden. He came as curate of Hawarden at Michaelmas 1883. In 1894 he spent eight months in South Africa, returning to act as temporary Warden at St Deiniol's, where under Gladstone's instructions he compiled the first catalogue of books. He was inducted vicar of Buckley, the adjoining parish, on 30 April 1897. Here he displayed his great gifts as a parish priest, and the generosity of his wife made it possible to carry out extensive restoration. The work was under the supervision of John Douglas and was paid for by Mrs Drew with the proceeds of publishing letters written to her by John Ruskin. When Stephen Gladstone resigned as rector of Hawarden in 1904 Harry Drew was chosen to succeed him. He came to the parish at a time when there was a crisis in Welsh education and the future of church schools were threatened against the background of the Welsh Church Disestablishment campaign. As a member of Flintshire County Council he made his views strongly felt. His lasting memorial in Hawarden Parish is the primary school named after him.

Mary and Harry Drew are remembered in Hawarden Parish Church by the Burne-Jones window of two minstrel angels on the south wall, and the three tablets showing the rectors of Hawarden and the seventeenth century seal of the Peculiar.

Stephen Edward Gladstone (1844–1920)[61]

Stephen Edward Gladstone was the third child and second son of William and Catherine Gladstone. He was educated at Eton and Christ Church, Oxford, trained for the Ministry at Cuddesdon, and spent sometime at

Gladstone family group, 1895
Back row (L–R): Rev. Stephen Gladstone holding his daughter, Edith; Annie Gladstone; Mary Drew; Rev. Harry Drew; Herbert Gladstone (holding the dog); Miss Helen Gladstone.
Middle row (L–R): Albert Gladstone; Miss Evelyn Gladstone; Catherine Gladstone; W. E. Gladstone, holding his grandson Stephen Deiniol Gladstone); Miss Constance Gladstone.
Front row (L–R): Charles Gladstone; Dorothy Drew; Catherine Gladstone.

Cumbrae College in Scotland. Much to his father's satisfaction he was ordained in December 1868. He served his title in the Tractarian parish of St Mary-the-Less, Lambeth, under Robert Gregory who was later Dean of St Paul's. When his Uncle Henry Glynne died in 1872, he succeeded him as rector of Hawarden at the early age of twenty-eight years, and sustained a long ministry of thirty-two years until he moved to Barrowby in Lincolnshire in 1904. During his thirty-two years in Hawarden, he had as many curates all of whom were paid out of his large but diminishing stipend. His temperament was idealistic and earnest, with a great sense of duty. He came to Hawarden at a time when the great Education Act was being implemented, and to avoid the creation of a School Board in the parish, with the support of his father, he established and maintained voluntary Church of England schools throughout the parish. These school-chapels at Sandycroft, Ewloe, and Shotton, became the basis of future churches. His emphasis in worship was Sacramental and he encouraged regular celebrations of the Eucharist, Communicant's Societies, and Quiet Days for Clergy, and music in worship with an annual week for Gregorian music. He did not neglect Parochial Visiting and developed the team of District Visitors introduced by his uncle. He was a great organiser of events and the parish magazines of his day show great parochial activity.

During his incumbency the fabric of the parish Church was well cared for. Through the generosity of Henry Hurlbutt, the south chancel was improved and fitted for worship in 1884. He patronised John Douglas, architect of Chester who provided the south gateway in 1874 in memory of Sir Stephen Glynne, 9th Bart. W. E. Gladstone commissioned Douglas to provide the memorial tablet to his eldest son, William Henry. The sculptural panels of the Ascension outside the main east window are in memory of two sisters, the Misses Rigby, descendants of Hawarden iron founders. They were both devout women and district visitors. Rector Stephen was also responsible for the introduction of stained glass, He favoured Edward Frampton 'a pupil of Clayton and Bell'. Four of his windows, two in the south aisle and two in the north aisle, depict Biblical scenes in a traditional manner. The fifth window in the north aisle next to the Gladstone memorial chapel is a tribute to Gladstone's defence of the persecuted Christians in the Balkans and Turkish Armenia. It represents St Bartholomew and St Gregory the Illuminator, the first Patriarch of Armenia (A.D. 314), and speaks of Christian suffering, 'the noble army of martyrs praise thee'. On Gladstone's eighty fifth birthday the Armenians of London and Paris presented a chalice to the rector, in remembrance of Gladstone, 'whose loving service on behalf of the persecuted Christians they desire humbly and gratefully to acknowledge.'

In 1885 Stephen Gladstone married Annie Wilson the daughter of a Liverpool doctor. It was a happy marriage, which produced six children, four sons and two daughters. All four sons served in the First World War. Albert served in the Dardanelles, Charles an observer in the Royal Flying Corps, was taken prisoner to the island of

Stralsund in the Baltic, Deiniol distinguished himself by winning the Military Cross in action up the Tigris, and the fourth son William Henry, joined the Coldstream Guards and won the Military Cross for a night raid on a German trench. He was killed in September 1918. His memorial is in the parish church.

Other Gladstone memorials include a window given by E. C. Wickham Dean of Lincoln, who married in 1873 Agnes, the eldest daughter of the Gladstones. The window is by Henry Holiday, and is a thank-offering for their marriage. In 1904 the family bought Wold House as a family residence. In the north chancel is a memorial window by Burne-Jones, to Mary Lyttelton (d.1857), sister to Catherine Gladstone. There are windows in the south porch to Lucy Cavendish, niece of the Gladstones, whose husband, Lord Frederick Cavendish, was murdered in Phoenix Park Dublin in 1882, and Helen, the fourth daughter of the Gladstones.

Stephen Gladstone died of pneumonia at Manley Hall in April 1920 and is buried in Hawarden churchyard.

Helen Gladstone (1849–1925)

Helen Gladstone, the youngest daughter of the Gladstones never married. Encouraged by her sister Mary, she went as a student to Newnham College Cambridge in 1877, and became Vice Principal in 1882. When Mary married in 1886, she took over her sister's work as political secretary. She left Newnham forever in 1896, and returned to Hawarden to care for her parents until their deaths. In 1901 she became Warden of the Women's University Settlement in Southwark. She had a house built in Hawarden 'The Sundial'; after she died in 1925 it became the rectory. Helen Gladstone made some contribution to education in Flintshire, and was a governor of the newly formed County School in Hawarden.

F. S. M. Bennett, Rector of Hawarden (1910–20)[62]

Frank Bennett was Rector of Hawarden at a critical time in the history of the nation and the parish. It was the first time since the eighteenth century that a cleric who was not a member of the Glynne/Gladstone family had been offered the Living. The Young Squire found some difficulty in filling the vacancy. He went himself on his bicycle to Christ Church, Chester, to see Frank Bennett in action, and offered him the living. Bennett came to Hawarden in 1911, and set about gaining the confidence of his parishioners and inspiring them with his Christian leadership. His churchmanship was in the Tractarian tradition and he encouraged beauty in worship through a musical setting. He encouraged sung celebrations of the Holy Communion and established a choral festival for united choirs. The district churches were encouraged to hold social events. Mrs Bennett strengthened the Girl's Friendly Society and the rector formed a Church Lads Brigade. A successful attempt was made to meet free church ministers through the formation of a ministers fraternal, a move which went some way to providing more understanding on the eve of the Disestablishment and Disendowment of the Welsh Church. Frank Bennett successfully completed Harry Drew's extensive programme of school building and refurbishment and improved the standard of Sunday school teaching. One of the most difficult areas of parochial administration is church finance. Hawarden had its own problem because it was expected that the rector would pay his assistant clergy out of his own pocket, and this had been the case until the appointment of Bennett. All his predecessors had overspent their stipends. Bennett could not afford to do so, and stipends would be drastically reduced when the Church was disestablished and its revenue reduced. There were eight assistant clergy in Hawarden and the rector needed a stable and regular income, which Bennett fixed at £500. He used the parish magazine, regular contact with his church officials, and considerable advocacy to implement a Free Will Offering Scheme, which raised money for clergy stipends.

Before the First World War a permanent church was built at Sandycroft, and a convenient building, half of Gladstone's iron Library, provided a church in Garden City. The Rector provided admirable leadership during the First World War when the steel works at Shotton and the munitions factory at Queensferry made a significant contribution to the war effort.

The Boer War (1899–1902)

The Boer War was fought to prevent the independence from Britain of the Transvaal and the Orange Free State, two independent Boer republics. The war began in October 1899, and concluded in May 1902. In 1910 the two former Boer republics, and the British Cape and Natal Colonies were joined in the Union of South Africa, Herbert Gladstone became its first High Commissioner and Governor General.

There was a military presence in Hawarden throughout the nineteenth century. Hawarden Park was open to

Hawarden soldiers returned from the war in South Africa
[B. Jones deposit, FRO D/DM/592]

the Volunteer Soldiers for their exercises, and local facilities were provided for their training at the Armoury and Drill Hall in the village and the Rifle Range along the riverbank. Hawarden was noted for its shooting team and won many prizes. One of its members was Tom Bailey who kept the Castle Inn from 1876 until his death in 1921. He was a champion marksman, and won the admiration of W. E. Gladstone when he shot the mad heifer, which charged him in Hawarden Park in August 1892. Herbert Gladstone as a young man was an officer in the Volunteers. The officers were usually selected from such families as the Davisons or Hurlbutts whilst many of the men in the ranks were estate workers or colliers. In 1887 the Hawarden B Company of the 2nd Volunteer Battalion of the Royal Welsh Fusiliers had an enrolled strength of 83.

Men from Hawarden took part in the Boer War. Eight men were given a send off in January 1900, and another fourteen men of the Hawarden Company of the Royal Welsh Fusiliers volunteered to relieve the thirteen who went when the first call was made. The parish gave an enthusiastic welcome to the Volunteers when they returned from South Africa in May 1901. There was a large parade in Queensferry and Shotton and dancing was arranged in the park. In June 1902 at the end of the war, men returning from South Africa where met at Hawarden Station.

Punctually to time the train steamed into the station, and amidst great cheering and the strains of 'Home, Sweet Home' from the band, the returned warriors arrived again at Hawarden and the men were conveyed on the carriage of the machine gun and drawn through the village by their comrades. From the station to the church the cheering was continued, and the bells rang out a merry peal. A short service was held in the parish church and afterwards the Volunteer Company escorted their newly returned comrades on the gun carriage to the centre of the village, where in front of the Gladstone Memorial Fountain, a platform had been erected, gay with draperies and flags. Here the Volunteers formed a square with the heroes of the hour in the centre. Mr T. Wright presented each of them with a half-hunter watch. A move was then made to the Armoury, where the Volunteers dispersed.[63]

The final celebrations were held on Boxing Day when a dinner was held in honour of the twenty-five Volunteers who went to South Africa, three of whom died on active service, Private Bailey and Troopers Fox and Toller.[64] A churchyard cross was erected as a memorial on the south east side.

Hawarden Grammar School (1606–1894)[65]

Hawarden Grammar School was founded by George Ledsham, a steward of the Inner Temple, London, who, in his will, proved at Chester in 1606, 'gave to the parishioners of Hawarden, three hundred pounds, to be paid within a month after his death, for the erection and maintenance of a free Grammar School in the Churchyard of Hawarden for ever.' George Ledsham came from Ewloe, and his benefaction followed a pattern which was common in the sixteenth and seventeenth centuries, that of the endowment of a school by a person who had gone to London and prospered.

The school is first heard of in 1614, in a letter by Sir Roger Mostyn to his father-in-law, Sir John Wynn at Gwydir. Sir Roger 'has sent for Mr Holmes to confer with him respecting the education of 'your' children and 'mine'; finds it difficult to find a convenient house; Harden, in respect of the English tongue, is a fit place, and there they may learn to dance, a musician being in the town. But there are very many children there, and the master in some brables with a neighbour and cannot be reconciled; which may hinder the school, for that he is cited before the High Commissioners at London.'[66]

We next hear of the school in 1637 from the evidence given 'concerning the Schole and the poore of Hawarden' on 14 March 1637, when evidence was given before a commission appointed to inquire into Flintshire charities.

It was reported to the commissioners that £50 of the original benefaction had been spent in 1608 for building a school in the west corner of the churchyard, also that the interest had been allowed to accumulate and the £50 repaid. Elaborate instructions were framed for the management of the endowment; and a body of trustees, of feoffees, as they came to be called, were appointed, They were responsible for the stewardship of the endowment, the payment of the schoolmaster, and the keeping of a book which faithfully record the 'acts dispositions and doings' of the trustees.

The school, built in 1608, consisted of a single room, 48 ft. by 20 ft. The first recorded election of a school master is in 1655, although, we know the names of previous holders of the office: in 1618, Robert Lloyd and in 1642, Mr Thomas Chaloner, rector of Much Wenlock, and headmaster of Shrewsbury School from 1636–52 and again from 1662–64. Thomas Chaloner came to Hawarden to replace the 'present schoolmaster' who was brought before the Hawarden Court 'for neglecting his duty to the Free School.' Chaloner was an outstanding schoolmaster whose life was disturbed by the Civil War. He had to flee from Shrewsbury because he was involved in the loan of £600 of the school fund to Charles I. He was offered the mastership of Hawarden Grammar School in 1646, and arrived with twelve of his old Shrewsbury pupils. Within three months he had attracted over 150 pupils. But the school was broken up on 28 June 1647 by the plague, which came to Hawarden, claiming the life of William Barlow, one of the most promising scholars.

The office of schoolmaster was generally combined with that of curate of the parish, and this was the case in Hawarden until the end of the eighteenth century, but even after that many of them were still in holy orders. In 1655 the Revd. John Robinson, a graduate of St John's College, Cambridge, was appointed. He was a member of a Royalist family from Gwersyllt, although the rector of Hawarden was a Puritan. Robinson married Eleanor, daughter of Mr Thomas Whitley, of Aston Hall, and in his will dated 1703 left fifty pounds to the poor of Hawarden 'on the account and kindness I had from wife Eleanor.'

Very little is known about the school until the middle of the eighteenth century, when the master complained that the school was crowded with little children, to be instructed in the first rudiments of the English language. As a result the trustees ordered that no boy should be admitted to the school before he could read the New Testament; and from that date, until the year 1768, the children of parishioners were all taught to read, and when required, the Classics, free of any expense. A change of policy occurred in 1768 when an inadequate income forced the trustees to reduce the number of boys entitled to receive a free education to eight, who instead of being taught to read only, were to be instructed in reading, writing, and arithmetic.

It appears that the most prosperous period of the school was during the mastership of Richard Willett, of which Nicholas Carlisle recorded in 1818:

> In 1778, the next regularly appointed Master was admitted for Three years only, and with Six Boys upon the Foundation. But in the following year, an influx of Boarders, amounting to 49, came to be educated at this School. This circumstance, which not only advanced the credit of the School, but caused a considerable circulation of money in the neighbourhood, excited unfounded suspicions of a preference given to Strangers; and, at the expiration of the Three years, the Trustees, at the importunity of the Parishioners, again threw open the School to all who could read in the Testament; but, at the same time, fixed somewhat higher terms for writing and arithmetic.
>
> The excellent Master, Mr Richard Willett, was reappointed in 1781, with deserved marks of approbation; and, during the long period of thirty six years, his house averaged nearly Fifty Boarders; and notwithstanding the hazard of infectious disorders, which, though their virulence may be abated, can neither be foreseen, nor arrested

in their progress, not one boy fell a sacrifice to their malignity; and two only died of incidental complaints; the one of the Iliac passion, and the other of Coma.

The number of Parish boys has usually been equal to the number of Boarders.

In 1773, the Trustees of the money paid by the River Dee Company to the Lord of the Manor of Hawarden and the Freeholders thereof, gave £27. 10. 0, to make up £50 from some savings of Interest of the £300.

In 1810, a further augmentation of £50 was made by it's kind and good Master, Mr Willett, for the purpose of educating Two boys, in the best practicable manner within the limited period of Four years; with an intent to show and convince the Parishioners, that it would be better to have six or eight boys completely educated, than to have a greater number merely taught to read; — and the plan has been attended with success.

The situation of the School overlooking the Estuary of the Dee, and within 6 miles of the City of Chester and 14 of the Town of Liverpool, is, perhaps, as pleasant and salubrious as any spot that could be selected in the Kingdom.[67]

The trustees with the help of the parishioners rebuilt the school 1813–4. The schoolroom was taken down and rebuilt, and an extensive dormitory to accommodate 40 boys placed above it. A convenient schoolhouse was built adjoining the school and the rector and the squire gave land for an extensive court yard. These improvements cost nearly a thousand pounds. Mr Willett retired in 1814 to write his book, Memoirs of Hawarden Parish, published in 1822.

Notice of the school is given in an advertisement placed in a Liverpool newspaper by Willett's successor Benjamin Smith for 5 January 1815.

Hawarden Academy, near Chester. Mr Smith returns his sincere thanks to his friends and the public for the very liberal patronage he has experienced, and takes the liberty of informing them that his School will re-open on 18th January next, where every attention will be paid to merit the continuance of their approbation.

At the above School young gentlemen are boarded and carefully educated in all the branches of classical and mathematical knowledge at 26 guineas per annum and one guinea entrance. The French and German languages charge is extra. The under mentioned young gentlemen have received silver medals and books as rewards of industry from the above school previous to the present vacation.[68]

The list includes twenty-three boys from Cheshire, Derbyshire Lancashire, Denbighshire and Flintshire; and nine boys from Hawarden, who are named as, Osborne, Boydell, Woodfin, and Barber. These received medals. Whilst James Hancock, Edward and Thomas Ballard, Paine, Moore, and Howell, were rewarded with books.

W. Bell Jones lists a regular succession of schoolmasters throughout the nineteenth century, and there are brief descriptions of the school's activities from time to time.

The first is the Charity Commissioners Report for 1837, which showed that owing to the insufficiency of the endowment, the trustees found it difficult in maintaining the school in a state of efficiency. Ten years later the report of the Commissioners on the State of Education in Wales is not very inspiring. It points out that there are three different groups of pupils, the subjects taught, and the general ignorance of the pupils.

Free Grammar School. — A school for boys, taught by a master, in a school built for the purpose. Number of free scholars, 8. Subjects professed to be taught the Church Catechism, reading, writing, arithmetic, English grammar, geography, and history. Entrance fee, 2s. 6d.

I examined this school March 1, when only 6 free scholars were present. I found 3 who could read with ease, 5 who could work a sum in the Rule of Three, and 3 who had just commenced learning geography; all professed to be learning grammar, but very little was known either of grammar or geography. No instruction is given in Holy Scripture, and although the Church Catechism is professed to be taught, I found no one who could repeat any portion of it. The master receives 12 pay scholars at terms, which exclude the poor, and 18 boarders. He conducts the school with the aid of two assistant masters.

The Trustees express themselves as dissatisfied with the manner in which the school is conducted.[69]

The government attempted to reform secondary education in the middle of the nineteenth century, and drew up schemes for the better use of endowments; this was the purpose of the Endowed Schools Commission and the visit of Mr Bompas on behalf of the Schools Inquiry Commission in 1867. He was not very impressed.

There are at present in the school 30 boys, of whom 10 are Welsh, 10 English, and 10 Irish, about half being boarders and half day scholars. Half of the day-scholars walk as much as two miles to the school. The condition of the school did not appear to me to be satisfactory; the discipline was very bad, and most of the boys appeared to know very little of any subject.

By 1875 the school appeared to be more efficient and to offer a wider and more demanding curricula on the appointment of a new headmaster. This was the headmaster who was in office when W. E. Gladstone presented the prizes in 1877. The school governors were S. E. Gladstone, the church wardens of Hawarden, W. H. Gladstone, W. Hancock, H. Hurlbutt (two industrialists), Dr T. Moffat, John Fox (brewer), and T. R. Roberts (gentleman farmer). The school had become accountable to outside bodies and offered a wider range of subjects, and advertised itself in the following way:

'This school has been entirely reorganised, repaired, and newly furnished, and is now in charge of a trained leader. The pupils receive a thoroughly sound commercial education (inclusive of Latin), and if required are prepared for the Public Schools, Oxford and Cambridge, Middle Class Examinations, the Civil Service, and the Government Examinations in Science and Art. Besides the ordinary English subjects, the syllabus of instruction comprises: Greek, Latin, French, Music, Algebra, Euclid, Mensuration, Bookkeeping, Animal Physiology, Botany, Geology, Drawing and Drill. Gentlemen appointed by the National Society's Middle Class School Committee will examine the boys every year. This Committee, which consists of all the Bishops, and many leading persons interested in education, such as Lord Lyttelton, the Rev. Canon Barry, D.D., the Right Hon. R. A. Cross, M.P. and others examine schools throughout the country, and publish class lists by which the proficiency of each pupil can be seen. Prizes and Certificates are awarded to the successful candidates.'

The 1881 census listed 17 boarders, the eldest 16 years and the youngest 10 years most of the pupils came from Cheshire and Liverpool and one each from Canada and Ireland.

A mixed report was received in July 1889 when Mr Arthur F. Leach reported to the Charity Commissioners. Part of his brief was to inspect the School buildings in connection with the erection of new premises.

The school buildings stand in a corner of the churchyard, with an open green in front and the churchyard at the back. The school is partly the original one, with later additions. In all there is room for 21 boarders; there are now 22, one being boarded out in a cottage near the school under the care of the assistant-master. The general effect of the buildings is mean. The school accommodation is very poor.

Leach's report on the school was fairly optimistic and there appeared to be no reason to doubt that there was a genuine reason for the contemplated building scheme.

At Easter 1888 there were in the school 30 boys — 12 boys from Hawarden and district, of whom eight were dayboys; all the rest boarders, of whom 16 were from Ireland. Of the dayboys, three were farmers' sons, and three of the boarders from the district were also farmers' sons. Four of the Irish boys were sons of clergymen, and the rest professional men and gentlemen. The instruction given is that of a first-grade school with a modern side, Greek, Latin, French, mathematics, English, singing, drawing, and drilling. Natural science is of an elementary kind and without experimental teaching. There is no laboratory or other provision, apart from books, for scientific instruction. Fees have been paid since 1781. There were till recently six free scholars, but none in 1867 or since.

Benjamin Sharp, formerly a master of Lancing College, left in 1891 to be headmaster of Thane Grammar School. His successor F. H. Sikes, resigned owing to ill health, and the school was therefore closed. In 1894 under the Welsh Intermediate Education Act, Hawarden Grammar School was transferred with its property and funds to the county governing body, and became one of Flintshire's county schools.[70]

W. E. Gladstone had erected his iron library almost within the shadow of the old Grammar School which was ideally suited to be converted into a hostel to provide accommodation for residents. The building was rented from the Local Authority and subsequently purchased in 1896 by Gladstone. It was demolished when the Residential part of St Deiniol's was built c.1905–6.

Hawarden County School

The story of this school is taken up to the year 1933. In the year 2002 the school is on the same site although much enlarged. The status of the school has changed through the introduction of comprehensive education and the reorganisation of secondary education in the former county of Clwyd.

Between the 1880s and 1920s Liberalism was in the ascendancy, and Wales benefited from the legislation, which created a new local government framework. In 1880 W. E. Gladstone appointed Lord Aberdare to Inquire into higher education in Wales and Monmouthshire. His commission's recommendations were implemented in the Welsh Intermediate Education Act of 1889. The Local Government Act of 1888 provided the executive machinery to administer the Education Act. The membership of the new county councils represented a bloodless revolution; power was transferred overnight from the Anglican gentry to the nonconformist liberals. Perhaps the main difference in Hawarden was that the Liberal party, which made these changes, was under the leadership of 'the People's William.'

The trustees of the old Hawarden Grammar School must have seen what was coming and no one was in a better position to read the signs of the times than Stephen Gladstone. He called a meeting in 1890 'to consider the advisability of claiming an intermediate school for that district (Hawarden). A committee of 60 was eventually formed, and at its first meeting a sum of £369 was promised on the spot by those who were present. In June 1890 an inquiry was held at which evidence was given by Mr W. E. Gladstone and a number of other gentlemen.

The Reverend Richard Jones of Mancot was appointed chairman of the local governing body. He was a much-respected nonconformist who enjoyed the confidence of the committee. The local committee submitted two proposals one of which was adopted, as follows: 'suitable buildings to be provided by the local governing body, as hereinafter constituted to accommodate 80 scholars, 50 boys and 30 girls, the county governing body to supply a capital sum of £800, on condition that a sum of not less than £1,200, including the value of a suitable site, be contributed by voluntary effort.' It was reported that they had practically £700 in hand, £380 had been promised by members of the Gladstone family.

The Flintshire County Scheme was published on 27 June 1894. The school catchment area was extensive and covered the parish of Hawarden, part of Hope, part of Northop, the townships of Higher Kinnerton, Marford, Horsley and Saltney. The subjects for instruction were the usual ones, together with a range of optional subjects: Welsh grammar, composition, and literature; Greek; mechanics; the principles of agriculture; navigation; mensuration; shorthand; working in wood and iron; moulding; modelling in clay; (and for girls only, cookery; needlework; cutting-out; laundry work). In the preliminary prospectus it was stated that the school was intended to provide a higher education for boys, to fit them either for a commercial career or for entrance to a university. The governing body was elected by the County Council, the County Governing Body, the Guardians of the Poor of Hawarden Union, the vestry of Hawarden ancient parish, Northop School Board, Hope School Board, and a parent of scholars at Hawarden, donors of £5 and yearly subscribers of 10s. 6d. and cooptative governors, by trustees of Hawarden Grammar School. The total number of Governors was twelve. The Reverend Richard Jones of Little Mancot was chairman and other representatives included Miss Helen Gladstone, Henry Swetenham, the agent to the Hawarden Estate, Sydney Taylor, Sandycroft Foundry, and Henry Hurlbutt of Dee Cottage, Queensferry. The school fees were £2 per term payable in advance. Two scholarships, tenable for one year, and providing free education at the school for that period, were to be awarded at the opening of the school; and two other scholarships were offered for competition to boys under 14, resident in the county, who had for three years been scholars in a public elementary school. Accommodation for a few boarders was provided by the headmaster at a charge of £12 per term.

Mr. Arthur Lyon, M.A. (London), was appointed head master, in July 1896, and was assisted by an assistant master, J. W. A. Young, B.A. and a teacher of drawing, J. H. Hutchings. The new school was opened temporarily on 8 September 1896 at the Gymnasium in Hawarden. The number of pupils in the first term was 27 and in the second term 31. A Girls' Department was opened in September 1898 with Miss Gibson as head mistress and 17 pupils in attendance. In December 1898 the headmaster reported that there were 48 boys on the school register who were offered a four-year course. The Central Welsh Board examined the school, and the boys were presented for the Oxford Examination. The school moved from the Gymnasium to its new building in January 1899. Miss Helen Gladstone opened the new school in May 1899. A good description of the School was given in the local press.

Hawarden County School was opened on Thursday by Miss Helen Gladstone. The buildings consist of two large central classrooms, divided by a sliding partition, which, when removed, gives an assembly room forty four feet long by twenty-two feet wide. To the west of this central block is the boys' wing, consisting of the head master's room, class room and laboratory, with the usual coat room and lavatory and boys' porch. To the east of the centre is the girls' department; while to the south of the central block is a large luncheon room and kitchen with access by means of covered ways from both wings. The kitchen is arranged to give special facilities for holding cooking classes and the wings are so disposed as to allow of future extensions.

The buildings are heated with hot water by means of ventilating radiators. The rooms have all high dados of beautiful enamelled bricks from Aston Hall Brickworks, chiefly of primrose tone with skirting and copings of brown glazed bricks. Externally the walls are of red Ruabon bricks, with dressings and mullioned windows of red terra cotta, from Mr J. C. Edwards' works, and the roofs are of red Ruabon tiles. The arms of the county appear in the central gable. The schools were designed to accommodate 54 boys and 44 girls. The architects are Messrs Grayson and Ould of Liverpool, and the contractors Messrs W. and T. Bailey of Hawarden.

Of the cost of the building, which was £2,450, exclusive of extras, which have yet to be calculated, there has been subscribed £1,162, and the county governing body have contributed £1,450, making a total of £2,612. The subscribers include the late Mr Gladstone £50; Mrs Gladstone £50; the late Mr W. H. Gladstone and trustees £200; Rev. S. E. Gladstone £50; and Miss Helen Gladstone £20. These subscriptions show the warm interest taken in the movement by the Gladstone family.

In the evening a Conversazione was held, at which chemical and electric demonstrations, and dumb bell drills were given as well as an enjoyable musical programme.[71]

The school appears to have captured the imagination of the locality and it began to expand. The pressure of growing numbers and the need for classroom accommodation was generally met as school numbers increased over the next decade. In 1899 a chemistry laboratory and a luncheon room were added and a gift of £500 was received from the Duke of Westminster. In 1901 Mr J. W. Summers provided a large and commodious pavilion and a school orchestra was started. School numbers increased to 110 (57 boys and 33 girls) in 1903, and 30 books were added to the school library, including John Morley's *Life of Gladstone*. The need for a house for the headmaster was requested, for 'his presence and supervision are required without a break from 8.15*a.m.* when the first train arrives, till 5.45*p.m.* when the elder boys and girls leave' In 1904 the county authority recognised the need for expansion and promised to provide funding to increase the accommodation from 100 to 200 pupils and on 17 September 1906 the Right Honourable George Wyndham, M.P., opened the new school extensions

The fourteenth report of the headmaster for the year 1909–10 pointed out the strengths and weaknesses of the school and gave a review of the pupils' entrance into employment. School numbers had surprisingly declined owing to the lessening number of pupil teachers. One of the reasons was the opportunity of boys of 14 and 15 to obtain well-paid positions in the Hawarden Bridge Works. It was estimated that the number in school represented about 1 per cent of the population. A summary of the careers of former boys stated.

Since 1896, 310 boys have passed through the school. Between 50 or 60 have either gone to other schools or left the neighbourhood before entering on a vocation. Of the rest, 38 have entered the engineering industry (including the first candidate to take the new engineering degree at Manchester University): 28 have entered the Hawarden Bridge Works; 36 have entered the various retail trades of grocers, drapers, &c; 31 have become clerks, together with 7 bank clerks; 27 have entered upon farming; 27 are elementary teachers, 4 secondary teachers 2 art teachers, and one is now assistant Professor of Physics at St Bartholomew's, London; 11 have become sailors, 6 are connected with the building trade, 5 are surveyors and 2 architects; 3 are connected with broker's firms; 5 have taken up analytical chemistry and 4 are pharmaceutical chemists. Two have entered the civil service; 2 are librarians; 4 have posts connected with mines and brickworks; 1 dentist; 1 brewer; 1 shipping merchant; 1 doctor; 1 post office assistant, complete the list.

In 1912–3 School numbers increased to 187 of which 70 partook of school meals it being reported, 'we now grow all the rhubarb and most of the green vegetables.'

The school's response to wartime conditions is seen in the headmasters report for the year 1915–6. By the autumn of 1916 school numbers reached 248 largely due to the growth of population through the Queensferry Ferry Munitions Works. Five members of staff had joined the army. Some ten Old Boys had given their lives for their country in France and Mesopotamia. 'The girls in school have continued their work as vigorously as ever in knitting and making garments for the war's necessities. The boys have offered their services to the neighbouring farmers for harvest work, both during term time and holidays, and on several occasions they have been used. The whole of them, however, have helped enthusiastically in the potato-growing scheme on the reclaimed land at the back of the school. Their efforts resulted in the substantial contribution of 3 tons of potatoes, grown under varied conditions of fertilising. More land is being broken up, and this amount we hope to surpass next year.'

An Army Cadet Corps was formed in affiliation with the Territorial Association. Among the old pupils, Ruth Allen was the first to be credited with a double first in the University of Wales. Numbers again increased in 1917–8, as did the school harvest recorded as 4 tons of potatoes, 12 hundredweight of onions, 6 of turnips and 2 of carrots and sufficient green vegetables to supply the school dinners. It was reported that academically the strongest side of the school was mathematics and science.

When peace came, the school playing field of four and a third acres was purchased for £700. Army huts were purchased from the gun station opposite the school as the headmaster reported 'giving us three extra large classrooms. The construction of a bungalow from two huts for the caretaker meets a long felt need.' In the spring term of 1921 the Lord-lieutenant of Flintshire, H. N. Gladstone, unveiled a bronze tablet to those who fell in the Great War. In 1922 plans for increased accommodation to cost £3,000 were approved. In 1922 attention was drawn to the formation of an Old Scholars Association, a Field Club, and Dramatic Society. The headmaster proudly announced that the new school hymnbook was the result of his cooperation with Sir Walford Davies.

The depression in industry particularly the steel works, led to the early withdrawal of pupils before the end of their four-year period in school. The teaching of the Welsh language was slowly beginning with five pupils being taught in 1924. In 1927 there were 341 pupils in school, 190 boys, 151 girls and 20 student teachers. The Right Honourable H. A. L. Fisher Minister for Education formally opened new school premises. Four new classrooms were built which could be converted into a large hall capable of seating five hundred people. It was reported that the school library had reached close upon one thousand volumes, including many valuable historical works presented to the library by the late Mrs Drew, in memory of Miss Helen Gladstone.

In 1928 Mr Arthur Lyon resigned as headmaster after thirty-three years of remarkable service, in which the new county school was placed firmly on its feet and excellence established in all departments of school life, particularly in the memorable musical activities in which he took the lead. The new headmaster was Mr Benjamin Morris Jones, who came to the School from Barry County School. In 1929 two and a quarter acres of land were purchased for £400 to extend the playground. The school was expanded. The old army huts were converted into a dining room, the old classroom into a woodwork centre. A new dining room and cookery centre were established, and a new kitchen built in 1930. By 1932 the number of pupils had arisen to 482 — 254 boys and 228 girls — which necessitated a new development scheme, which included three new classrooms, an enlargement of the dining room, and a domestic science block. Shortage of teaching space had meant that the headmaster was using rooms in his private house as an office, and even for class teaching. The school orchestra had thirty-five performers and the number taking school dinners had reached two hundred and fifty.

Hawarden Church Schools (1834–1977)

Earlier we described the establishment by Rector Neville of elementary schools in 1814 for boys and girls, which were held in the Tithe Barn. Henry Glynne's new school of 1834 was for boys only, who were transferred from the mixed school of boys, girls and infants, held in the Tithe Barn, to the mellow sandstone building in Gladstone Way. All the schools in the parish, with the exception of the British School in Mancot, were run according to the principles of the National Society of the Church of England. In 1870 they became known as Voluntary Schools because they continued to be administered and in the main financed by the local Anglican church, instead of being the responsibility of local School Boards elected by the ratepayers.

We look at Hawarden Church Schools in two ways. The first approach is a description of the schools and their buildings against the background of government reports and legislation, and the second approach is to examine the school log books in order to give a brief glimpse of school life.

A valuable but somewhat biased insight into education in Wales in the middle of the nineteenth century is to be found in the Report of the Commissioners Inquiring into the State of Education in Wales. John James visited the schools in Hawarden in March 1847, and wrote the following detailed reports.

Hawarden Church School for Boys — a school for boys, taught by a master, in a school built for the purpose. Number of scholars, 96; number employed as monitors, 4. Subjects taught — the Scriptures and Church Catechism, reading, writing, arithmetic, English grammar, geography, history, agricultural chemistry, and music. Fees, 1d. Per week. Salary, £70.

I examined this school on the 2nd of March, when 85 boys were present; 39 were above 10 years of age, and 46 had attended the school for periods varying from two to above five years. I found 30 who could read with ease, and 5 with fluency and expression; only 34 of the scholars present were learning to write upon paper, the rest practice upon slates. I saw only two copybooks, which contained good writing. The children are required to provide themselves with copybooks; 55 boys were learning arithmetic, 35 of which were learning the four first rules, and 9 had commenced Proportion and the higher rules, 2 of the latter number having very considerable merit. In mental arithmetic there was no proficiency. A class of 16 had acquired some knowledge of geography, and a class of 10 were learning English grammar. In the History of England there were 18 who knew a few simple facts, 14 somewhat more advanced, and 3 decidedly intelligent; 31 were able to answer Scripture questions, and 4 possessed a competent knowledge of the subject. Among 66, who could repeat parts of the Church Catechism 29 were perfect.

The master is 36 years of age, and was formerly a courier. He was trained at the Central School, Westminster, and has been a schoolmaster for about seven years. Besides the last-mentioned office, he fills those of agent to an insurance company, and assessor and collector of taxes.

The classes were large and the members unequal in terms of attainments. Some of the monitors were intelligent, and capable of discharging their duties well.

The building is a very fine one. The furniture and materials for instruction are sufficient. The latter include apparatus for experiments in agricultural chemistry, which the master occasionally uses. The outbuildings are very insufficient.

The organist of the parish church occasionally visits the school to teach vocal music — John James, Assistant.

Church School for Girls — a school for girls, taught by a mistress and an assistant, in a building set apart for the purpose. Number of scholars 70; number employed as monitors, 4. Subjects taught — the Scriptures, the Church Catechism, reading, writing, arithmetic, and geography. Fees, 1d. per week. Salary of mistress, £40, with a house rent-free.

Thirty-six girls are above ten years of age, and 18 have attended the school for more than five years.

I examined this school March 1, when 58 scholars were present. I found 18 able to read a chapter of the Bible. Among 27 copybooks belonging to the whole school 9 were legibly written; 9 children were learning arithmetic, but none were proficient in the rules, which they professed to know. A class of 19 had commenced learning geography; 19 were able to repeat parts of the Church Catechism, 9 of them perfectly. I found none who possessed a competent knowledge of Holy Scripture, although 7 were able to answer some easy questions.

The mistress has not been trained to teach. The clergy frequently visits the school. It is well provided with religious books for reading and catechising. The

School House, Hawarden Church School for Boys, c.1905. The headmaster, George Spencer, watches boys leapfrogging
[FRO 28/N/42]

children attend Divine service in the church every morning before school hours.

Instruction is given in needlework every afternoon.

Hawarden Infant School — a school for Infants of both sexes, taught together, by a mistress, in a building set apart for the purpose. Number of boys, 37; of girls, 45. Subjects taught — selections from Scripture, the *First Steps to the Catechism*, and reading. Fees, 1d. per week.

I examined this school March 1, when 52 children were present, 10 of whom had been members of the school for more than two years. They were employed in learning to read the alphabet, and words of one syllable, in counting and repeating rhymes. Some were learning to knit. As soon as they are able to read words of one syllable correctly they are removed to the upper schools.

The mistress has spent six weeks in an infant school in London to learn the system. Her school is visited by the clergy.'[72]

The 1870 Education Act was aimed at providing elementary education for all children, to fill up the gaps in the Voluntary system by providing new schools whose cost was to be met with out of the rates. Voluntary schools would continue to receive money from the Treasury but all schools had to reach an acceptable standard as far as its buildings were concerned. Thus the parish of Hawarden if it wished to remain in the Voluntary system was required to build new schools in the districts of the parish, which lacked them and bring those that had them up to a standard approved by the government. The government stipulation was that new schools were to be built at Shotton, Sandycroft, and Ewloe, with the addition of a new classroom at Hawarden Boys' School.

Subscriptions raised over a thousand pounds. Some from local industry; Queensferry Colliery Co., Sandycroft Foundry, and Rylands, Saltney. Local landowners were generous. Lord Spencer gave £200 and the site for Shotton School, the Glynne Gladstone family £370 and sites, and the Duke of Westminster £100. The River Dee Company Trust gave £370, and the National Society £90. The contract for the provision of a classroom for the Boys' School by Messrs Bailey was £312 11s.

The responsibility for raising the money and completing the building of schools was that of the National School Managing Committee inherited from Rector Glynne, and now put to good account by his successor, Stephen Gladstone. It was composed of the rector, churchwardens, clergy of the Parish, and an elected member from each of the districts of the parish. The scheme for the parish took almost five years to complete. Details are to be found in the accounts below for the various districts.

During his long incumbency at Hawarden, Stephen Gladstone raised money by voluntary subscription to maintain these schools. The schools

Canon Drew Memorial School, Gladstone Way (now demolished)
[FRO 28/M/79]

provided education for the majority of the children in the parish. The attendance at the eight day schools in 1894 — on the books, 1,162, average, 867. The average in 1872 was 348. The day-to-day management of these eight schools fell on the shoulders of the rector.

In 1899 it was estimated that 517 persons in the parish subscribed £366. 9s. 4d. to the maintenance fund for the eight schools, the equivalent of 7s. 10d. in the pound, towards the education of every school child. At the beginning of January of that year, Stephen Gladstone wrote a letter of resignation from the chairmanship of the Schools Management Committee because he could no longer cope with the incessant business and anxiety involved in the management of elementary education, which was so costly and complicated. He confessed that he found it a strain he could no longer bear.

Worse was to come. When Stephen Gladstone resigned the living of Hawarden in 1904, his successor Canon

Harry Drew, was forced to begin all over again in the never ending task of bringing buildings up to the standard demanded by the government. The Education Act of 1902 was opposed by the Welsh local authorities and they threatened to confiscate Church schools and bring them into the state system. Amidst this confusion, which lasted until 1907, Harry Drew was forced to carry out works of repair to the eight schools in the parish. The strain of this burden eventually killed him. He died on 31 March 1910 after a short incumbency of five and a half years.

It was decided that the most fitting memorial to Canon Drew would be to complete his task and build a new mixed boys and girls elementary school in Hawarden on a site adjacent to the 1834 boys school. His daughter Dorothy Drew laid the foundation stone of the school on 17 November 1911. The *Parish Magazine* described the building.

> The plan of the school is a central hall about 50 feet by 32; round one end cluster four boys classrooms and teachers' room, round the other end, three girls' classrooms and cookery room. A folding screen divides the hall; by folding other screens two classrooms are thrown into each division; or all screens may be folded. So we may have two halls of about 25 feet, or one great hall of 50 feet, or one of 90 feet. The red tiled building outside is very attractive — inside, spacious, convenient, light and airy. The boys have most sun, the girls a splendid view. The Education Committee has been able, owing to recent judgments, to supply all new furniture found necessary; this is a great pleasure. The cordiality of that committee and much valuable advice from its chief officials must be gratefully recorded.

A. G. Edwards, Bishop of St Asaph, opened the school on 14 September 1912. The newspaper account acknowledged that 'Canon and Mrs Drew gave a spirited and self-denying lead to the large fund it was necessary to raise, and during his incumbency no less than £7,500 was raised for this purpose. The sudden death of the canon for the time ended the project, but the parishioners resolved to complete the scheme as a memorial to him.' The Bishop of St Asaph said, 'there were two things in Canon Drew's school policy which had left an indelible impression upon his mind. At Buckley, and again at Hawarden, Canon Drew and Mrs Drew kindled the enthusiasm of others by their own splendid generosity. In one of his letters as rector of Hawarden Canon Drew said he was prepared to devote the whole of his net income as rector on the work of school building.'[73]

School life as seen through the Log Books (1863–1964)

In 1863 the government decided that it was the duty of the headteacher of every school to keep a log book, which could be inspected by the school managers, and the government Inspectorate. The log book recorded attendances, staffing, examination reports, reasons for school closure, accidents, the punishment of pupils, and what was most important, anything else which the headteacher thought might be relevant to the life of the school community. Hawarden was no different, and here are a few extracts from the Boys' School Log Books given in chronological order.

One of the first entries for most schools is the celebrations surrounding the marriage of Albert Edward, Prince of Wales to Princess Alexandra of Denmark, for which schools were awarded three days holiday. In September 1863 Robert Wilson began his duties as headmaster. He made the following observations:

Nov. 6. rather a lazy day: not much work done.

1864 Jan 15. near the fire as possible

1864 July 14. Clock stopped — kept boys in half an hour too long.

1865 Feb 6. the paid monitor in this school is not equal to his post. The school can hardly said to be in a satisfactory condition. The attainments of the children are inferior. The issue of the master's certificate is suspended for a better report.

1865 July 13. Chancellor's son Mr W. H. Gladstone elected yesterday to representation of the city of Chester was drawn through the streets of Hawarden today in his carriage by about sixty persons.

1868 School Report 15 January — this school is in thoroughly good order, & is well classified. The boys have passed a very successful examination in the elementary subjects. There has been a large influx of new scholars during the past year in consequence of the closing of schools in the neighbourhood.

1868 Aug. 31. George Spencer new headmaster

1868 Oct 2. Introduced through the liberality of the Rector H. Glynne Mr Williams Harrisonian Abacus or Arithmetical Apparatus into the school.

1869 March 22. Struck John & Joseph Lovell's names off the books — they and their parents going to New York tomorrow.

1869 May 31. read a letter I received yesterday from J. Lovell to the boys.

1869 April 12. Allowed boys to go out from 9. 45 to 10. 10 to see a number of caravans — some drawn by elephants &c pass by the school.

1869 June 8. Many boys absent in afternoon owing to a collection of waxworks in the village.

1870 Feb. 11. Robt. Fidgett & W. Burbridge absent today. They left 'home' last evening about 6 it is supposed & made for London via Chester. Nothing has been heard of them at present. [They were probably from the Orphanage]

1870 June 20. Rec'd & distributed a quantity of cut currant bread, seed do [*sic*] & bread & butter not consumed at the festival amongst the boys, the same being the gift of the Hawarden Lit. & Scientific Institution.

1870 Nov. 10. Very cold all day: a native of India came into school — begged to warm himself.

1872 July 8, 9 & 15. site of schoolhouse started out by Mr J. Bailey under the direction of the rector. Foundation of schoolhouse commenced. First stone of schoolhouse laid

1881 May 23. all the orphanage boys absent, on account of fever being in the home. July 1 used disinfecting powder & chloride of lime freely about the school today. July 4 Robert Lloyd who was at school last Wednesday died this day (Monday). July 8 Closed school today for four weeks on account of the scarlet fever being so prevalent.

1887 June 21. Jubilee of the Queen. Holiday in afternoon, a Treat given in the Park to all children of the parish under sixteen years of age. Provided by subscription. A rosette & medal given to every child at its own school. Monster procession formed in the village & children marched to the Park. Tea served in front of the Castle followed by games &c till 7.15.

1890 April 30. brought a large case for the purpose of forming a school museum. May 2 several objects brought for museum by boys including pumice stone & a piece of an Atlantic cable made at old Wire Works.

1892 July 28. Holiday in afternoon the boys all being invited to tea by Mr & Mrs Spencer. All had tea in the field near the school. The boys assembled at 8*p.m.* and were briefly addressed by Mr Spencer, who then bade them 'Farewell' having been Master of this School for nearly twenty-three years.

August 29. Opened school after the Harvest holidays having received the appointment of Head Master, J. H. Adkins Certificated Teacher.

Oct. 6. There was a half-holiday to day to celebrate the marriage of the Master at Hawarden.

1896 Oct. 14. School assembled at 8*a.m.* and marched to the Wynt Gate of the Castle to witness the procession to the station of the remains of His Grace the Archbishop of Canterbury who died suddenly at morning service at Hawarden Church on Oct 11. The cortege left the church at 8.30 and reached the Wynt at 8.45 where they paused to sing a hymn the boys uncovering (removing their caps) as the coffin passed.

1897 May 10. Visit of the Prince & Princess of Wales to Hawarden Castle. The school closed at 11.30. The boys assembled in the afternoon at 1.30*p.m.* and marched through the village in fours. The school children lined the Park from the Lower Lodge to the Little Home.

1897 June 22. Commemoration Day of the sixty years of the reign of the Queen. School closed all day. The boys assembled at 12.30 in the playground each bearing flowers & coloured ribbon. They marched to the Ewloe Road where they joined the other schools of the parish numbering in all about 1,200. Then accompanied by the Hawarden Band they proceeded through the village halting at the Golden Wedding Memorial Fountain where Mrs Gladstone and Miss Helen Gladstone were awaiting them. Here the schools were grouped and the National Anthem sung conducted by the Master. Mrs Gladstone's carriage then headed the procession, which entered the Park by the Moor Lane Lodge. Here a hollow square was formed in front of the Terrace and the National Anthem & Doxology were sung by all assembled. Mr Gladstone addressed the children & Mrs & Miss Helen Gladstone distributed medals. Tea was provided for the children & sports were indulged in afterwards. Each child was presented with a bun & an orange when leaving the Park.

1898 May 19. Ascension Day The death at the Castle of the Rt. Hon. W. E. Gladstone which took place at 5 *a.m.* The boys attended Church in the morning. May 24. told the boys of the sad colliery accident, in which two men were killed, one of them being the father of a boy in the third standard, which occurred at Aston Hall. In the afternoon about 50 of the elder boys in two batches, went with their teachers to view the body of the Rt. Honble W. E. Gladstone lying in his doctor's robes in the Library at the Castle.

1900 March 1. Relief of Ladysmith. On receipt of the news, the Master announced the contents of a telegram received in the village. Cheers were given, the National Anthem sung, and the boys let out early.

May 31. Announced news of entry into Pretoria to boys. National Anthem sung, the flag hoisted & a map flag placed in capital of Transvaal.

There are references to the boys from the Orphanage. They had a cricket ground in Hawarden Park on which the school matches were played. In September 1905 Henry Gladstone invited seventeen orphan boys to spend the day with him at Burton Manor. It was recorded on March 1 1912 that the 'Home established by the late Mrs Gladstone for orphan boys was closed. The boys names taken from the registers'.

1911 April 6. The boys of Standards 5, 6, & 7 under care of the Master visited the Queensferry Colliery. After inspecting the surface works the party descended the pit 180 yards & travelled 1200 yards below ground. Mr James Hampson Manager kindly accompanied the boys. Preparatory lessons had been given.

1912 April 22. There was a day's holiday to celebrate the marriage of Miss Dorothy Drew at St Margaret's Westminster. The head master was present at the ceremony. April 23. each child received an iced almond cake with the letter 'D' upon it from the bride & bridegroom.

Sept. 14. the new school opened today Sept 30 began work in the new school.

There are references to the First World War. In 1915, the death of Lieut. W. G. C. Gladstone is recorded with the entry and the boys, instead of sending a wreath, desired to have a framed portrait of the brave squire as a permanent memorial in the school. It was estimated that over 70 old boys were serving their country. In October 'One of the boys brought a Turkish shell to School sent by his father Sergt. Major Bellis from Gallipoli. It was shown to the boys in a lesson given on ammunition. In 1916, on 17 May, the master visited the woodwork centre and recorded 'The boys have been making splints, crutches &c for the Red Cross and Ambulance Societies.' In 1917 in February after Miss C. Gladstone had distributed the school prizes the senior boys gave a display of 'some stretcher drill.' Miss Wright left to take up work with Women Police in London and was presented with a thermos flask and a fountain pen by the boys. In May there was a Royal visit by King George V and Queen Mary to the Munitions Factory and the new housing estate at Mancot Royal, and when they came to the Castle to inspect the wounded soldiers the boys had a good view of the proceedings. In 1918 the last year of the War the school was used by the local Food Control Committee. In October the school was closed for a week to allow the boys to assist the farmers with the potato crop. In December after the Armistice Mr C. Littlewood visited school. 'He had been reported killed in France and the greatest pleasure was felt by boys and staff that the report proved untrue: he was for a time assistant master here. But the greatest killer of all in 1918 was the influenza epidemic, which hit Hawarden in October and led to the closure of the School.

In 1919 Mr J. H Adkins retired in May as headmaster after 27 years service. Previously he had served in Shotton for 18 years. The new head master was H. Maldwyn Davies. He introduced a meteorological station into the School garden and sixteen boys were given individual plots to cultivate. The Hawarden Estate gave 75 shrubs for the shrubbery, the school manager's seeds, and the teacher manure. When war broke out in 1939 the head master was called

School children take part in the procession to celebrate the coronation of King George V in 1911. Note the old Post Office building on the right
[B. Jones deposit, FRO D/DM/592]

up for duty in the Middle East and returned to teaching in June 1941. In January 1945 he was appointed headmaster of Shotton Council School. His successor was Mr Morris Averill from Sheffield who died on 4 November 1952 and Mr Peter Rowlands succeeded him in 1953.

In 1977 a new school, the Rector Drew School was opened in Cross Tree Lane by Mrs Dorothy Parrish, the daughter of Canon and Mrs Harry Drew, who had laid the foundation of the former school in 1911.

Hawarden Methodist Church

Hawarden Methodist Church belonged to the branch of the church called the New Connexion, which in 1797 seceded from the Wesleyan Methodist Church and in the union of 1907 was incorporated in the United Methodist Church. The leader in 1797 was Alexander Kilham, whose main difference with Wesleyan Methodists was his belief that Methodists should have the right to receive Holy Communion from their own preachers. The New Connexion differed from Wesleyan Methodists chiefly in the matter of church government and the exclusion of any use of Anglican worship.

The Methodist Church was founded from Chester at the beginning of the nineteenth century. The first notice I have seen refers to the re-opening of the church in April 1832. It was reported that the services were well attended. A week later there was a crowded meeting of the Hawarden and Buckley branch. On these occasions two ministers from Chester, T. Waterhouse and W. Chapman, conducted the meetings. There is a list of ministers 'who have been stationed in the Hawarden Circuit' from 1847 to 1881. The Hawarden Circuit in 1881 covered Hawarden, Pentrobin, Bistre, Penymynydd, Dublin (Alltami), Wepre, Bretton, and Kinnerton.

It was decided to build a new chapel in 1860 and that the Grecian Style be adopted. To raise funds for the new chapel lectures were given by ministers. In May 1861 Mr John Wright produced a drawing of an elevation by Mr Kendrick of Brierley, which was greatly approved of. Ten thousand bricks were purchased at 16s. per thousand, and Messrs Hodge, Hancock, and Podmore offered to give a day each for carrying them. Ellis Wainwright and David Williams cleared the site of the new chapel and agreed to pile up the bricks. The site of the chapel was on the Highway on the outskirts of the village.

The foundation stone of the new chapel was laid in May 1862 by George Pennell of Liverpool, an event, which was reported, in the local press.

> Its erection has been rendered necessary by the want of accommodation, the old fabric for a long time, having been found insufficient for those who belong to the Denomination. Seats will be provided for between 200 and 300 persons, and the external appearance and interior arrangements of the structure will reflect great credit on the architect, Mr William Kendrick of Hawarden. Mr Bailey is the contractor, and Mr James Humphreys, Buckley, the builder. The expense including the land will be £600, half of which has been raised. Several ministers from Liverpool, Manchester, Chester, and other places, and the trustees took their stand on a temporary platform. The Revd. James Candelet, the esteemed superintendent of Hawarden, read the 84th Psalm and a portion of the second chapter of Haggai. An interesting feature, introduced after the laying of the foundation by stone by Mr George Pennell, was the Christening of the Revd. James Candelet's youngest child by the Revd. J. Addyman, on the newly laid stone. No less than 500 partook of the 'refreshing cup'. The proceedings lasted six hours.

The new chapel was opened on 6 April 1863. 'A more excellent meeting we have seldom had the privilege of attending. The erection of an edifice so commodious and beautiful was the subject of general congratulation. It is an ornament to the village and a credit to the architect, Mr Kendrick, and the trustees. Mr Bailey of Hawarden was the builder. Mr G. Williams presented a handsome Bible for the pulpit and other ornamental articles'.[74]

The good relationship between the members of the Hawarden New Connexion Church and Mr Gladstone is illustrated by the following story.

Hawarden Methodist Church (now demolished)
[J. H. Davies deposit, FRO N/31/23]

Hawarden Methodist Church Manse
[J. H. Davies deposit, FRO N/31/23]

Several weeks ago, the friends of the Methodist New Connexion Chapel Hawarden decided to renovate their school at that place and in their endeavour to keep out of debt, they applied to their illustrious neighbour for a little pecuniary assistance. A few days after the application had been made, the valet of the right honourable gentleman called at the Manse, with a letter for the circuit minister, the Revd. J. Stark, who, on opening the letter, was agreeably surprised to find not only the desired reply (a cheque), but also an invitation to lunch at the Castle with the band of the Royal Welsh Fusiliers on the occasion of their visit. Mr Stark was introduced to Mr John Morley, late Chief Secretary for Ireland, and shewn over the Castle and grounds and he left highly pleased with the reception he received there.[75]

The First World War

The parish of Hawarden made its contribution to the war not only with the number of lives that were sacrificed, but particularly the special way in which various communities came to the forefront. In Shotton and Garden City, John Summers supplied materials for shells and trenches. Queensferry and Sandycroft became one of the largest Munitions Factory in the country with Mancot Royal providing houses and a hospital. The potential of Sealand as an aerodrome was recognised towards the end of the war.

The village of Hawarden played a different role. In April 1915 W. G. C. Gladstone, a lieutenant in the Royal Welsh Fusiliers, was killed by a sniper at Laventie in France. Writing from the Front before his death he expressed the wish that men from the R.W.F. convalescing in the old Orphanage should be allowed to wander freely in the Park. By the time the home was closed in December 1916 107 NCOs had been cared for under the supervision of Mrs W. H. Gladstone. In 1917 the Army Council accepted the offer of Hawarden Castle as a convalescent home for officers, as an annexe to the hospital established at Eaton Hall. In February Colonel Berthon arrived as commandant.[76] A letter from the Commandant to H. N. Gladstone in August 1917 states, '16 officers came yesterday, the total here now is 34. Roughly we are half full. Yesterday I got a couple of lads from Chester paid for by the Red Cross. On Friday the Whiz-bang pieretto troupe are coming over to give an entertainment. Do tell Mrs Gladstone that the Music on Saturday made a great hit.'

On 14 May 1917 King George V and Queen Mary visited the hospital as well as inspecting the munitions factory at Queensferry.

By the end of the war the number of officers received at Hawarden Castle for convalescence was over 860, and weekly shoots were organised for them, and the facilities at St Deiniol's Library were also available. It was noted in February 1919 that the Castle, 'which has been in use as a hospital for wounded officers, is now assuming its former state. All the patients have gone, and the hospital effects are being speedily removed. The villagers will miss the familiar sight of the R.A.M.C. orderlies and officer patients, which has so often enlivened the streets during the past year or two.'[77]

In 1917 Wold House was offered to and accepted by the War Office as a paraplegic hospital but in the end it was not used as such.

Hawarden parish with the rest of the world was hit by the devastating influenza pandemic in 1918–9, which was said to have started in Spain, hence its description as the Spanish 'flu, but most probably the pandemic came from the United States. The influenza attacked the age groups of children under 5 years, adults between 20–40 years,

The presentation of an ambulance from the Parish of Hawarden
[FRO 28/P/72]

and the elderly. The signs of this epidemic were horrific: before death the lungs were filled with fluid and the victim effectively drowned. There was no means of relief. Estimates of the number of deaths vary between 40 and 100 million, effectively killing more than perished in the First World War. In March 1918 the County Medical Officer, because of widespread illness, closed schools for three weeks. A meeting of Hawarden District Education Committee in October heard that attendance at schools was down by 50%. It wasn't until the middle of 1919 that the pandemic began to wane.

The Armistice was signed at 5.00*a.m.* on 11 November 1918 and the news reached W. Bell Jones, postmaster at Hawarden, at 8.30*a.m.* The names of those who sacrificed their lives in the conflict may be seen on the War memorial designed by Sir Giles Gilbert Scott in 1919–20 which stands at the Junction of the Highway and Gladstone Way .

The Hawarden Estate Sale

In January 1918, Henry Gladstone advised the tenants of the estate:

It is my duty to announce, and I do so with very sincere regret, that my nephew, Captain Albert C. Gladstone, the tenant for life of the Hawarden estate, now on active service, has, on my advice, and with the consent of the trustees, decided to sell a considerable portion of the property. The portions to be offered by public auction within the next few months include farms and cottages in the districts of Pentrobin, Buckley, Ewloe, Aston, as well as in Broughton and Saltney. As soon as particulars can be got out occupying tenants will be communicated with in order to give them an opportunity of purchasing their holdings should they elect to do so. The decision to sell a portion of the property is in conflict with my father's life-long desire and efforts to keep it intact, and to maintain without break the happy relations between landlord and tenant that have so long existed. Unfortunately recent legislation and in particular the Finance Acts of 1910 and 1914, have made this inevitable.[78]

The Hawarden Event Book records the extent of the property to be sold.

1918 April–May. Valuation made of property to be sold; 2,467 acres with a rental of £4,455 comprising 3 residences, 2 public houses, 8 farms over 100 acres (including Well House, Catherine and Mary farms), small farms and smallholdings, and 73 cottages, amounting to *c.*£97,000. Holdings were offered to existing tenants, and unsold lots went to auction in July.

There is the additional comment. 'In August the workmen in the estate and the 'decrepit men in the Gardens' threatened to strike for higher wages — due to enormous wages at the Munitions Factory. Labourers wages raised from 33s. to 36s. for those in the woods.'[79]

In January 1920 there was an auction sale of the remaining holdings at the Glynne Arms, Hawarden, when the total realised was £1,400.[80] An account of the sale in the local press reported that the properties which had been offered to the tenants in 1918 had realised £112,000, and the land sold in 1920 had brought £225 an acre for agricultural land, with £295 each for four-roomed cottages and six-roomed ones for £320.[81]

Henry Neville Gladstone, Lord-lieutenant of Flintshire with his wife Maud E. Gladstone, were the life tenants of Hawarden Castle and played an important part in the life of the community.

Roman Catholicism
The first Roman Catholic Chapel

The first Catholic chapel in Hawarden was opened on the site of the existing church in May 1922. The local newspaper gave this account.

A Catholic chapel of wood and zinc, which has been erected on the Ewloe Road on the outskirts of Hawarden, was opened on Wednesday last week. The building has been provided by a benefactor for the use of those who have hitherto have had to attend mass at Connah's Quay or Buckley and will be under the superintendence of Father Pochard, the priest in charge of Buckley.

The clergy present were the Archbishop of Cardiff, Father Pochard, who assisted by the Revd. Dr Barron of Mold was the celebrant at High Mass, the Revd. Monsignor Canon Nightingale, of Menevia, and Father Ryan of Neston. The choir of the church of Our Lady of the Rosary Buckley sang St Cecilia's Latin Mass.[82]

A demonstration that the church and congregation were becoming established is seen three years later in the following description.

On May Day morning Sir R. Terry's mass was sung, and by chance the composer himself was present. Mr Sharpe was at the organ. There was a large procession at 6.30 *p.m.* which included 16 altar boys and more than 20 girls arrayed in white. Miss Wilde assisted by Mrs Toller and Mme. Sergeant carried banners. Four girls in white carried the statue of Our Lady of Lourdes. After the procession a sermon was give on the circumstance and benediction of the Blessed Sacrament.[83]

Between 1966–7 the Church of the Sacred Heart was built on the same site to the design of the architects, Weightman and Bullen.

The Poor Clare Community of Tŷ Mam Duw[84]

Tŷ Mam Duw means house of the Mother of God and is the name given to the Monastery of the Poor Clares, which stands on the site of the former residence known as Aston Bank. The Poor Clares were founded by Clare; a follower of St Francis of Assisi in *c.*1212. The Colettines is a branch of the Poor Clares founded by St Colette in France in the fourteenth century.

On the 30 June 1928 Mother Cherubina Clare with six other sisters travelled to North Wales to stay for a few days with the Benedictine Sisters of Talacre before settling in their small house at 67, Church Street, Flint. They came from Notting Hill at the request of Bishop Francis Vaughan, the newly appointed Bishop of Menevia. His cousin, Mother Mary Felix Clare Vaughan, was at that time Abbess of the London Community.

Flint they regarded as a temporary home until they found a site to found their convent. Early in June 1930 Mother Cherubina came to Hawarden to view some land for the community. Here she met Mrs Toller of Aston Bank. The house was for sale and Mrs C. B. Toller persuaded the trustees of the estate to allow the community to purchase the property on generous terms. The press announced the purchase in August 1930.

The well known half-timbered residence of Aston Bank has been purchased by the Convent of the Poor Clare Colettines, Flint. Part of the community is expected to remove there about the middle of next month. Extensive alterations are to be carried out, and much of the panelling in the main rooms will be utilised in making a chapel. Aston Bank has now twenty-two bedrooms; these are to be increased in number. The grounds of about five acres have been acquired by the Convent, and will allow for further extensions.[85]

On 22 April 1931, Bishop Vaughan laid the foundation stone of the new chapel which was completed the following March, the first Mass being offered on Easter Sunday.

The great day came for the new community on 19 May 1932 when the Interior Order of the Sisters of the Poor Clare Colettines at Aston Bank were to be enclosed at a solemn ceremony conducted by Cardinal Bourne, Archbishop of Westminster. The day's events were described in detail:

At present there are ten nuns on the premises, seven belonging to the Interior Order and three lay Sisters to the External Order. A new wing has been added to the original main house, and two churches have been built, one for each order. The premises are equipped to hold a maximum of twenty-three sisters. The present sisters arrived on the premises in September last. According to the rules of the Order, the nuns will live on the charity of the faithful, and the obtaining of alms, if necessary is part of the work of the external sisters.

Cardinal Bourne, the Archbishop of Cardiff, Dr Mostyn, the Bishop of Menevia, Dr Vaughan, and about forty priests from the diocese lunched together at the Glynne Arms, Hawarden. The afternoon's solemn events then began.

Aston Bank Convent. The Poor Clare Community of Tŷ Mam Duw. The building has been demolished and replaced by a new convent [FRO 28/N/80]

At the Convent there was a congregation of about five hundred waiting when his Eminence arrived at the marquee, where a solemn service was held, and an address from the Cardinal Archbishop. A temporary altar had been erected in the centre of the marquee, and members of the hierarchy were arranged in their full and splendid vestments. In addition to the forty or fifty priests present, there were about the same number of nuns from various parts of North Wales, including the Holywell, Holyhead, Rhyl, Wrexham and Pantasaph Convents. The local Scouts and Guides formed a guard of honour. Cardinal Bourne gave a very fine address on the value of prayer. The sermon was followed by the Benediction of the Blessed Sacrament given by the Bishop of Menevia.

His Eminence the Cardinal Archbishop headed the procession with full ritual round the premises, the general public who so desired, following in the rear of the ecclesiastical procession. Every room and cell received a blessing, and his Eminence finally entered the Church (technically known as the Choir), while all the visitors left the building and the premises beyond the enclosure. Then stepping into the courtyard he handed the key to the Mother Abbess, who locked the door from the inside, performing the ceremony known as 'locking in.'[86]

After which the Sisters sang the *Te Deum*, and then to work scrubbing the muddy floor made by those in the procession.

On the weekend at the outbreak of war in September 1939, the Sisters helped to find homes for the Catholic children evacuated from Birkenhead. Several large rooms in the Convent were used as temporary schoolrooms, and three teaching nuns and a dozen children were accommodated in the external quarters for a few months. On 21 April 1941, while the Sisters were singing vespers, an aeroplane came down in the garden, narrowly missing the house.

In 1944, Bishop Bannan of Menevia granted permission for the community to build a new convent designed to meet all the needs of the convent in a more practicable way. This work was delayed until 1955 because of post-war building restrictions and lack of funds. However, on 23 February 1960, the Sisters moved into their new convent buildings. The demolition of Aston Bank, the home of the Hancocks and the Tollers, in the nineteenth and twentieth centuries, took place in 1961, and the site of the old house was drained and turfed and laid out as part of the convent garden.

By this time members of the founding community had been in residence for thirty years and were becoming an ageing group of Sisters. On 14 June 1982 the convent was reinvigorated by the arrival of a large number of Sisters from Notting Hill. To mark this renewal it was decided to call the monastery Tŷ Mam Duw in honour of Our Lady. The name derived from that inscribed over the door of the chapel at Courtfield, the ancestral home of the Vaughan family.

In 1983–4 the convent (which is referred to as 'monastery' on the gatepost) was adapted structurally to meet the needs of guests and retreatants who wished to spend time in prayer and reflection. In 1985 a new public chapel was built in which was incorporated a small shrine to Our Lady of Schoenstatt. In 1986 Archbishop Bruno Heim, formerly Papal Pro Nuncio in Britain, returned from Germany to presided at the dedication of the new chapel, at which Bishop Hannigan preached and received the picture of Our Lady for the public shrine.

Tŷ Mam Duw is now known as a retreat centre for individuals and groups from various denominations who come for a day of reflection to share with the Sisters in their prayer and praise.

The Use of the Old Rectory

The Knutsford Test School

The Knutsford Test School came to the Old Rectory in Hawarden in December 1926. The purpose of the school was to give the necessary academic qualifications for entrance to university or theological college for students to train for the full time ministry of the Church of England. The word 'Test' refers to the necessary matriculation qualifications, which the students required. The subjects taught for matriculation were English Literature, European History, New Testament Greek, Latin and elementary Physics. The Revd. Tubby Clayton (the founder of the 'Toc H' movement) had the vision to realise that after the war young men from the three services would wish to offer themselves as candidates for the full time ministry of the Church of England. This idea received full support from the Bishops and after the Armistice Clayton gathered men together at the old Machine Gun School at Le Touquet, and on demobilization they reported to Knutsford Gaol on 26 March 1919. The first intake of students numbered over two hundred, and in October, sixty-seven went on to further education. The first

Principal was F. R. Barry, later Bishop of Southwell. The Gaol closed in 1922, and the Test School moved to Kilrie, a suitable house in Knutsford to accommodate the number of students now reduced to thirty-six. Here they remained until December 1926 when they removed to Hawarden Old Rectory.

The last rector to occupy the large Parsonage House was the Reverend C. F. Lyttelton, M.C. When Miss Helen Gladstone died in 1925 her residence, the Sundial, was made available as the new rectory. Mr Henry Gladstone offered the Old Rectory to the Test School, together with £3,000 towards necessary alterations to the building. These were reported in the press:

> The architects have made full use of the Old Rectory, and a new three-storey wing has been added to give accommodation for forty students. There are three floors in the new wing, and nine bedrooms on each floor. The huge library of the Old Rectory has been converted into a junior common room, and a permanent stage has been fitted. The delightful gardens and wooded grounds will be available to the students, and from the front door of the college a special path has been made to the side chapel of Hawarden Parish Church, the chapel having been set aside for the use of the students.

A distinguished congregation assembled for the dedication of the building by the Archbishop of Wales, A. G. Edwards, on 26 February 1927. With him were the Bishop of Chester, Luke Paget, the Bishop of Manchester, William Temple, who preached the sermon, and the Bishop of Pretoria, Neville Talbot, together with the Dean of Chester, F. S. M. Bennett, Tubby Clayton, and Mervyn Haigh, later Bishop of Winchester. By July 1928 the school was fully occupied with thirty-eight students in residence. They were no longer ex-servicemen but students wishing to obtain the qualifications needed to embark on theological training. The Bazaar and Garden Party held in the grounds went very near to reaching the £9,000 required to pay for the alterations.

In 1930 a room was set-aside within the house to provide a chapel, furnished by a small chamber organ, originally belonging to W. H. Gladstone. The gardens were put to good use in the summer season, and in 1931 a pageant was presented to emphasise missionary activity. In 1937, the Principal of the School, R. V. H. Burne, left the school on his appointment as Archdeacon of Chester. A former tutor at Knutsford, the Revd. E. S. G. Wickham, a grandson of W. E. Gladstone, succeeded him. Between the years 1922–37 the school had provided training for 365 men of whom 180 went on to Universities, and 136 to theological colleges. This was to come to and end in 1940 when war led to the closure of the school. In 1939 the local District Council on behalf of Birkenhead commandeered the Old Rectory for a home for blind and infirm patients. Sir Albert Gladstone invited the dispossessed school its twenty-five students and staff, to take refuge in the Castle where they used the Temple of Peace for the Chapel. By 1940 most of the students left to join the armed forces.[87]

Some of the students were later consecrated as bishops. One of them trained at Hawarden was Tom Greenwood, later Bishop of the Yukon.

1946–8 Church of England Training College
Between January 1946 and July 1948 the Old Rectory was used by the Church of England for the training of ex-service candidates for the Ministry. It was one-year course under the supervision of the Principal, the Revd. Roger Lloyd, an ex-naval chaplain.

1948–53 The William Temple College
The newly formed William Temple College to provide theological education for Women spent five years in Hawarden before moving to Rugby.

1956 Flinthire County Council
The Old Rectory was purchased from the Test School Trustees in 1956 at a cost of £3,605 to be used as the headquarters of the County Library. Extensions were made at the south end of the building. The Record Office, established in Mold in 1951, moved to the north end of the building in 1956, and after the building had been fully adapted for storage and research purposes it was officially opened on 23 June 1962. When new County Buildings were erected in Mold, the space used by the Library was taken over by the local branch library. The Old Rectory is now shared between the Record Office, the Branch Library, and the Registrar of Births, Deaths and Marriages

Twentieth Century Buildings in Hawarden Village
This list is by no means comprehensive but it does indicate that the character of the village has changed through the addition of completely new buildings, the demolition of old buildings to be replaced by new buildings, and the obvious change in the use of building materials, the most drastic being the replacement of thatched roofs by slate and the use of brick in place of stone.

1900 Lloyd's Bank
A description is given in July 1900.

> The new bank buildings which have been sometime in course of erection are now completed and form a striking architectural feature of the village. No cost was spared. The interior fittings were of mahogany and brass, the flooring of teak blocks, on the public side of the counter the flooring was of Italian mosaic and 'From the outside, the building, which has been erected at a cost of about £4,000, is imposing in appearance without being obtrusive. It is faced with red Ruabon brick, with oak gables relieved by cement after the style of many of the Chester houses, and the roof, which is covered with brindled tiles, gives a finish to the building. The porch is of Runcorn stone beautifully moulded and carved with a mosaic floor. Mr A. E. Lloyd Oswell, of Shrewsbury is the architect, and the work has been carried out by Messrs Freeman of Chester.[88]

1904 Wold House (purchased by the Dean of Lincoln).
Dr E. C. Wickham was the son in law of W. E. Gladstone and the husband of Agnes his eldest daughter. He spent over £3,000 in reconditioning and making additions to the property, including a drainage system, with the addition of three bedrooms on the third storey with the intention of occupying the house. When he died in 1910, the house was sold to Henry Gladstone and subsequently in 1921 to the Hawarden Farmers Co-operative Society.[89]

1906 The Glynne Arms
Was refurbished in 1906 when it was leased to the People's Refreshment House Association.

1907 The Sundial
Built for Helen Gladstone, the architects were Douglas and Minshull of Chester. When she died in 1925, it became the rectory from 1925–1980. It is now called Hawarden Grange.

1909 Hawarden Building Improvements
It was reported in September 1909,

> ... at present there are two large spaces in the main street caused by the demolition of some of the older houses in

the village. The picturesque thatched cottages, which were cramped and unsuitable to modern times, have been pulled down, and soon will be replaced by more up-to-date dwellings. What is lost in picturesqueness will be more than counterbalanced by the convenience of the new erections, which will be in harmony with the rest of the houses in the village. The *Blue Bell Inn* is also in course of re-erection.[90]

1909 The Post Office

Originally in Rectory Lane and later moved to Glynne Way It moved to its present site in 1909.

1913 Hawarden Drill Hall

The new Drill Hall at Hawarden in connection with the 'B' Company 5th. Battalion of the Royal Welsh Fusiliers has been completed. It is a spacious building situated on the main road from Hawarden to Northop. In the basement is a large drill hall, with officer's rooms, orderly rooms, armoury, and cloakrooms. In the rear a miniature rifle range, and on the upper floor are recreation rooms for sergeants and men. At the rear of the building is a sergeant and inspector's house. The building, which is substantially built of plain brick with a brown brick dado around the inside and white bricks above, has an open roof. The architects were Messrs John Davies and Sons of Chester, and the builders George Wright and Sons of Hawarden.

1920 The Midland Bank

The cottage facing the village on the east side of Rectory Drive was leased to the London City and Midland Bank for new premises. This house belonged to Dr Thomas, in whose service was Nelson's Lady Hamilton, a native of Ness, Neston, Wirral, who subsequently lived in a cottage now pulled down opposite Church Way. Dr Thomas is believed to have moved across the Rectory Drive to the Clergy House now occupied by W. Bell Jones (Kentigern), and Emma may have moved with him.[91]

1923 Wynt Lodge,

Construction began in August 1922 and was completed in twelve months. It was the gift of Mrs H. N. Gladstone to the Hawarden estate and was designed by her nephew H. S. Goodhart-Rendel. The Lodge was said to be a replica of one seen by Mrs Gladstone while on holiday in the south of France.

1926–7 Queen Mary Cottages

Three cottages at Trueman's Hill were completed in the autumn of 1926. Permission was obtained from Queen Mary to call the Wold Croft group of five houses 'Queen Mary Cottages'. The newspaper reported, 'The Queen has taken an active interest in the problem of making good the shortage of cottages, throughout the country, and has inspected the design of these cottages prepared by Mr Fred Davies of Chester, which Mr H. N. Gladstone recently had the honour of submitting to Her Majesty.'[92] In 1927, a second group of cottages known as Wold Croft, and located next to Queen Mary Cottages, was completed as well as two new estate houses in Rectory Drive.

1927–8 The Tithe Barn

October 1927. 'The old Tithe Barn was opened as a parish room in memory of the Revd. Stephen Gladstone. Mrs Stephen Gladstone and her family gave the building. There are two rooms in the building, a large and a small one, and they are nicely coloured and panelled and lighted with electricity.'[93] 'Modernising and extending of Church School cottage completed by executors of Miss Helen Gladstone. Hawarden Estate enlarged and improved the outbuilding near the Tithe Barn as a memorial to Rector Gladstone for use as a sexton's house which was leased to Hawarden church authorities'.[94]

1928–30 New Offices of Hawarden Rural District Council

The Hawarden Estate sold the site to the council. The architects were John Davies & Sons of Chester who produced a neo-Georgian building in distinctive red brick. The offices were opened in July 1930 by W. Bell Jones, who said 'if he was asked what the new offices represented, he would say 'Progress and Pride'. It would interest them to know that all the bricks for it were got from Buckley and Shotton, the stone work from Broughton, whilst all the window and door frames were made by Flintshire craftsmen in Flintshire workshops'.[95]

Hawarden Cricket Club[96]

Hawarden Park Cricket Club has had a distinguished career. The club was founded in 1866 and played its first match at Holywell on 29 July 1865. It received the support of the Glynne and Gladstone families, Herbert Gladstone played for the club at the age of 16 years as did his nephew W. G. C. Gladstone over thirty years later. The Gladstone cousins, the Lytteltons, were a noted family of cricketing parsons and two of them played for Worcestershire, the Revd. A. V. Lyttelton curate of Hawarden in the 1870s and when he returned from South Africa Priest in charge of Pentrobin, 1905–18, and his nephew C. F. Lyttelton, rector of Hawarden from 1920–28. A feature of the late 1920s and early 1930s was an annual match between the club and the castle side selected by Patrick Parish, great grandson of W. E. Gladstone, after the match they were entertained to dinner at the Castle by Mr H. N. Gladstone.

A notice in the *Chester Chronicle* for the year 1870 shows that the cricket ground was established in Hawarden Park by this date:

> It having been thought desirable to establish a cricket club at Hawarden, a large number of gentlemen met at the Glynne Arms Hotel, on the 28th ult. to take such steps as might be deemed necessary for the purpose. Sir S. R. Glynne, Bart. with his accustomed generosity, has very kindly placed a portion of his beautiful and extensive park at the disposal of the committee, and steps have already been taken for putting the ground in order. The approaching season will commence on Easter Monday.[97]

There is an account the same season of the match against Northop:

> This match was played in Hawarden Park last Wednesday, in splendid cricketing weather, and upon a very true wicket, for which great credit is due to R. Moffat. Hawarden won the toss and sent their men in, and when the last wicket fell, one hundred and seventy five had been scored. W. Johnson's eighty-one being a very hard hitting innings, making one five, fours &c and only two singles; but H. Gladstone's twenty-four without doubt was the best innings of the day, showing good defence as well as hitting.[98]

Hawarden won by an innings and 62 runs.

In the 1871 season twelve matches were played, of which seven were won and five lost, the highest individual score being made by the schoolmaster, George Spencer.

The club prospered and was able to engage the services of a professional. Five were employed between 1892 and 1911.

An influence over the years on the availability of guest players has been the St Deiniol's Residential Library, which has attracted University men as Readers. Between the wars there were players such as P. H. Phelps of Worcestershire F. A. Obeyeskere, a brilliant all-rounder from Ceylon, who later became Speaker of his country's Legislative Assembly, and Harold de Soyza, a good all-rounder, later Bishop of Colombo. In the years after the war the club was strengthened and enlivened by two brilliant overseas stars. In 1947 A. H. Kardar an Oxford blue, an Indian Test player, and later Pakistan's first Test Captain, assisted the club whilst spending his long vacation at the Library. One of the young Pakistani players who toured with Kardar in 1954 was Khalid Wazir who remained in this country at Hawarden for the next three summers and 'gave countless exhibitions of all-round brilliance unequalled in the Club's long history. In the three seasons 1955, 1956 and 1957 he scored 2,210 runs (average 40.93) and took 261 wickets at 5.88 per wicket and made three centuries.' The club also received the assistance during the 1950s of Peter Greenwood.

The *Centenary Booklet* of 1966 pays tribute to the many homegrown players of

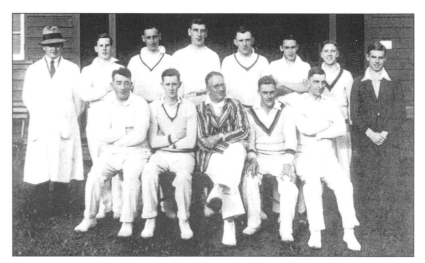

Hawarden Cricket Club, c.1950
[FRO 28/P/95]

outstanding skill. Harry Phillips, Leslie Shallcroft, Tommy Weigh, W. H. B. Roberts, Alex and George Reidford, Gerald Temple, Eric Higham, Harry Bonnewell, Grover Cowper, Leslie Burdekin, George Ede, Malcolm Bowyer, Ron and Glyn Williams, Alan Wright, Ted Stockton, Jack Russell, Ron Roberts, John Reidford, Michael Burdekin, and Ken Wellings.

The Gladstone Playing Fields

Henry Neville Gladstone was created a baron in the birthday honour's list of June 1932 'for political and public services.' He had been resident in Hawarden Castle as life tenant since the death of his nephew W. G. C. Gladstone in 1915, the estate being vested in another nephew Captain A. C. Gladstone. He was a generous man and gave freely to many causes and in 1934 made an outstanding gift to the village of Hawarden. He presented a Park in connection with the Playing Fields Association of about twenty acres in extent. The ground was laid out with four tennis courts (two hard and two grass), a cricket pitch, and a bowling green. There were two sections for football, one for juniors and the other for seniors. Hockey was also provided for, and, a space reserved for children where organised games could be played.

The official opening of the Gladstone Playing Fields, 17 July 1937
[FRO 28/P/21]

Field Marshal The Earl of Cavan opened the Playing Fields on 17 July 1937. Henry Gladstone intended them to be a memorial to his brother Herbert Viscount Gladstone (1854–1930), but owing to the death of Henry, Lord Gladstone in 1935, the Memorial Committee decided to call them 'The Gladstone Playing Fields' in memory of both brothers, and a Memorial Gateway to Henry Lord Gladstone was erected at the entrance by public subscription.

Following a vote of thanks to Lord and Lady Cavan by Mr A. C. Gladstone, Lord Cavan then proceeded to formally open the Children's Playground, which was the gift of Mr A. C. Gladstone in memory of Lord Gladstone. Other memorials to Lord Gladstone were the Children's Shelter given by the Wickham family and the pavilion clock given by the office staffs of Ogilivy Gillanders & Co., and Gillanders, Arbuthnot & Co. The cost of laying out the land for the Playing Fields was shared between various bodies. Lord Gladstone £3,500, the Dee Embankment Trust £1,500, and the National Playing Fields Association and Carnegie Trustees gave a grant of £800. In addition a legacy of £1,800 left by Lord Gladstone to the Hawarden Parish Council was handed over to the Memorial Committee.[99]

Herbert John, Viscount Gladstone of the County of Falkirk (1854–1930)

Herbert John Gladstone was the youngest child of William and Catherine Gladstone. He was the most politically gifted of their children. He was born at No. 12 Downing Street when his father was Chancellor of the Exchequer and educated at Eton and University College, Oxford where he obtained a first class in Modern History in 1876 and lectured on the subject at Keeble College 1877–80. He represented constituencies in Leeds as a Member of PArliament from 1880 to 1910 and served in junior posts under his father. He was Liberal Chief Whip in 1899 and was placed in charge of the General Election campaign of 1906 when the Liberals achieved a landslide. As a reward for this success he was appointed Secretary of State for Home Affairs and as such piloted 22 Bills through the Commons in this great reforming parliament, including the Workmen's Compensation Act of 1906 and the Children's Act of 1908. In December 1909 he was appointed the first Governor-General and High Commissioner of the Union of South Africa and was raised to the peerage as Viscount Gladstone of the County of Lanark. He served with distinction in South Africa from 1910–14. Returning home he became Treasurer of the War Refugees Committee and gradually withdrew from politics. He married Dorothy Mary Paget of Cranmore Hall, Somerset, in 1901. They had no children.

As a young man Herbert Gladstone was a great favourite with the people of Hawarden for the energy with which he became involved in the organisation of the great fetes and for his melodious singing voice. He was

Vanity Fair, 'Spy' caricature of the young Herbert Gladstone, 1882

devoted to his family and was an avid correspondent. In 1918 he wrote a memoir of his nephew W. G. C. Gladstone and, ten years later, published a volume *After Thirty years* which gives a delightful picture of the home life of the Gladstones. He was a noted sportsman and excelled at cricket, golf, shooting and fishing.

Henry Neville, Baron Gladstone of Hawarden (1852–1935)

Henry Neville Gladstone inherited the business acumen of the family. He was more like his grandfather Sir John Gladstone, than any of W. E. Gladstone's children. Not considered academic enough for Oxford, he was sent to King's College London before setting out for Calcutta to spend fifteen years in India and becoming senior partner in the firm of Ogilivy, Gillanders & Co., East India merchants. He made his fortune and returned to England to become his father's financial adviser and secretary and in 1890 married Maud Ernestine Rendel and settled down at Burton Manor on the Wirral. The Gladstones lived there for twenty-five years, within a stone's throw of Hawarden and close to his parents and siblings. He was close to his nieces and nephews in their childhood, and encouraged their careers and was fiercely loyal to his parents. As a mark of respect he commissioned Richmond's imposing monument to his parent's in St Deiniol's parish church. When his brother Willy died in 1891, he became one of the trustees of the Hawarden estate and with his brother Herbert and sister-in-law Gertrude gave the young Squire the role model of a good landlord and a Christian gentleman. When Will Gladstone was tragically killed in 1915, he was seen as the best person to guide the estate, and was made tenant for life to exercise the necessary stewardship as his father had done after Oak Farm in the 1850s. His abilities were recognised in Wales as Lord-lieutenant of Flintshire, Treasurer of the National Library of Wales, and member of the Representative and Governing Bodies of the Church in Wales during, its vulnerable infancy. At home in Hawarden he enjoyed with his wife the role of philanthropist. He presented 'Sundial' to the Church in Wales as the new Hawarden Rectory and gave the Old Rectory to the Knutsford Test School in memory of Sir Stephen and Henry Glynne. He bought the Munitions Factory Hospital at Mancot and presented it to the county as the Catherine Gladstone Maternity Hospital. He was particularly conscious of the part played by the men of Flintshire in the First World War and caused a record to be made of all who served in the conflict. Under his direction the Hawarden estate gave war memorial plots of land at Shotton, Queen's Ferry, Buckley and Broughton. He guided St Deiniol's Library with assurance, imagination, and generosity, extending the Library and Hostel. He instituted Founder's Day, an annual celebration of the life and achievement of his father. Henry Gladstone commissioned W. Bell Jones to write the history of Hawarden Castle, Manor, Church and Family, the Hawarden Deeds to be deposited, listed and published by the National Library of Wales, and the Gladstone Papers to be sent to the British Museum. This list of his generosity is not exhausted but may be found elsewhere in this study.

The Second World War

By the middle of the 1930s, Hitler began to make his territorial ambitions clear to the rest of Europe. The Ruhr was occupied; Austria taken over, Czechoslovakia destroyed, Poland invaded on 1 September 1939 and two days later Britain was at war with Germany. After the Munich Agreement in September 1938 between Chamber-

Henry Neville, Baron Gladstone of Hawarden

lain and Hitler, which guaranteed 'peace in our time' the British government began seriously to prepare for war. Factories were built for the production of aircraft, and orders made to steel works for the production of air-raid shelters Already we were re-arming. After Munich measures were taken to protect civilians against gas attacks, air raids, and invasion. Plans were made to evacuate women and children from the big cities because of their vulnerability to air attack.

The part that the village of Hawarden played in the Second World War is gathered from newspaper reports and outlined in the Hawarden Events Book.[100] In 1938 two rooms in the basement of Hawarden Castle were prepared as air-raid shelters. It was announced on 25 November that 'what has been described as the largest aircraft assembly factory in the British Isles is to be established shortly near Hawarden (at Broughton).' The managers of Vickers Armstrong gave this information. On the site acquired for the factory stood St Mary's and Catherine's Farm, Broughton. It was estimated that 4,000 workers would be employed in the factory, with the need for housing accommodation for 2,000 workers, and that 500 houses should be erected immediately. The Hawarden Estate provided 600 acres at Broughton. The aircraft factory was in production by October 1939.

On 1 September 1939 Hawarden became a reception area for evacuees from Birkenhead and Merseyside although only half this number arrived by rail. Thirty crippled evacuees were housed at the Old Rectory in the Knutsford Test School and 30 blind persons found accommodation in St Deiniol's Library. The Knutsford Test School was transferred to the Castle. Miss Thom placed her large house Springfield at the disposal of the Hawarden Ladies Committee of Management for use as a voluntary hospital, intended primarily for evacuee children. A hundred pounds was raised to fund it, a sewing circle established for sewing and mending for the evacuees. Six local nurses offered their services and were assisted by British Red Cross workers.

A Deeside Division of the ARP (specially trained wardens who were on duty during air raids from enemy planes. ARP meant Air Raid Precaution), was organised and classes given on anti-gas measures, first aid and incendiary bombs were held. These were in charge of local women. The Hawarden centre of the WVS (Women's Voluntary Service) was organised by Miss Catherine Gladstone and Mrs M. Harris; they worked from sixteen centres in the Rural District Area. Later in the war they organised a rest centre at Canon Drew School to provide temporary accommodation, food and clothing for people who had suffered from enemy action.

In the autumn of 1939 three hundred territorial troops were billeted in Hawarden at the Tithe Barn, Institute, Drill Hall the Old Boys School, St Winifred's and the Ewloe Club Officers and men of the Flintshire R.A.S.C. (Petrol Supply) Coy. occupied Broadlane in October.

1940 was a crucial year of the war with the evacuation from Dunkirk in May, the beginning of the Blitz and the war in the air, the Battle of Britain, in September. Hawarden became an important R.A.F. establishment for maintenance, and three hundred men from the unit were billeted in Hawarden village. In June a fighter pilot school was started. In the Park masses of huts and buildings were put up and the greater part of Manor Farm militarised. Towards the end of the year huts were built on the Racecourse in the Park with the object of dispersal against air raids. Fields at Park Farm and Broughton were also filled with aircraft for the same reason. When the Knutsford Test School dispersed from the Castle in the summer it was handed over to the R.A.F. for the accommodation of officers. The first bombs that fell in the district were on Mr Youd's farm at Broughton on 27 June. A few days later bombs fell in the officers' quarters in Sealand aerodrome and further bombs were dropped in the neighbourhood on at least a dozen occasions. On 18 August an enemy bomber was plainly visible, dropping about 24 bombs in fields at Sandycroft. The instructors shot down four of five German bombers. The Home Guard was established in Hawarden at the end of May. James MacCallum, estate agent, was battalion commander. In the autumn, Miss Gladstone organised a mobile and a hut canteen at the aerodrome, under Y.M.C.A. control.

By 1941, most of the arrangements for the accommodation of air force and civilian personnel were already in place. The officer's mess at Hawarden Castle was reserved for senior officers, and WAAFS were also housed there. The aerodrome was expanding. In 1942 the R.A.F. fighter school left after twenty-eight months in residence to be succeeded by Army Reconnaissance School No. 41. A 'Warship Week' for the area including Shotton was held in March and raised £213,000. All private petrol was banned in May, since when the Morris has been kept in action only to enable Catherine Gladstone to do Land Girl supervision duties. There are 92 girls in her area, 50 of them in a hostel Sealand. In June the King and Queen passed through Hawarden at speed on a munitions tour.

1943 — a circle of lights sixteen miles in circumference was put up round the aerodrome. It ran across the Cherry Orchard, under the Old Castle and through the orchard. Church bells were allowed for Easter, and later all restrictions on their uses were removed. Manor Farm house was turned into a Women's Land Army Hostel.

In February 1944 the R.A.F. Officer's Mess moved from the Castle to premises in the camp. The castle has since been used for a dormitory for about a dozen W.A.A.F. officers. In August because of the flying bomb attacks, boys from Harrow School were evacuated to the Castle.

In 1945 the war ended in Europe on 8 May and on 14 August the Japanese government unconditionally surrendered.

In 1946 Sir Albert Gladstone relinquished his life interest in the Hawarden Estate and handed over the life tenancy to his brother Charles Gladstone who arrived with his family on 2 September.

Sir Albert Gladstone inherited the baronetcy on 12 February 1946. The baronetcy was that originally conferred on Sir John Gladstone, the father of W. E. Gladstone, his fourth son. Charles A. Gladstone retired after serving for thirty-four years as a master at Eton College.

6. Modern Broughton and Bretton

Modern Broughton came into existence in 1798 when Parliament passed an Act for 'dividing, allotting and inclosing all the commons and waste lands in the townships of Broughton, Pentrobin and Bannell within the manor and parish of Hawarden, containing in estimation six hundred acres or thereabouts.' This included the Warren, the open rough hillside to the south of Hawarden, upon which there was a rabbit warren, the preserve of the Glynne family as lords of the manor. The diaries of Sir John Glynne for 1770 record that, between 1762 and 1769, a total, of 5,232 rabbits were killed in the Warren.[1] The Act was brought into being as the result of the petition of the principal landowners agreeing to the enclosure. In this case they were named as Sir Stephen Richard Glynne, Richard Earl Grosvenor, Lloyd Lord Kenyon, Dame Mary Glynne widow, Sir George William Prescott, the Reverend Randulph Crewe, Rector of Hawarden, and several other persons and proprietors.

The intention of the Act was to improve farming by enclosing the wastes and common lands, which made up a greater part of the land in the area. Enclosure had taken place since the fifteenth and sixteenth centuries, but there was an increased demand in the eighteenth century. The agricultural revolution led to an improvement in breeds of cattle through the experimentation of such men as Robert Bakewell and Thomas Coke, and the development of the four-course rotation of turnips, barley, clover and wheat. These improvements could only be achieved by enclosure of scattered holdings of the open-fields and the commons. Common rights included the right to graze cattle on the common, the right to cut turf for burning, and the right to gather firewood. To carry out the work of enclosing hundreds of acres of land, the Act of Parliament appointed commissioners. Three were appointed to carry out the work in Broughton, Bannel and Pentrobin townships, Josiah Boydell late of Rossett, Josiah Potts of Chester, and Thomas Wedge of Sealand.

The commissioners were charged with making an accurate survey of the lands to be enclosed, giving directions for fencing, mounding, ditching and draining the allotments, preserving watercourses, making bridges, gates, stiles and other works and making and laying out public and private roads. The commissioners meetings were public and notice was given in both Chester newspapers, the first of which was held at the house of Lydia Howell at the sign of the Fox on 8 May 1798. This gave the opportunity for all persons with a right of common and their tenants to give particulars of their claim to land. Some of the evidence given to the commissioners has survived:

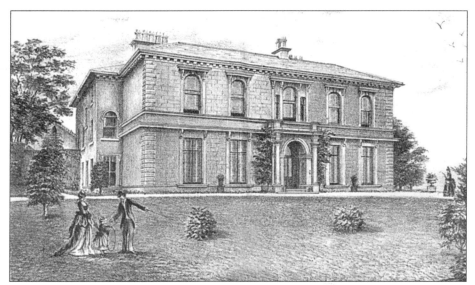

Mr Clarke of Broughton aged 76 has lived there 50 yrs says the Bretton people used to leave sheep upon Broughton Common when Saltney was flooded. He never heard that Bretton sheep or cattle were drove off or interrupted.

John Hornby of Broughton, Warrener to Sir Stephen R. Glynne, he has been in that capacity 24 or 25 years. He remembers lambs belonging to

Warren Hall, c.1872
[FRO PR/F/195]

John Thomas of Aston on Broughton Common about 22 years ago. That Wm. Rogers tended them. He thinks the lambs belonging to John Thomas were turned on two summers and taken away in the winter. They were never drove off or interrupted according to this examinant. He does not remember that sheep or cattle belonging to any other persons in Aston, Shotton or Mancot were turned on these commons.

William Leach of Bretton aged 67. Born in Bretton say he has known all the commons in Hawarden as long as he can remember. His father held a farm in Bretton about 7 or 8 acres part thereof being in Broughton township. He used to keep sheep on Broughton common which were depastured there and never interrupted upwards of 40 years ago, and he kept a few heifers at times and after his father's death the examinant did the like. The Bretton people pulled down the fences of Slaughters Inclosures. They did the same 3 times, the first time of their own accord and afterwards by order of Lord Grosvenor who had about 50 acres of land in Broughton.

When the commissioners met in Chester in September 1799 they disallowed the claims of right of common upon the commons and waste lands in Broughton in respect of lands in the several townships of Aston, Shotton and Mancot, but allowed them for the township of Bretton.[2]

The commissioners were empowered to sell off allotments in order to recover their costs. £2,516 was raised in this way, Lady Glynne paid £1050, Josiah Boydell £506, Mr Rigby £255 and Mr Willett £455. The expenses incurred included journeys to London, the expenses of the three commissioners, and the payment to William Williams of his account as road surveyor of £970. 16s. 11d.

The commissioners made their Award on 20 November 1802, the results of which changed the topography of Broughton, Pentrobin and Bannel from wastes, commons, open fields and straggling foot paths and crooked roads to straight fenced and hedged fields, and well appointed public and private roads of statutory width.[3]

The Award designated public carriage roads of a breadth of forty feet, between and exclusive of ditches. The Mill Road leading over the Bowling Hill towards Hawarden Mill Road. Lower Mill Road. Hope Road leading from the village of Hawarden to Hope. The Penyffordd Road, the Kinnerton Road, the Leycester Lane Road, the Broughton Green Road, leading out of the Mold Road at the village of Broughton into an ancient highway that leads to Broughton turnpike. The Pentrobin Road leading from the Mold Road to Buckley Mountain, the Smelting House Road leading from the Pentrobin Road towards the Smelting House, and the White Well Road leading out of the Penyffordd Road towards Buckley Mountain. The chief beneficiary in the allotment of land was Sir Stephen Richard Glynne who received almost five hundred of the estimated six hundred acres enclosed. Lord Grosvenor was allotted fifty-eight acres.

In the nineteenth century Broughton and Bretton remained primarily agricultural communities. In Bretton in 1841 there were 36 houses, a population of 224, with 14 farmers and 11 households with the head occupied as an agricultural labourer. In Broughton 76 houses, a population of 404, with 12 farmers and 29 households with the head employed as an agricultural labourer. Forty years later the number of houses had increased to 86 in Broughton and 33 in Bretton, with respective populations of 415 and 162. In addition the inmates at the workhouse in Broughton numbered 52. The 1881 census gives more details of farms than any of the previous enumerations: Catherine Farm; Hope's Place, Benjamin Youd 28 acres; Bretton Hall, Benjamin Jones, 245 acres; Digly Lane Farm, Susannah Mitchell, 30 acres, Bretton Farm; William Brailsford, 140 acres; Broughton Hall, William Johnson, corn miller; Green End Farm, John Fisher, 250 acres; Broad Oak Farm, Arthur Fdk. Davies, 125 acres; Warren Hall, James Bower, retired manufacturer; Warren Bank, Samuel Tudor, 10 acres; Park Farm, R. C. Griffiths, 268 acres; Green Lane Farm, Daniel Sheen; St Mary's Farm barn, John Jones, cattle dealer. There were other farms but they were unnamed in the census return.

St. Mary's Church, Broughton

As a result of the enclosure of the districts of Broughton and Saltney, the draining of the marshland, the establishment of improved road communications, and an increasing population, the Rector of Hawarden, George Neville, turned his attention to the building of a church for the district. He was a man of energy and fervour, with a desire to reform the lives of his parishioners by giving them the opportunity for schooling and religious worship. Buckley was the first place to see the fulfilment of these ideals with the building of a church, parsonage, school and master's house in 1822. In this endeavour he received a Parliamentary grant of £4,000 from the Commissioners appointed to build churches in England and Wales, and the assistance of the Glynne family. Neville was well connected in society and was determined to use this advantage for the benefit of the people of

142

Watercolour of St Mary's Church, Broughton, 1824. John Oates architect FRO PRF/F/109

Broughton. He obtained a grant of £400 from the River Dee Embankment Trustees, £300 from the Church Building Society, and the rest from subscriptions solicited from his highly influential friends. The foundation stone was laid in March 1824 and the church consecrated and dedicated to St Mary the Virgin on the feast of her nativity, 8 September 1824, by the Bishop of Chester, Charles James Sumner. As at Buckley, Neville maintained the right of the parish to exercise its rights as a Peculiar and Exempt Jurisdiction not subject to the authority of the bishop of the diocese. He demonstrated this by the procession of officials to greet the bishop: the Apparitor of the Peculiar Court, the Parish Clerk, the Registrar, the Hawarden Yeomanry, and a band of music. The architect John Oates attended with a plan of the church.

Oates designed a number of Commissioners' churches, 'which are often more picturesquely composed, and more carefully detailed than most of their kind.'[4]

The church consists of a nave with a battlemented western tower, the base of which is the main entrance to the church. Before the church was altered in 1877 there was a small sacrarium at the east end, with a vestry on the south side; and a western gallery. One of the unusual features of the church is the carved oak of the Tudor and Jacobean period. The pillars, which support the gallery, are said to have been the posts of a massive bed belonging to Henry VII. They demonstrate the monarch's interest in genealogy and his desire to display his claim to the English throne, amongst which are the heraldic badges of the Neville's of whom the Rector was a descendant. Elizabeth of York, the Queen of Henry VII, was the granddaughter of Cicely Neville, mother of Edward IV and wife of Richard Plantagenet.[5]

Both Rector Neville and Rector Glynne collected carved panelling which was worked up into the pulpit, desk, gallery, and vestry door. The panels of the pulpit bear figures of our Lord, Faith, and Charity, and a representation of the Crucifixion. Now lost was the carved figure of a monk which formed part of the prayer desk. The carved panels on the front of the gallery include griffins facing right and left, a group composed of the Holy Child, the Virgin Mary, and her mother St Anne. There are a benefaction board relating to the Broughton Charities, and the Royal Arms of George I.

The original font was a Norman piscina (a basin with a drain for washing the Communion vessels), and was said to have come from Lincolnshire. It now forms the base of the credence table in the sanctuary. The original east window was made up of pieces of ancient glass probably collected by Rector Neville. It was replaced in 1851 by a window to the memory of Lavinia Lyttelton, the wife of Rector Glynne. It was made by William Wailes, and was of three lights: central light our Lord in glory, and either side the Adoration of the Magi and the Presentation in the Temple. This window was placed at the east end of the new chancel in 1877 and replaced in 1916 by another window presented by Gertrude Jessie Glynne, Lady Douglas Pennant, daughter of Henry and Lavinia Glynne, by Powell of London, representing the Adoration of the Magi. The two stained glass windows either side of the chancel are by C. E. Kempe, and were the gift of William Johnson of Broughton Hall, for the new chancel in 1877. The window on the north side depicts The Annunciation and on the south the Flight into Egypt. A beautiful set of Communion plate the gift of the Neville family, was brought together for the opening of the church. 'This consists of two Communion cups, two patens and a large flagon. They are of different dates', and bear inscriptions relating to the donors.[6]

The church was enlarged in 1876–7 at the expense of Mr William Johnson, corn merchant and miller in Chester, who resided at Broughton Hall. He wished to commemorate the year of his office as Mayor of Chester by generously building a new chancel to the church. The building was closed for more than a year and reopened in June 1877. The *Chester Chronicle* gave this account:

After having been closed for rather more than a year, to allow a thorough internal restoration and extensive addition to the building, the pretty church of St Mary Broughton was reopened for the conduct of divine service by the Lord Bishop of St Asaph. The addition of the fabric consists of a spacious chancel and north and south transepts, which are the gift of W. Johnson, Esq., Mayor of Chester, and have cost about £1,400. This new portion of the church is in the Gothic order of architecture, in accord with the older portion of the building, and, though the stone used in the building is of a different kind and colour, the effect is not displeasing. The exterior part of the fabric is of Cefn stone, carefully dressed, with a slate roof of a tolerably high pitch, and ornamental iron eaves and spouts. In the south transept, which is to be used as a vestry, there is a small oak Gothic door, opening into the churchyard. Inside the appearance of the chancel is very pleasing. The three windows have handsome tracery heads, the east window being in three divisions and supported at the point from which the arch springs by two well-carved half-length figures of angels.

The interior walls are of Stourton stone. The north transept is open to the chancel, and is to be used as an organ chamber. On the south wall of the chancel is a tablet of Yorkshire stone, in a handsome carved Gothic border of Runcorn stone, at the head of which are the arms of the city of Chester, and the motto, *Antiqui colant, antiquum dierum* and following it the inscription in antique capitals, 'of your charity remember William Johnson, Esq., Mayor of the city of Chester, during the third time of his mayoralty, at his charge erected this chancel, A.D. 1876, to the glory of God and in memory of H. R. H. Prince Consort.

The floor of the chancel is paved with handsome encaustic tiles, of a very chaste pattern. The altar furniture is entirely of oak; the chancel stalls are of pitch pine polished with ornamental ends, and are four in number. The ceiling of the chancel is of pitch pine, semi-octagonal in form with the principal beams picked out in green and scarlet with gold beads. On the outside of the east window are carved heads of the late Prince Consort and her Majesty the Queen, one on either side, and in similar positions in relation to the north chancel windows are portraits in stone of W. Johnson, Esq., and Mrs Johnson. The carver is Mr Griffiths of Chester.

St Mary's Church, Broughton
FRO 9/40

Inside, the whole of the old church has been restored, and the ceiling and walls have been decorated in a manner which it would be hard to describe, but which considerably improves the appearance of the interior of the church. An ornamental brass lectern has been presented by W. Aaron, Esq., The architects for the restoration and extension are Messrs. Kelly and Edwards of Chester and Messrs. Cook and Moulton of Chester, have carried out the work.[7]

St Mary's School

An account of the Commissioners Inquiring into Education in Wales on 1 March 1847 gives the following information:

A school for boys and girls, taught together, by a master, in a school built for the purpose. Number of scholars, 81; number employed as monitors, 4. Subjects taught-reading, writing, arithmetic, English grammar and etymology, geography, history, and music, the Holy Scriptures, and the Church Catechism. Fees 1d. per week. Salary, £60.

I visited this school on the 1st of March, when 78 scholars were present; 40 boys and 38 girls. Among these, 23 were above ten years of age, and 17 had attended the school from four to above six years. 21 could read rather better than usual, while 11 could not say the alphabet. Among 38 who were learning to write on paper, only 2 could write well. Among 38 who were learning arithmetic, only 4 understood compound rules, and 21 were imperfectly acquainted with Simple Addition. Very little was known of mental arithmetic or of the history of England. A class of 17 were learning English grammar, and a class of 20 geography, but neither class had made much progress. Only one possessed competent knowledge of Holy Scripture. 22 were able to repeat the Church Catechism perfectly, and there were only 5 children present who could not repeat some portion of it. The girls are taught needlework by the master's wife every afternoon. The boys in this school commit to memory a catechism upon agricultural chemistry, by Professor Johnston.

St Mary's School
[H. G. Kay deposit, FRO D/DM/856/1]

The master was previously engaged in husbandry. He is 32 years of age, and has been a teacher for about three years. Before commencing his present employment, he spent two years as an assistant in a school at Chester. He endeavours to follow the national plan of education. His classes are so large that sufficient graduation is impossible.

Connected with this school there are lavatories for the children of both sexes — John James, Assistant.

In the 1870s St Mary's school was used as a reading room and recreation club for the workingmen in the district. When the parish of Hawarden had to up-grade its school accommodation as a result of the 1902 Education Act the new Rector Canon Harry Drew with the Broughton local committee decided that there should be a new church school. The Duke of Westminster generously gave an acre of land and a thousand pounds. On 17 September 1908, the Countess Grosvenor opened the school and the Bishop of St Asaph read prayers of dedication. The mixed school provided accommodation for 154 pupils. The school closed in 1955 as a result of the provision of a new school by the Flintshire Education Authority. The old school became the church hall.

Bretton Methodist Chapel

There are few documents relating to this chapel. It was built between July and September 1859 on land purchased from Robert Dutton Grindley, a Chester druggist. The members of the Methodist New Connexion church involved in setting up the new chapel in Bretton were William Wilkinson, Kinnerton, farmer; Richard Parry, Saltney, shopkeeper, John Williams, Bretton, builder and John Wilkinson, Pentre Moch, shopkeeper. In 1902 the chapel was extended by the building of a new Sunday school on land given by the Duke of Westminster. In 1920

Broughton Hall (now demolished)
[H. G. Kay deposit, FRO D/DM/856/1]

a memorial porch was added to the chapel to commemorate members of the congregation who died in the First World War. In 1926 the chapel was registered for the solemnisation of marriages. The buildings were improved by new kitchen facilities at the rear of the Sunday school in 1949 and the installation of a new heating system in 1953. Centenary celebrations took place in September 1959.[8]

Broughton Primitive Methodist Church
In May 1880 the piece of land on which the Church stands was purchased from Mr William Hignett of Liverpool and put into the care of trustees who came from a large area: Kinnerton, Penymynydd, Buckley and Hope. There was a small society in existence in the 1840s, which joined the Chester Methodist circuit in 1852, and the newly formed Buckley circuit in 1871. Before the chapel was built 'there were meetings in a cottage occupied Mr Knight, at the ' back of the town ' and a Mr William Davies of Kinnerton placed his house 'at the disposal of friends.'[9]

The Hawarden Union Workhouse
From Elizabethan times onwards parishes became responsible for the care of the poor and infirm through the vestry. Overseers of the poor were the officials nominated by the vestry to use the parish rates to meet their obligations. In the eighteenth century Parliamentary legislation allowed parishes to join together, or form a union, to build poorhouses or workhouses to give institutional relief to the poor and destitute. With the growth of population and the coming of the industrial revolution, there were more poor people to be cared for in an environment that was more hostile and parochial vestries could no longer cope. The Poor Law (Amendment) Act of 1834, introduced new legislation, which shifted responsibility from the vestry to an elected body the board of guardians who administered the new poor law over larger areas called unions, which were composed of groups of parishes financed by a poor rate. One of the objects of the 1834 Act was to deter applications for relief from the able-bodied. It was doubtful if this worked, for it was the crippled, the destitute aged, the poor widow and her children, the orphan and the imbecile, who made up the workhouse inmates. Until the 1850s the parish of Hawarden, in the Chester diocese until 1849, had been part of the Union, whose workhouse was in Chester. The

Hawarden Poor Law Union was set up in 1853 and the Workhouse opened in Broughton in the spring of 1855.

Boards of Guardians were elected bodies and it was they who appointed the Master and Matron to control the harsh environment. The first couple to take charge of the Broughton Workhouse were Mr and Mrs Bamber who were succeeded in

Workhouse treat at Hawarden
Rectory, c.1900
[FRO 28/G/1]

1878 by Mr and Mrs Dodwell. When the 1891 census was taken, there were fifty-seven inmates in the Broughton workhouse. Twenty-one were under the age of fifteen, five were imbeciles, four crippled or paralysed, two blind, and there was a group of middle aged inmates of both sexes who could not cope with the world outside, and the aged with no one to care for them. Some attempt was made by the Guardians and sympathetic friends to give the inmates some entertainment at Christmas time or an occasional outing.

In Jubilee year 1887, Mr J. Bowers entertained forty-two of the inmates at Warren Hall. They were conveyed there in a lorry lent by Mr John Roberts of Well House Farm, Saltney. Arriving at three o'clock, they were escorted round the gardens and then sat down to a knife and fork meal. Afterwards each was supplied with a sponge cake, an orange and a plate of muscatels. Subsequently, all adjourned to the lawn in front of the hall where various games were indulged in until half-past seven, the inmates in the meantime being regaled with lemonade, port wine and biscuits. They were each given a new shilling before leaving.[10]

On New Year's Eve 1902, the annual Christmas Tree and entertainment were given at the Workhouse with the guests including the Board of Guardians, a large number of friends and the Rector and Mrs Stephen Gladstone. 'The Christmas tree was a magnificent spectacle and contained such useful presents as shawls, stockings, tobacco pipes, teas, tam o'shanter, ties, sweets, *etc*. After the distribution of the presents, a miscellaneous concert followed by local artistes and when this concluded the Ohio Troupe of Minstrels gave a most enjoyable entertainment from Chester. A delightful evenings enjoyment was brought to a close by the singing of the National Anthem.[11]

In 1921 the inmates were taken to Llandudno, by charabanc and had a perfect day. Blind Mary was so anxious to realise that she was by the sea that she said 'Do let me stroke a donkey, and let me feel the pebbles, and let me dip my hand in the tide'. Another old gentleman said 'I shall live ten years longer after that glorious treat'.[12] In 1929 the Poor Law was again reformed and the Workhouse at Broughton closed as such. From June 1919 it had been known as Laburnham House. From 1856 to 1930 seven hundred and thirty one inmates who had died in the workhouse were buried in Broughton churchyard. In 1933 Laburnham House was converted into a home for the feeble-minded, and the inmates removed to Holywell.[13] During the Second World War the patients and staff vacated Laburnham House, going to Rhyl, and the premises were taken over by Vickers Armstrong.

Broughton and Bretton War Memorial Institution

The first meeting to discuss what form the memorial to those from Broughton and Bretton who gave their lives in the First World War should take met in October 1919, and decided that it should take the form of a public room to be used as a reading room, in which a tablet would be placed recording the names of the men who fell in action and the names of all the men from the district who served in the Forces. Henry Gladstone offered a piece of land, and work began in 1925 to prepare a recreation ground. It was not until 1933 that a decision was made to commence building the Institute, when a grant of £300 was made from the Hawarden Embankment Trustees. The progress being made was reported in the *Chester Chronicle* in February 1935:

After months of work, most of which has been done voluntarily by local village brick setters, joiners, painters, plasterers, labourers and farmers, the village Institute is nearing completion. The project would probably never have been realised but for the generosity of

The Ratcliffe family outside the Glynne Arms, Broughton
[FRO 9/41]

Lord Gladstone of Hawarden, who gave the ground on which the Institute has been built and the ground surrounding it for a recreation ground for the village children. Lord Gladstone has taken a personal interest in the scheme from the beginning, and selected the site on which the Institute has been built. The interior measurements of the main room are 40 ft. by 24 ft. Everything is complete, with exception of the installation of the heating apparatus, and the seating accommodation. Before the official opening in the spring, the trustees have decided to build a kitchen at the rear of the Institute and are anticipating another grant from the Hawarden Embankment Trust. A billiard room will probably also be added. Mr G. Reidford, architect, Hawarden, prepared the plans and supervised the work *gratis*.[14]

Lord Gladstone died in 1935 and his nephew Mr A. C. Gladstone opened the new Institute at the beginning of April 1937 when it was decided to call the building the Broughton and Bretton War Memorial Club.[15]

The Women's Institute

The inaugural meeting of the Broughton, Bretton and Warren branch of the Women's Institute took place at the new Institute on 10 April 1937 and they began to meet once a month.

The Broughton & Bretton Cricket Club[16]

The first notice of a cricket club in Bretton occurs in 1880 when cricket was played upon the Brook Field. Mr Sandbach of the Dogs public house in Bretton managed the team. There was a notice in the *Hawarden Parish Magazine* for April 1882 saying 'After Easter cricket may be expected to become general. The Broughton Club is preparing to start for the season and the Bretton young men are anxious to start a new club'. In 1900 Mr Horace Mayhew reformed the club and players from Broughton and Bretton played in the same side on a ground between the plantation and Broughton Hall. In 1904 Mr Henry Roberts of Mancot laid a cricket square in the Halls Hay Field. During the First World War the pavilion was loaned to a squad operating a searchlight.

Broughton Cricket Club XI, c1900
Back row(L–R): Ellis Williams (joiner, of The Warren, emigrated to Canada); Walter Jones (engine driver NE Railway); Tom Youd (signalman); Ernest Cecil Jones (commercial traveller); Harry Roberts (plumber); Edward Nicholas (G.W. Railway) of Digby Cottage, Bretton.
Sitting (L–R): Jim Maddocks (plumber) Eaton Estate, later farmer of Hopes Place, Bretton; Arthur Mills (station master, later post master); Jack Bartley (bricklayer) small-holding, The Warren; Tom Connah (brick-maker & kilnsman) The Warren.
Front: Ted Ratcliffe (Sandycroft Foundry, later Fords of Dagenham).

[H. G. Kay deposit, FRO D/DM/856/3]

The club was reformed from time to time, and in 1929 they were looking for a field to play. From 1934–9 the club played in the Chester and District Amateur League. No cricket was played after the outbreak of the war in 1939 until hostilities ceased in 1945. In 1946 Broughton and Bretton won the Boughton Hall Cricket Club knock-out competition, beating Helsby in the final by 4 wickets. At this time they used the cricket ground at the Gladstone Playing Fields. The club restarted again in 1966, only to close in 1974.

Broughton and Bretton Railway Station

The Mold Railway Company constructed a line of double track from Saltney Ferry, the junction with the Chester and Holyhead Railway, to Mold, a distance of ten miles under an Act of 9 July 1847. Edward Ladd Betts constructed the line. The main line was opened in September 1849. Broughton and Bretton Station is four and three-quarter miles from Chester. The London and North Western Railway acquired the Mold Railway Company in 1858. The station buildings on the Down platform were designed by Francis Thompson. The station was originally named 'Broughton' when the line was open, changed to Broughton Hall to avoid confusion with stations of the same name, and finally changed to Broughton and Bretton in 1908. With the coming of Vickers-Armstrong Ltd. in 1939, a branch line was laid to serve various parts of the factory. It continued in use until 1969 and the line was removed in 1971. Ratcliffe's Iron founders, Hawarden, used the railway yard as a base for the transport of their boilers and engineering manufactories in the nineteenth and twentieth centuries. The line closed to passenger traffic on 30 April 1962, and freight traffic on 15 June 1964. It was from this station that the body of W. E. Gladstone was taken to London for his State Funeral in Westminster Abbey in May 1898.

Broughton Airfield and Factory[17]

The name of Broughton is known throughout the world because of the present Airbus UK Factory. Its origins as a factory for the production of aircraft goes back to 1935 when the government began to prepare for war by building shadow factories. Broughton fitted the criteria for locating these factories near but not too near centres of population. The land was ideally suited for laying out a large airfield, which would be suitable for the dispersal of finished aircraft, and other uses to which the RAF might wish put it. The decision was taken in 1937 that the new factory was to be used for the production of the Wellington. It was to be government owned and leased to Vickers-Armstrong who would share the adjacent aerodrome with the RAF. The factory would be used to assemble the Wellington from parts made elsewhere. Broughton had its satellite assembly plant at Byley, near Middlewich in mid-Cheshire. The first Wellington was built in a temporary Bellman-type hangar on a site near the Glynne Arms, Hawarden: begun on 3 April 1939 it was finished by 2 August. The new factory became fully operational the month of the declaration of war, September 1939.

Gradually the work force was increased from 697 on January 1 1940, to 5,546 by the end of September 1943, with another 1,500 on the staff. The total production from 1939, until it ceased in October 1945, was 5,540 Wellingtons and 235 Lancasters, built between June 1944 and September 1945.

The airfield was used as an Officer Training Unit for various purposes during the war. No. 7 OTU, later renumbered No. 57 OTU, was used principally for Spitfires, until they move to Eshott in November 1942. No. 41 OTU, was stationed here in September–October 1944 to train tactical reconnaissance personnel of the Fleet Air Arm. In March 1945 the day-fighter wing located at Poulton moved to Broughton and became No. 58 OTU, until it closed down at the end of hostilities in July.

The Broughton Wellington, R1333. which was subscribed to by the workers at the Broughton factory. Seven days after completion (7 November 1940) it was damaged in Hawarden's only air raid. After repair it was allocated to No 99 Squadron and was destroyed on take-off on 18 December [FRO 9/35]

Facing page
Top: Lancaster bombers under construction at Broughton, 1944   [FRO 9/42]
Bottom: De Havilland 125 executive jets under construction at Broughton, 1963   [FRO 9/49]

At the beginning of the war Broughton maintained an unofficial Battle Flight of three Spitfires, permanently armed and available for use by any of the instructors. They were exercised on three occasions in August and September 1940. On 14 August a Heinkel 111, which had bombed Sealand, was brought down at Saltney; on 7 September a Ju 88, after a running fight, crash-landed on a mountainside in Merionethshire. Their final encounter of the war was on 18 September when a Dornier 215 was sent down into the sea off Anglesey.

Broughton airfield was also used by a civilian organisation, the Air Transport Auxiliary, for the ferrying of aircraft. No. 3 Ferry Pilots' Pool, disbanded in November 1945, was responsible for the ferrying of many types of aircraft both during the war and afterwards when many were scrapped. On two occasions, after D-Day 1944, US troops were transported from Broughton to Normandy in C-47s.

It was not until 31 March 1959 that the RAF Station was finally closed at Broughton when No. 631 Gliding School was transferred to Sealand.

At the end of the war, production at the Broughton Factory changed from aircraft to pre-fabricated aluminium houses (pre-fabs), with an order for 11,250 units. By the time the Vickers government lease of the Broughton Factory expired in April 1948, a total of 28,000 housing units had been completed.

Vickers Armstrong were followed in 1948 by the de Havilland Aircraft Company, who were allocated the Broughton Factory to enable them complete their orders for £10 million worth of aircraft. Broughton gave them scope for expansion to meet government demands, which came with the Korean War in the 1950s, the growth of overseas orders, and the development of civil and commercial aircraft.

3,548 aircraft of eight de Havilland types were produced between mid–1948 and the end of 1959 —Mosquito (81), Hornet (149), Vampire and Vampire Trainer (1,236), Chipmunk (889), Dove (209), Venom (834), Heron (129) and Comet (13).[18]

From 1949 a branch of the de Havilland technical school was established at Broughton to train apprentices and tradesmen to produce a highly skilled work force, which has enabled the factory to adapt over the years and become a strong argument in the continuing location of production at the factory.

By 1965 the De Havilland Company was incorporated into Hawker Siddeley Aviation Limited. Components for Nimrod aircraft were produced until 1970, the twin engined executive transport, the D. H. 125, 'an airliner in miniature', sold 621 between 1962 and 1985.

Meanwhile, 1971 saw the commencement of Airbus Wing construction, and in April 1977 the Government created British Aerospace (B.Ae.). By March 2001, the total number of the various types of Airbus Wing Sets made at Broughton had reached 2,666. The Broughton Factory operates integrally with the Airbus UK management, design and manufacturing centre at Filton, Bristol. The UK industry is part of Airbus Industrie (UK, France, Germany and Spain), with assembly centres at Bremen, Toulouse, and Hamburg. Improvements to the main runway in 1996 allowed the fleet of Airbus A300-600ST Super Transporters, the world's most voluminous cargo aircraft (nicknamed 'Beluga', due to its resemblance to the sturgeon of that name), to transport completed Airbus wing sets to the final assembly centres in Europe.

At the northeast of the Broughton site is the Raytheon Aircraft Services Limited, which continues to build the airframe structure kits for their Little Rock, Wichita, plant. The 450-acre Broughton factory-aerodrome site employs a workforce of around 4,000 from north-east Wales and north-west England.

7. Modern Ewloe

There were two townships in the ancient parish of Hawarden, Ewloe Town and Ewloe Wood, which were often simply known as Ewloe. Modern Ewloe is discussed here as what remains in Hawarden ecclesiastical parish after the constitution of the parish of Buckley by Order in Council on 12 December 1874. The new parish of Buckley was created out of 2,048 acres of the parish of Hawarden, which gave up the township of Ewloe Wood and parts of the townships of Ewloe Town and Pentrobin. The census return for 1881 identified the area of Ewloe Town, which remained in Hawarden. The total population was 1742, of whom 386 remained in the parish of Hawarden, and 348 inhabited houses, of which 77 remained in Hawarden parish. In the township as a whole there were ten brick works, three potteries, and two collieries. The following places were listed by the census enumerator as being in the ecclesiastical parish of Hawarden. Level houses, Wood Cottage, 14 dwellings, mostly colliers, with Thomas Hughes farming 10 acres. Old Hall Farm — Mary Johnson, farming 30 acres. Wood Lane: 20 dwellings, mostly colliers. Paradise Farm, Edward Weigh farming 30 acres. Owlet's Hall, (Hole), Nicholas Collins, blacksmith farming 13 acres. Aston Hall Colliery. Kearsley Farm, Mary Hughes, farming 70 acres. Hawarden Heys Farm, Hugh Davies farming 70 acres. Oaks Farm, Herbert Hearst, farming 38 acres. Hill Farm, Mary Nield, farming about 40 acres. Pantile Houses, 5 dwellings. Ewloe Lanes, 29 dwellings, which includes Ewloe Toll Gate with Margaret Roberts, keeper. Broom Cottage. Castle Hill Brewery — John Fox — brewer and farmer of 130 acres, employing 14 men, 3 women and 2 lads.

This study looks at the community until about 1950.

The Primitive Methodist Church

On 12 October 1862 a new Primitive Methodist Chapel was opened in the place, which is now the Methodist schoolroom opposite the Crown and Liver Public House. The following account is give of the opening:

> Sermons were preached by brothers J. Eastwood, J. Postlethwaite, and E. Kershaw. One soul found salvation in the prayer meting at the close of the evening service. The services were continued on the following Sabbath. Mr W.

Hughes, of Queensferry, has made a handsome pulpit, and fixed it in the chapel at his own expense. The chapel is 32 feet by 22, and 13 feet from the floor to the wall plate; is well lighted, and fitted up with ten pews on an elevated floor; and will cost (including £24 paid for land) £126 10s. The inhabitants in the neighbourhood seem highly pleased with the accommodation now afforded them for meeting to worship God, as there is no other place of worship within about a mile, and we trust that much lasting good will result from the rearing of this house of prayer, and our ardent prayer is, 'Peace be within thy walls'. J. Eastwood.[1]

*Ewloe Methodist Church
[John Davies deposit, FRO N/31/23]*

Thirty years later the growth in numbers inspired the members to contemplate building a new chapel to hold at least 220, and with the vestry to hold 250 adults. In 1894 'sixteen yards of land in width down to the lower hedge' was purchased from Mr F. G. Wright for £25. In this time of industrial depression and bad harvests money was scarce and certain economies were imposed: it was resolved 'that we do not present any silver trowel, mallet, or books to any of the stone layers.' The initial cost of the building was reduced from £893 to £675. Thirty trustees were nominated in February 1895, which reflected the occupational make up of the membership; fifteen were colliers, two insurance agents, two farmers, two grocers and one the Broughton postmaster. The chapel was opened on 7 May 1895 beginning with an out-door service after which a key was presented to Miss Hartley of Liverpool, who unlocked the door and declared the chapel open. 'After the service tea was provided in the old chapel, at which upwards of 200 sat down. At seven o'clock Mr Watkin delivered his popular lecture on Christmas Evans to a crowded gathering. The new chapel is a splendid piece of workmanship. A clock was presented to the chapel by Mr Francis Jones, of Mold; also a cloth for the communion table by Mr Owen Hughes of Buckley.[2]

Music was encouraged in the chapel by the purchase of a cornet, the gift of a double bass fiddle, and the introduction of an organ. The first decade of the twentieth century was marked in Wales by the fervour of religious revival, which must have been felt in Ewloe. By 1903 the accommodation of the chapel was inadequate and the chapel was enlarged, and the money was raised by the sale of the schoolroom to the Co-operative Society for the sum of £250. On 29 October it was proposed, 'that the opening of the new chapel and preaching services for the first five Sundays be put on the big bills for publication, that we have plain bread, currant bread, seed bread and a sandwich tea with a special table for the higher classes, price of tea 1s.'.[3]

In 1953 a proposal to build a new Sunday school and make improvements to the premises at a cost of £12,000 was rejected. In February 1964 a plot of land was sold to the Birkenhead & District Co-operative Society for £750. In 1990 significant improvements were made to the chapel, which was dedicated on 9 March 1991 as Ewloe Highway Methodist Church.[4]

St Winifred's School Chapel

The reaction of the parish of Hawarden to the Education Act of 1870 was to build school chapels in the outlying districts of Sandycroft, Shotton and Ewloe, rather than establish schools, which would be under the jurisdiction of elected school boards. The first proposal was to erect a timber building but in September 1875 it was announced that the school would be of brick if the sum of £500 could be raised. For this purpose the daughters of the gentry collected money. The Miss Davisons from Stafford House and Shotton Cottage, and Miss Hancock from Aston Bank were zealous in the cause, and an anonymous friend sent £50 through Miss Mary Gladstone. Messrs Kelly and Edwards of Chester were the architects. Whilst the school was being built in the winter of 1876–7 Monday evening services were held at the house of the Weighs which it was reported 'has swelled at times beyond the capacity of the room and that several time the number has reached 50.' The work was delayed by a strike of bricklayers and carpenters and the absence of the Rector. In August 1876 a magnificent two day fancy bazaar was held on the green of the old Hawarden Castle with seven stalls manned by members of the Gladstone family, for example on stall one in charge of Mrs Moffat, Hawarden and Mrs Frederick Thompson, Aston Hall had on it a number of model yachts

St Winefride's Church interior
[FRO 18/47]

St Winefride's School Chapel, 1895
[S. E. Gladstone]

and other vessels; hand-painted finger-glass mats, illuminations, ottomans, fretwork, and other ornamental articles. A prominent feature was a talking doll, for which a very reasonable price was asked.

The school chapel was opened and dedicated in the presence of the Right Revd. N. J. Merriman, Bishop of Grahamstown, South Africa, on Tuesday, 14 August 1877. The Rector, the Revd. S. E. Gladstone, and the Curate, C. Gamlen conducted services. The day was fine, and Mr Hancock provided luncheon for a large party of friends. Next day a Tea was held in the afternoon and a Concert in the afternoon. The school opened as a day school for infants on 8 October 1877 under the charge of Miss Ore. Pupil numbers increased quickly from 18 on the opening day to 52 by the end of the month. A monthly celebration of the Holy Communion began on Saturday, 1 September. In the winter of 1877 a night school for men and lads were opened on Monday and Wednesday evenings with a weekly fee of 2d. The attendance was made up of 16 men and 18 boys. In January 1878 it was reported that 'the Reading Room for men has now fairly started. The room is open every night except Thursday from 6.30 p.m. until 9.30 p.m. On Saturday afternoon it opens at 3 o'clock. Draughts and Dominoes and other quiet games are provided as well as the *London Daily News*, and a weekly local paper, the *Cheshire Observer*.

A routine was soon established with Sunday and weekday services, and a Bible class. The church members became responsible for the organisation of the reading room and other social activities. A cricket team was formed in the summer of 1878 and were invited by Mr Hancock to practise at Aston Bank, and latter a soccer team. In September 1879 a Mutual Improvement Society was formed to meet in the winter months. The Ewloe community dependent on the coal industry was at the mercy of economic forces. The *Hawarden Parish Magazine* announced in September 1881:

> The Aston Hall Colliery Distress Fund. Some eight weeks ago this Colliery stopped payment, and over 400 men and lads lost their work and wages; there has been in consequence no little distress. A Relief Committee began to investigate cases under the chairmanship of Mr W. H. Gladstone, at the Ewloe School on Monday 22nd, and to distribute food. Gifts of money are invited for this purpose.

St. Winifred's School was closed in 1922 and pupils transferred to Ewloe Green School. The building continued to be used as a worship centre until a new church was opened in 1938. St Winifred's was then used as a clinic and for meetings of the Women's Institute.

The Church of the Holy Spirit

In April 1936 the Rector of Hawarden announced that Lady Maud Ernestine Gladstone had expressed her desire to build a church at Ewloe in memory of her late husband Henry Neville, Baron Gladstone (d. 1935). This was to be the seventh daughter church built in the ancient parish of Hawarden in less than 120 years. The site presented by Lady Gladstone was on the top of Aston Hill commanding a magnificent view across the Cheshire plain and the Dee and Mersey estuaries. Lady Gladstone's nephew, H. S. Goodhart Rendel, President of the Royal Institute of British Architects, was

Lady Maud Ernestine Gladstone, 1924
[FRO 28/B/29]

Left: Church of the Holy Spirit
[Bell Jones, FRO 18/56]

Below left: Church of the Holy Spirit interior
[Bell Jones, FRO 18/65]

Above: Consecration of the Church of the Holy Spirit
[FRO 18/66]
L–R: F. S. M. Bennett; Nugent-Hicks (Bishop of Lincoln); A.
Edwards (diocesan Chancellor); Lady Maud E. Gladstone; Bishop
Wentworth-Shields (Warden St Deiniol's); Bishop W. T. Harvard
(St Asaph); Saunders Rees (Rector of Hawarden); Curate of
Ewloe; Bishop N. H. Tubbs (Dean of Chester)

commissioned as the architect. The architect expressed the meaning behind his choice of a style derived from the Byzantine school.

> The practical demands of a small church have been met in an original way, and care has been taken to prevent as far as possible the feeling of isolation produced by the wide parallelogram of the normal nave when the attendance is small: and at the same time to make it possible for the priest at the altar to be visible from every seat when the church is filled.

The corner stone was laid in May 1937 by the Bishop of St Asaph W. T. Havard, and consecrated by him on 14 September 1938. The sermon was preached by the Bishop of Lincoln Nugent Hicks, an old friend of Lord Gladstone and a trustee of St Deiniol's Library. Other clergy present included Bishop Wentworth-Shields, Warden of St Deiniol's library; Bishop N. H. Tubbs, Dean of Chester; and Bishop M. S. O'Rorke, former Bishop Accra.

The roof slates came from Llangynog, the stone from Talacre, and the bricks were local. An unusual feature is the lantern dome surmounted by a large golden cross which when lighted is visible from the Liverpool Bar. The whole of the interior is plastered. It was hoped that this would give the opportunity for wall paintings. As a protection against fire the interior is entirely vaulted in reinforced concrete. Practically all the windows look to the south and west to catch the maximum of warmth and sunshine. Over the south porch is the figure of a dove in gold mosaic, a symbol of the Holy Spirit. There are two porches, the south porch being a little more than halfway from the middle of the nave, and the other at the west end of the church. The placing of the organ and choir in the centre of the north wall leaves the large west window on which the interior is mainly dependent for light, entirely unobstructed. On the north side is a bell-cote containing two bells The priest's vestry is at the rear of the high altar, the server's vestry at the rear of the side chapel, and the choir vestry is against the north wall between the organ and the west end of the church.

Under the dome is a large circular chandelier carrying fourteen lamps. In the Lady Chapel dedicated to St Winifred, hangs a large circular painting of the Virgin and Holy Child. The crucifix on the high altar dates from *c.*1650 is Italian work in ivory and carved mother of pearl and came from Cerlossa Abbey in Pavia. On its base are carvings of St Francis and St Antony and our Lady, and on its shaft the seven sorrows of Our Lady, the Agony in the Garden, the '*Ecce Homo*', the Scourging at the Pillar, the Carrying of the Cross, and at the top, the Resurrection. The candlesticks were designed by the architect to match the Crucifix. The communion plate consists of a chalice made from domestic silver belonging to Lord Gladstone, and engraved on the hexagonal foot is the Crucifix. It has the inscription 'To the glory of God and in memory of Henry Lord Gladstone from Ishbel Aberdeen'.[5]

Castle Hill Brewery

In 1844 John Fox and his brother-in-law James Heyes founded a brewery at Castle Hill Ewloe. The Fox family were yeomen farmers in the neighbouring township of Shotton, and John Fox himself farmed at Castle Hill. James Heyes' family were potters from Bistre. On the death of James Heyes in 1870 John Fox became the sole proprietor.

The Brewery guaranteed a sale of its beers by owning many of the local public houses such as the Castle Inn, Shotton, the Crown and Liver, Ewloe, the George and Dragon, Flint, the Hawarden Castle Hotel, Queensferry, the Mechanics Arms, Pentre, the New Inn, Sandycroft, the Plough Inn, Aston, the Ship Inn, Connah's Quay, and the Stag's Head, Ewloe. Other local inns such as the White Bear, Mancot, were leased to the Brewery.

The water for brewing was obtained from natural springs in Wepre Wood and the barley malted at Swndwr malt kiln near Northop. The barley was bought locally and cheaper varieties came from California and Chile. Hops came from Worcester and Kent. The brewing took place in a building a short distance behind the farmhouse. Some beer was put into barrels and the rest bottled. The work force at full strength numbered between twelve to fifteen men. The three beers brewed at Castle Hill were Mild Ale, India Pale Ale and Lamb's Wool, an extra strong beer brewed

Above: John Fox   [FRO 18/91]

Below: James Hayes   [FRO 18/93]

Fox's Brewery Bottling Department
[FRO 18/81]

for the Christmas season. During 1930s and '40s the brewery bottled Guinness stout and Bass pale ale.

In 1948 Castle Hill Brewery was sold to Burtonwood Breweries of Warrington, whilst Cecil Fox farmed the Castle Hill until his death in 1978 when the estate was sold.[6]

The Second World War

Ewloe Green school logbook includes entries, which report some of the incidents, which happened in the community during the Second World War. On the day Britain declared war on Germany, 3 September 1939, the school was opened at 9.30 *a.m.* so that evacuated children might assemble prior to attending divine service at Ewloe Church. The children were from Brassey Street Central School, Birkenhead. On 17 November at 11.20*a.m.*,

> … this morning an air raid warning was sounded. At a given signal from Mr J. Champion the scholars deployed to their allotted positions in the fields.

The week 26 April to 3 May 1941,

> … this school was a centre for War Weapons Week for Deeside, Hawarden and District area. Although on duty until 8.30 *p.m.* each night I found joy in doing a little towards the effort. The total taken was £1189 10s. Such a figure reveals in significant fashion the patriotism of our neighbourhood.

1941 June 11, the headmaster recorded,

> … at 10.35 *a.m.* this morning I was told that a Liverpool evacuee had fallen down a disused coal shaft in a plantation near the school premises. I immediately ran for help calling Mr C. Price who was working near the school. I suggested at the same time that a large rope would be needed. Mr Price found one and raced to the shaft. Mr Robinson soon afterwards hurried along. Mr Davies of Ellery, Ewloe Green also joined the party. The Police were informed. In the meantime Mr Price had been lowered down to the boy whom he brought up safely to the surface.
>
> 1942 September 23. School dinners were inaugurated today and 126 scholars sat down. On the whole a good beginning.
>
> 1943 August 31. As all scholars over eleven years of age have been transferred to Queensferry Senior School, we now become a Junior and Infants School.

8. Modern Mancot

The township of Mancot was relatively small in both acreage and population. In the 1861 census it was divided into three:

Little Mancot	21 houses, 52 males, 56 females, total 108
Pentre	11 houses, 22 males, 31 females, total 53
Big Mancot	26 houses, 53 males, 62 females, total 115
Total houses	58 *Total population* 276

By the 1891 census there were 75 inhabited houses with a total population of 365. The work force was almost equally divided between coal miners, workers on the land, labourers, and foundry workers. The township had two grocers, a butcher, draper, tailor, shoemaker, and a fisherman. The census enumerator recorded families living in Mancot Bank, Scotch Row (7 dwellings), Little Mancot Farm, Well House, White Cottage, Lower Ash Farm, Lower Ash Cottage, New Row (5 dwellings), Mancot Village, Mancot Square, the White Bear, Mancott [*sic*] Farm and Pentre Mancot. Mining went back at least three hundred years, and by the end of the nineteenth century the collieries had been worked out.

A significant increase in housing and population took place in the First World War with the building of housing for the key workers at the Queensferry munitions factory.

Mancot Royal

King George V and Queen Mary visited the new housing estate on 14 May 1917 when they came to see the Queensferry munitions factory. As a result, the new area of the township was aptly named Mancot Regis perhaps to distinguish it from Great or Big Mancot and Little Mancot.

The wartime emergency brought a workforce to Queensferry, which grew to about 7,000 workers. It was necessary to have key workers and the emergency services living on the spot. Houses were built for firemen, policemen, certain process workers and tradesmen. Nothing should be allowed to interrupt the smooth running and maximum output Lloyd George

Above: Plas Mancot
[Mancot Womens Institute deposit, FRO D/DM/306/1]

Right: Scotch Row. Note the unusual height of the windows in relation to the front doors
[Mancot Womens' Institute deposit, FRO D/DM/306/1]

demanded from the new munitions factories. Senior management, assistant superintendents, section managers, the heads of the maintenance and engineering departments, and some chemists were given houses. Morale was equally important. Married men were provided with family houses. By February 1918 there were more than 170 children under 14 years of age living in the township. Single people lived in hostels to encourage corporate identity and provide comradeship. There were two hostels for male chemists, one for welfare supervisors and female shift officers, and two for the women police. A fire station in Crossways and a hospital were included on the estate.

The site chosen for Mancot Royal was situated between Big Mancot and Pentre and set between Mancot Lane and Leaches Lane. Here about 160 houses were built in an estate, which received the praise of post war planners:

> Following the medieval precedent of Flint, its designer Mr Raymond Unwin, laid down its main axis at right angles to the coastal road. In house planning and disposition of houses on the site, as well as in the planning of its main axis, this village is a model for the future residential development of the Region.'[1]

Theodore Fyffe came to the factory in February 1916 to supervise the building works which went on until their final completion in March 1918.

The creation of Mancot Royal brought about a social grouping, which resembled a small university campus. They had their own motto *Semper Floreat Mancot Regis* ('May Royal Mancot always flourish') and they soon developed their own distinctive social organisation. They set up their own committee, which was inaugurated in January 1918, with the support of eighty residents and the presence of the Chief Constable of Flintshire, Yarnell Davies and the Rector of Hawarden, F. S. M. Bennett. The Mancot Royal Circular was issued fortnightly to advertise local events, which showed the breadth of their interests and enthusiasm. A whist drive with musical thrills was held at the Queensferry Co-operative Hall. An orchestral concert was held in Mancot Church Hall. The Mancot Royal book club was established, 'a splendid brainstorm of somebody's, to give you all the best in fiction to while away the hours at the factory'.

In March 1918 it was announced that 'a preparatory school for children has been opened in the church hall, Mancot Royal, by Miss Jarvis.' The agenda of the committee was concerned with 'allotments, seed potatoes, post box Sunday delivery of mail, a notice board and the committee room.' Mundane parochialism had soon established itself. A more destructive virus was the influenza epidemic of 1918 when three members of the factory clerical staff died in November and scores of workers were seriously affected.

With the coming of peace, production at the munitions factory ceased, and the houses in Mancot Royal were vacated and gradually inhabited by local people. The fire station in Crossways became first a garage, and then a grocery store. One of the hostels became a private school run by Miss Jarvis. The St Deiniol's Church committee bought a carpentry shed in Crossways to be used as St Michael's Church and church hall.

Mancot Presbyterian Church
Mancot Presbyterian Church was established in 1818 when some people in the township came under the influence of members from Northop.

Above: Munitions Village, Crossway, looking towards Hawarden Way
[FRO Deeside Regional Planning Scheme …]

Left: Leaches Lane, the house occupied by Sir Stafford Cripps (c.1915) when he was Assistant Superintendent at the Queensferry Munitions Works during the First World War
[Mancot Womens' Institute deposit, FRO D/DM/306/1]

The new followers of the Presbyterian cause first gathered together in the open air and began to be ministered to, and very soon afterwards they showed a desire for their own place of worship. When the Revd. John Parry preached at Mancot in 1822, one of his hearers John Bennion was moved to offer his cottage as a place to meet, but this soon became too small and they had to move to another one in an old row of cottages near the present chapel. This church began to grow through the influence of newcomers like Andrew Williams a preacher of Lady Huntington's denomination, and Joseph Wright a native of Rhosllanerchrugog by 1826 there were eight members and a Sunday school of thirty scholars. Ten years later the number of members had risen to thirty-six, and it was decided to build a chapel. Encouraged by Captain Cole, R.N., agent to the Dundas estate, John Jones leased the land in 1838 for a site for the chapel, which was built at a cost of £300. His granddaughter later married the Revd. Richard Jones, a distinguished and much loved Presbyterian Minister, who became a county councillor and chairman of the governors of the Hawarden County School. A schoolroom was attached to the chapel in 1842 to encourage

Mancot Presbyterian Church
[Mrs Sylvia Roberts]

the children. John Reed was appointed schoolmaster and taught at the school from 1842–6, being succeeded by John Prichard from Amlwch. John James, one of the Commissioners Enquiring into the State of Education in Wales, visited the school in February 1847 and left this report:

The Calvinistic Methodists, who contribute £20, towards the support of the master, established Mancott Chapel School — May 1846. The later is required to preach in the chapel. The school is open to persons of all denominations, and no test is required, or catechism enforced. It is a School for boys and girls, taught together by a master in a room attached to the Calvinistic Methodist chapel. Number of scholars, 25. Subjects taught — the Scriptures, reading, writing, and arithmetic. The master is 25 years of age, and has not been 12 months engaged in teaching. He preaches at various places in the neighbourhood, by which means he derives a small addition to his income. He has never been trained to teach. He speaks English incorrectly. When I entered the school I found him reading *Butler's Analogy*, and more than once during my stay he returned to the same book, leaving me to pursue the examination by myself. His pupils are disorderly.

The building is damp and badly drained and ventilated. On the occasion of my visit the place was dirty. The door of the outbuildings, which opens on the public road, was off its hinges, and lay across the doorway. The master said it was intended to adapt the premises for the purposes of a British school, and to reduce the terms to a level with the National schools in the parish.[2]

In the 1870s the Schoolroom was enlarged at the cost of £150 and improved for the sum of £50 in 1882, when £350 was spent on renovating the chapel. Later the same minister served the chapels of Mancot and Sandycroft.

In April 1913 the Lancashire and Cheshire Presbytery met at Mancot when members gave an account of the Cause at Mancot. They were the Revd. Richard Jones and the Revd. R. Norman Jones, pastor, together with J. A. Wright, John Wright and Herbert Jones. Since October 1908 the Cause had flourished and the membership increased from 27 to 44 as well as the congregation. About 12 houses had been built in the immediate neighbourhood during the past twenty years. An encouraging feature

Mancot Presbyterian Church and Sunday School
[Mancot Womens' Institute deposit, FRO D/DM/306/1]

was the number of young people attached to the church who were willing to render whatever service was required of them. The average attendance at the Sunday school was 75–80 although there was a tendency to lose them between the ages of 16 and 20. The weekly Band of Hope and Bible Class were well attended.[3]

Ambitious plans for the future were announced in December 1923 following a successful two-day bazaar.

The history of the small chapel dates back nearly a century when two or three men and women met in a cottage and laid the foundation stone of the cause of the Calvinistic Methodist Church of Wales in this straggling village. The first church seating 150 was built in 1838, and the present Sunday school with an accommodation for 120, formerly an old British school, was annexed later. Since then progress has been steady until it was given a spurt by the war with the addition of 250 houses. It is now proposed to build a new school and a minister's manse, and since the average attendance of the Sunday school alone is 160, there is certainly scope for such progressive building. The expected cost will be around £2,000, and a church member has already given a piece of freehold ground. Some £250 is already in hand, and as a result of the bazaar last week another £300 will be most probably added. The officials of the bazaar were the Revd. E. P. Hughes, minister of the circuit, which included Sandycroft as well as Mancot, Mr T. Nield, bazaar treasurer, and Mr J. A. Wright, secretary.[4]

The new Presbyterian Church at Mancot was opened in July 1929. The opening ceremony was performed by Mr E. Buckley Jones, county councillor of Rhyl, after which the President of the English Conference led the congregation in prayer. A presentation key was handed to Mr Buckley Jones, who, after a short speech, opened the doors and declared the magnificent new church open. The congregation then entered the church for a service conducted by the Revd. E. P. Hughes, a former pastor. The Revd. J. H. Howard of Liverpool preached the sermon. In the evening the church choir, which had been augmented by other choirs in the neighbourhood gave a performance of Messiah. The Revd. Robert Rees, B.A., was the pastor of the church, which was erected to the designs of Messrs J. H. Davies & Sons of Chester.[5]

Hubbard describes the design as, 'low and chapel-like in form. Much conventionalized and mechanical Perpendicular tracery.'[6] The exterior is of red brick with stone facing on the windows and central front entrance approached by steps. On the roof is a slated turret.

In 1969 the original nineteenth century buildings were demolished and replaced with a modern hall, which is widely used for church activities.[7]

The Catherine Gladstone Memorial Home

The obvious future of the Munitions Factory hospital was to retain it as a hospital for the community. Once again Henry Gladstone was sensible and generous in enabling this to take place. He brought about a meeting and decision from Flintshire County Council when the adaptation of the hospital for peacetime use was worked out at a conference held at the hospital on 19 October 1923.

Present at the meeting was P. E. Watkins, secretary of the Welsh Board of Health, the County Medical Officer, Dr D. Llewelyn-Williams, senior Medical Officer and members of the County Council. Dr Llewelyn-Williams made a strong case for the establishment of a Maternity Home in Flintshire and the adaptation of the building for this purpose. The proposals were modest: that one ward is temporarily used for an antenatal clinic, and an infant welfare centre, that the Home should commence with five beds and cots. A plan of the hospital was discussed and suggestions were made as to its use as a Maternity Home, and the minor alterations, which would be necessary. The financial question was fully discussed and correspondence from Mr Gladstone submitted.

Henry Gladstone was prepared to make a gift of £7,000 to be applied in the following manner: £2,000 for the purchase and improvement of the hospital, £1,000 for equipment, and the balance of £4,000 to be invested as an endowment fund, on condition that the gift was subject to the maternity home being called the Catherine

Left and below: The Catherine Gladstone Maternity Home
[Mancot Womens Institute deposit, FRO D/DM/306/1]

Gladstone Memorial Home, to be vested in trustees and administered under a trust approved by the Charity Commission. Representatives of Mr Gladstone were on both the trustee body and the administrative body.

Salaries were discussed. The nurse matron would receive £90 per annum and a day and night nurse £50 respectively, the cook general £40, ward housemaid £30, laundries £50, man (part time) £50. Thus making the total staffing costs £360, other running costs would bring the total cost of maintaining the hospital to £1,000. It was estimated that a sum of £80 would be received from patients who were able to contribute, for the first year, leaving the sum of £920 to be provided from interest on the endowment fund, grants from the Ministry of Health, and the balance from rates raised by the Flintshire County Council. The charge on the County Council was estimated to be about £260 per annum. Alderman Henry Gladstone who was present at the meeting submitted a memorandum setting out the terms with regard to his offer.

The formal opening of the Catherine Gladstone Memorial Home took place in August 1924 with Countess Beauchamp performing the ceremony. The *County Herald* reported:

A notable feature of the gathering was the striking speech delivered by Professor Sir Ewen Maclean, head of the Welsh National School of Medicine, Cardiff, on the unenviable position of Wales in the matter of maternity mortality.

The hospital has been transformed into a magnificent maternity home, where the equipment represents the latest word the science can utter, and is everything that money and medical knowledge can procure. There are two wards, which provide accommodation for twelve beds, but at present only six are installed. There is a charming entrance hall, where the visitor at once gets the impression of comfort, brightness and peace. There is a small isolation ward, a medical theatre, and accommodation is also provided for the establishment of an antenatal clinic, to which the donors and management attach great importance. The home is well provided with various and well equipped offices and outbuildings. The matron is Miss Eleanor Newton who is assisted by Sister Shepherd.[8]

In August 1928 The Hon. Mrs Gladstone sent out over two hundred invitations to all the mothers who had been in the home during the previous three years, and well over one hundred accepted the invitation to return to the maternity home for the celebrations, the chief event of which was a baby show.

The number of patients in 1926 was 38; 1927, 54; 1934, 72; 1935, 71. The maternity home was extended in 1938 and the number of patients in 1939 was 324. Through the foresight and generosity of Mr and Mrs Henry Gladstone, Mancot had led the way for maternity care in Flintshire twenty-five years before the introduction of the National Health Service.

The building closed as a hospital on 31 May 1992 when patients were transferred to the new community hospital.

The Church in Wales

Rector Stephen Gladstone during his long ministry in Hawarden (1872–1904), established mission churches in the township of Mancot. The first was in Little Mancot, near Scotch Row, with the dedication to St Sylvester. Sylvester was Bishop of Rome from 314 to 335 and his feast day 31 December. Stephen Gladstone usually dedicated his mission churches to the saint commemorated nearest the day of opening. A church dedicated to the Holy

Innocents, feast day 28 December, was opened at Pentre in 1889.

After the building of St Deiniol's Library and Residence in the first decade of the twentieth century, the iron building was taken to Mancot but later transferred in two halves to Shotton and Garden City by the Rector F. S. M. Bennett. When a carpentry shed in the Crossway, Mancot Royal became available at the end of the First World War, Bennett obtained the building and had it converted into a consecrated church, dedicated to St Michael and All Angels, and a church hall. The hall became the centre of community activity being used for a school, clinic and library. The parish purchased the building in 1936.

Mancot and District Residents Association (MADRA)[9]

Established in the 1950s, the president was Wing Commander Goodchild, with a committee made up of Messrs Wood, Lamb and Councillor Griffiths. Their achievements included the establishment of a library in St Michael's Church Hall, a clinic in Pentre Mission, and the building of a new school to replace St Ambrose's, opened in Leach's Lane in 1958. In 1968 a new clinic and library were opened at the junction of Mancot Lane with Ash Lane and Hawarden Way. This new centre became the meeting place of the Young Wives, the Women's Institute founded in 1948, and other organisations.

New Clinic and Library, Mancot
[Mancot Womens Institute deposit, FRO D/DM/306/1]

The Farms in Mancot, *c.*1970

Mancot Township was predominantly agricultural. When the Women's Institute compiled their history they listed the remaining farms.

Starting from the lower end of Mancot, there is Mr Wainwright's farm of Lower Ash, where the Leach family once lived and gave their name to the rest of the Lane. The outhouses of this farm were once dwellings themselves and the farm is about two hundred years old. Higher up Leach's Lane, beyond Plas Mancot and near to Scotch Row, stands Mr Brown's farm, and beyond it stands the old Bellis property where Mr Brown's brother now lives. The other two farms of Mancot stand on either side of the White Bear. Between this inn and the new library, there is the old farm, which belonged to the Racket family before it passed to the late Mr Wilcock. Mr Wilcock's father used to be a valet to the young Squire Gladstone, who was killed in World War One. The new library and clinic stand on land which once belonged to this farm. On the other side of the White Bear stands the farm, which used to be called Wright's farm, but it had its name changed to Mancot Farm when it passed into the ownership of Mr and Mrs Johnson and family. The acreage of this farm was once vast, but like all the other Mancot farmlands, much of it has now disappeared under houses and bungalows.[10]

Pentre

Hywel Wyn Owen suggests that this hamlet was probably built by the colliery owners, Rigby and Hancock, for the miners, since there is a footpath shown on all maps, except 1815, leading from Pentre to the colliery north of Big Mancot.[11]

Welsh Wesleyan Chapel

When John Taylor moved his foundry from Rhydymwyn to Sandycroft in 1862, a number of Welsh-speaking workmen came with him. They were Wesleyan Methodists by persuasion. They settled in Welsh row, and at first met to worship in each other's cottages. This was unsatisfactory, but fortunately the Sailor's Home Queensferry, welcomed them and provided a place to meet until they were able to erect their own building in Pentre. A plot of land was purchased for £20 in May 1876 at Mancot Lane End. Foundation stones were laid by Mr David Williams of Chester and Mrs Redfern of Halkyn. The total cost of the land and the building was £313. Services of dedication were held in December 1876. Members of the chapel included colliers, bricklayers, pottery workers and foundry men. Membership numbers in 1905 were adherents 100, communicants 40, Sunday school teachers and scholars 66.

Pentre Mission Room and Holy Innocents' Church

In the autumn of 1878 the reading room, common room and night school were opened and were available on Tuesdays, Thursdays and Saturdays. Here the *Daily News* and *Illustrated London News* were provided, together with books from the library. Night School classes for all above 13 years of age were held on Mondays and Fridays. Miss Rigby, the daughter of the iron-founder, used the rooms for her mothers meetings and the annual entertainment 'which she arranged year by year for the edifying and amusement of the people in this district when songs, readings, pianoforte and violin solos where presented.' The value of these gatherings it was remarked, 'should be much felt as spreading a neighbourly feeling among workers and people alike.'[12]

This building was used as a Church of England Mission Room from 1887 onwards, with Miss Rigby playing the organ. In October 1889 a fund was launched for a new iron church which was opened on 28 December, Holy Innocents Day, in the presence of W. E. Gladstone, members of his family, and the parochial clergy.

Pentre was badly drained and the lack of inadequate drainage made the low lying place insalubrious and a breeding ground for frequent epidemics. 1894 was such a year when it was reported:

> We have had a very broken year at Holy Innocent, Pentre, owing to the ravage of diphtheria; we mourn the loss of several members of the school. The Tea given on Monday last, by Mr and Mrs Sydney Taylor. Mr Taylor delighted and mystified us all by his conjuring and thought reading. Miss Rigby, Mrs Sydney Taylor, and the teachers, joined the young men's class at tea later on. The inspiring words of Mr Gladstone, who with our old friends, Mr and Mrs Drew, were also present, added largely to the success of the evening. After tea there was a dance to which the teachers and elder scholars were invited, and which we all thoroughly enjoyed.[13]

Holy Innocents' Church, Pentre, 1895
[S. E. Gladstone]

Faithful women workers supported the hamlet. The Misses Rigby spent their lives as voluntary church workers amongst the poor. When they died Miss Helen Gladstone took over and when she left to return to educational work in London a paid worker Miss Hoste took her place. Pentre at this time, in 1895, was busy and central enough to have its own Police Constable William Andrews. There were a few shops and the Mechanics Arms, which catered for cyclists and tourists.

9. Pentrobin

Pentrobin Township was divided between the ecclesiastical parishes of Buckley and Hawarden in 1874. The division in the 1881 census shows that Buckley received the greater part of the population: the total in the township 1251: Pentrobin 194. Inhabited houses in the township 249: Pentrobin 87. The areas in Pentrobin included parts of Bannel Brook, Bannel Road, Little Mountain, Dirty Mile Road, Dobshill, Hawarden Road, Chester Road, Stony Hill, St John's Lodge, Hawarden Gate, Wood Cottage. It was part of the early colliery workings owned and developed by the Glynne family in the eighteenth century and was on the Sandycroft Tram Road. The largest occupational group in the 1881 census was coal miner. There were 18 houses listed as farms: 7 were under 10 acres: 3 between 10 and 20 acres: 5 between 20 and 50 acres: the remaining 3 were John Tomlinson, Bryn Tygg, 141 acres; John Mackintosh, 113 acres, and George Moore, Hawarden Road, 98 acres. Many of the small farmers were colliers. The census does not provide any evidence for the survival of the Smelting House for lead ore which Richard Richardson, goldsmith of Chester, was allowed to build on waste land at Pentrobin Green leased from Sir John Glynne in 1751.

Pentrobin New Connexion Methodist Church, Bethesda

The Society at Pentrobin was started from the Chester Circuit of the New Connexion. The members first met in an old barn known as Newton's Barn in Burntwood in 1820. A small chapel was built by the members 'after the normal days work was over', and was ready in 1823. It stood on ground behind the present buildings and accommodated 150 people, and the old building was converted into two dwelling houses. After the chapel was built, a Sunday school was added to serve also as a vestry. In the early days members gathered for a prayer meeting on Sundays. With the expanding population it was decided to build a new chapel.[1]

The chapel was built on land on which the lease expired in 1874. It was said to be the oldest chapel in the Hawarden Circuit. A special Sunday meeting was held in April 1874 in a large brick shed lent for the occasion by Messrs Ward & Co. The preacher in the morning and evening was the Revd. J. H. Robinson of London, the editor of the *Methodist New Connexion Magazine*, and in the afternoon, the Revd. W. Jeffries, Wesleyan Minister of Buckley.

Bethesda Methodist Church, Pentrobin
[John Davies deposit, FRO N/31/23]

The attendance was good in the morning, better in the afternoon, and best at night, some 2,000 persons being present. On the following Monday a public tea meeting was held in the same place and between 400 and 500 sat down to tea. The object of the meeting was to raise a fund towards the building of a new chapel at Pentrobin and more than £65 was promised.[2]

An account of the opening of the new chapel was given in the *Chester Chronicle* in March 1878. It informed the reader that the foundation stone was laid the year before by L. Lindley, Esq., Sheriff of Nottingham and the architect and builder was Mr Williams of Buckley:

The new chapel, which has cost about £600 reflects credit on his skill and taste. The exterior of the building is plain, but very effective, and it is only at the front there is any attempt at ornament. The walls are of red brick, with recesses of white brick, with stone sills and arched tops, for the windows. The windows at the sides are of plain ground glass, while those at the front are of a little more handsome character. On each side of the principal doorway there is a two-light window, and over it is a small three-light window. The centre of each light is of ground glass, but the borders are of a very pretty stained glass, and this with the divisions and arches of white brick, produces a very pleasing effect. The doorway, which is approached by a flight of three steps, is also arched, in uniformity with the windows, and the door, which is ingrained in oak, has ornamental iron hinges. The roof is of a high pitch, and is covered with blue slates. A small stone tablet, bearing the name of the chapel, Bethesda, is let into the wall immediately above the centre window. The interior of the building is even more attractive, than the exterior. The walls are stuccoed, in imitation stonework, and the ceiling, which is corniced, is white. The roof is supported by three massive cross and transverse beams, and these are stained dark, contrasting strongly with the whiteness of the ceiling. Artificial light will be provided by six oil lamp chandeliers two of which are hung from each of the crossbeams. The entrance from the front is by a vestibule, with doors opening on either side. The seats, which are open, and will accommodate over 250, are very well arranged. The floor slopes slightly from the vestibule to the Communion area, which is covered with carpet, and enclosed by a polished pine rail, mounted on handsome iron supports, coloured and gilt. The pulpit or rostrum is a very pretty piece of workmanship. In addition to the chapel a Sunday school, which will also serve as a vestry is being built at the rear and when this is completed the old building will be abandoned. The first of the opening services was held on 3 March, when the Revd. J. Medicraft, President of the Methodist New Connexion Conference, preached morning and evening, and the Revd. D. Thomas, Congregationalist Minister of Buckley, in the afternoon. At the evening service between 200 and 300 persons were unable to gain admission.[3]

When the centenary was celebrated in 1920 it was reported that the Church had been renovated and a pipe organ installed which came from the United Church, Pepper Street, Chester.

Penymynydd, Mount Tabor Chapel

The congregation, which built Mount Tabor Chapel in 1824, first met in the stone cottages close by. The chapel was built by local labour that carted stone quarried nearby. It was a simple plain building sparsely furnished and warmed by a coal and log burning stove in the centre of the floor. It was decided to rebuild the church towards the end of 1913, and with the advent of the United Methodist Church, Penymynydd, became part of the new Buckley and Mold circuit. During the period 1927–9 the interior of the church was modernised and central heating and electric light introduced. The church was active, and meetings were held on weekdays such as Bible Classes, Men's Own and Women's Own meetings. A male voice party was formed from the Men's Own meeting with Joseph Shone, choirmaster, and Albert Kirkham organist. A presentation was made to them on 6 March 1955. One hundred and fiftieth anniversary celebrations were held from 19–26 May 1974.[4]

The church was closed for worship in September 1994, and the congregation joined in the local ecumenical project at Trinity Chapel, Penyffordd. The site and buildings were sold during 1996 and the buildings demolished in May 1997. A set of photographs and a measured site plan were deposited with the property committee of the Methodist Church in Manchester.[5]

The Church of St John the Baptist, Penmynydd[6]

This was the third district church built in the parish of Hawarden within twenty years. It is situated between the two earlier ones erected at Buckley and Broughton on Glynne land at Penymynydd. Although the cost of £3,000 is said to have been borne by Sir Stephen Glynne, Bart., it was really a family gift which is said to have been inspired by his mother, Lady Mary Glynne. The township of Pentrobin was experiencing great industrial activity in the growth of collieries, brickworks and increase of population, and the Glynne family gave to its tenants a church, parsonage and school, and more importantly their continuing support.

The church was consecrated on 22 July 1843; the sermon being preached by Dr W. F. Hook, vicar of Leeds, who was highly regarded as a parish priest and trainer of clergy. The architect was John Buckler, who must have appealed to Sir Stephen Glynne because of his assiduous devotion to carefully recording churches. By the end of his life he is said to have made over 13,000 sketches, mainly of topographical subjects.

Built in the Early English style of local grey stone, with yellow sandstone dressings, St John's is slightly raised up silhouetted against the sky, and a little detached, looking down on the traffic roundabout below. Externally

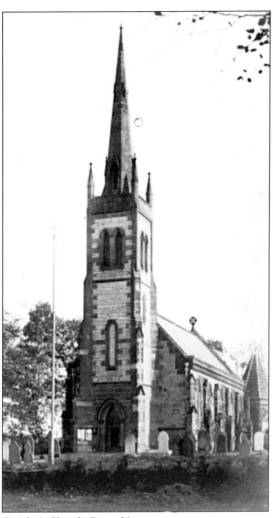

St John's Church, Pentrobin
[FRO 28/Q/5]

the church appears narrow. This is emphasised by the tower, set off by pinnacles and surmounted by a steeple, which from a distance looks like a finger pointing to the heavens. The whole length of the walls has an effective corbel table. The internal plan is simple, no aisles, a short chancel with a south vestry and a nave with a west gallery. The main entrance to the church is through the base of the western tower. The chancel is divided from the nave by gates and a richly coloured screen. The roof principals are supported by projecting corbels with angels. On the south side of the chancel is a *sedile* (a seat for the priest), a *piscina* (a stone basin for washing the communion vessels) and an entrance to the vestry, through which access is made to the stone circular pulpit. At the west end is a stone arcading which supports the gallery, the pointed arches having the arms of the Glynnes and others on the spandrels. Underneath the south side of the gallery is a small Baptistery, the font being transitional Norman surmounted by a canopy. The church is lighted with lancet windows.

St. John's church is unlike any other in the benefice because of the enrichment made by the first priest in charge, the Revd. J. E. Troughton (1843–64). Troughton gloried in the faith and expressed its revelation through the scriptures in the interior decoration of the church. W. E. Gladstone was impressed by his work and caused a memorial tablet to be placed in the church in 1898, with the inscription. 'He used his rare gifts of genius and taste in himself adorning all the interior of this church by colouring, frescoes sculpture and window staining. With much labour, but no detriment to the faithful discharge of his Parish duties.'

The spaces on the walls between the windows and over the chancel arch and east window are filled with large paintings in oil some of them copies of pictures by a German artist Friedrich Overbeck (1789–1869). The pictures are surrounded with painted framework and canopies and others with diaper pattern decoration. Troughton was indebted to his friend R. P Pullan, an architect and archaeologist, who worked in Italy and Greece, for much advice.

The overall theme is the events of our redemption from the Fall to the Day of Judgment. Over the west gallery is the Fall, Our Lord's Baptism is over the east window and the Day of Judgment on the chancel arch. On the walls the Annunciation, the Nativity, the Adoration of the Shepherds and the Wise Men, the Presentation in the Temple, the first Miracle at Cana, Healing the sick, Raising the Dead and the triumphal entry into Jerusalem.

Troughton carved the woodwork of the screen on which is pictures of the twelve apostles each with the instrument of his martyrdom. The angels in the pulpit panels bear scrolls upon which are inscribed the beatitudes. The altar is of fine sandstone 6ft. 2in in length, and on its front is our Lord in Majesty and the four evangelists. Round about the altar is a reredos in gold, on red, black and blue ground; and on shields are painted the instruments of our Lord's suffering. The walls are painted stone colour. Four angels are drawn on them representing, invocation, beseeching, sorrow, adoration. On the east wall are two figures, one veiled, and holding a broken reed representing the Law, the other unveiled, and with the Cross, representing the Gospel. Two angels look down from the roof, one bearing a crown and the other a palm. The roof principals are supported by projecting corbels with angels, which Troughton decorated with rich colouring. The colouring of the chancel roof was improved in a restoration by Robert Heaton, 1979–80, following fire damage.

Troughton was responsible for the stained glass in all the lancet windows, except those at the east and west ends. The windows have each a central medallion in illustration of the Passion, Cross and Resurrection; and are a memorial to Lavinia, (d. 1852), wife of Henry Glynne, rector of the parish. At the extreme west on the north side is the Agony in the Garden; and going east are the Betrayal, Pilate washing his hands, the Scourging, the

Crowning with thorns, and crossing to the pulpit window, we have the bearing of the Cross, until after further windows we come to the Resurrection, at the Baptistery. In 1910 new stained glass was inserted into the east window by Powell and Co., the subject, The Virgin and Child, placed there in memory of Canon Harry Drew, Rector of Hawarden.

Some of the silver is rare and unusual. There is a silver gilt paten, unmarked, which probably belongs to the sixteenth century, and a gilt communion cup with an inscription which is dated 1637.[7] The other silver is modern. In 1908 a church clock was presented by W. E. Gladstone's eldest daughter Agnes, Mrs Wickham, the wife of the Dean of Lincoln. A custom, which survived until the beginning of the twentieth century, was the division of the sexes at the time of Service, the women sitting on the south side of the nave and the men on the north. The Lychgate was given as a memorial to Thomas Henry Ashcroft and was placed there in 1911.

The former Parsonage, now in private hands, was built in 1846, at a cost of £1,500.

St. John's School

The Report given by Commissioners Inquiring into the State of Education in Wales in 1847 is one of their most complimentary and does great credit to the school at Penymynydd established in 1844.

St John's School — a school for boys and girls, taught together, by a master, in a school built for the purpose. Number of boys, 58; of girls, 51; number employed as monitors, 4. Subjects taught — reading, writing, arithmetic, English grammar and etymology, geography, history, and music, the Scriptures, and the Church Catechism. Fees, 1d. per week. Master's salary, £70., with a house and garden.

Forty-eight of the scholars have attended the school for more than two years, and 33 are above ten years of age.

I examined this school on the 2nd of March, when 90 children were present. I found 24 able to read with ease, and 18 ignorant of the alphabet. Out of 22 copies shown, only one was well written. 43 were learning to write upon slates, 7 of whom wrote well. There were 27 learning arithmetic, 12 of whom understood compound rules, and 2 excelled in Proportion. I found but little knowledge of Geography, and nothing of etymology or English history. Out of 71 examined in the Church Catechism, 31 repeated it well; and among 25 who could answer Scripture questions, 3 possessed a competent knowledge of the subject.

The children were well behaved and very clean. There are lavatories connected with the school. The attendance is very regular. The master's wife teaches the girl to sew.

The master was formerly employed in husbandry. He is 31 years of age, and was trained at Chester for 12 months, in 1844. His treatment of the children is good, and is considered by the minister to be the main cause which has restored the school from the state of decline to which a previous master had reduced it. The children would consider it a punishment to be kept out of the school, to which it is stated that nearly every teachable child in the district belongs. He employs monitors only for the mechanical part of teaching, and changes them every week. The attendance is very regular. 19 scholars were absent during my visit, owing to the prevalence of measles in the neighbourhood. A medical man regularly visits the school, and every other church school in the parish of Hawarden, and the children receive gratuitous medical aid.

The schoolroom is very healthily situated, and altogether a very good one — John James, Assistant.

10. The Making of the River Settlements

One of the fascinating things about the history of the parish of Hawarden is the changing settlement pattern from the medieval period through to modern times. Particularly interesting is the way the northern boundary of the parish was shaped by the action of man and nature on the course of the river Dee. Nature, time and tide, affected the river over the centuries, giving the course of the river ample opportunity to shift its sand at will in the broad tidal estuary. When man intervened, it was an attempt to correct and discipline the river by setting its limits within man-made embankments. It was the creation of this new course of the Dee, which brought into existence the new river settlements of Shotton, Queensferry, Sandycroft, Saltney and Sealand.

Sand was the chief enemy. It was ever shifting, it choked the river, and made the depth of water unreliable for safe navigation to the ancient city of Chester: there was no safe channel for the smooth passage of vessels in order that trade would flourish. In 1377 there was a reference to the 'ruinous state of the city and of the haven', a complaint made with more vigour in 1449, 'the navigation had been so much impeded by sands from the frequent changing of the channel, that it occasioned the total ruin of the haven.' Successive generations of the city fathers continued to voice their alarm, but with little agreement on the acceptance of an adequate solution. In the sixteenth century there was an attempt to construct a safe new haven for larger vessels at Neston, but this failed through the lack of financial provision. In the last decades of the seventeenth century, a number of schemes were put forward to improve the navigation: by Andrew Barry in 1687, Evan Jones in 1693 and Francis Gell in 1698. All of them, for one reason or another, were unacceptable to the Mayor and Corporation of the City of Chester. In 1700 an Act of Parliament was passed to 'enable the Mayor and citizens of Chester to recover and preserve the navigation of the river Dee.' But the work, which was done by means of the Act, was expensive and ineffective, and when in 1720 flooding destroyed a newly built wharf and warehouses, the scheme was abandoned. However, the seriousness of the situation was revealed in 1731 by a Parliamentary enquiry, which found that for a distance of ten miles below Chester, 'the river bed was being still further filled up with sand, so that even with the aid of the tide, it was extremely difficult to reach the city from the sea.' To overcome this unsatisfactory situation it was decided to adapt a plan, which had been proposed over fifty years before in 1679 by Andrew Yarranton.

Yarranton proposed making the river 'to Chester Navigable by a New Cut', by which, 'there would be Three Thousand Acres of land gained out of the Sea, and made rich land, besides, the Coles from Aston will be brought to the City of Chester by water, which now are brought by land, and all Goods and other things carried and recarried from England to Ireland, and from Ireland into England with much less charge than now it is.' The New Cut, Yarranton proposed, was to run in a straight line from Alderman Wright's House, Chester, as far as Flint Castle. He further recommended:

> There must also be a cut drawn along the Welch shore, and so from Aston Pits, and dropt into the Main Trench, whereby the waste water, that comes from the Hills and Mountains will be voided, and the Coles that are now carried by Land to Chester will then be carried by water, and at least 1000 *l per Ann*. Saved in Carriage; This Trench must be very large, that two Ships may Sail one by the other and the Sea Banks must be made very Firm and Strong, not upright, but very much sloaping. There must also be made five very strong Locks or Sluces of Stone, which is there very necessary, at the end of the Trench. This will be done for £15,000.[1]

In 1733 an Act of Parliament 'to recover and preserve the Navigation of the River', authorised Nathaniel Kinderley, the engineer and principal undertaker, to proceed with the work. Whereas Yarranton had proposed two channels, Kinderley proceeded to make one, and whereas Yarranton's scheme sought to prevent silting, Kinderley's ignored it. But whatever the faults of Kinderley's scheme, it was to prove immensely beneficial to the parish of Hawarden.

The old course of the river was along the Cheshire side of the estuary, and the decision of Kinderley to set the New Cut along the Flintshire side gave rise within the course of a century to the growth of new settlements. It made communications between collieries, brickworks and the river channel, shorter, cheaper, and more convenient. The New Cut marked the future site of bridging points across the river at Shotton and Queensferry. Above all it was to provide thousands of acres of rich farming land to the north and south of the new channel.

By the 1733 Act the city of Chester relinquished all its rights to the estuary; Kinderley and Company received all the lands from Chester to the sea, and the levying of tolls on shipping tonnage. Such parts of the estuary as were grassed over were reserved to the Lords of the Manors. To finance the making of the New Cut, Kinderley issued 400 shares of £100. The first sod of this gigantic work was cut in April 1733. The work took four years, and the water from the old river channel was directed into the New Cut on 3 April 1737. The work took four years to construct the 14,000 yards of the new channel. It was tackled by means of 'ploughs and eroders', the surplus water being pumped out by means of portable windmills. George Lloyd, with his own experience as an engineer, described the digging out of the New Cut:

> Through the marsh, a trench, eighty feet wide by eight feet deep was excavated and the spoil material was thrown up to form the right or north main bank of the channel. The river face of this bank was pitched with stone to above high water level and at the Golftyn end, which was open on both sides to high waves from the estuary; both sides of the bank were faced with stone.[2]

George Lloyd estimated that the approximate work of excavation was one million cubic yards, with the removal of 1.4 million tons. The building of the south embankment was not completed until 1780. Kinderley promised to maintain a depth of sixteen feet of water, on a moderate spring tide, from the sea to Chester. This 'standard' depth, as it was known, wasn't realised, and the standard was reduced to fifteen feet of water in 1743. The work on the New Cut was completed by 25 March 1740. By an Act of Parliament in the same year, the undertakers were incorporated as, 'The Company of Proprietors of the Undertaking for Recovering and Preserving the Navigation of the River Dee.' They were known as the River Dee Company and began their work with a capital of £52,000.

The River Dee Company's jurisdiction was on the north side of the New Cut. They were the owners of the land within the manor and parish of Hawarden, which stretched as far as the Wirral side to the boundary of Wales and England. By Act of Parliament in 1743, the company became responsible for providing and maintaining two ferries, the Higher at Saltney Ferry, and the Lower at King's Ferry, 'in case the channel shall become so deep as that at low water, when the tide of sea is out, and no flood of fresh water is in the river, the same shall not be fordable for passengers on horseback or for carts or carriages.'

The River Dee Company were anxious to exploit, either by sale or lease, land they were to reclaim, but before they could legally do this, it was necessary for them to obtain the extinction of any claims to rights over the land by the Lord of the Manor, Sir John Glynne, Bart. and other freeholders. Sir John Glynne was equally determined to exploit what rights remained to him, chief of which related to income from tithes due to the rector of Hawarden. He therefore caused to be entered in the court rolls of the Manor of Hawarden, a record of the boundaries of the Lordship, ' in particular to so much as lies on the North side of the New River or Cut on Saltney Marsh commonly called the Navigation and having justly measured the Land as well as that part thereof which is now Greensward commonly called Salt Marsh and that other part known by the name of White Sands.' Glynne was anxious to determine the ancient course of the river Dee, as the boundary between the County Palatine of Chester, which coincided with those of the Manor and Parish of Hawarden in Flintshire.

The outcome was a formal agreement between Sir John Glynne, Bart., Lord of the Manor and several freeholders and occupiers of land, and the River Dee Company, by Act of Parliament in 1753. Basically what this did was to give the River Dee Company the right to reclaim and enclose the land on the north side of the New River channel, through the surrender of the rights of common by Sir John Glynne and his associates to the company. In return the River Dee Company agreed to pay Sir John Glynne and fellow trustees the sum of two hundred pounds a year to be 'applied to some public uses for the benefit of the Lord and Freeholders of the Manor of Hawarden.' The act empowered Sir John Glynne and his trustees to make a new cop or bank on the south, Saltney, side of the river, with one or more sluices, for the water to be let off into the river, and make another cut or channel, 'at some little distance from the present bank in a parallel line.' In order to carry out this work the River Dee Company promised to pay the Hawarden Embankment Trust, (as they became known in

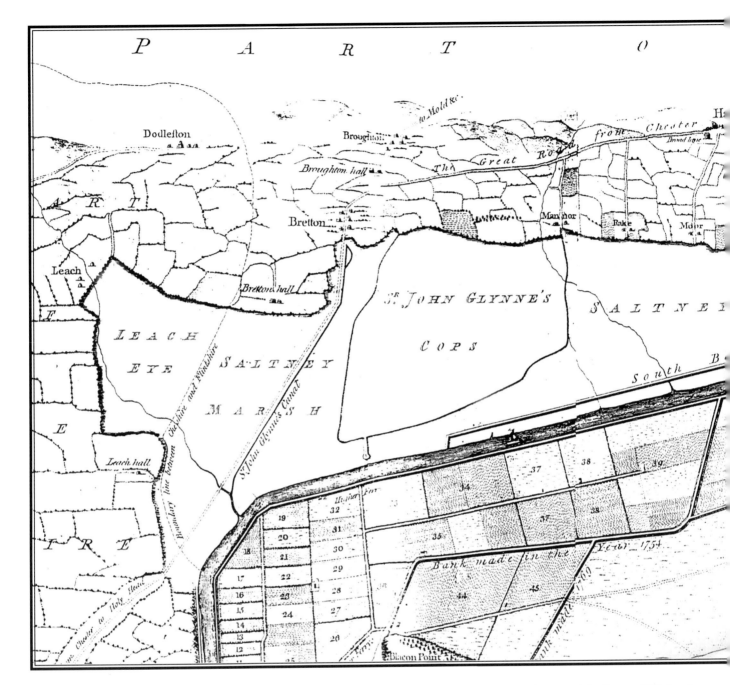

Part of 'A Plan of the Lands & Premises belonging to the River Dee Company as lye between the City of Chester and the Towns of Flint and Park Gate shewing particularly the several Imbankments and Improvements already made. Taken in the Years 1770 & 1771 by Thos Boydell' [FRO D/DM/819/1]

Of particular interest on this plan are:
1. the 'Great Road from Chester to Holy Head' following a straight route across Saltney Marsh, the same route as that followed by the A5104 and B5125 today.
2. the way in which the former coastline settlements of Bretton, Manor, Rake, Moor, Mancot, Aston and Weppra have 'moved' inland after the canalisation of the river Dee and the drainage of the marshes.
3. the route of 'Sr John Glynne's Canal' through Saltney March.

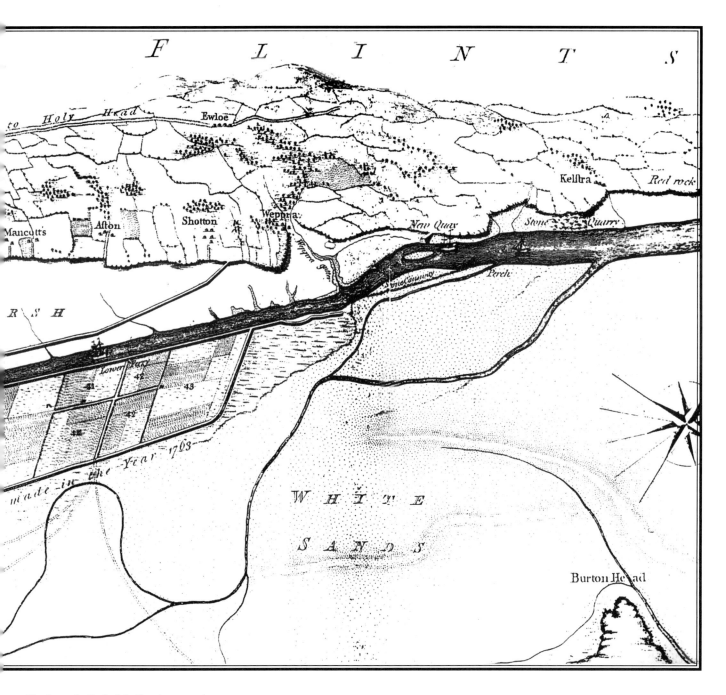

The legend attached to the plan records:
  'By the Bank made in 1754, laid out and Lett in Lotts from No 1 to No 30 inclusive contains 1411A. 3R 0P.
  By the Bank made in 1763, Lett in Lotts No 40, 41, 42 and 43 contains 664A 1R 38P
  In the third Embankment being laid in Lotts No 44 and 45 contains 348A 0R 31P

1804), the sum of six hundred pounds, and also the yearly sum of fifty pounds for the maintenance of the new bank. In consideration the River Dee Company would be discharged from paying or making good any damage that might happen to the common salt marshes within the manor and parish of Hawarden.

The River Dee Company was now free to reclaim the land on the north side of the New Cut, which was done, systematically between 1754 and 1916, by means of building embankments. Cohen gives the following figures for reclamation on the north side.[3]

Date	Embankment length (yards)	Area reclaimed (acres)
1754	4,775	1,661
1763	4,445	664.5
1769	1,495	348
1790	3,124	964.5
1826	1,980	400
1833	1,800	158
1857	2,310	514
1887–90	5,060	1,195
1869–1916	3,750	1,250
Totals	42,739	7,155

This is seen in George Lloyd's map (below).

Saltney Marsh

The area which concerns us here is that part of Saltney Marsh which was within the boundaries of the parish of Hawarden. It extended on the north to the south bank of the New Cut, on the east to the boundary between England and Wales at Saltney and on the west to Wepre Brook. The southern boundary gives an indication of the

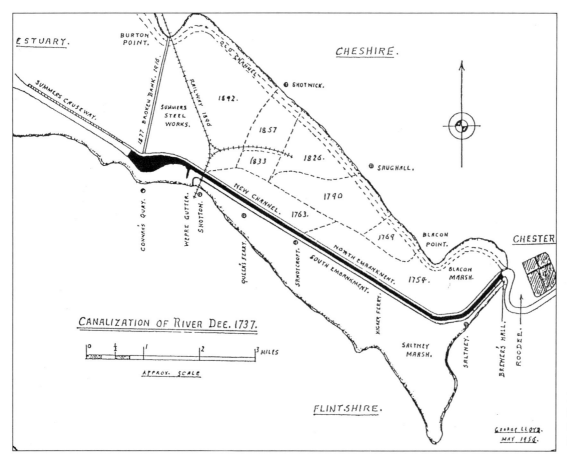

The canalization of the river Dee. Diagram by George Lloyd [FHS Vol. 23]

worth of reclamation to the Lords of the Manor, the rector of Hawarden, and the freeholders of the parish. This area is shown on the survey, which Thomas Boydell made for the River Dee Company, 1770–1. The survey in the form of a map shows that Hawarden parish is crossed from east to west along the ridge by the 'Great Road' from Chester to Holyhead, which rises from the marsh on the outskirts of Chester and passes through Bretton, Broughton, and Broad Lane, to the small market town of Hawarden. Another line of settlements is strung out in a line below, northwards, on the edge of the marsh, these are connected by minor roads. ' Moor Lane from Hawarden to the river at Moor Mark, Mancot Lane from Hawarden through Mancot to Mancot Mark, and the road further west leading to the river at Latchcroft.'[4] Pennant defines 'The Mark' as a place 'where the vessels lie to receive or discharge their lading.'[5]

There is an indication of work completed as a result of the agreement between the River Dee Company and Sir John Glynne and his associates in 1753. Boydell indicates on the north side of the New Cut land reclamations from Chester to opposite the Weppra brook. On the north side Chester is connected by road to the Higher and Lower Ferries, but with no roads from the southern bank. Four features stand out on the south side: Sir John Glynne's Cops, a line to the south of the bank of the New Cut, Sir John Glynne's Canal and the Saltney Marsh.

Sir John Glynne's Cops

The previous Lords of the Manor of Hawarden, the Stanleys, had reclaimed about 600 acres of land as early as 1472, in Bretton, Manor, Rake, and Saltney. Another area enclosed by them, and in existence by 1642 in Bretton and Saltney was known as Harden Copp. These areas of reclaimed land were on the edge of the marsh. The method of reclamation was to raise up a projecting mound or embankment surrounding the area taken from the marsh. In 1730 Sir John Glynne enclosed about 620 acres of land, which is shown by Boydell as the Cops. 'A substantial bank was erected around the area with a series of drains cut, within, and the interior divided into large fields, shown on a map of 1733, with field names including Big Cops, Lesser Cops, Long Cops etc.'[6]

The South Bank

Boydell shows the south bank running parallel to the south bank of the New Cut between Shotton Lane and the Upper Ferry, a length of four and a half miles. It is intersected by gutters or sluices, which drained into the Dee. The plan of the south bank is dated 25 March 1752 and its cost is given as £553 14s. 6d.[7] This was the first embankment to protect the vulnerable south bank of the New Cut and restrictions were enforced to prevent damage by trespass by horses and cattle along the new cop, and its use as a footpath or crossing place except at the new ferries.[8]

Sir John Glynne's Canal

The Glynnes controlled the way across Saltney Marsh by making and maintaining at their own expense a narrow pavement for which they were remunerated by a toll taken at the tollhouse in Bretton. Upon the creation of a turnpike road in 1757, the Commissioners compounded with them for this toll, which was purchased by them about 1800.

The Glynnes also made a canal which is marked on Boydell's map as immediately west of and alongside the Great Road from Bretton to the shoulder of the first bend of the New Cut between the Higher Ferry and Brewer's Hall. The canal was cut on behalf of Sir John Glynne in 1768 to ease the burden of transporting his coal across the Marsh on its way to Chester. The coal was brought from mines in Buckley and Ewloe in carts and in panniers on the backs of droves of donkeys. It was then loaded on punts constructed for this purpose, unloaded at the end of the canal, and reloaded once more on to punts on the river, to begin its short journey to Chester. This operation was tedious and expensive, and the coal was broken with too much handling. Mr George Prescott joined Sir John Glynne in this enterprise. It was adjudged to be a failure and the canal was filled up.

The Enclosure of Saltney Marsh

The purpose of enclosure was to divide and fence off areas of land, which were suitable either for growing crops or grazing cattle. It was argued that the 'fencing off' would make for better crops and the more selective breeding of cattle. As for the enclosure of marshland this would enable land to be properly drained, sown and brought under cultivation, with the rich alluvial deposits yielding bumper crops. Landowners, who were prepared to see these complex measures through Parliament and see to their implementation by the growing ranks of

Sir John Glynne's Enclosed Marsh (note the drainage ditch and, on the right, the boundary fence of Broughton Airfield) [CPAT PRN 37743]

commissioners and surveyors, conducted the movement for enclosure. The people who suffered most by enclosure were the poor who lost the right to graze their cattle on land, which was previously held in common. The piecemeal work of the enclosure of the Saltney Marsh which had begun in the fifteenth century and accelerated in the eighteenth century, was completed between the year 1778, when Parliament passed an 'Act for Dividing, Inclosing and Preserving a Certain Common, waste ground or marsh, called Saltney Marsh, within the Manor and Parish of Hawarden', and the granting of the Award made by the Commissioners on 21 February 1781. This enclosure act was different in the respect that one of its purposes was the erection of embankments and sluices on the south side of the New Cut, thus completing the work begun in 1733.

For centuries the commons on both the Flintshire and Lache side of the border had been grazed. In the thirteenth century, Robert de Montalt had granted the monks of Basingwerk Abbey pasturage on Saltney Marsh. In a deposition made by Edward Roberts of the city of Chester in 1770s he said 'that he remembered the Hawarden people ride the Boundaries of Hawarden on Saltney Marsh at Whitsuntide in every year, and amongst the rest, often put this examinants cattle and put them in the Pinfold at Hawarden, but upon application they were immediately delivered up without any satisfaction or imputation of trespass. He generally grounded his sheep upon the land which lyes on the other side of Saltney Bridge, which lyes within the County of Flint because that part was always thought to be the best pasture.'[9] By the Act of 1778 this unimpeded grazing was abolished. The chief landowners applied for the Act: Sir Stephen Glynne, Bart. the Lord of the Manor; the rector of Hawarden, as owner of the glebe land; the Earl of Plymouth; Ann Whitley, spinster, and others, proprietors of lands and tenements entitled to rights of common.

Commissioners were appointed to implement the Act by providing an exact survey, plans and maps of the land to be enclosed, public and private roads to be made, and rights to be protected. Some money towards the cost of enclosure, two thousand pounds, was obtained by mortgaging the £200 a year received from the River Dee Company, which was used to pay annuities. Further advantage was received when the newly enclosed land became the legally designated township of Saltney placed by the Act on equal terms with other townships in the parish of Hawarden and with the authority of the vestry to raise a rate for various purposes. The Commissioners were Samuel Wyatt, Burton, Staffs; Edward Stelfox, Dunham Massey, Cheshire; and John Earl, Frodsham, Chester. They were instructed by the Act that 'no allotment was to be made in respect of the Copps in the tenure of Sir Richard Glynne, and containing more or less 620 acres of land, 'and that the 'Rail or Frame Road, of George Hope, extending from Great Mancott Lane and across Saltney Common, to Mancot Mark, adjoining the new channel of the Dee shall remain free and open for the purposes of carrying coals and other minerals.'

The expenses involved in the enclosure of Saltney Marsh were relatively high because of the extra work involved in strengthening the south bank of the New Cut by building embankments and making sluices. The account of the Treasurer, James Boydell, for 22 September 1781 shows a credit balance upon the assessment of the proprietors of £720 2s 7d. The total cost of the work was £10,195 19s.

The major costs were the embankments. The lower bank undertaken by Mr Heald, £1760 18s 8d for work done, 30 June 1779 and 13 January 1781. The bank between the two ferries undertaken by Mr Edson £897 2s 6d. The sluice at Stoop Bridge. Sept. 30 1780 and Sept. 20 1781 £354 7s. 3d., which included payments for bricks, timber, stone, oak, slabs and repairing damage. Drainage payments between 18 March 1780 and 20 September 1781 £245 2s. 9d. Roads. The canal to Higher Ferry, Road from Mancot Rail road to the Manor, from the Manor to Upper Ferry, Moor Lane to the main road. Sanding, levelling, rounding. Total £817 16s. John Bayley & Co. in full for their several contracts for making sundry roads £307 17s. 6d.

The legal bills in this border area were very high. The total cost was £2,263; the highest were those of Sir Stephen Glynne, who had to defend 26 actions.

The money to fund the works was raised from the sale of annuities £3,000. Two assessments raised upon several proprietors £7,149 14s. 6d. Surplus land in Sir S. R. Glynnes £39 14s. 6d.

The award made on 21 February 1781 stated that the Commissioners had surveyed the whole work of the commons and erected the embankments and sluices and that there were 2050 acres 3 roods 26 perches of commons to be divided exclusive of the public roads and the new embankment. The owners of those awarded allotments were to maintain good and sufficient fences. The proprietor of Sir John Glynnes Canal 'was to have free liberty with Horses, Carts and Carriages, or otherwise to convey their coal or other lading.'

The land appropriated for roads and ways was 48 acres. Public highways were to be 40 feet wide and private roads, 20 feet wide. The list of roads is included to show how the opportunity was taken to establish good roads across the newly drained area, which linked the riverbank with the rest of the parish at a time when coal and brick were being exploited. It is these public and major roads, which remain the major lines of communication today. Amongst the roads designated in the award were:

Public Roads, 40 feet wide.
   Wepre Road: to run in an easterly direction to Lower Ferry and adjoin the Turnpike road leading from
      Hawarden to Chester.
   Shotton Road: beginning at and leading from Shotton Lane end.
   Lower Ferry Road: beginning and leading from Aston Lane in a straight direction to Wepra Road.
   Great Mancot Public Road: leading from out of Great Mancot Lane to Wepra Road in the same direction as
      the frame road of George Hope, Esq.
   Newtown Road, Moor Road, Rake Road.
   Manor Public Road: beginning at and leading from Manor Lane across the N. W. side of the same copp to
      Wepra Road.
   Private Roads 20 feet wide.
   Great Mancott, Little Mancot, Sandycroft Road, Reads Road, Manor Private Road, Bretton Lake Road,
      Hope's Place Road, Bretton Hall Road.

The main beneficiaries of the Commissioners Award were Sir Stephen Richard Glynne, 900 acres; Anne Whitley (became Dundas property in the nineteenth century) 194 acres; Lord Grosvenor 91 acres; and Charles Mainwaring 134 acres.

The enclosure award created a stable and more ordered landscape along the New Cut in the township it created in Saltney. A reasonable depth of water, width of river and cheap land encouraged the setting up of trading facilities, manufactories, and shipbuilding with an outlet for a flourishing hinterland of coalmines and brickworks easily accessible along the new tramways and railroads.

Enclosure was enacted to promote agriculture with its square fields and straight fences. The success of this was soon apparent on both sides of the New Cut. Walter Davies writing in 1810 spoke of the success of enclosure on the north bank of the Dee:

'3,100 acres are now covered, even the inner sides of the embankments with good crops of corn, of Lucerne, and of other grasses: and the whole redeemed waste is incorporated into a township, bearing the very appropriate name of Sealand.'[10]

George Kay noticed the success of the Saltney enclosure in 1792.

The gentlemen of this county have not been entirely remiss in improving wastelands. Two thousand acres were gained from the Dee, by embankment, about 12 years ago the soil is for the most part clay, and is now rented at 20s per acre. Two thousand four hundred more have been recently embanked in the vicinity of Chester, the soil whereof is a pure sand, on which a very great variety of artificial grasses have been sown, but the white clover prevails, and already produces good pasture, appearing as if it would soon equal the best in the country. To make it capable of producing good crops of corn would require a long series of years of cultivation, besides a great command of dung, which in a short time will make the most sterile land productive, by a total alteration of soil.[11]

The ground was prepared for the making of the river settlements and the creation of industrial communities.

11. Queensferry

Queensferry has been the place name used since the accession of Queen Victoria in 1837.[1] An Act of Parliament in 1743 created two toll-free passages across the canalised Dee, the new cut, to compensate for the loss of low water fords. The Lower Ferry here at Queensferry, and the Higher Ferry, above Saltney. For a period in the 1760s and 70s it may have been known as Connah's ferry. In honour of George IV's accession in 1820 it was given the name of King's Ferry, which was changed to Queensferry in 1837, when Victoria came to the throne, although it took some time for people to realise the change. Queen Victoria did not make a personal visit but merely passed through by train. W. E. Gladstone recorded in his Diary '… came on to Queen's Ferry where I waited with Catherine and saw the Queen's blinds as she flew by'; she had been visiting the Britannia Bridge at Anglesey and was returning to Windsor by train.[2]

Nevertheless, by 1844, *Slater's Trade Directory* announced that King's Ferry had been

The King's Ferry on the river Dee. 19th century watercolour
[FRO PR/F/111]

… brought into prominent notice from the number of travellers now crossing the Dee by this route; besides which, in the summer months it is resorted to by many respectable visitors, for whose accommodation there is an excellent inn — this is the 'Hawarden Castle Hotel', an admirably arrange establishment, containing every convenience and comfort, whether for families or the commercial visitant. Hot and cold seawater baths are provided on the premises; and post-horses, with vehicles of various descriptions are constantly at hand.

The population of the township of Saltney of which 'King's Ferry was an integral part' had risen from 172 inhabitants in 1831 to nearly 600 in 1841. This population was scattered along the river from Shotton to modern Saltney in Wales. A miniature spa failed to develop at Queensferry because of the coming of the Chester–Holyhead railway in 1848.

James Boydell, the 'Father' of Queensferry

James Boydell, Jnr, (1803–60), the agent of Sir Stephen Glynne, lived at Dee Cottage, later Queensferry Hall, until about 1841. Living next door to the ferry, he was well aware of the dangers and difficulties experienced by travellers, and that the crossing was 'impassable for carts and carriages at times, during the rapid flowing and ebbing of the high tides, and those periods when the river is very much swollen by heavy land floods.'[3] This was the problem Boydell was asked to solve by the local landowners, and he set himself the task of finding a practical way in which the ferry boat could cross the river safely and directly at all times and on every stage of the tide.

His solution was simple and effective, described by the newspaper, as 'an application of the principle of 'the endless chain', invented by Mr James Boydell, junr.' Its success revolutionised the Lower Ferry and improved communications between Liverpool and north Wales so much so, as to delay the building of a road bridge here for over sixty years. The experiment was described in great detail in the *Chester Chronicle*, 15 May 1835:

On one side of the river, the Cheshire side, a large pulley is firmly fixed, near the bank, in the bed of the river, and on this revolve a strong iron chain, the other extremities of which are attached to a whimsey, on the Flintshire side, similar to those used at the mouth of coal pits, and worked by one horse. To one side of this chain the ferry boat, a flat, was used in this experiment, is moored by a chain, called the bridle; and as the main chain at the bottom of the river travels round the block, when the whimsey is put in motion, the boat travels with it from side to side, as may be required — the bridle, or mooring chain being placed over one bow or other of the boat' so that her head shall form an angle of 45 degrees or thereabouts, with the chain in crossing, in order to give her the benefit of the current, whichever way it may be setting — and thus dismiss the power necessary to wind her from side to side. The main chain passes under rollers at low water mark, so that throughout the whole breadth of the navigation, about 65 yards, the chain is at or very nearly at the bottom of the river, and thus can offer no impediment to the passing or repassing of vessels while the boat is in transit. The day was very favourable for a fair experiment; there was a very high tide, twenty feet by the Liverpool tide table, and a breeze of W.N.W, which occasioned a strong current as the tide was setting in. As at this time, the company's large ferry boat, upon the ordinary construction could not cross the river, but the flat, with which this experiment was made, did so repeatedly with the utmost facility, two vessels and a steam boat having passed close under the bows, of course without any inconvenience, during the experiments. Mr Boydell also exhibited an ingeniously contrived working model of the apparatus, with an improved slip or landing place on the Flintshire side. The boat of this working mode also was of an improved construction affording increased facility of shipping and unshipping carriages, coaches, *etc*. We are in candour compelled to admit that this experiment was completely successful.

Boydell's invention received the praise of the Mayor and Corporation of Liverpool and the appreciation of the Flintshire neighbourhood, when in September 1836, he was given a piece of plate worth a hundred guineas ' in

The ferry boat, c.1900
[FRO 51/4]

testimony of the acknowledged superiority of his plan for effecting a certain safe, and speedy passage at all times over the river Dee, at the King's Ferry in the county of Flint.'[4]

James Boydell built ships on the riverbank near Dee Cottage.

Ships built at Queensferry, 1836–1851

1836	Sloop *Rossett* 55 tons. The suitability of the Rossett in bad weather was questioned
1836	Schooner *Honoratus* 70 tons. Lost at Bull Bay Point near Amlwch, October 1843
1837	Schooner *Anna Maria* 77 tons
1839	Schooner *Skimmer* 150 tons owner James Boydell merchant 64 shares
1839	Schooner *Skimmer* 76 tons propelled by steam, converted to sail, 1846, James Boydell 43 share, Sir Stephen Glynne 6, W. E. Gladstone 1, William Lyttelton 1
1840	Flat *Collier* 49 tons. Owned by Rigby and Hancock
1840	Flat *Oak* 39 tons co-partners 'Oak farm ironworks'

Ships built by John Powell timber merchant Queen's Ferry

1842	Sloop *James* 64 tons owner John Powell
1848	Schooner *Margaret* 79 tons owner John Powell
1851	Schooner *Ann and Mary* owners' the spinster daughters of John Powell[5]

Boydell moved to Stourbridge in 1840 to manage the industrial enterprise of Sir Stephen Glynne on the Oak Farm estate. Here he showed prodigious energy. 'He was a man of fervid and infectious enthusiasm. He greatly extended the works, building new furnaces, forges and rolling mills; he sank new shafts and drove new galleries. Iron plates and other parts for steam boats, rails and gates, and the manufacture of special steels for edge tools, were specialities.'[6] Unfortunately he lacked commonsense and business acumen. Worse still all the partners, including W. E. Gladstone, bore unlimited liability. When the crash came in 1848 there was a loss of £267,000, which placed an impossible burden on the Hawarden Estate, only rescued after thirty years of wise stewardship by W. E. Gladstone. He had complained in 1843 of the extravagance of Boydell and his 'making a fancy steam engine while the company's concern continues unproductive.'

After the Oak Farm debacle Boydell was seeking the fame and fortune that would come to the first person to harness steam power

James Boydell's 'Steam Tractor'
[Illustrated London News]

successfully to cultivation. Boydell's novel proposal was the 'endless rail', a series of hinged boards attached round the perimeter of each wheel; like a skier on soft snow, his steam horse would spread its weight and thus avoid becoming bogged down.[7]

An experiment with Boydell's steam engine was held near Louth Lincolnshire in the summer of 1858 with an international audience. 'Boydell was rewarded with three hearty cheers, and his men shared £4 collected from bystanders.' When he died in 1860 the *New York Times* spoke sympathetically about him.

One of the greatest mechanical worthies of his age died about three weeks since of decline, brought on by cold caught through exposure on Woolwich marshes, while waiting for the officials to test his engine. He was a man of giant frame, simple and noble disposition, untiring industry and great genius.[8]

Boydell died on the verge of fame with success in his grasp having witnessed the approval of his steam engine.

The Ferry 1842–97

In 1842, the King's Ferry Trust advertised for a contractor, for working and maintaining the ferry, who was 'to employ practical and experienced Boatmen, and to furnish all Horses, Boats, Chains *etc.* and every other article necessary to work the Ferry; and to keep the same and the Slips, Whimseys, Chains, Stables *etc.* in good and substantial order and repair.'[9] Various reports over the succeeding years throw light on the working of the ferry. In 1853 a large iron boat was built at Messrs Williams and Mowles foundry in Egerton Street, Chester. It was so large, wide and heavy and had to be drawn through the city by twelve horses at an early hour in the morning.'[10]

In 1872 the River Dee Company proposed 'to convert the present ferry into a steam one' and to change tolls for the use thereof. The Commissioners also proposed, 'that the ferry should be closed from 10 o'clock at night.' The protestors maintained, 'that the number of passengers in the day time averaged 1,000 per week, and 150 at night, while 300 carriages went over during the week.'[11] Repairs to the boat were necessary from time to time, as in 1883, when ' it was found to be in a most dangerous condition the planks not having been properly bolted together, and that, 'without a moments warning, its deck might have opened and passengers and cargo have gone through into the river.'[12] The next spring the manager of the ferry William Povall was sued 'for damages sustained through detention while crossing the river', by Henry Tozer who had arrived from Holywell, on his way to Neston, with his horse and trap loaded with fresh meat. The chain was faulty and the boat swung into the centre of the river and was stuck for a number of hours. In his defence Povall stated that 'he was employed by Captain J. P. Davies, who was an officer of the River Dee Company. He was paid £30 a month, and out of this he had to find two horses, four men, two boys, coal, light, shafts, shackles to piece the chain when broken, and sundry other things. Samuel Molyneux, the boatman was in his employ.'[13]

At the end of 1884 Captain J. P. Davies was charged with, 'feloniously killing and slaying William Jackson, at Queensferry, on 20 December.' Jackson, his wife, and their child, three years of age, were drowned. They were members of a party who had attended a raffle on the Cheshire side, and were returning to Queensferry on a dark night, in an overcrowded and unseaworthy boat, when she sank. Captain Davies was acquitted but judge and jury condemned the ferryboat. In May 1888 the river became impassable. 'The water is so low as to enable persons to wade across in perfect safety.' Two accidents occurred in 1890 when low water made the boat passage unpredictable. Cattle drovers, frustrated when the ferry boat went aground twelve yards from the Welsh shore, forced their cows into the water to wade to the bank, only to find that the animals made for the opposite bank.'[14] At the end of July a party of Birkenhead ladies returning from Hawarden in a four-wheeled carriage alighted to allow the coachman to drive across. All went well till midstream was reached when both horse and vehicle got into deep water and began to sink in the sand and had to be rescued by the ferryman.'[15]

The Waterfront, Warehouses and Wharfage

The river had been canalised to make it navigable for sea-going vessels to conduct trade. It was in every ones interest that there should be transport to the waterfront and adequate warehouses and wharves for the storage of their goods. Tramways were constructed to carry coal and brick from as far as Buckley. There were two wharves at Queensferry, one on Glynne land, and the other the extensive wharf of the Dundas family, built on the land the Whitley family received from enclosure in 1781.

The Glynne warehouses were advertised in 1839. 'Warehouses are provided, particulars of freight may be had at the King's Ferry Wharf.' There is a 'new steam conveyance, a new packet the *Skimmer*, built expressly for the trade plying between Liverpool, the King's Ferry, and Chester, designed to carry goods of all description and tow all vessels entering the Dee.'[16] Another vessel used for towing in the Dee was the steam tug the *Conqueror* under the command of Captain Benjamin Bennett, a licensed pilot for the Dee. The agent was Timothy Gregory of Queensferry.'[17]

In May 1844 Sir Stephen Glynne's warehouse, used by Messrs Davison and Bennion, general carriers, was completely destroyed. It was 'stored with treacle, flour, tar, about a ton of gunpowder, and other mercantile commodities, and was surrounded by a large timber yard, and several other warehouses in which a considerable quantity of highly inflammable articles were deposited. The gunpowder ignited and a most terrific explosion took place, which was heard for miles, and the effect resembled the shock of an earthquake. The estimated damage was about £3,000.'[18] Glynne was represented at Queensferry by his agent James Boydell, and Benjamin Bithell of Wepre. Bithell was responsible for directing the trading activities of Glynne's fleet of schooners on the Dee and was responsible for the purchase of livestock, grain, and other commodities, and the export of coal and bricks to Dublin, The wharfage accounts for Sir Stephen Glynne and the proprietors of the lower wharf in 1839, include receipts for bricks, the shipment of pig iron and coal from Buckley and the Alltami Colliery Company. The rental receipts of the wharf from 1839–41 were £1,080.[19]

After the death of Charles Davison of the King's Ferry Carrying Company, in 1849, notice was given that the wharf was being put into an efficient state of repair 'and will be found a most commodious place for loading and discharging vessels on the Dee being provided with an excellent Crane, Store House and other conveniences.'[20] Captain Thomas Hector was in charge of the wharf. A table of the wharfage rates anticipated a vigorous trade in foodstuffs — flour, meal, sugar, raisins, treacle, tea, wheat, oats, barley, hops, potatoes, turnips, mugs of butter, wines, spirits, ale, porter, furniture, tin, copper, lead, wire, cordage, rope, timber, alum, and manure — but no mention is made of coal, brick, and pottery ware. However, an account of goods shipped from wharfs on the Hawarden estate, in the period 1849–54, record several tons of Buckley earthenware, bricks, coals from Castle Hill, iron and castings from the Rhydymwyn Co., and an item in November 1854, 'Mr. Cram 29 tons of timber', most likely for the building of the *Royal Charter*.

A plan of the Aston Wharf in 1861 shows the frontage; coal stages, weighing house, stable, whimsey, engine house and tramways. The tramways were let to: 1. Catherall's bricks and tiles. 2. Hancock's coal, bricks and tiles 3. Davison's bricks and tiles and 4. the Royle Patent Fuel Company.

Evidence in 1860, from a Committee of Enquiry, into the building of the Buckley Railway, given by Samuel Edwards the Harbour Master at King's Ferry, calculated the amount of tonnages received at the Dundas wharf as 32 thousand tons in 1859. This, he said, 'would entail 8,000 wagonloads in 4 ton capacity wagons or 4,000 trains (each with one horse). Over a period of 308 working days'. Edwards maintained that King's Ferry was safer anchorage than Connah's Quay as vessels could lay two abreast there. They had no steam tugs of their own, but some where available at Saltney.[21]

The Sailors' Home

In 1842, under the patronage of Admiral Dundas, a Sailors' Home was opened on the wharf side. The home was to be used as a place of worship under the auspices of the Wesleyan Methodists, and as 'an Evening School, a Depository for Bibles, Prayer Books, Tracts and a Loan Library. By which means it is hoped that the 1,600 seamen, who assemble in the course of the year, may be induced to spend their winter evenings in obtaining useful knowledge, instead of, as at present in the beer shop.'[22] In January 1843 a special service was held 'for the benefits of the Shipwrecked Fishermen and Mariners Society, and for those afflicted widows and orphans who have become so from the violence of the late storm, and who reside in the immediate neighbourhood of the Dee.' The sermon was preached by Captain Hudson of Liverpool from the text, 'Thou didst blow with thy wind, the sea covered them; they sank as lead in the mighty waters, 'to a crowded and attentive congregation principally composed of sailors and colliers'.[23]

The Coming of the Railway

With the opening of the Chester & Holyhead Railway in 1848, Queensferry became the first station out of Chester. It was designed by the architect Francis Thompson. A goods warehouse was built in a loop in 1870. In 1900, the Thompson building was swept away with a widening scheme. During the First World War platforms for munitions workers were erected at the station and the Dundas sidings on both sides of the line were increased. Some 300 yards to the east of Dundas signal box were the platforms of the HM Factory. The 600 ft. timber platforms were reached from an adjacent bridge and electric light was installed in 1916. Queensferry station was closed to passengers on 14 February 1966.

The Sailors' Home, Queensferry
[FRO 51/140]

Early Industry

Early industry at Queensferry was located between the Lower Ferry and Chymistry (1781), which became Chemistry (1839). This area is also known as Pentre, which is almost equidistance from Queensferry, Sandycroft and Mancot. The first record of industry, other than coalmining occurs at the end of the eighteenth century, and is mentioned by Richard Willett in 1822.

1781. Henry Thorp of Chester

In the year 1781, Mr Thorp, a button manufacturer in Chester, purchased a small allotment upon the lately inclosed Saltney Marsh, and near to Big Mancott-lane-end, where he erected the Chemistry. To this place he sent down his refuse horn and bones, from which he extracted Glauber's salts, and sal ammoniac, and ground down the calcined residuum into ivory black. Mr Rigby purchased this concern, about the year 1793. It passed next into the hands of his brother Mr John Rigby, by whom, in conjunction with his nephew Mr Leigh Rigby, the above articles continue to be manufacture to a considerable extent.[24]

By 1850 Honoratus Leigh Rigby was in financial difficulties and the buildings in the Chemistry, together with six cottages, were conveyed to the Chester bankers T. P. and J. Williams. The equipment, warehouses and sheds were sold to David Murgatroyd of Tranmere in 1853.[25]

George Lloyd observed in the 1950s:

In recent years a number of cast iron pots were found below the ground level of the site. I was told they were as big as dustbins. They were probably used for what was known as 'destructive distillation' of raw materials. In all probability, production ceased sometime in the 1840s. It is thought that a pottery followed on the site, but about 1850 we learn that this later establishment made the wire hangers for the *Royal Charter*, launched in Cram and Coy. Yard at Sandycroft in 1854.[26]

Wireworks

In the 1850s Fenton, Hyde & Co. made wire cables at Pentre for the Electric Telegraph Company. In May 1855 the Companies steamer the *Monarch* collected two cables weighing 290 tons with a joint length of 140 miles 'to ship the cables at the same time, across to Howth in Ireland.'[27] Another Wire Rope Works, Hemingway and Scott, (late Murgatroyd & Co.), advertised their wares in the 1856 *Trade Directory*, as 'manufacturers of improved wire rope of every description for collieries, mines and for ships standing rigging with wire cables for submarine and other telegraphs.' By 1868 the Queensferry Wire Rope Company were the only makers advertising. The 1870 Ordnance Survey map shows the wire works in Chemistry Lane as disued but the buildings were taken over in 1873 by Warrington Wire Rope Works Ltd.

The North & South Wales Patent Steam Fuel Company

In the 1850s twenty-five acres of land on the Aston Wharf were leased to the North and South Wales Steam Fuel Co. Ltd. They had 'a licence for use within the Principality of Wales, of Wood's 'Patent Inventions for Improvements in the Manufacture of Fuel.' Unfortunately it was found that the local coal was unsuitable for their process, which, with purchase of expensive equipment, led to voluntary liquidation.

The site was advertised as being capable of adaptation with excellent prospects for marketing.

The frontage towards the river affords ready means of water carriage to Liverpool, and on the other side is the Chester Holyhead Railway, with an ample and most convenient siding, from which a branch railway communicates direct into the works, described as 'an extensive factory, with drying floors, two engine houses, two lofty chimney stacks, a large coal depot, dwelling house for the manager, smith's and carpenter's shops, stables offices, weighing houses *etc*.[28]

The Chemical Works — Joseph Turner & Company

Joseph Turner & Co. who made good use of the facilities as is seen from their advertisement in *Slater's Directory* of 1862 acquired the site of the Patent Steam Fuel Co. They manufactured anti-friction greases for locomotive and railway carriages, and lubricants for trams, engines and machinery. Anti-corrosive paints, quick drying varnish, and printer's inks, were supplied to the market. They specialised as manufacturing chemists and general distillers in naphtha, benzol, nitro-benzol, carbolic acid, ammonia, salts, spirits of tar *etc*. Farmers were supplied with artificial manures.

Joseph Turner was a Northumberland industrial chemist. Morris Jones recalled that it was very much a family business, both in the management and the work force. The chemical works had its own horse-drawn vehicle pulled by two horses to extinguish fires. When the hooter sounded the fire alarm, the horses would be at the gate of a nearby field ready to be tethered. The Chemical Works was known locally as the Black Works, and it was a thrill for the local children to watch the motor vessel *Water Witch*, being steered by 'black Jack Massey', along the river from Chester, loaded with coal tar.[29]

In the 1890s they manufactured a heart drug, which continued production until the 1970s. In 1924 Messrs. Joseph Turner & Co. was amalgamated with the Midland Tar Distillers who joined with Yorkshire Tar Distillers in 1967. The trade suffered from the impact of North Sea Gas in the 1950s and the closure of local gas works. The company ceased trading in the 1970s after more than 125 years of continuous production. In its last years Synthetic Chemicals concentrated on manufacturing heart drugs for the export market, a product made for 77 years by the Queensferry Co.[30]

The Opening of the Jubilee Bridge, 1897

The opening of the Jubilee Bridge in 1897 emphasised the importance of Queensferry as the gateway into north Wales. The second phase of the development of Queensferry began in the 1870s and continued until the beginning of the First World War in 1914. It was marked by the opening of local collieries, and the revival of shipbuilding. Sales of land between 1869–1913 encouraged the development of private housing. Shops, schools and religious buildings were erected for the needs of a growing population, which was further increased by the workers at John Summers Iron Works, and Willans and Robinson's Engineering Works.

Thousands of people assembled to assist in the opening ceremony of the Jubilee Bridge in June 1897. Some 3000 ticket holders were admitted within the barriers, where was erected a covered platform for the accommodation of Mr and Mrs. W. E. Gladstone, members of their family, representatives of the Cheshire and Flintshire County Councils, and businessmen of both counties. The presence of the county police ensured that good order prevailed. Streamers and flags were hung across the new bridge; the boats on the river, sported bunting, and the strains of Buckley band enhanced the festive aspect of the occasion. In the interval of waiting for Mr Gladstone, the visitors had the pleasure of witnessing the launch of a new steamer hard by the bridge, the vessel having been built by a local firm for service in the Isle of Man. During these proceedings the centre span of the bridge was opened for river traffic to emphasise the fact that Mr Gladstone's function was to open the bridge for vehicular and pedestrian traffic by closing the telescopic span.

The newspapers reported that Mr Gladstone looked exceedingly well. He sported a large red rose and seemed in uncommonly good spirits, as his, subsequently more than usually humorous speech proved. This began with a formal declaration of the opening of the bridge, and through the desire of the sponsors and spectators he formally named it the Victoria Jubilee Bridge. In the course of his speech he reminded the spectators of his wife's interest: 'you may not be aware that the boat which has performed the duty of carrying people backwards and forwards over the ferry was named after my wife and her sister, the *Catherine and Mary*. She cheerfully and generously surrenders her interest in the title and she rejoices to contemplate the new bridge as a great social improvement.' Gladstone reminded his listeners that he was born in 1809 and without vanity considered himself in some sense a man of the nineteenth century and spoke of the great changes that had taken place as regards the increased facilities of communication all over the country and the world. He

W. E. Gladstone is escorted through the crowds at the opening of the Jubilee Bridge, Queensferry, 1897
[FRO 51/7]

The ferry boat Catherine &
Mary, *c.1880*
[FRO 51/146]

mentioned in particular the advantages brought by Sir Rowland Hill and his penny postage and Cook's Tours. When he was a boy the mail coach was not more than a fourth part of the size of a railway carriage, but now we have railways carrying goods, minerals, and general merchandise, and the telegraph carrying our messages and the telephone our voices. He concluded that he hoped the Victoria Jubilee Bridge would have the advantage of a continuous communication between north Wales and Lancashire. Mr Gladstone then pressed the button, which set the machinery in motion.

The cost of the bridge was met by a number of interested parties. The Dee Conservancy Board contributed £4,000, Cheshire Council £3,000: other contributors were the Hawarden Embankment Trustees, neighbouring landowners, the major cost being borne by Flintshire County Council who were authorized to raise a loan of £6,000. The bridge was free for foot passengers, but the Queensferry Bridge Act provided a toll of three pence 'for every bicycle, tricycle' and other like carriage', with a weight limit of twelve tons. Flintshire County Council were responsible for the construction and offered a prize of a hundred pounds for the best design. The prize was awarded to Mr T. W. Barber of Hastings whose plans were adopted. The contractors were the Teeside Bridge & Engineering Company Limited of Middlesborough.[31]

An account of the bridge of 1897 was given in the official programme for the opening of a new replacement bridge in November 1926.

The bridge was of wrought iron girder construction and it was divided into three spans with a total length of

Ships passing through the open
Jubilee Bridge, Queensferry
[FRO 51/12]

four hundred feet; the centre span was arranged to open in two moving parts, which were cantilevered out from over the river piers at the central ends of the fixed spans. Each moving part was carried on a twelve wheeled carriage, which rolled along a girder track set between the main girders and under the roadways of the fixed spans; the roadway on the moving span was very ingeniously carried on cast iron swinging arms, which allowed the roadway to be lowered through nearly two feet, so that when it moved back it cleared the fixed span roadway; on both the fixed and the moving the roadway is placed over the main girders and is supported by pressed toughing. The original road surface of the bridge was wood blocks both on the fixed and moving spans, but about twenty years ago the fixed spans were resurfaced with hard blue bricks, which were specially made at Buckley. This unusual road surfacing stood up very well to the heavy traffic which it was called upon to carry and, at the time of the demolition showed remarkably little signs of wear. Under all weather conditions, except possibly frost, it formed a non-slippery surface, which was equally suitable for horse and vehicular traffic. Hydraulic rams were used for opening and closing the bridge and movement was effected quite quickly; the hydraulic pressure was obtained from steam-driven pumps and an accumulator place in the building on the south abutment.

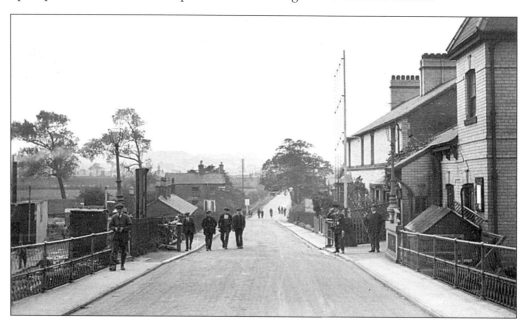

Queensferry Bridge and tollgate (right) [FRO 51/18]

George Lloyd's Memories of Queensferry[32]

George Lloyd, a distinguished engineer, was born in Shotton and trained at Queensferry. After his retirement he became an active member of the Flintshire Historical Society and contributed extensive notes on the Deeside area which are deposited in the County Record Office. In one of these he describes the smallness of the Queensferry community which he remembered as a boy. He takes a tour around the village —

   At the entrance to the river bank near the Hawarden Castle Hotel there was a small wooden building, which contained a barometer with a flagpole outside, flying a weather cone. At the time of the Queen's Jubilee in 1887, there were a number of buildings on the Ferry hill. Amongst them a stone built bungalow, with latticed windows, occupied by Mr John Hough, a cashier at the Aston Hall Colliery. Along the road leading to the Chemical Works were a cottage and a one-storey shop both of which were dismantled when the first Dee Bridge was built. A group of buildings close together were Dee Farm, occupied by George Povall, the Sailor's Home, a small cottage, Messrs Hancock's shipping office, the Chemical Works, four workmen's cottages and the Hawarden Castle Hotel. Nearby was the residence of Henry Hurlbutt, formerly Dee cottage, but now proudly named Queensferry Hall. By the railway station were about a dozen cottages, and a smithy, worked by the blacksmith, William Hough. In one of the other cottages, where the Midland Bank now stands, lived John Jones, a shoemaker. There were about five houses, near where now stands Zion Methodist Chapel, and in the largest of them resided Thomas Nicholls, who was a most capable millwright and engineer. This skill is to be seen in the iron railings he made for part of the Roodeye racecourse at Chester. In one of the other cottages lived John Hughes, the Post Man, who in the daytime kept a little shop selling everything. When evening came he would set out for Flint, with the mail, driving his horse and trap, and emptying the letterboxes on the way. The next residence, at the Cross Roads, was the Toll Gate house, occupied by John Thomas. Opposite lived Tom Cooper, a general grocer, in a small one-storey house and shop. On the Shotton road, there were two houses, owned by Mr John Bannister. In his adjoining workshop he carried out an extensive business as a wheelwright. The house at the junction of the Hawarden road was in the occupation of Joseph Whithead. Jesse Hughes occupied the house, which was built into the old draw bridge buttresses, along the Sandycroft road.

The first drawbridge was erected in 1790 to carry the iron railway from Mancot to the river. When the road was widened in 1911 the Flintshire County Council removed the old bridge and replaced it with an iron bridge, which was dismantled in 1942, and the scrap used for war purposes. When Queensferry began to develop in 1888, the first four houses built in Station road were, Mona, Heath, Epworth, and Beaconsfield cottages. Other houses and shops quickly followed.[33]

Building land was made available in a sale of over 64 lots at the Hawarden Castle Hotel on 3 September 1902. The area sold formed a square between Station Road, the London North Western Railway, the Aston Colliery road, and the Flint Saltney road. In the next ten years Queensferry was to take shape with the main residential and shopping area situated between the Chester Holyhead Railway line and the Flint Saltney road and divided by Station road leading northwards to the river with Fairfield Road, Gladstone Street and Pierce Street on the west side and Glynne Street, Queen Street and Dundas Street on the east.

Station Road, Queensferry
[FRO 51/64]

In 1904, the Spring Brewster sessions reported the population of Queensferry as 'now 500 but expected approach before long 2,900. The employees of the new works of Willans and Robinson number 350, and it is anticipated the new colliery will employ a large number of men. There are about 500 passengers a day at the Queensferry Station.'[34] It was a young community, in February 1908; there were 330 names on the register of Queensferry Council School, and 177 pupils at the Infant School.

An example of the bonding between the communities developing along the river Dee was the welcome home given to the local volunteers returning from the Boer War by the inhabitants of Shotton and Queensferry in May 1901. A demonstration of welcome was arranged with a procession along a route, which led from Shotton School to Queen's Ferry Bridge, thence to Connah's Quay and back again to Shotton. Volunteers were represented from the companies of Hawarden, Connah's Quay, and the Sandycroft battery.

In front of the military, who were led by the drums and trumpets of the Sandycroft battery, came a gun crew dressed in white sailor costume, consisting of boys from Shotton School, and dragging a mounted naval gun made by Mr T. W. Toby. This was considered the chief feature of the procession, and added much to the spectacular effect. Behind the band came the eight warriors in whose honour the demonstration was organised, easily distinguished by their stained uniforms. The volunteers came next, followed by the Queen's Ferry Fire Brigade under the command of Mr Bartley, and then followed by the civilian element. This was composed of the Connah's Quay band, a wagon on which was placed a wounded soldier, with nurse attendants, another containing a number of girls from Shotton School, representing Britannia seated, trident in hand, surrounded by representatives of other nations, all clad in appropriate costumes. Quaintly dressed cyclists brought up the rear. The only drawback was the state of the road, but the men stepped out with military smartness to the strains of the music, and cheerfully endured the discomfort. The houses were decorated with bunting and coloured devices. In Shotton also the decorative effect was striking, and gave to the village an appearance such as it never before presented. A discharge of rockets, which were evidently aimed at the venerable and tottering structure which does for a railway station, but unfortunately without any effect, concluded a demonstration which gave pleasure to several thousands.[35]

Zion Primitive Methodist Chapel, 1896–1984

The foundation stones of a Primitive Methodist Connexion Chapel were laid in September 1895 by Mr John Roberts, J. P., Saltney; Mr John Roberts, Ewloe; Mrs. John Roberts, Alltami; the Revd. Joseph Davies, Buckley; and Mr John Weigh, Superintendent of the Sunday School, Aston, on behalf of the scholars. The Church at Aston, the parent body, was purchased in 1878, for £350. The block of buildings, which included a licensed beer-house, were made suitable for public worship, until the capacity of the room failed to hold the increasing congregation. In August 1895, Mr George Hughes of Queen's Ferry offered a plot of ground in the centre of the village and also offered to erect a chapel to seat 250, for £600. He became its architect and gave £50 to its building fund.

Zion Primitive Methodist Chapel, 1985
[FRO 51/130]

The chapel was opened at the beginning of February 1896, which was considered 'to be the model chapel of the district, being perfect in symmetry, built of the best material, and original in design.' In 1905 there were 11 deacons, 250 communicants, 16 teachers, 117 scholars under 15, and 73 scholars over 15. As well as Sunday and weekday services, a popular event in a number chapels, was the monthly PSA or Pleasant Sunday Afternoon. This, for example, was held at Zion in 1903 to celebrate the New Year, and is an example of the way people came together and contributed to the entertainment.

> A programme prepared by Mr C. Cliff, of vocal and instrumental music, was performed before a large and appreciative audience. Solos were sung by Miss Lewis, Sandycroft; Miss Bessie Hughes, Queensferry; Mr W. Challinor, Hawarden; Master J. H. Cliff, Pentre; duets by Miss Lewis and J. H. Cliff; recitations by Miss E. Challinor, Hawarden and Mrs. H. Green, Shotton. The instrumental music was given by Shotton Orchestral Band, consisting of first and second violins, mandolin, cello and cornet: conductor Mr A. Barker. Accompanist, Miss Manifold and Miss Eva Cliff. The Reverend William Barrett, presided.[36]

In February 1924 the Chapel was extended by the building of a new Sunday School Room to provide facilities for the teaching of the large number of young people receiving religious instruction at Zion.[37] An extensive renovation to the chapel took place in 1930. In February 1945, the fifty years Jubilee, was celebrated with a public tea and two concerts by local artists and the Leeswood Male Voice Choir. The Chapel closed in 1984 and was later used as shop premises.

Trinity, Wesleyan Methodist Church, 1906–63

The Welsh Wesleyan Methodists worshipped in the Sailors' Home for nearly fifty years. In April 1895, the Sailor's Home Chapel, was re-opened after a much needed renovation. Worship and social activities continued. A Social-Tea was held in January 1903, presided over by Mr Olsen, circuit evangelist. After tea a very interesting programme was given, consisting of songs, organ selections, cornet solos, recitations and selections on the gramophone.

By 1904 the members realised that they would have to move, 'times are changing, the neighbourhood is rapidly growing and it seems out of character to see a bright attractive congregation packed into an uncomfortable little building', they argued, as if to justify the purchase of 'a splendid site for a new chapel' on the corner of Chester Road and Glynne Street. This was opened at the end of August 1906, when the newspaper reported:

> The need for a new cause had been a pressing one, and the erection of a new and more commodious building has been eagerly looked forward to. These hopes have now been realised, and the friends are to be congratulated upon the excellently built chapel and its commanding position. The room is well designed, every detail being in perfect harmony and good taste. The architects were Messrs Green, Knowles and Russell of Liverpool. The building, which was entrusted to Messrs E. Blane and Son, Connah's Quay, has been very well done, the

Cutting the first sod for Trinity Wesleyan Church, 1906
[FRO 51/141]

ornamental work being in exceedingly good taste. The chapel is designed to seat 400. The opening ceremony was unique and picturesque. At half past three the assembly met at the Sailor's Home. Miss K. Evans formally locked the old place of worship, and this little formality was not without its touch of pathos. The procession commenced its journey from the old to the new. Upon arrival at the new chapel, which was gaily decorated with bunting, Mr S. Beresford CC of Mold stepped forward and unlocked the building. The Reverend John Wilson of Liverpool preached an excellent sermon. Tea was provided in the Primitive Methodist School, kindly lent for the occasion, and about 300 sat down.[38]

In its early days the church was used for overspill school accommodation. At the beginning of the First World War, British soldiers at the Prisoner of War Camp at the Pentre were allowed to use the vestry for a reading and writing room, and the kitchen for refreshments and games. In 1916 the members cleaned the church, rather than renovate it, in order 'to send our lads with the colours, the money for a Christmas present.' The adjoining land was divided into six plots for allotments. By the 1920s the Church was free from debt. Trinity Wesleyan Church closed in 1963 when it was sold to the Roman Catholic Diocese of Menevia.

The Council School, Queensferry

The building of chapels and schools in the decade gave the emerging working classes a sense of confidence. The rector of Hawarden, S. E. Gladstone, established a school in Queensferry in the year he left the parish in 1904. In the same year, Flintshire Education Committee, negotiated with the Hawarden estate, representing the new rector, for the purchase of the school building and the land attached, upon which to build a substantial council school. The price paid was £2,204 6s 9d and the school opened in the autumn of 1904. This relieved Queensferry children of their journey to attend the school at Sandycroft.

In November 1905 a Tender of £3324 2s 2d was accepted to build a mixed school to accommodate 300 pupils. Early newspaper reports and information given by school inspections show how necessary the provision of school buildings was for the growing community of Queensferry.

The school was opened in April 1907 when the newspapers commented:

It is evident that the handsome building has attracted a great many

Chester Road, Queensferry. Trinity Church is on the left
[FRO 51/122]

The Council School (now demolished) [FRO 51/177]

parents who are desirous of obtaining for their children the combined advantages of a good elementary education and also hygienic surroundings.

The school was inspected in February 1908 and a favourable report given.

MIXED DEPARTMENT — The fine premises were opened for the first time last April, and already there are as many as 330 names on the register of this department. Each class occupies a liberally equipped classroom of its own and there is also a central hall large enough to accommodate the whole of the scholars, when they assemble together for collective work. It is a pity that the playground was not asphalted when the school was erected, as the surface is rather too rough for the physical exercises to be executed in the open air during favourable weather.

The energetic and able Head Teacher has organised the school most judiciously and has framed a scheme of work, which shows that the standard he has set before himself and his colleagues is a very high one. Discipline is easily maintained, and an excellent spirit of work prevails. There is much intelligence and energy in the teaching. The children are beginning to respond to their teachers' efforts by doing some good work.

INFANT'S DEPARTMENT — This Department is sensibly conducted, and its tone is extremely pleasant. The methods of teaching are sound and intelligent, and the progress made by the pupils is very gratifying. The babies' class, which is cleverly handled by its teacher, has increased greatly of late.

By July 1908, with accommodation for 120 children, there were 177 names on the register. Numbers dramatically increased and in May 1914 there were 447 names on the registers of the mixed-department, and 230 in the infants department. The opening of a new council school in Garden City relieved this pressure.

There was a desire for education and with few free secondary educational opportunities evening schools made a real contribution towards meeting the needs of local industry. In 1907 evening classes were held in arithmetic, composition, elementary drawing, reading, and elementary science. The report for the session 1907/08 was encouraging:

This is a flourishing school. There are over forty students on the registers, all young men, nearly all of who are engaged in local industries. Rewards offered by Mr Summers and Mr Sydney Taylor, the chief employers of labour in the neighbourhood, have stimulated the students to attend regularly.

In 1911 classes were held in office routine, commercial correspondence, arithmetic, sick nursing and dressmaking.

The Liberal Club

The building of chapels and schools in Queensferry in the years before the First World War gave the emerging working classes a sense of confidence. They had buildings, which belonged to them. They ran their own committees; they had a platform on which to perform. It was quite natural that major political parties should court them. In 1910 the young squire of Hawarden, W. G. C. Gladstone, leased the Queensferry Liberals a site adjacent to the council schools on which to build the new Liberal Club. The *Flintshire News* reported:

It is a structure of pretty design, and when finished will not only be useful, but an ornament to the village. There is to be a reading room, billiard room, library and game room. No intoxicating drink will be allowed to be sold or brought on to the premises. Messrs Cowason of Glasgow, are the contractors.[39]

Miss Helen Gladstone opened it in February 1911 when 'some 200 members and friends sat down to an excellent tea in the Council Schoolroom and in the evening an exhibition of billiards was given by Messrs. Millar and F. Jones'.

The Gymnasium

In March 1911, Mr F. Hurlbutt presided at the Dee Side Gymnasium, in Queensferry, for a benefit performance given by twenty-four local boys, on behalf of their instructor, Mr Davies. He had given his services gratuitously two nights a week during the winter.

Physical drill, barbells, Indian clubs, dum-bells were all given with great precision and in good style, while the entertainment was lightened by brilliant feats on the parallel and horizontal bars. Some really clever tableaux on the former were much enjoyed by those present.

At the conclusion, Mr F. Hurlbutt, thanked Mr Davies for his goodness to the boys, and pointed out to the parents what an excellent outlet for superfluous energy gymnastics were to high spirited boys. Energy, which if not provided with a safety valve, spent itself in mischief and even in downright harm. Boys trained in the healthful atmosphere of a gymnasium, would make better workmen when they went to work.[40]

Queensferry fielded a football team named, the Ironopolis, because the members worked at Sandycroft Foundry. In 1895–6 they won the Welsh Junior Cup. They were an amateur side, which contained future Welsh Internationals.

Enough has been said to prove that Queensferry was a growing community. *Bennett's Business Directory*, 1913–4, listed two-dozen shops, most of them in Station Road. In addition there were tradesmen: builder, painter, decorator, surgeons, and three hotels, the Hawarden Castle, the Queensferry Hotel and the Mechanic's Hotel, Pentre. To the west of Station Road, between the river embankment, the railway and the main road with the main drive bordering on the former Eleanor Colliery was Queensferry Hall.

Queensferry Hall

This was known as Dee Cottage when it was the residence of the agent to the Hawarden estate. Henry Hurlbutt, a timber merchant, lived there in two spells between *c*1870 and 1912. He married Mary Joy Davidson of Shotton Cottage. They had four sons and seven daughters, some born at the hall and the others at Wold Court, Hawarden. Queensferry Hall was set within an area of about 80 acres. The hall was built of yellow brick and contained a

morning room, library, dining and drawing rooms, conservatories, a ground floor billiard room, and a large square entrance hall. The staircase formed a miniature picture gallery leading to ten bed and dressing rooms, bathrooms, with maids bedrooms, approached by a secondary staircase. The domestic offices comprised a butler's pantry, a large kitchen and two cellars. In the grounds

Queensferry Hall
[FRO 51/77]

were stables, shippons, chauffeur and gardener's cottages, coach house, motor garage, and a brick-slated lodge or bailiffs house, all standing in extensive grounds of six acres where there was a large octagonal summer house and a brick slated ivy-covered castellated tower with an outside spiral iron staircase leading to the roof, from which, as the sale catalogue described it, a very extended view of the Dee and the surrounding country is obtained, whilst the inside has wood dado and coloured glass forming a charming summer house.

Henry Hurlbutt had bought Queensferry hall, from Earl Spencer in 1877, when the conveyance was subject to maintaining and using a tramway ten feet wide from Eleanor Colliery to Queensferry Wharf.

Shipbuilding — the Second Phase
Shipbuilding was a major industry at Queensferry for over forty years from 1885 to 1935. Evidence for this is found in a manuscript of the Dee shipbuilding works in the Flintshire Record Office, which is supplemented by newspaper accounts of launches at the two yards.

Smith & Company
Morris Jones states that George K. Smith, a Scottish engineer, who resided at Station Cottages, was the manager at the Queensferry shipyard until 1892. Another source[41] refers to material in the Abdela and Mitchell papers, which included drawings of vessels by R. Smith, Engineer and Ship Builder of Old Quay, Preston, and by Richard Smith of Liverpool. A Preston firm of Richard Smith & Co. built ships from c.1869 and eventually from 1893, becoming the Lytham Ship Building & Engineering Co. This coincides with the Shipyard at Queensferry being idle from 1892 to 1894.

Smith & Co. were building ships at Queensferry in the yard used by James Boydell in the 1830s. Their operations, using metal in the structure of the ships, created a high pitched screeching sound, which Henry Hurlbutt at Queensferry Hall found intolerable and at the beginning of 1891 the yard was moved to a site near the terminus of the Aston Hall Colliery Railway.

The first reference to the shipyard of Smith & Co. is a newspaper report of 6 July 1888. It refers to the completion of a steel screw steamer for passengers and cargo traffic on the river Amazon.

The vessel, which has first class accommodation for passengers has a light awning deck from stem to stern above the main deck, and supported on galvanised iron stanchions, with single iron frame, light canvas curtains being hung all around as a protection from the weather. The comfort and convenience of passengers have been studied everywhere in her construction. The after part of the boat is set apart for passengers, with a partition and doors between the main and awning decks, seats being fitted on each side and around the stern. The bulwarks are of steel, with wooden rails. The machinery consists of a steel return tubular boiler, with the furnace constructed to burn wood, high pressure engines, donkey pumps, inspirator and ejector, everything being on the most modern and approved principle. She (the vessel is not named) underwent a steam trial on the river to the entire satisfaction of all concerned. Subsequently the superstructures were removed and packed in the vessel, which was fitted up for sailing out to South America, ketch rigged with a good spread of canvas. Everything completed she commenced her voyage on Thursday of from 5,000 to 6,000 miles, under the command of Captain Brown, who expects to reach his destination in about two months.

The account concludes with a statement, which implies that Smith & Co. had been building ships for sometime, but without any indication of the situation of the shipyard.

Vessels constructed by the firm have at various times been despatched to the Congo, the Levant, and Spain, as well as a number of surf boats to various other places.[42]

In December 1888 there is a report of the trial trip of a new steamer *Ambas*, built by Smith & Co. *en route* for the west coast of Africa, for Mr H. M. Smith of Waterloo, Liverpool, and under whose superintendence she has been built.

In May 1889, a small steamer, SS *Daisy*, built by Smith & Co., for Count Joseph Raffo, left Queensferry bound for Tunis, to be used partly as a pleasure vessel and also as a means of communication between the fishing fleet owned by the count.

The vessel fully came up to the expectation of her builders, and behaved admirably on her first voyage, her speed being 10 knots. She will follow the English coast, stopping at all places of interest, and then across the English

The Francia, 1908
[A. M. Langford deposit, FRO
D/DM/1036/1]

Channel to France, sail up the Seine, stopping at Paris to allow those who accompany her to visit the Exhibition and then across France by canal.[43]

Three other vessels are recorded as being built in 1890 similar to SS *Daisy*: the *Alerta*, the *Nora*, and the *Foxhound*.

A newspaper report of November 1891 gives significant information about shipbuilding at Queensferry. First that 'during the seven years they have been building here they have sent quite a fleet of craft of almost every description, to various countries.' This puts the date of the beginning of Smith & Co. to 1894. Second, it confirms the establishment of another shipyard at Queensferry in 1891.

In the beginning of the present year more suitable premises were acquired, and the plant considerably improved by fusion with other firms in the iron trade, and when the work of laying out the yard is fully completed will be one of the best places in the kingdom for constructing vessels such as the river will allow.

The ship was launched by Miss Smith and named the *Reliance*. She was built to the order of Messrs. J. H. Beckwith & Co. Colchester, 90 foot long, 18-foot beam, depth of hold 7 foot 6 inches, constructed of steel throughout.

The Queensferry Ship Building and Engineering Co. Ltd.
In 1893 a new company was formed to buy out Smith and Co. The shipyard had been idle for two years. The new company was the Queensferry Shipbuilding and Engineering Co. Its managing director was Mr Charles Myers, the inventor of the Myer's patent propeller. In May 1894 Mrs. Myers launched a vessel named the *May Queen* and it was reported:

She will be taken to Sandycroft foundry in a few days to receive her engines and boiler by the kind permission of Mr Sydney Taylor.' The boat was built for Messrs. Crosbie and King, especially for a passenger and towing service on Lough Neagh, Ireland.[44] Another vessel, a 'smart and powerful steam tug', fitted with one of Myer's patent propellers for Grimsby fish merchants, was named the *Monarch* by Miss Cissie Mould, the daughter of the landlord of the Hawarden Castle and was launched at the beginning of October 1894.[45] Other vessels built at this time were the *John O'Gaunt* and the *Escott*. Three vessels, the *Thistle*, the *Rose* and the *Shamrock*, were built in 1897, under the supervision of Mr M. W. Hanson, for the Douglas Steam Ferries Co. of the Isle of Man.[46] In February the following year, Hanson built a steamship the *Research*, for Mr J Waddington of Liverpool, for work on the Klondike.[47] There is no information for the years 1898–1906 which names particular vessels. In spite of the silence the shipyard continued to thrive. A twin screw, steel vessel, was launched in July 1906, for tropical service. There was great activity the following year. At the beginning of April the steel lighter, the *Pike*, of 350 tons, was launched. It was built for the Rea Transport Company, Liverpool, as a sister ship to the *Tunny*, *Tarpon* and *Pilchard*, to be employed in the cross-river coal carrying trade. The newspapers mentioned other vessels.

The firm have this year already completed the conversion of HMS *Bulldog* into a grain carrying barge, and a small steam tug for Valpariso, together with a motor driven salvage launch, have also been delivered. On Saturday their small Amazon steamer, the *Hercules*, underwent satisfactory trial trips on the Dee, and was subsequently delivered to Liverpool, after having her deck erections dismantled and shipped for Peru on Tuesday. Another steam launch for the same quarter is being framed at present, and among other craft on the stocks and in hand are two stern wheel launches for Egypt, two twin screw steamers for the East, and a wood tug for South America.[48]

In September 1907 another vessel, the *Conger* was launched, to join the fleet of the Rea Transport Co. It was reported, 'the builders have three more similar vessels on hand, besides a number of smaller craft.' On this optimistic note the life of the Queensferry Shipbuilding & Engineering Co. ended.[49]

Isaac J. Abdela & Mitchell Ltd.[50]

Isaac J. Abdela, a member of the Jewish community in Corfu, was three years old when his family fled from Turkish persecution to Manchester. Here he studied engineering and naval architecture. Eventually he went into partnership with Messrs. Mitchell Ltd and they acquired the works of Edwin Clark & Co. Ltd., steamboat builders of Brimscombe, Gloucestershire, on the Thames and Severn canal. Here they were restricted by the canal lock system. Their search for a place to build larger vessels led them to take over the Queensferry shipyard in 1909.

The first Abdela launching was the *Pepuhy*, a diminutive tug, followed by two tugs for a French firm at Marseilles. Their move to Queensferry was a success as the newspaper confirmed that, 'since taking over the Queensferry yard the firm have placed themselves in a splendid position for the quick and cheap building of craft up to 200 foot for their yard, being easy for delivery to Liverpool, and convenient both for getting materials delivered and away.'[51] In 1911 great interest was shown in the building of the150 foot *Labao*, the newspaper described her as a 'handsome screw passenger steamer which is intended for service on the river Amazon, between Para and Manoes. The vessel, which is the largest built on the river Dee since the days of the *Royal Charter*, over half a century ago, contains three decks and has been specially designed for the passenger and cargo traffic in the Brazils, where she is to be employed chiefly in the rubber trade.' Isaac Abdela's mother-in-law performed the launch. 'The banks of the river were lined on either side by people, whilst the children from the Queensferry Council School were provided with accommodation in the shipyard and afterwards regaled by the firm. The neighbourhood was *en féte* with bunting.'[52]

The main years of production by Abdela and Mitchell, were between, 1909 and 1925. A list of ships built in these years is too great to include here. But it is possible to indicate certain trends.

The production of lighters and barges. 1910, *Dory*. 1911, *Cod, Oyster, Plaice, Sole*. Lighters built for Rea Transport Co. Liverpool. Another group, in 1913, were the *Anchovy, Sardine, Hake, Haddock, Whiting* and *Whelk*. In 1915, the *Yumbi, Zambi* and *Dolo*. Ten grain barges, powered by sail, were built for the G.W.R. in 1913 and 1914.

War time production up to 1919, included two tugs, two boom defence vessels, two floating pneumatic grain elevators and six steam driven trawlers, for the Admiralty in 1918–9.

Post war production included: 1920 two drifters and five lighters. Between 1921 and 1928, ten tankers.

The only known side-wheel steamer built by Abdela was the *Menai*, for the Caernarfon ferry service. It was specially designed by the builders, in conjunction with Messrs. Esplen and Sons Ltd., naval architects, Liverpool, and was intended to carry vehicular traffic. The Mayoress of Caernarfon, Mrs. A. H. Richards launched it.[53]

Isaac J. Abdela & Mitchell Ltd's yard, Queensferry, c.1912
[FRO 51/47]

Left: Pepuhy, the first ship built at the re-opened Abdela yard
[FRO 51/46]

Below: The Manuel Thomaz
[A. M. Langford deposit, FRO D/DM/1036/1]

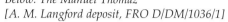

Left: Dignitaries await the launch of a new ship at Abdela's yard
[A. M. Langford deposit, FRO D/DM/1036/1]

Below: Launch of the Lobao *at Abdela's yard*
[A. M. Langford deposit, FRO D/DM/1036/1]

Ships built for John Summers & Sons Ltd.[54]

When John Summers & Sons, came to Shotton in 1896, they bought cheap land on the Dee estuary, and found the river indispensable for bringing in building materials and plant for their new works. R. S. Fenton lists twenty-seven ships, which belonged to the firm between 1897 and 1967. Six of these were built at Queensferry by Abdela and Mitchell Ltd. All of them had Spanish sounding names. *Carita*, 1913; *Fleuriat*, 1913; *Sir William/ Felita*. Built for John H. Vernon, Liverpool 1914, and bought by Summers, 1915 and renamed, *Felita*; *Warita*, 1919; *Indorita*, 1920; *Eldorita*, 1920. All these vessels had oil engines made by Bolinders of Stockholm.[55]

Outward bound, the Summers Fleet carried a cargo of basic slag, a by-product of steel making, used as a fertiliser and sent to south west Scotland and Ireland. On their return they carried a cargo of scrap iron.

In 1925, Abdela and Mitchell fell on uncertain times. Trade was falling off, there was an uninsured fire at Brimscombe and the Company name was transferred to Isaac J. Abdela and Mitchell (1925). One of the directors, Mr Walter Smith, took the leading role and built the tanker *Energie* in 1928 and in 1930, the coaster *Brightside*. The shipyard came to an end in December 1933 when the plant was dispersed. On a nearby site, between 1939 and 1940, ferro concrete barges of about 100 tons were constructed and launched sideways in the river. Shipbuilding at Queensferry came to an end having lasted, intermittently for just over a hundred years.

The Aston Steamship Co. Ltd.

Three ship owners are listed for Queensferry in Slater's Directory of 1868. John and James Powell, James Shone, and a Thompson. R. S. Fenton mentions the Aston Steamship Co. Ltd. owners of one of the earliest cargo steamers on the Dee, the *Aston*, built for J. & F. Thompson of Queensferry in 1867. W. E. Gladstone was one of the subscribers. The Thompson's trade was the shipment of lead ore, and bricks and earthenware goods made in Buckley or Ruabon, to Ireland. They added another steamer, the *Shark*, in 1880. The Company was wound up in 1882, and the *Aston* and *Shark* sold.

Willans & Robinson[56]

The arrival of Willans and Robinson in 1900 from Rugby to found a subsidiary company at Queensferry was greeted with extreme optimism, a rapid expansion of Deeside was expected: 'it is more than probable that in the course of two or three years, there will be one line of houses from Connah's Quay to Sandycroft, with a total population of something like 10,000 or 12,000 persons', and a work force of 800 men, houses are springing up in all directions.' Thirty two acres of land on the Gladstone estate was leased on a site adjacent to Chemistry lane between the river Dee embankment and the Chester and Holyhead Railway.[57]

The factory buildings were in blue brick with 'Belfast' roofs, and in the centre was a tower ninety feet high, to accommodate four hydraulic accumulators. The architect was H. B. Creswell. Nicholaus Pevsner, hailed it as, 'the most advanced British building of its date.'[58] Between the main factory and the river embankment were the steel and iron foundries, equipped with a thirty ton open hearth Siemens-Martin melting furnace, six crucible furnaces, one cupola furnace for cast iron, and drying ovens.

The workshops were equipped with hydraulic and compressed air installations, overhead travelling cranes, central heating equipment and broad and narrow gauge railways connecting with the Dundas sidings.

On the river embankment was a jetty complete with an electrically operated jib crane for unloading anthracite coal for the gas producers and for pig iron for the foundries. The materials were conveyed direct from the ships into the works by an overhead ropeway with automatic tilting skips or buckets, thus reducing labour to a minimum.

The main factory was equipped with a small steel-section electrically driven rolling mill, a 2,000 tons hydraulic forging press, two 1,000 tons hydraulic piercing presses, hydraulic plate-bending machines, heavy plate shears and riveters hydraulically operated, chain draw benches for the drawing of solid drawn steel tubes of the highest quality and all the necessary auxiliary machinery for the production of many products. All machined work, including tube header cones, crankshafts, gears *etc.* were made to a tolerance of plus or minus one-thousandth part of an inch. The working pressure of the hydraulic installation was 1,500 lbs per square inch when necessary.

The Queensferry works was ostensibly laid out for the manufacture of Niclausse water-tube boilers, which held a French patent, designed for land and marine work. Although the French navy were partial to this type of rapid steaming boilers, the British Navy, after an experimental trial, did not adopt them. Boilers were installed at generating stations at Pontypridd, Cleveland, and Durham, at Basingstoke and Birmingham University.

Willans & Robinson [Edward Hubbard, The Buildings of Wales: Clwyd, Penguin Books]

For the first time in the history of steel smelting, vanadium steel was produced in this small foundry. It was an alloy steel of high tensile strength with ductile characteristics, and at that time revolutionised the making of engineering components. A chrome vanadium steel was also produced for the manufacture of spiral and leaf springs. Other products were high-grade steel and iron casting and thirty ton steel ingots supplied to Firths of Sheffield for the manufacture of large gun barrels. The patentees were Captain Sankey, director, and Mr Kent Smith, works chemist. At the close of the Queensferry works, Mr Kent Smith took up an executive position with the Carnegie Steel Works of America, which took over the patents.

Other products were super heated feed water heaters, steel boiler chimneys, auxiliary plant for the generation of steam, crankshafts and gears in vanadium steel for light and heavy motor vehicles, and steel and iron engineering castings. There was a workforce of five thousand men. Factory hours were 6a.m. to 5p.m., Saturday 6a.m. to 12.30p.m. A works canteen, cricket and football teams, with an occasional canteen concert, formed part of the social life at Willans and Robinson's.

Hopes of a successful business at Queensferry were dashed from the very beginning. In 1903 the steel works ran at a loss: £22,000 in the half year ended on 31 December and the next half years loss was £25,902. However, by 1906, there was an improvement, and the chairman Mr Mark Robinson stated that:

the success achieved by the company's steel made at Queensferry was remarkable, and there was already a profit from it, which promised to become considerable.' In the steam turbine branch of their business the company were doing well. During the past half year, they received a fair proportion of orders, which had been placed in this country, for land service turbines of large size, and their patented system of blading had been adopted for the turbines of the two great Cunard steamers which were now being built under special arrangements with the government. The one profitable part of the work done at Queensferry was owing to connections with the shipbuilding world at Liverpool.[59]

The situation blackened and in August 1908 it was proposed that the works at Queensferry be discontinued and offered at auction. The works closed in 1910, and in 1911 the whole of the plant was sold by auction. The original Company of Willans & Robinson Ltd. continued at Rugby until the late 1920s when the English Electric Co. Ltd. absorbed them.

The First World War
Within days of the declaration of war, the disused works of Willans and Robinson was requisitioned and became, as the press described it, 'the Queensferry concentration camp for German prisoners.'[60] German internees, like Baron von Trutychler, who had his sixteen hunters and his motor car commandeered, found themselves in custody. By the end of September, the first prisoners of war captured on the Belgian battlefield were received at Queensferry. With increased pressure of numbers, it was reported that, 'the bill of fare at the camp has undergone revision, the men are to be contented with war rations and one ounce of tobacco instead of two per week.' There were sixteen hundred prisoners in the camp. By May 1915, they had all departed to the Isle of Man, the press stating succinctly' 'the premises are to be utilised for other purposes.'[61]

The Munitions Factory
The Willans and Robinson site was quickly vacated to become the site of a munitions factory. In May 1915, Lloyd George was called to solve the crisis of the supply of munitions, ammunition, explosives, and guns, to the

Western Front. The army demanded 200,000 high explosive shells a day, far in excess of delivery of 150,000 per month. Lloyd George solved the problem within a year by drastic solutions. First, he gathered together a team of men who were the best brains in the country. Second, he constructed sixty new munitions factories. Third, he solved the problem of the labour supply by an agreement with the trade unions, who gave up the right to strike in munitions factories, and agreed that women should be allowed to do the work previously done by skilled men.

Negotiations began in April 1915, to take over the former site of the Willans and Robinson factory and adjoining land belonging to the Hawarden estate, between that site and Sandycroft foundry. Henry Gladstone sought to impose restrictions on the use of the site. He was strongly against the manufacture of nitric and sulphuric acid, but time and circumstance rendered his protest impotent. However, he was successful in diverting the discharge of toxic effluent from the river Dee to the river Mersey.[63]

German internees arrive at Queensferry
[FRO 51/96]

We have a description of the building of the Queen's Ferry Explosives Factory between May and December 1915:

Thousands of men invaded the area, new plant arrived, new buildings sprang up where once was marsh, and very soon the interiors of the existing structure took on an entirely new aspect. By day, the air resounded with the noise of riveter's hammers, band saws, cranes, locomotives and all manner of things that an engineer holds dear. By night the work still continued in the light of numberless arc lamps that, viewed from Hawarden hill, made the place look like a huge and magnificent fair ground. As a result of much forceful work, the first charge of cotton was able to be nitrated in the afternoon of 1 December 1915, just about six months after the first sod had been turned, and from that day, the process has practically been continuous.[63]

The factory site was designed by Kenneth Bingham Quinan (1878–1948), a consulting chemical engineer from South Africa. Lloyd George employed him in the construction of HM factories at Queensferry Sandycroft and Gretna.[64]

Chosen to be the assistant superintendent of the Queensferry factory was Stafford Cripps, who lived in a house in Leach's lane, Mancot opposite the hospital. Medically unfit for the army, Cripps volunteered in 1914 as a lorry driver in the Red Cross. Because of his knowledge of chemistry he was brought from France to Queensferry to take up a senior post at the explosives factory. Here, 'he learned and contributed much. Through his gift for administration and capacity to work long hours and master intricate problems he made Queensferry the most efficient of all the munitions factories.'[65]

The Site — Existing buildings in the disused Willans and Robinson factory were adapted for the manufacture of guncotton. It was early decided to increase the functions of the factory by providing, trinitrotoluene — T.N.T., and tetryl sections. New land was secured on the riverbank, south east of the old works, by the Asiatic Petroleum Company, who built a factory for the production of mono-nitro-toluene, M.N.T, adjacent to the T.N.T. section. The M.N.T. factory was subsequently incorporated into HM Factory Queen's Ferry. Plans were prepared for a Grillo Oleum section, which was situated south west of the main factory and separated from it by the L. & N. W. Railway. Wet guncotton was first manufactured here, and packed ready for despatch, by Christmas day, 1915. The total area of the factory, in its various sections, was 343 acres.

Queensferry Munitions Factory
[FRO 51/97]

The Manufacturing Process — Guncotton was produced on a large scale at the factory, to be used as an explosive to propel the shell from the bore of the gun. It is made up of cotton waste, which is manufactured into cellulose. It is cleansed, teased and immersed in acid, and then boiled, washed, dried and incorporated with nitro glycerine.

Also manufactured was the high explosive trinitrotoluene (T.N.T.), used for filling shells. To produce TNT Mononitrotoluene, M.N.T., was transferred from Sandycroft to Queensferry, by pipeline, for further nitration. The mixed acid for the M.N.T. stage came from Queensferry, and spent acid was then returned there. The various pipelines between the two factories were carried on an overhead gantry, about $^3/_4$ mile in length. Over 37,000 tons of M.N.T. were produced for consumption on the T.N.T. plant. Production in the M.N.T. section began in January 1916, and the first of the T.N.T. units was producing in March 1916. Over 55,000 tons of T.N.T. was despatched to Gretna during the plants 2 $^3/_4$ years of operation.

T.N.T. was found to act more satisfactorily as an explosive in combination with a charge of tetryl, to act as a booster. The manufacture of crude tetryl began in November 1916, and about 460 tons were produced. The purification of crude tetryl, by means of acetone, was introduced in September 1917, and about 160 tons of Grade 1 tetryl was produced by this method for despatch to Gretna. The Queensferry and Gretna factories had much in common: the production of nitro cellulose, nitric and sulphuric acids, the treatment of spent acids from nitrations, and acid mixing plants.

Transportation — The factory site was linked to the national railway network and extensive sidings were laid down for factory use and the internal railway system, exclusive of the M.N.T. section, extended to about thirteen miles. As many as three hundred railway wagons were known to have been received at, or, despatched from, Queen's Ferry, in the course of a single day. Some idea of the amount of goods traffic may be seen from the fact that about two hundred express goods engines were still standing in the Sandycroft siding, exposed to the elements, as late as 1924.[66]

Electricity and Power Equipment — The factory was equipped with three 1,500kw generators, and one of 1,000kw. In November 1917, 2.5 million units of electricity were generated in the factory.

Water Supply — This was largely piped from the Halkyn mines drainage system for process work. The maximum supply per day was four million gallons. Water from the river Dee was used for cooling purposes with a capacity of 6.3 million gallons per twenty-four hours. The effluent from the several sections was treated and then pumped to the Mersey at Ellesmere Port.

The Workforce — At its period of maximum output, the work force on the Queensferry and Sandycroft sites, numbered, 4,093 males and 3,232 females, totalling, 7,325. The largest number was employed on process work: a total of 3,418 of whom 2,492 were females. It was observed, 'that contingents of female workers are repeatedly proceeding to and from the various towns to the employment centres. The Flint Labour Exchange officials have been carrying out extra duties with the rush of females for employment.'[67]

The work force was transported from a wide area. Crosville Motor Co. Ltd. provided sixteen motor charabancs from Ellesmere Port, Wrexham, Heswall, Saltney and Mold. Three railway companies ran workmen's trains: London and North Western, Great Central, and Great Western lines, starting from Crewe, Whitchurch, Ellesmere Port and Wrexham. Other workers came by train from Chester.

Female workers were the responsibility of twelve supervisors who dealt with the women's welfare and answered their complaints.

Because of the toxic nature of their employment every effort was made to see that strict regulations designed to protect their health and safety were observed. They were provided with special clothing, changing rooms and bathing facilities, which were obligatory. Those on special processes received regular medical examination. The welfare and canteen arrangements were good, the women had a smaller sickness rate than the men, and good working results were attributed to eight hour shifts.

Outside the factory, recreation clubs were available for men and women: the Y.W.C.A, Y.M.C.A. and G.F.S. The government tried to stamp down on drunkenness in 1916, by cutting down the public house opening hours, from 12.30–2.30*p.m.* and 6–9*p.m.* In spite of this, the Flintshire Education Authority, received complaints, of the neglect of children through drunkenness, by munitions workers of both sexes.

The environment of the process work was hostile, and every care was taken to make medical and first aid arrangements available. Nursing staff was always on duty. The common accidents in 1917–8: acid burns, 3,813; eye injuries, 2,128; industrial dermatitis, 763; and other accidents, 12,778. Mancot Hospital opened at the end of 1916, received 411 cases, with an average stay of ten days. There were five cases of toxic jaundice, all of whom recovered.

The Royal Defence Corps, the Factory Police, and the staff of the explosives area office, shared the responsibility for the safety of the factory from explosion, fire, air raid or other circumstance. A factory fire brigade, consisting of chief fireman, nine firemen and nine firewomen, were on a shift rota. They were provided with special fire hoses to withstand the acid, a Dennis motor fire engine, and automatic and controlled sprinklers.

The policing of the Munitions factory strained the resources of the relatively small Flintshire Constabulary. They looked for assistance from the Lancashire Police Force, and the introduction of women police officers, to handle the large female work force. Eventually the police force was composed of eighty-seven male police and sixty women police. What it was like to be a policewoman at Queensferry is vividly recounted in the diary of Miss G. West, who recaptured the conditions, which prevailed there:

20 December 1916
The factory is about 5 miles from Chester and you go by train. On morning shift you have to rise at 4*a.m.* Horrid! Still you get the afternoons to yourself. The work consists of the following duties: searching for matches, cigarettes, spirits *etc.* (*i.e.* in the pockets, baskets, *etc.*); keeping guard at the gate, and allowing no one to enter without a pass; conducting stray visitors around and dealing with new workers, lost passes, lost clock-cards *etc.*; keeping guard in the office, where matrons, supervisors *etc.*, sign on, and enquiries made; patrolling to see there is no larking or slacking. We generally do these jobs, in turn, an hour at a time and have two hours off, for meal times, sometimes more so, it's very easy.

5 January 1917
But I haven't told you anything of this place yet. The factory is occupied in making the following: sulphuric acid, oleum, and gun cotton, T. N. T. The result is the most terrific collection of stinks or fumes, to put it less baldly, that you could possibly imagine. For patrolling purposes it is divided into four areas.

1. The grillo, consisting of five sulphur burners, acid coolers, platinising plant, *etc.* The burners each have 40 furnaces, 20 doors on either side. Occasionally, for cleaning purposes, the ' the blowers are taken off', exactly what that means, I don't know, but the result is most fascinating. Out of each furnace door,

This rather indistinct photograph shows the visit of King George V and Queen Mary to the Munitions Factory, 14 May 1917
[FRO 51/135]

and each damper, comes a huge sky blue flame, 3 or 4 feet long, so that the whole place is an avenue of gorgeous colour. The first one, and then another flame begins to get pink at the base and then pink all over, then they begin to have flame coloured tips and lemon yellow bases and then they gradually turn from yellow to pink to green and green to deep rich blue. After that, they begin to flicker out, but while it last, it is the most wonderful display of colour you could possibly see. Devonshire Park fireworks are mere glimmers to it. When the blowers are on, the grillo hasn't much to recommend it, being enriched with an evil sulphurous smell, such as I always imagined was reserved for the Devil and his angels, exclusively. I wonder if they even take the blowers off down there?

2. Gun Cotton. The first few times you go round, you think, what an interesting place, and are just brimming over with questions: but, the gun cotton, soon ceases to interest you, and the evil smells from the gun cotton retorts, become more noticeable.

3. The T.N.T. stinks, no other word describes it, an evil sickly, choky smell, which makes you cough, until you feel sick. But, even the T.N.T. is not so absolutely suffocating and overwhelming as

4. The Middle Section, oleum. Here, sulphuric is turned into nitric, and nitric, into oleum. The air is filled with white fumes and yellow fumes and brown fumes. The particles of acid land on your face and make you nearly mad with a feeling like pins and needles, only more so, and they land on your clothes and make brown spots all over them, and they rot your hankies, so that they come back from the laundry in rags, and they get up your nose and down your throat and into your eyes, so that you are blind and speechless, by the time you escape. All over the place, to cheer you on your way, are notices telling you what to do if anyone swallows brown fume. If conscious give an emetic. If blue in the face, apply artificial respiration and, if necessary, oxygen. Being quite sure, that you have swallowed numberless brown fumes, this is distinctly cheering. Each time you emerge from the Middle Section, you feel like Dante returning from hell.[68]

Henry Gladstone, by now Squire of Hawarden and Lord-lieutenant of Flintshire, was concerned that, 'the fumes given off, could not fail, to have a serious effect on the vegetation', in the neighbourhood. Later in the year, he noted the remarks of George Spencer, churchwarden and head teacher: 'I do not know which was the worse, incense fumes inside the church' or 'the Queensferry fumes in the churchyard!' Gladstone, noted: 'On several occasions in crossing the river Dee bridge, in broad daylight, dense yellow and white fumes, totally obscured the munitions works $^1/_2$ mile to the S.E. and Summers large iron works to the N.W.' In August and September, trees and hedges were stripped of their leaves, but just managed to produce some fruit.'[69]

A description of the houses built to accommodate the workers at the munitions factory is given under modern Mancot.

Between the Wars, 1918–39

These were not very prosperous years but some of the services drawn to Queensferry remained: Lloyd's Bank, the London City and Midland Bank, a firm of solicitors, T. M. Dutton's Motor Garage, Roberts & Son, Motor & Cycle Garage, and two chip shops. The Liberal Club of 1911, through lack of support, became the War Memorial Institute. One innovation of which all approved, was the establishment of the cinema, and Queen's Ferry had its share. The Cosy Cinema above the Co-op in Station Road was the place to see the latest silent film, and receive other entertainment. At Christmas, 1922, Mr Worrall, the cinema manager, with the co-operation of the traders of Queensferry, entertained 'the inmates of Broughton workhouse and made the season jollier and happier ' for them. The Enterprise Cinema was the venue for a concert, when in 1924, Zion P. M. church, held a concert there for extension funds. Great was the day when the Plaza Cinema opened, just in time to show the abdication of Edward VIII. Such was the popularity of cinema going that the Plaza was built to accommodate between five and six hundred people.

The munitions factory was gradually dismantled and the site sold off in piecemeal fashion. The last workers were paid off in August 1921. In 1922, Chester Town Council purchased the electric power installation at the factory. Throughout this period there were regular sales by the Disposal and Liquidation Commission.

H. Morris-Jones, recollected an area known locally as the 'ornament'. The area within the arc of the old Aston colliery railway and the Chester, Holyhead railway, in the centre of which, was a man made ornament, on which had been erected a tall yellow brick ornamental building. It was probably placed there by one of the Hancock family in the nineteenth century. The east of the mound was a willow pond where boys used to enjoy themselves standing on a raft floating on the surface, whilst they caught newts. Between the willow pond and the Chemistry area was a large undeveloped area.

In the 1920s a Gloucester man named Lane erected a works to manufacture and repair wagons which became known as the North Wales Wagon Co. Unfortunately a fire destroyed the works, there was a change of ownership and the business was moved to a new site near the Connah's Quay Docks. Another industry which occupied the former munitions site at Queensferry and Sandycroft was Scientific Roads (Western) Limited who made tar macadam and bought tar from their next door neighbours, Midland Tar Distillers. In addition they manufactured 'Bitrin' Products, tar bitumen compounded to prevent 'bleeding' on roads during hot weather. 'Bitrin Emulsion' for grouting and disinfectants was sold to sanitary authorities. The number employed in the mid thirties was about forty. In 1934 a considerable area of land was sold to Hanson's Dairies for their wholesale milk and delivery business.

Serious unemployment was not avoided on Deeside. Men were laid off at John Summers & Sons Ltd and there was short time. Attempts were made to do something for the unemployed and the *County Herald* reported in February 1933:

Queensferry Co-Operative Stores, 1920s [FRO 51/137]

On Monday morning last about forty men, all of whom are wholly unemployed, presented themselves on the site of the new recreation ground at Queensferry, situated near the old colliery shaft, and during the week they have been engaged in levelling out the ground. The men work in two shifts, twenty work for three hours in the morning, and the remaining number for three hours in the afternoon. The foremen on the job are also unemployed. The morning shift have a meal before they start work, and the other shift enjoy theirs when their afternoon work is over. Chits, which could be exchanged for food, are given to the men each week. It was announced that upwards of a hundred men had enrolled for voluntary labour.

Edward Prince of Wales accompanied by Lord Gladstone inspected the work in May 1934. Sadly Lord Gladstone died before the official opening, which was performed by Master John Parish, W. E. Gladstone's great grandson, in August 1935. Mr. T. Ketland who had worked with Lord Gladstone on the scheme recalled, 'when the men were working on the site they called it 'heartbreak hill'. At the word given by Master Parish there was a rush by the children, and it was not long before the swings and roundabouts were in full swing.

Slowly the local economy began to recover, particularly at John Summers & Sons Ltd, under the shadow of war. In January 1937 between thirty and forty men were found work at Queensferry smokeless fuel industrial plant for the production of Stellite smokeless fuel.

At Pentre over seventy young women were employed at Nutona Limited manufacturing various kinds of food from fruits, nuts, cereals, *etc.* A large quantity of the raw material was imported from Spain, Italy, France and Brazil.

The 1926 Queensferry Bridge

When the Jubilee Bridge was opened in 1897 it was designed to cope with regular river traffic but not with an increase in road traffic. The roadway on the bridge had over the years felt the stress of the increased weights of commercial vehicles, the structure of the bridge was affected and weight and speed limits had to be imposed which resulted in frequent delays and the tail back of the traffic.

The only solution to these problems was to build a new bridge and this was facilitated expeditiously by the close co-operation between the Ministry of Transport, the local authorities, the Board of Trade and the Dee Conservancy Board to ensure a smooth and swift passage through Parliament. In 1924 the tender of Messrs Sir William Arrol & Co. Ltd, bridge builders and public works contractors of Glasgow was accepted for the sum of £78,377, of which the Ministry of Transport contributed 75%. The Consulting Engineer was Mr. Basil Mott in collaboration with Mr. R. G. Whitely resident engineer.

The new bridge was opened in November 1926 by Colonel W. W. Ashley, Minister of Transport who was accompanied by Captain A. C. Gladstone, eldest grandson of W. E. Gladstone. The weight of steel in the structure was 1,200 tons. The bridge was electrically controlled and took $2^1/_2$ minutes to open and close.

The old and new bridges at Queensferry, 1926
[FRO 51/22]

The Queensferry By-pass and New Bridge

The scheme for major road works to banish the traffic congestion that had blighted Queensferry for years was inaugurated on 29 July 1960 when Flintshire County Council became the agent authority for the Minister of Transport. The first phase of this scheme consisted of the construction of a new road to form a by-pass to the east of Queensferry on the Dolgellau–south of Birkenhead Trunk Road (A494). The road is approximately 1.7 miles in length.

The scheme included the erection of a new river bridge which, in order to suit the road layout for the by-pass, was set on a skew and curved both horizontally and vertically. The bridge crosses the 416-foot gap of the river in three spans of 113 ft., 190 ft. and 113 ft. respectively with two 24 ft. carriageways, two 6 ft. footpaths and a 10 ft. wide central reservation.

A new railway bridge was erected on the site of the old bridge. An underpass was provided at Foxes Lane and a pumping station was erected to ensure that surface drainage water was not flooded from the Queensferry drain. These works were completed by 1962.

Educational Arrangements

The arrangements for primary and secondary education over the last 60 years are rather complicated for Hawarden, Shotton and Queensferry.

St. Ethelwold's VP school moved from its position in the centre of Shotton to a new site in Aston next to the Community Hospital. The Roman Catholic school, the Venerable Edward Morgan School, replaced the first school built in Charmley's Lane. Canon Drew School in Gladstone Way and the infant school in Church Lane, Hawarden, became Rector Drew School in 1977 when they moved to a new school in Cross Tree Lane.

In 1945, grammar school education continued to be available in Hawarden and the selection arrangements were continued whereby those narrowly failing the 11+ examination went to Deeside Central School, Shotton, and other children to the secondary school in Queensferry.

A new secondary modern school was opened in Saltney in 1954.

In 1958, a five-form entry school to accommodate approximately 600 pupils was opened and named Aston County Secondary Modern School. In 1966, a new four-form entry secondary school for approximately 700 pupils was built on land adjacent to Aston County Secondary School. This became a split-site school linked with Hawarden School on the introduction of comprehensive education. Hawarden became the lower school for Deeside Senior High School that comprised Aston and Queensferry Schools. Further developments resulted in Hawarden becoming Hawarden High School in the 1970s. Queensferry became Deeside Community High School and then John Summers High School. The Aston block was sold to ASDA and then demolished.

The Deeside Central School for a time became the lower school to Connah's Quay High School until it closed in the early 1980s.

12. Sandycroft

Sandycroft was part of the new township of Saltney created by the enclosure of land in 1781. Its northern boundary is the canalised river channel of 1737 and the southern boundary is with the township of Moor. The place name derives from the Sandycroft old colliery near Lloyd's Hills, Buckley, mentioned in a lease from Sir John Glynne dated 1751 to John Dutton and Walter Stubbs, of Beckbury, Shropshire. They were permitted to lay tram-roads from the colliery, past the lead smelting works at Pentrobin, and northwards, along the Moor lane, Hawarden, to the river at Fowl Pool Gutter, known as Sandycroft Mark. A tram road leading to Sandycroft Gutter existed by 25 March 1752. A railroad extending from near Lane End, Buckley, down to the riverside at Sandycroft Wharf, a length of four and a half miles, was built around 1790, and after 1800 in iron, and leased to Rigby and Hancock. This was abandoned about 1840.

Rigby probably supplied the iron rails from his Hawarden iron works. The Rigby family built the iron foundry in the 1770s. It stood in the rear of where now stands the Institute. Willett describes it in 1822:

> In the Town of Hawarden also, is an Iron Foundry, with a Boring Mill, all on a large scale. This is an old Establishment, of great deserved note, originating in the late highly respected Mr Rigby, father of the present worthy proprietor, and where articles are fabricated from the great Fire engine of sixty horse power, to the smallest kitchen utensil; and this work affords employment, and support to about one hundred persons.[1]

William Hancock in partnership with John Rigby founded Wm. Hancock & Co. in 1792. Hancocks were one of the largest brickmaking firms in Wales. As a result of this partnership, a tram road was constructed to join the Aston tramway, to give access to the river at the Dundas wharf, for the export of bricks, tiles and coal.

Rigby extended his ironworks by opening a branch in Sandycroft. The date is uncertain. George Lloyd gives it as 'sometime after 1822', another source as 'erected 1836'.[2] John Rigby began building ships at Sandycroft, using his skills to become a specialist in steam engines and construction in iron.

Morris-Jones lists the following ships, launched at John Rigby's shipyard: *Kingfisher*, 1830, paddle steamer, 120 tons; *Lapwing*, 1842, paddle steamer, 33 tons; *Alexandra*, 1835, paddle steam, 83 tons; *Princess Royal*, 1841, schooner, 2 masted, 64 tons; *Guapicen*, 1841, gunboat; *Sarah Davison*, 1842, flat, 42 tons; *Gamon*, 1847, schooner; *Prince of Wales*, 1843, schooner, 2 masted 47 tons.

The following are known to have used iron in their construction: *Prince of Wales*, 1843, paddle steamer, 38 tons; *Star*, 1845, paddle steamer, 92 tons; *Birkenhead*, 1846, paddle steamer, 132 tons.

A report of 1846 states:

> We have often had occasion to notice the extensive operations carried on by the Hawarden Iron Company, at Sandycroft. At present the company are engaged in putting a pair of 500 horsepower engines into the *Fury* steam frigate, now lying at Liverpool, which we are assured, for beauty of workmanship and engineering talent, will compete with any in the navy.[3]

A prestigious commission came from Sir John Gladstone, of Fasque, and the Duke of Buccleuch, for an iron steam packet, to serve the Burnt Island and Granton Ferry on the Forth. She was named the *Forth*, of 150 feet in length and fitted with 120 h.p. engines. The launch took place in October, when the tide was 20 ft. 5 in. and was not without incident, and foreshadowing future difficulties

> When the steam vessel touched the water, she stuck in the cradle; and all the efforts of the *Cymro* steamer were unavailing to move her. However, the launch was easily perfected in the subsequent tide.

Celebrations went ahead and a considerable party were entertained to dinner by the Company, at the Hawarden Castle Hotel Queen's Ferry, when John Rigby, presided.[4] Her trial in April 1847 was noted with satisfaction: 'from her power of engines she will prove as effective with a head wind or side sea and keep her course straight.'[5]

Perhaps, because of the ill health of John Rigby or financial difficulties, the Sandycroft premises of the Hawarden Iron Work, were advertised in July 1847 and again in 1853, as' Sandycroft (machinery and ship) works.'

The *Royal Charter*[6]

The Sandycroft shipbuilding yard was leased by George Cram from, Williams' Brothers, bankers, Chester. Cram was established at this time as a shipbuilder at the Roodeye, Chester.

The press reported extensively on the construction and launch of the *Royal Charter* in 1855.

Great interest attaches to the vessel on account of its vast proportions, the novelty of the construction of such a ship on the banks of the Dee, and the situation of the spot where the launch will take place. During the last three weeks thousands of people have been down to visit her, both by water and along the cop. We understand that the walk presented the appearance of a fair last Sunday, and we have no doubt that next Tuesday will be a general gala.[7]

The dramatic launch of the ship received wide coverage:

Despite the heavy soaking rain on Tuesday last, thousands of people assembled on the banks of the Dee, from Chester, Liverpool, and all parts of Flintshire, to witness the launch of the magnificent screw steam ship *Royal Charter*, which has been built at Sandycroft, for the Australian Steam Ship Company of Liverpool. From Chester everything that could roll was on the road, and every thing that could float was on the water, with people eager for the spectacle.

To show more clearly the difficulties attending the launch, we may explain that the river Dee is at this part much too narrow to allow the vessel to be placed across it, and she therefore had to be built and launched almost in a line with the stream, her stern up the river, so as to let her take the water in the same direction as the flood tide runs. To add to the difficulties, the Sandycroft side of the river is impeded with banks of mud and sand just above the building yard …

A party of about sixty ladies and gentlemen from Liverpool went by the railway, amongst whom were Mr Nathaniel Hawthorne, the American consul at Liverpool, many shipbuilders and nearly all the gentlemen from the large establishment of Messrs Gibbs, Bright and Co., the agents here for the company to which she belongs.

Handbill advertising voyages on the Royal Charter
[FRO PR/F/155, National Museums &
Galleries on Merseyside]

The ROYAL CHARTER'S extraordinary passage of 59 days to Melbourne is the fastest ever made.

LIVERPOOL & AUSTRALIAN NAVIGATION COMPANY.

Steam from Liverpool to Australia.
UNDER 60 DAYS.

THE MAGNIFICENT STEAM CLIPPER
"ROYAL CHARTER,"

2719 Tons Register and 200 Horse Power, with Fire-proof and Water-tight Compartments,

F. BOYCE, COMMANDER,

IS APPOINTED TO LEAVE THE RIVER MERSEY FOR

MELBOURNE, PORT PHILIP,
ON THURSDAY, 2nd OCTOBER.

This noble Steam Clipper, built expressly for the Company, one of the finest models yet constructed, combines all the advantages of a Steamer with those of a Clipper Sailing Ship, and offers the only opportunity yet presented to the Public of certainty in the time required for the voyage. She has just made the extraordinary passage of 59 days to Melbourne—a performance never before accomplished. On this voyage she ran one day 358 knots, during which she attained the astonishing speed of 18 nautical miles in the hour. Her daily average for the whole distance to Melbourne was 223¾ knots, or 10½ miles per hour. Her accommodations for all classes of Passengers are unrivalled.

FARES TO MELBOURNE.

AFTER SALOON—60, 65, and 75 Guineas. | SECOND CLASS,......25 and 30 Guineas.
THIRD CLASS,......16, 18, and 20 Guineas.

Including Stewards' Fees, the attendance of an experienced Surgeon. and all Provisions of the best quality, except Wines, Spirits, and Malt Liquors, which will be supplied at very moderate prices on board.

Children from One to Twelve Years, Half Price. Infants free.

Passengers booked to be forwarded by the First Opportunity after arrival to SYDNEY, ADELAIDE, HOBART-TOWN, &c., at an extra charge of 7 and 8 Guineas 1st Class; 4 and 5 Guineas 2nd Class; 3 and 4 Guineas 3rd Class.

In the AFTER SALOON every requisite will be provided, including Beds, Berths, Bedding, Plate, Table Linen, Crockery, Glass, &c.; supplied with the best articles of Food, and an abundant Dietary Scale. Live Stock, Poultry, &c.

The AFTER SALOON is fitted with Ladies' Boudoir, Baths, &c., &c., &c.

DECK.—The Poop aft is appropriated to the After Saloon Passengers alone. The Deck amidships to the First and Second Class Passengers, and forward the Third Class Passengers.

No Passenger can be accommodated in a State-room by himself, so long as he can be placed with other passengers, unless the State-room is specially arranged for; Berths may be changed, if necessary, unless a whole State-room is secured.

DEPOSITS.

One-half of the passage-money must be paid before a Berth can be secured. The Berths are appropriated in rotation as the Deposits are paid. Passengers in the country can have Berths secured by enclosing a Bank or Post-office order to the undersigned for half the amount of passage, and they are requested to give their Christian names, ages, and trades, and if married, names and ages of each member of the family.

LUGGAGE.

THE REGULATIONS BELOW WILL BE STRICTLY ADHERED TO.

Forty Cubic Feet allowed each Adult Passenger in After Saloon
Thirty do. " " " " Second Class
Twenty do. " " " " Third do.
Children in proportion.

Freight on any excess, not exceeding 10 feet, will be charged at 3s. per foot. If, however, the excess be more than 10 cubic feet, it must be previously engaged as cargo. Such overplus must be along side the vessel six days prior to sailing, or it cannot be taken on board: and unless specially engaged previously, cannot be taken if the ship is full.

PASSENGERS MUST TAKE CHARGE OF THEIR LUGGAGE UNTIL ON BOARD SHIP.

Before Luggage can go on board all Passage-money to be paid. The Luggage to be distinctly marked with Paint, two inches long. with the owners name and destination, and cannot be delivered elsewhere. State-rooms, Berths, and Cabins to which it belongs.

The owner's are not responsible for loss or damage to Luggage. Merchandise cannot be carried as Luggage. All Bullion, Specie, Watches, Jewellery, or Treasure, above the value of £150, must be declared, and pay the Freight.

DOGS are charged £5 each.

SERVANTS—Females are charged one-half After Saloon Fare. Men Servants are charged Third Class Fare, and are berthed and

Nathaniel Hawthorne described his arrival at Sandycroft:

Here the train stopped, and absolutely deposited our whole party of excursionists, under a heavy shower, in the midst of a muddy potato field, whence we were to wade through mud and mire to the ship yard, almost half-a-mile off.[8]

The three fine boats, *Rattler, Sampson* and *Pilot*, belonging to the Liverpool Steam Tug Company, were in attendance to tow the vessel round to Liverpool. Spectators from all the surrounding neighbourhood lined both banks of the river, and presented a terrible array of umbrellas!

At one o'clock, the tide being just on the full, and everything declared in readiness Mr William Patterson, the builder, who constructed the *Great Britain*, at Bristol, gave the word …

The ship began slowly to move; Mrs. — threw the bottle against the bow with a spasmodic effort that dashed it into a thousand pieces, and diffused the fragrance of the old port all around, where it lingered several minutes. I did not think that there could have been such a breathless moment in an affair of this kind.

The ship moved majestically down toward the river; and unless it were Niagara, I never saw anything grander and more impressive than the motion of this mighty mass as she departed from us. We on the platform, and everybody along both shores of the Dee, took off our hats in the rain, waved handkerchiefs, cheered, shouted, — 'Beautiful!' 'What a noble launch', 'Never was so fair a sight!' — and, really, it was so grand, that calm, majestic movement, that I felt the tears come into my eyes. The wooden pathway adown, which she was gliding, began to smoke with the friction; when all at once, when we expected to see her plunge into the Dee, she came to a full stop. Mr —, the father of my friend, a gentleman with white hair, a dark expressive face, bright eyes, and an oriental cast of features, immediately took the alarm. A moment before his countenance had been kindled with triumph; but now he turned pale as death, and seemed to grow ten years older while I was looking at him. Well he might, for his noble ship was stuck fast in the mud of the Dee, and without deepening the bed of the river, I do not see how her vast iron hulk is ever to be got out.[9]

On the tide falling it was discovered that the failure of the launch was owing to the ground having given way under the starboard 'ways'. The *Chester Chronicle* described the *Royal Charter*:

The outline of her hull is beautiful, her model is well proportioned, and her clipper lines must ensure great speed, when she is used either as a sailing ship or steamer separately, or as both combined. Her dimensions for tonnage are, length, 320 feet; beam, $41^1/_2$ feet; depth of hold, $26^1/_2$ feet; measurement 2, 785 tons . . . the engines will be of 300 horse power, with boilers to work up to 500 horse power . . . she is provided with Trotman's patent anchors, manufactured at the Dee ironworks, Saltney, by Messrs. Henry Wood and Company.

At the end of August another attempt to launch her failed; but eventually,

… with very little exertion, she floated almost of herself, and the launch was greeted with hearty cheers and the event announced by the firing of guns. On Thursday at one o'clock in the afternoon, at the time of high water, the *Royal Charter* was taken in tow by three steam tugs, and proceeded down the river on her way to Liverpool. She was gaily decorated, and as she passed Queen's Ferry and other places much cheering took place. By the time she got to Flint Castle the tide had ebbed considerably and on passing a corner where two channels meet, she took ground, and became safely embedded without any strain or shock. At the flood yesterday about 1*a.m.* she again floated, and at the return of the tide she proceeded.

The maiden voyage of the *Royal Charter* was announced 'for Melbourne direct, on the 17th January 1856, forwarding passengers for Sydney, Adelaide, Hobart Town &c. Fares from 16 to 60 guineas. She left on time with 260 passengers, but was detained in Plymouth Sound, to repair and strengthen her upper works.[10] She arrived at Melbourne, on the 16 April, after a passage of 59 days from Plymouth, the shortage voyage yet made by the regular ocean route.

We hear nothing more until the *Royal Charter* was wrecked close to Moelfre, Anglesey in the early hours of 26 October 1859. She left Melbourne in August with 388 passengers, many returning from the gold fields, and a crew of 122. On leaving Holyhead she ran into a hurricane. The captain attempted to let her ride out the storm on her anchors but these parted at 1.30*a.m.* and soon after 3 o'clock she was aground on the rocks at Moelfre. A local farmer roused the villagers, but the Moelfre lifeboat crew found it impossible to get out to sea. Contact was made with the shore when a sailor from the *Royal Charter* with a rope attached to his body reached the land and was preparing to haul passengers ashore on this life-line when a freak wave smashed the hull in two and began the

Gold ingot imbedded in iron from the wreck of
the Royal Charter
[Illustrated London News]

disintegration of the stranded vessel. As the *Chester Chronicle* put it,

> … that journey so nearly terminated was fated to end in the destruction of the noble ship, in a watery grave for 455 people, and that within a few yards of land, and less than 50 miles from their port of debarkation. In a few hours the *Royal Charter* was smashed into scraps of iron and timber, only 39 out of 493 souls being saved.[11]

The wreck captured the imagination of the nation and Charles Dickens was stimulated to write his book *The Shipwreck* to tell the tragic story of the doomed passengers and crew. Unfortunately the return of the *Royal Charter* coincided with one of the worst storms of the century. On the same night and following day 195 vessels were wrecked and 648 people lost their lives. Ironically most of the treasure was recovered from the wreck. The force of the storm is seen in the illustration of a gold ingot embedded in plate of iron recovered in the salvage operation.

> The mass of gold impacted in the fissure is part of an ingot of the purest quality imported, worth more than £4 an ounce. Divers employed in recovering the sunken treasure, who found the gold so firmly fixed that it was impossible to separate it from the iron, sent it up in its present form from the wreck. The remainder of the ingot, of which an engraving is also given, was found subsequently near the same spot, and has been identified, together with nearly £300,000 worth of gold of the original shipment of about £320,000. The weight of the ingot is about 211 ounces, and it is worth about £860.[12]

Sandycroft Foundry

The career of George Cram was wrecked before that of the *Royal Charter*. Sandycroft Quay was not quiet for long. The tradition of Rigby's engineering skills was revived, enhanced, and developed by John Taylor, a respected figure in the Flintshire lead mining industry. Taylor showed his qualities as manager of the Mold mines situated in the Alyn Valley. In 1837 Taylor established a foundry at Rhydymwyn to provide machinery for the lead mines and develop an overseas market. Taylor saw the vacant site at Sandycroft as an opportunity to be more favourably situated for the export of mining machinery to all parts of the British Empire. Taylor occupied the site in 1862 and established an iron foundry under the management of his eldest son, John Taylor, junr. In less than a

decade the Sandycroft Foundry enjoyed a worldwide reputation as noted by the *Mining Journal* in December 1871. 'At the Sandycroft Works, the largest in the northern part of the Principality, they are busy in engines, boilers and pumps for home mines, Spain &c.'[13]

Like every Victorian entrepreneur the Taylor's were expert publicists. In 1887 they invited their neighbour, W. E. Gladstone to tea and had the event reported in the press:

The remains of Sandycroft Quay
[PRN 34/252 CPAT]

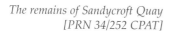

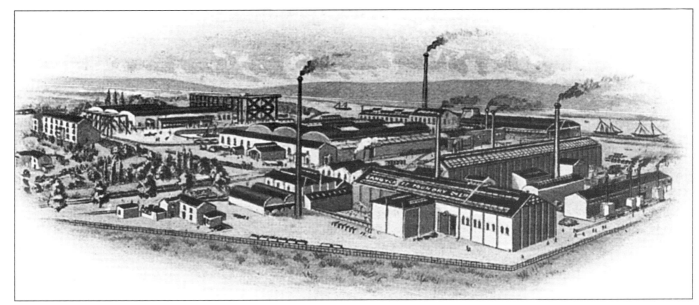

Sandycroft Foundry, c.1908
[H. G. Gregory deposit, FRO D/DM/158/3]

The Sandycroft Foundry is principally engaged in the manufacture of machinery for the extraction of gold from quartz, for which particular class of work they have established a great reputation. Mr Taylor and Mr Kelly the works manager explained the machinery and processes through which the quartz passed. Mr Gladstone also inspected some steam engines in the course of manufacture, and saw the processes of casting, forging by steam hammers, and by hand, and the operations of the lathes, planing and boring machines *etc*. The Sandycroft Works are upon the Hawarden estate, and the majority of the hands, numbering upwards of 400, are natives of Hawarden or the surrounding district.[14]

The company was overwhelmed with orders from India, Brazil, Australia, New Zealand, and the newly opened gold mines of South Africa. The *Mining Journal* remarked in 1899 that, 'there is hardly a mining field in the world where Sandycroft stamp mills are not in evidence.' At a dinner given in 1891, Mr Herbert Gladstone remarked, that the Sandycroft Company was most fortunate in being allied to the eminent firm in London, Messrs. John Taylor and Sons. Mr Frank Taylor, the manager at Sandycroft, replied proudly, stating the extent of the foundry's five-year output. 'Gold mining machinery', he remarked, 'is our speciality, and of stamp mills, the machine chiefly used, we have made 3,300 during the last five years, which if placed in a line would reach from Hawarden Castle to Sandycroft, or a distance of a mile and a quarter. The turner's work in that period such as the lifters, camshafts and so forth, would reach ten miles. The stamp mills crushing three tons of rock in two hours would crush three million tons per year. From each ton of rock I estimate an ounce of gold would be extracted, which total up to 56. 25 millions of money in five years. In addition we have made engines representing a total of 20,000-horse power, and something like 300 boilers.'[15]

Under the supervision of Frank Taylor, grandson of the founder, the manufacture of electrical machinery was added to the firms business and the works extended and altered. It was reported that, 'the last shop which the company erected measures in length 160 feet by 115 feet in width and 60 feet to the gables. There are three electric travelling cranes and nine motors drive the whole of the machinery in this department. The shop is heated with the patent steam-circulating apparatus. The company have also erected a new forge, and are about to commence building a new moulding shop.'[16]

In 1900 the L.N.W.R. Co. made extensive improvements to Sandycroft Station with new platforms and waiting rooms emphasising the growing passenger traffic. The company continued to export mining machinery of the highest quality up to the First World War. By 1920 there was much competition, order books were empty, and the firm closed in 1926.

The foundry was offered for sale on 11 October 1927. 'Engineering Works and Foundries. On the river Dee, eight direct sidings to the L.M.S. Railway. Ground area of about 14 acres with ground floor buildings, having a floor space of 118,000 square feet. and a block of six cottages known as river row cottages.[17] No offers were made

Sandycroft Foundry, 1907. A pair of winding engines made for an Indian gold mine
[FRO 60/27]

Sandycroft Foundry apprentices
[FRO 60/45]

for the engineering works and foundries. The dispersal of the entire contents of the works, offices and yards occupied the auctioneer three days. Good prices were obtained. In 1930 the premises were leased to the International Electrolytic Plant Company and sold to them in 1951. They manufactured plant for the production of hydrogen and oxygen, employing at times over 100 people.

For over sixty years the Taylor family had a tremendous influence on the community at Sandycroft. They provided work accompanied by training in engineering skills so that those who had been apprenticed at Sandycroft could obtain employment, anywhere. An Institute was founded in 1875, to provide their workers with congenial surroundings for their leisure, and an opportunity for education and improvement. The building was built of wood on a brick foundation, and situated in the centre of the village, near the Drill Hall and railway station. The grounds enclosed a bowling green and quoiting ground. The use of the institute to the whole community was described in the local press:

> The library and reading room was opened last winter and has up to the present time, been fairly patronised. The first festival of the Sandycroft Institute took place on Saturday last. An excellent tea was provided to which over 200 sat down. Messrs. Taylor and Bicknell of the Sandycroft Foundry rendered support to the Institute. After tea dancing commenced on the bowling green, to the music of the Sandycroft Foundry Band, till nine o'clock, when all quietly dispersed.[18]

A sea trip to Llandudno, the previous August, to raise funds for the Institute, was not quite as successful.

> Through the kindness of Messrs. Taylor and Bicknell, it was arranged that the trip should be made by the steamer *Swiftsure* on Tuesday last, at the low fare of 2s. 6d. there and back. 250 tickets were disposed of, and the steamer left Sandycroft about 9 a.m., stopping on the way down the river at Connah's Quay, where a considerable addition was made to the number on board. All went well and pleasantly for some time. The Sandycroft Brass Band accompanied the excursionists, and dancing commenced right merrily to its strains: but one by one the dancers found themselves obliged to retire, and by the time the vessel reached the Irish sea most of those on board had felt the effects of the voyage to an unpleasant degree. The sea was so rough that it was deemed advisable to give up going to Llandudno. Some of the party preferred stopping at New Brighton, the rest went on to Liverpool, where they arrived about 2.30p.m., and a stay of an hour was allowed. Many of the party however had quite enough of the sea, and took a more pleasant mode of travelling, preferring the train to the steamer. Those who returned by the steamer arrived at Sandycroft about 9p.m. with no mishap beyond the loss of a few hats, and a drenching or two from the spray.[19]

The paternalistic attitude of the Taylor family was echoed when the Institute was replaced, 1899–1900, by a new building. It was noted:

> Although the present buildings hardly meet the requirements of the members they have served the purpose for which they were erected by generous spirited and gratuitous hands, and the facilities thus offered have been beyond doubt the means of helping many into good positions who were formerly apprenticed at the Sandycroft engine works.

The new building was two storied with spacious rooms: reading room, library, council room, games room, two billiard rooms, caretaker's house, baths, lavatories, and surrounded by a veranda, with the gymnasium approached by a corridor way.[20]

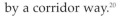

The vice president of the Sandycroft Mechanics Institute demonstrated how much control the Foundry exercised over the lives of its employees. 'He was sanguine to hope for a much greater membership, seeing that there were about 500 employed at the works, and 311 only were members. The probable cost of the building and furnishing would be

The Institute
[FRO 60/23]

between £1,650 and £1,700 which sum had been advanced by the Engine Work Company.[21]

Further education by way of evening classes was available. For example, in 1908, eight out of the eleven candidates who attended the machine construction and drawing classes were successful in obtaining certificates from the Board of Education.

The foundry had its own fire brigade, founded in 1886, under the command of Superintendent E. S. Taylor, and Deputy Superintendent W. Kelly, the works managers. The villagers turned out en mass to greet the arrival of the new fire engine in 1889. Its capabilities were described to reassure the populace. 'It can be worked by 22 men and is capable of discharging about 100 gallons per minute and of throwing a jet of water to a height of 120 feet. It is of the utmost importance to owners of property between Sandycroft and Rhyl.' In 1891 a special demonstration was staged by the Fire Brigade at Hawarden Castle for the benefit of W. E. Gladstone and members of his family.

An ambulance corps was formed in 1887. It met fortnightly to practise bandaging, stretcher drill, and rendering first aid.

An annual festival and sports in connection with the Institute commenced in 1875 and was held in the grounds and on the field adjoining, under the presidency of one of the Taylor family.

In December 1932, Lord Gladstone of Hawarden, generously conveyed freehold land, the dwelling house and institute to the trustees, to be used, as in their opinion, 'will best tend to promote the moral, physical, and intellectual welfare and rational recreation of residents in Sandycroft and the neighbourhood.'

The institute was used until the l970s by the youth club, old age pensioners committee, and a keep fit class, and dancing class. A public meeting was held in October 1970 to discuss its future, which was unfortunately, decided by a fire on 11 June 1971. Eventually a new infant school was built on the site in 1974. The county council promised to provide community facilities at the school and the trustees made a capital contribution towards the cost of this provision from money received from the fire insurance and the sale of the land.[22]

R. Graesser Ltd.

New industry came to Sandycroft in 1934. The Graesser family, experienced chemical engineers, moved from Acrefair (which overlooks the Pontcsyllte Aqueduct, built by Thomas Telford, 1805), to a site of about seventy acres. The founder of the firm was Robert Ferdinand Graesser, who was born in Ober Mosel, in Saxony in 1844.

Phoenix Street
[FRO 60/22]

He started his own business at Acrefair in 1867 in partnership with a Manchester lawyer. They were major producers of phenol and its by-products. In 1921 N. H. Graesser went into partnership with the American Company, Monsanto. The partnership ended in 1928 and Graesser's came to Sandycroft in 1934 as Graesser Salicylates. By April 1935 their new plant was in production and in 1939 a co-operative scheme with the Lancashire Tar Distillers and various gas companies ensured the long-term supply of tar and tar acids. In 1945 R. Graesser Ltd., merged with Lancashire Tar Distillers Ltd., and the Litherland, Liverpool, refinery was operated in conjunction with the Sandycroft Works in the production of refined tar acids and its by-products — phenols, cresols, xylenols, cresylic acids and high boiling tar acids.

In 1960 Aspro Nicholas, an Australian Multinational Group, acquired the Graesser Thomas works. Following a recession in 1981 the workforce was reduced from 250 to 150, which was quickly followed by an increase in products. To reflect the change the name was changed from Aspro Nicholas to Graesser Laboratories in 1984. Further changes came in 1988 when the firm was acquired by B.T.P. plc and later merged with NIPA laboratories.

The School Chapel of St Ambrose, Sandycroft, 1875

A Sunday school was opened in the Vaults public house by Miss Helen Gladstone, which formed the nucleus of a school-chapel, named after St Ambrose of Milan. Her brother Stephen, the rector of Hawarden, opened it on 10 April 1875 Amongst those present on that day were a number of gentlewomen, who worked with the poor in the parish as district visitors, including the two Misses Rigby, Miss Burnett and Miss Helen Gladstone. A year later the school was being used for Sunday worship, a Sunday school, weekday services, and as a 'night school for lads', and on Saturday evenings for girls'. A mothers' meeting was held on Wednesday afternoons.

The entries in the school logbook for the first year are typical. About thirty children presented themselves during the first week after the opening, and twelve of these, above the age of seven years, were unable to read. A strike amongst the local workmen kept children at home because there was no money for school pence. There were rejoicings in honour of the return home of W. H. Gladstone with his bride. In the next year, W. E. Gladstone, Miss Helen Gladstone and John and Frank Taylor made regular visits from the foundry. Over the years epidemics of chicken pox, scarlet fever, measles and mumps were frequent.

1885 was a very cold winter:

February 24. The children have not done knitting or needlework this week because of the cold, their fingers being too numbed. It was decided the next year that, 'during the cold weather the classes take their turns in front of the fire alternately.'

May 11 1896 was a red-letter day for the school when Miss Ada Jones took charge. Here she stayed as headteacher until retirement in December 1930. She was an excellent teacher, full of ideas. The school report for 1903 recognised this. 'This school is pleasantly and efficiently conducted. Miss Jones is progressive and new features are constantly being introduced into the curriculum.' For the nature lesson boys brought rabbits to school.

A balloon was sighted in February 1910 on a voyage to Dublin and a lesson given on the same theme. On 29 May 1911, a passenger boat was launched at Queen's Ferry, and in the afternoon those who witnessed the ceremony were given a lesson on ships past and present. In 1912 free meals were distributed to necessitous children whose fathers were laid off owing to the coal strike. In November 1913 four boys were allowed out of school to make a sketch of the new church. The logbook recorded the changes made by the building of the new church, and the Great War.

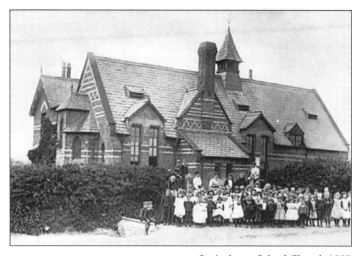

St Ambrose School Chapel, 1895
[S. E. Gladstone]

1914 Jan. 21. The stained glass windows have been removed from the east end of the main room and plain glass put in, consequently the lighting has much improved.

May 28. older boys visited the shipbuilding yard.

July 2. Lesson taken on the assassination of the heir to the Austrian throne.

August 27. Great interest is being taken by the children in the progress of the Great War. A war map has been purchased and coloured by the boys.

1915 March 23. Current events, the operations in the Dardanelles.

1916 February 2. Current events, Zeppelin raid over eastern and midlands counties

1917 Jan. 11. Geography lesson. Our farms and farmers, taken in connection with food problems.

May 14. Visit of King and Queen to H.M. Factory. The children taken to see their Majesties.

In 1918 the influenza epidemic reduced the numbers attending school. The closing of the Foundry was felt:

1929 April 22. Five children (one family) have left the school for Canada, sailing under the emigration scheme.

The radio began to play a part in school life:

1930 June 4. Scholars listened in to a commentary on Derby Day, broadcast from Epsom.

On 18 December 1930 Miss Ada Jones retired after 34 years service as headteacher of Sandycroft School and was presented with a handsome grandmother clock. When the school closed in 1957 Sandycroft pupils attended the new County Primary School at Pentre, opened the same year.

St. Francis Church, Sandycroft

St. Ambrose was used as the centre for Anglican worship from 1875 to 1913. The first service, harvest thanksgiving, was held in October 1875. Lady Frederick Cavendish and Mrs. Wickham, provided an altar, and Holy Communion was celebrated for the first time on 7 September 1876. An apse, added to the school-chapel, was dedicated in October 1892, for which Lady Stepney gave a stained glass window the work of Edward Frampton.

In 1907, a meeting was held to discuss the provision of a new church. It was evident that the district and the congregation had outgrown 'the accommodation and conveniences, (or lack of them), which the school building provided'. They thought they might be better served by 'a comely little iron church, which might be devoted entirely to sacred purposes and be an immense boon to this active and growing community.' A building fund was launched in 1907, which was greatly enriched in 1912, when Mrs. Frank Taylor gave £1,000 towards the cost of building a chancel in memory of her husband, who died in 1908. This was made practical when W. G. C. Gladstone gave a site for the new church.

There were two outstanding memories of the laying of the foundation stone of the new church dedicated to St Francis of Assisi. The first was the very heavy autumnal rain, and the second, was the deference paid to the deceased benefactor, Frank Taylor, by his Masonic brethren. An occasion which the *County Herald* described with great gusto.

On Saturday the foundation stone of the new church at Sandycroft was laid with full Masonic ceremonial by the Right Worshipful Provincial Grand Master, North Wales, Colonel Platt, C.B., who was supported by a number of Grand Officers of England, Provincial Grand Officers, and brethren of the Province of North Wales and neighbouring provinces. Those present at the ceremony included Mr W. G. C. Gladstone, Lord-lieutenant of

Left: St Francis Church
[Church booklet]

Below:The chancel St Francis Church
[Church booklet]

Below: St Francis Church Hall, 1958
[Church booklet]

Flintshire, who gave the site, Miss Helen Gladstone and the Hon. Rev. A. W. Lyttelton, and the Rector of Hawarden. The procession from Sandycroft Institute to the site of the new church included members of the various choirs of the parish. When the site was reached the brethren halted and formed an avenue, through which the Provincial Grand Master passed, and his arrival at the site was heralded by a flourish of trumpets. Worshipful Brother E. Sydney Taylor, requested the Grand Master to lay the foundation stone, presenting him with a trowel, and with the accustomed ceremonies strewed corn and poured wine and sprinkled oil over the stone.[23]

Rector Bennett reported the event in the Hawarden Parish Magazine. He reminded the readers of the rain, the ancient Masonic Ceremonial, and went on to thank Mrs. Frank Taylor the church's chief benefactress, adding,

But it would ill become us to forget that those who have laboured before us at Sandycroft, named our School Chapel after the great Bishop, St Ambrose, and on the north side of the chancel of the Church of St Francis will be built a beautiful little chapel, which we shall call the chapel of St Ambrose, and to it will be transferred from the apse in the school, the altar and its ornaments, the prayer desk and the windows in accordance with the wishes of Mrs Drew, and in memory of Canon Drew. He reminded his readers that they were within 'some £300 of the £2,640 needed for the building of the chancel, the chapel of St Ambrose, the vestries, and two bays of the nave, which will give us before this time next year accommodation for 230. Later on two more bays will be added to the nave, and our Church will then hold between four and five hundred worshippers.[24]

The architect was Sir Charles Nicholson. The church was built in a simple Gothic style with a dark brick exterior and plastered interior, and a square bell-turret at the junction of the north aisle and the northeast chapel. A. G. Edwards, bishop of St Asaph, dedicated the church on 20 December 1913, in honour of St Francis of Assisi and in memory of Frank Taylor. Admission to the service to which 350 were invited was by ticket only.

This dedication marked the end of the golden age of Sandycroft. The foundry was an early victim to economic changes and the depression; the heart went out of the community when it closed. Plans to add two more bays to St Francis' church were not carried out, but alterations were made to the west end, providing extra accommodation and a gallery for the organ, at a cost of £1,500. To mark the official completion of the building the

St Francis Church and school
[FRO 60/24]

church was consecrated on 10 July 1935. On 6 December 1961, the feast of St Nicholas, a chapel was dedicated to the honour of that saint, which replaced the former children's corner. When the school closed in 1957, money from the sale of the building was generously made available to the parish by the Gladstone family, and this paid for a new church hall, erected in the grounds of the church, and dedicated on 14 December 1958, by the rector N. S. Baden-Powell.

Sandycroft Primitive Methodist Chapel

The Primitive Methodist Chapel was erected in 1864. This building incorporated a house. When the chapel was extended about 1900, it took in the house, the kitchen of which was used as a vestry until 1972. A pipe organ was installed in 1920, electric light, and a solid fuel heating boiler. Major changes took place in the 1970s. In 1974 the vestry and outhouse were demolished and a schoolroom erected. The chapel was refurbished, 1984/5, and the pipe organ replaced by an electronic organ.

Tradition has it that before the chapel was built, services were held either in the open air, or, in various houses, particularly those of Mr and Mrs. Thomas Roberts, Duckworth Row, and Mr and Mrs. Robert Carter, 1 Pritchard Street. In the 1905 Report, the chapel had 160 sittings, 4 elders, 21 communicants, 55 adherents, 13 teachers, and 55 Sunday school scholars.

The Anglicans and Primitive Methodists joined together in 1883 to hold gospel temperance and blue ribbon movement meetings, to encourage people to abstain from intoxicating liquors. The meetings were held partly in the Primitive Methodist Chapel and partly in St Ambrose Schoolroom.

Each meeting was crowded and enthusiastic, and the mission proved to be a complete success, as the following figures show. Numbers who have taken the blue ribbon, (the pledge), in Sandycroft, total 228. Many of this number were total abstainers previously; but the great number of them were drinkers, and some of the number very notorious ones. A Gospel Temperance Society has been formed, and efforts will be made to extend the good work and make it permanent.[25]

Sandycroft English Presbyterian Church

In the 1905 Report, the chapel had 150 sittings, 37 Communicants, 150 adherents, 12 teachers, scholars under 15 years of age, 101, over 15, 33. A report of 1908 gives the following information.

Presbyterian Sunday school — The members had their treat on Saturday when over eighty scholars were entertained in the schoolroom to tea. Afterwards the scholars adjourned to a field lent by Mr Duckworth. Games and competitions were taken part in. Refreshments were again provided. Mr H. R. Williams and Mr H. A. Lewis, superintendent and secretary of the Sunday school carried out the arrangements.[26]

Sandycroft Methodist Chapel
[John Davies deposit, FRO N/31/23]

13. Saltney

Old Saltney, Saltney Common, part of the salt marshes of the river Dee, was the waste area of two extensive parishes, St Mary's, Chester, and St Deiniol's, Hawarden, both part of the diocese of Chester, until Hawarden was transferred to St Asaph diocese in 1849. The border between England and Wales cuts through Saltney. The Welsh side is part of the Lordship of Hawarden and in the county of Flintshire; the English portion is a suburb of Chester. The Enclosure Act of 1781 formed a new township of Saltney. The Welsh side of the township in 1896 was administratively divided into two. West Saltney embraced the area from Wepre brook to the Higher Ferry and included the new settlements of Shotton, Queen's Ferry and Sandycroft. The area from the Higher Ferry to the English border was known as East Saltney. It is in East Saltney, in Flintshire, where the main industrial development took place. It is assumed that the topics dealt with in this chapter refer to this area, unless specifically noted as being in England.

The prospects for and the beginnings of the industrial development of Saltney were noted in the *Chester Chronicle* in October 1858.

> There are few places which have so rapidly sprung up as Saltney. A few years ago, and the Shepherds was the only house. Now there is a population of the industrious classes numbering from two or three thousand. Facilities of land and water carriage, and cheapness of the land doubtlessly have been the great inducements. We do not know how any locality which can urge superior, or even rival pretensions, the great essentials for manufacturers, coal being here almost as cheap as at the pit mouth. It is pleasing to recount this progress. It cannot be denied that the Great Western Company have been a direct means of its advancement. Messrs. Woods Brothers, who have obtained a world-wide reputation for their Trotman's Patent Anchor, were the first to lay down works upon any extensive scale; then came the firm of Messrs. Proctor and Ryeland; then the unceasing energy of a Taylor produced the Rubicon Works which is presently to be a enlarged by a transept from the Manchester Art Treasures Exhibition. Mr William Charles of the Merridale Oil and Grease Works, is removing to Saltney, and we are also told that several other large manufactories are in contemplation.[1]

Thus the main features of the industrial development of Saltney to the end of the nineteenth century were anticipated in this report. The location of industry along the river and at the junction of two major railways, the establishment of Wood Brothers, anchor smiths and chain makers, the oil industry, and the arrival of agricultural chemists principally concerned with the manufacture of fertilisers. Saltney Wharf was opened on 1 July 1847, and the Shrewsbury and Chester Railway Company operated motor tugs to enable vessels to get up and down the river and transport their cargoes further afield. Maintaining sufficient draught of water in the canalised river from Connah's Quay to Saltney was a major concern. The success of the wharf depended on railway goods traffic and this was the main attraction to industry. For example, the North Wales Mineral Railway, in operation by November 1846, brought coal, iron and brick manufactures to the wharf at Saltney Junction. The line from the Junction to Chester was shared with the Chester Holyhead Railway, opened on 12 October 1848. The Shrewsbury Chester Railway and the Shrewsbury Birkenhead Railway were amalgamated into the Great Western Railway in 1854. The use of Saltney wharf and the G.W.R. tugboats will be discussed later.

Wood Brothers, Dee Iron Works

The firm was founded in 1780 at Stourbridge. After 1825 it was known as Wood Brothers and *c.*1827 one of the brothers came to Liverpool and opened a branch under the name of Henry Wood and Company. In 1871 on the death of Henry, the last survivor of the Wood brothers, his son Albert, with his business partner William Coltart acquired the Stourbridge, Saltney, Liverpool and London businesses. The firm became a private limited liability company in 1891 under the name of Henry Wood and Company.

Right: Employees of Henry Wood & Co, c.1900
[FRO 58/58]

Below left: Chainmaking at Henry Wood & Co
[FRO 58/60]

On their arrival at Saltney in 1847 Wood Brothers announced that their premises, the Dee Iron Works, was for the manufacture of cables, anchors, scrap hammered uses, and forged iron of every description, ship's windlass, castings, shovels and spades, anvils, vices, nails and all kinds of chains. Because of convenient facilities for traffic by rail and river, they were able to deliver their products to their stores in Liverpool and London at a reduced rate.[2]

They were in production by the autumn of 1847. 'We observed with much pleasure' purred the *Chester Chronicle*, 'large trucks laden with anchors rolling along our railways from this new establishment towards Liverpool.'[3] At the Great Exhibition in 1851 the firm obtained the prize medal for chain cables. Again success attended them in 1852 at the anchor trials of all nations held in Hull from May to October. The Trotman and Porters anchors made at Saltney were found to possess the greatest holding powers of 40%. They also patented an anchor known as Wood's 'Improved Solid Palm' an improvement on Trotman's.

This universal success was much to their advantage and in 1857 Isambard Kingdom Brunel commissioned the Saltney Works to make anchors for the *Great Eastern* steamship. It was observed:

This firm has gained universal renown for the manufacture of all kinds of anchors, but particularly of Trotman's, which may now be seen on board every large steamer in the Mersey. The largest ships afloat have Messrs. Wood's anchors, the Cunard Company's steam ships, The Peninsular and Oriental Company's, the Australian Companies, *etc*. and they are to be found on board Her Majesty's yacht, Victoria and Albert. The three large anchors for the Great Eastern are to weigh seven tons each, having a shank 18 feet long, with a space of 8 feet between the points of the anchor. The smaller ones are to weigh five tons each, with proportionate dimensions.[4]

By 1860 such was their reputation that their Saltney works were regarded as an international showpiece.

On Thursday, a large party connected with the mercantile shipping of Liverpool, agents of the Admiralty, and Consuls of foreign governments, visited these celebrated works, at Saltney. The party included French, Spanish Russian and Ottoman Consuls. The whole process of anchor and chain cable manufacture was shown. The greatest object of interest was the testing machines for their valuable and costly machinery was put into full work, and the general testimony was, that it far exceeded anything of the kind in other works. The whole party were entertained to a splendid lunch and later conveyed to Birkenhead in special trains.[5]

Although the testing of anchors and chains was taking place at Wood's in 1860, there was eventually established next door to the Dee Iron Works, Lloyd's Cambrian Chain and Anchor Public Testing Company Works, known locally as 'the test'. The testing of anchors and chains was licensed by the Board of Trade and managed by the Committee of Lloyd's Registry of British and Foreign Shipping. It was sensible that a testing works should be near to the anchor makers. According to E. L. Roberts, Lloyd's was established in Saltney in 1866. As late as 1875 anchors and chains were being sent from Liverpool and Birkenhead to Saltney to be tested.[6] The mode of anchor testing at Woolwich was shown in the *Illustrated London News* of 19 September 1857. 'The proof of an ordinary anchor of five tons weight, the largest used in the navy, is 67 tons strain; but in this instance Trotman's anchor will be proved to 105 tons.'[7]

The street names are a memorial to the foundation industry of Saltney. Cable Street, Chain Makers Row, the Anchor Hotel and the Wood Memorial Schools. The labouring force came from Ireland and the chain makers and anchor smiths from Worcestershire, Warwickshire, Lancashire, and Durham.

Oil Works

Charles & Maxwell, 1858

The first oil manufacturer mentioned as being associated with Saltney was William Charles, of the Merridale Oil and Grease Works. In the autumn of 1858 the *Wolverhampton Chronicle*, advised that Charles was coming to Saltney.[8] In July 1862 there was a serious and extensive fire at his works. It was reported,

> There were between 400 and 500 casks of American oil in the place at the time the fire broke out, besides several hundredweight of grease all of which was consumed, together with the whole of the machinery, the damage being estimated at £3,000.[9]

In 1862 and 1863 Charles and Maxwell were accused of causing a public nuisance at the Petroleum and Blubber Works because of the stench, and a public petition, signed by 600 people was set to the Mayor and City Council of Chester. A perpetual injunction was sought in January 1863 restraining the defendants from carrying on their business. Charles and Maxwell offered to remove their works from Saltney if they were paid £250.

The Mineral Oil Company

Ebenezer Fernie, and Hussey Jones, of Leeswood, founded the company in February 1861. Works were established at Leeswood and Saltney, to use the process patented by James Young for obtaining paraffin oil from bituminous coals by slow distillation.' There was a supply of cannel coal in Flintshire from the mines at Nercwys, Coed Talon, Leeswood, Mold, and Padeswood. The combined production of cannel coal in Flintshire in 1862 was 28,816 tons which had risen in 1865 to 150,000 tons, 'almost the whole of which was consumed in the extensive oil works in Flintshire. The cannel coal was raised chiefly for the manufacture of paraffin oil by distillation at a low red heat. As much as 80 gallons of crude oil to the ton were obtained from curly cannel, 35 per ton from smooth cannel and 33 gallons from the 'oil shale'.[10]

The site chosen by Fernie and Hussey for their oil works was the St David's works. Here they provided 115 retorts for the process of distilling into crude oil the 230 tons per week of curly cannel supplied by the Leeswood Cannel & Gas Coal Co. Ltd. Saltney was also the site of the refinery, where the crude oil sent from the Leeswood works, and crude distilled at Saltney was refined in 45 stills of sizes ranging from 350 to 2,600 gallons, of which 15 were of the latter size.'[11]

The site of the oil company, St David's, was originally part of the Shepherd's House farm, and was sold to the company in 1864 by Sir Stephen Glynne.

The Flintshire Oil and Cannel Co. Ltd.

The Flintshire Oil and Cannel Co. Ltd purchased the works from the Mineral Oil Company in 1864, paying £75,000 for the concern at Saltney, and the same price for the Leeswood plant. In 1865 the value of both works was estimated at £54,763. Nevertheless the new company anticipated they 'could supply Chester with from one to two million cubic feet of gas every week, of an excellent quality, at three shillings per thousand, with considerable profit to the company.'[12] In 1885 the St David's works were sold to the Dee Oil Co., for £120,000.

The Dee Oil Company

The Dee Oil Company arrived at Saltney in 1867 and set themselves up adjacent to the St David's site. Under the management of William Charles Deeley from Liverpool, they proved to be the most successful of the Saltney oil manufacturers, and by 1881 their works covered ten acres of ground with a work force of about three hundred. In the 1860s the production of oil from curly cannel became unprofitable and the coal commanded a better price

Saltney in 1905. The Red Lion Inn
on the corner of River Lane
[FRO 58/55]

in the overseas market for supply to South American gas works.

The Dee Oil Company was involved in a different process, the manufacture of the heaviest bodied hydrocarbon oils, derived from the American residuum, the residue after a portion of the oil is taken away. From this the company manufactured cylinder oil, engine oil and lubricating oil. The American scale or crude wax derived in the manufacture of oil was sold on to the candle-makers. However, by 1880, there was a glut on the market of this material and the company decided in 1879, to erect large new works near to their oil works, to manufacture their own candles, at an estimated 120 tons of wax candles per month. To achieve this output they made their own sulphuric acid works, put in a steam plant, and worked on improved appliances for refining the wax. The basic material was the American residuum, oil exported in 5,000-barrel cargoes at a rate of 800 tons per month. When emptied the barrels were steamed and sold to gas works or filled with creosote and exported back again to America. A candle-making machine manufactured the candles. This consisted of a series of moulds capable of producing 96 to 112 candles with their wicks in place. After being inspected and packed they were despatched from the company's railway sidings. Other products were 'fatty oils', olive, neat's-foot, grape, *etc.* stored in tanks capable of holding 225 tons. The company manufactured their own gas.

In 1885 the Dee Oil Co. bought the ailing Flintshire Oil and Cannel Co. for £120,000.

Proctor & Rylands Agricultural Chemists

Proctor & Rylands Agricultural Chemists came from Stourbridge to Saltney in 1856. They were manure merchants and manufactured superphosphates. In order to boost their market they offered premiums to successful competitors using their products who grew the best crops of swede, turnip, mangold *etc.*[13] There is a record of the firm chartering a large steamer, the *Sarah Blanche* of Douglas, in April 1895. 'The vessel arrived at mid-day on Friday, and was loaded with 220 tons of manure, and left again about one o'clock for Bristol.'[14]

Edward Webb & Sons (Stourbridge) Ltd., Seed Growers and Merchants

This firm took over from Proctor and Rylands in the 1890s as agricultural chemists, manufacturing sulphuric acid, super phosphates, and organic and inorganic fertilisers. In the 1930s they employed 50 persons.

The Great Western Wharf

Industry was attracted to Saltney because of the excellent facilities available for the transport of raw materials and finished goods, by river and railway. The railway company owned the wharf at Saltney Junction and it was their policy to attract business by offering to the traders whatever assistance it could, and for this purpose it employed tugs to tow shipping traffic up the river to Saltney. In 1854 the steam tug *Conqueror* was in service on the Dee between Chester and Holywell and to and from Liverpool. Tugs were needed because of the problems associated with silting, to prevent vessels going aground and to give their owners confidence. In 1884 before a Select Committee of the House of Lords, evidence was given by Mr T. Barrett, on the state of the G.W.R. quays at Saltney. He said:

> The quays and sheds were in good repair, and the wharves would hold seven vessels at one time. There were steam-travelling cranes there. The largest vessels coming to the wharf generally were about 300 tons burden.

Barrett reported that,

> … he travelled up and down with the tugs, and found that the channel was a very shifting one. There had been no falling off of the trade at Saltney, and the company did everything to develop that trade to their own interests. The premises had not been enlarged since the company took them in 1854.[15]

Early on in the life of the Hawarden Bridge, Shotton there is a report of damage to one of the Saltney tugs.

A collision occurred on Wednesday afternoon, causing damage to the steam tug *Derby*. As the schooners *Useful*

The Manxman
[J. L. Bennett deposit, FRO D/DM/383/4]

and *Robert Brown* were being towed towards Connah's Quay from Saltney, the *Robert Brown* collided with the *Derby*. One of the middle paddle boxes was entirely broken, and the funnel knocked with great force into the river. The cause is attributed to the swing bridge being closed against them although the tugboat carried out full regulations when approaching the bridge.[16]

In 1892 Mr Wheatley was appointed as goods agent at the G.W.R. wharf. He was anxious to build up trade, and traffic increased. During the first week in April 1894 eleven vessels had laden or discharged at Saltney. If the river traffic was to be developed, 'the *Derby* was no longer able to meet the requirements of the service, and the directors resolved upon securing a boat better able to cope with the traffic. Captain Lecky, the marine superintendent of the G.W.R., was deputed to look for a suitable vessel, but the task was by no means a light one, as the kind of boat required had to be of great power in order to tow perhaps six or seven vessels at a time. Captain Lecky succeeded in dropping across the *Manxman* at Hull. ' He found a strong boat of 56 tonnage with compound engines of 240-horse power and a mean speed of over eight knots. She was overhauled and tested at New Milford and successfully reached Saltney. 'The steamer was available for towing vessels from Liverpool, Fleetwood, Holyhead, and other points in the neighbourhood, into the river Dee.'[17] When the *Manxman* underwent repairs in 1897 she was replaced by the *Palmerston*, 'a paddle boat of fine dimensions, good speed and plenty of power.'[18]

River traffic was busy in the summer of 1894 when in the last week in June, 'no less than six schooners and four steamers were dealt with, some bringing iron ore and wheat and some loading with flour and coal at the Great Western Wharf.'[19]

Crichton's Shipbuilders and Engineers, Saltney Shipyard[20]

Crichton's brought business to the river at Saltney, and a great deal of pride to their workmen over a period of nearly thirty years because of the inventiveness of their employer, James Crichton. In a space of thirty-two years, 1913–35, over five hundred vessels and other craft demonstrated the ingenuity of James Crichton and the engineering shipbuilding skills available at the Saltney yard.

James Crichton was born in 1885, the son of Charles Crichton, who founded the firm of Messrs. C. & H. Crichton Ltd. of Liverpool, shipbuilders. He was educated at Liverpool University and took an engineering degree before serving his apprenticeship with Messrs David and Rowan Co. Ltd of Glasgow, as preparation before entering the family firm.

James Crichton commenced shipbuilding in Saltney in 1913. The firm was reorganised in 1921 as C. & H. Crichton Ltd. Crichton built up a reputation in the light shipbuilding industry and was a member of the Shipbuilders Employers Federation, the National Shipbuilders Security Ltd, and other associations. The work at the Saltney Yard was that of general engineers, shipbuilders and repairers, boilermakers, founders, sheet metal workers *etc*. The firm described itself as Contractors to the British Admiralty, War Office, Dominion Governments, Foreign Governments and the principal Railway Companies.

Crichton's were specialists in shallow draft vessels, oil tankers, tugs, barges and coasters. The river at Saltney was able to cope with these kinds of vessels and was adapted to their needs. In 1924 the *Times* described the site:

The Saltney yard has 20 berths for vessels up to 200 foot and is entirely equipped with electric and pneumatic tools. It has an extensive water frontage, and a private fitting-out wharf where vessels can lie afloat at all states of tide. Of recent years tugs up to 1,200 h.p., coasters of 500 tons, and barges of all sizes have been launched and completed from this yard.[21]

The work force at Saltney varied according to trade demand from 200 to 300 men. Some of them, experienced in light shipbuilding came from Essex and Gloucestershire. James Crichton was concerned for the welfare of his employees and he provided a wide range of recreation facilities. Two large wooden huts were erected at the rear of the lodge, together with a bowling green. The huts had billiard tables, a bar, tables and a small stage. Crichton's also supported a football team in the Cheshire League and billiards and snooker teams in Chester and district leagues.[22]

James Crichton gathered around him at Saltney a skilled team of draughtsmen to put into practise his ideas for specialist vessels. It was Crichton's inventive, innovative and practical ability to solve marine problems, which attracted orders from home and abroad and kept the Saltney yard open during the years of depression.

A review of production at Saltney shows their extensive markets. This was brought about to some extent by

their ability to obtain orders by promoting themselves. In 1924 they issued an illustrated booklet,

> … containing a wealth of information on the various types of tugs which they have constructed, both for commercial and special purposes, and for colonial and foreign clients, intimating that they are ready to undertake the construction of tugs of any size, whether single or twin screw, steam or motor machinery, and if steam driven with boiler adapted for either oil or coal burning or a combination of both, for river and harbour tugs, export, estuary and sea, ocean work, small motor tugs, and sea-going motor tugs.[23]

In the 1920s Crichton's built ferry steamers for a world market. The *Traz-os-Montes* and *Alentejo*, sister ships, each having accommodation for 300 first and 300 second class passengers, were built in 1924 as passenger ferry steamers for the Portuguese government, to link up the service of the state railways between Lisbon and Barreiro across the Tagus. The following year the *Lurgurena*, a double-ended screw steamer, was built for the Tasmania government, for vehicular and passenger service in the Derwent River between Hobart and Bellerive. She was 550 tons, with accommodation for 50 vehicles and 120 passengers. At the launching, the Tasmania agent congratulated Crichton's and 'expressed the hope that many orders would come to them as a result of the splendid advertisement which will be shortly leaving for Tasmania under her own steam.' Orders followed from the Sydney Ferries Ltd., for Sydney Harbour, Australia, for two steamers, the *Kalang* and the *Kara Kara*. Both were launched in March 1926 and completed in sixteen weeks. Reviews[24] of work at the shipyard in 1926 mention other vessels. The coaster *Radstock* built for the Southern and L.M.S. railways to carry locomotive coal, the steam-tug *Marie Regina*, for the Ceylon Wharfage Co. Ltd., and delivered under her own power at Colombo. The steam tug *Hazel* was shipped complete ready for work. An unusual commission was the forty-foot boat beacon, the *Beta*, for the Mersey Docks and Harbour Board. The *C. C. Mengel junr* was lifted on board the Elder Dempster steamer *Egba* and delivered for service on the Gold Coast. Two forty-foot special type high-speed passenger launches were despatched for government service in South America at Puerto Cabeib and Maraccubo. In 1927 the twin-screw steamer *R. H. Carr* was built for passenger and cargo service on rivers and coastal work in British Guiana.

It was the specialised patented work of Crichton's at Saltney, which attracted the public imagination. In 1928 the cigarette manufacturer Wills issued a set of cards under the title, Strange Craft. Three of the cards featured vessels built at Saltney. One was an oil separation barge built for the Mersey Docks and Harbour Board to carry out the purification of oil contaminated waters, at the rate of 200 tons per hour, specially designed for cleaning the holds of oil tankers.

Another patent was for a marine slipway installation, which enabled dry-docking. They used one of them at

Connah's Quay for the repairs of vessels up to about 300 tons. In 1924 it was announced that:

'Four small barges now await delivery, together with hauling-up slipway for Central America. This is a somewhat special slipway, and interesting for the fact that it is not designed for the usual purpose of hauling up vessels for effecting repairs, but in conjunction with ordinary slipway rails there is a transfer platform enabling the barges hauled up to be brought to a level keel, and the ordinary cradle has an additional side shipping cradle fitted, the whole apparatus forming a novel but rapid means of handling goods from steamers lying off the coast directly inshore without transhipment from the barges. An endless cable will be operated by the main capstan on the slipway, which loaded barges will pick up, bringing them on to the main slipway carriage, from whence they will be carried up the incline and on to the level rails via hydraulic transfer platform and so to unloading sheds direct. The barges and slipway work have all been carried out under the superintendence and to the design of Mr W. Gordon Glover, consulting engineer.[25]

The following year two further orders were received, one for an electrically driven slipway of 400 tons to be laid down in the Gambia Colony of West Africa, and another from the Lewis and Harris Welfare Development Co. Ltd. for a 350 ton longitudinal marine slipway to be laid down at Leverburgh in Scotland, and capable of handling trawlers.[26]

The work of Crichton's at Saltney, which captured most publicity, was the floating grain elevator. Eight of these were built at Saltney in the 1920s. The design and manufacture of the main grain pumps and the superstructure were by Messrs Spencer of Melksham, Wiltshire, and the weighing apparatus by Messrs Avery. Crichton's assumed responsibility for the whole contract and completion of the elevator, the design and construction of the pontoon, installation of the engines, boilers, pumps and the erection of the superstructure.[27]

An account of the delivery of one of these giant elevators in September 1929 was given by the local paper. ' The feat of navigating the 600-ton pneumatic elevator down the river Dee from Messrs. Crichton's shipyard at Saltney was safely accomplished on Saturday afternoon. The first part of the journey from Saltney to Queensferry, the most difficult of the whole journey, owing to the sandbanks in the river, a distance of three miles, took one and a half hours, the huge elevator being towed by three powerful tugs, the *Taliesin* from Connah's Quay, and the *Felgarth* and the *Edengarth* from Liverpool. On the elevator nearing the Queenferry Bridge the leading tug gave a blast on its siren, and the bridge quickly opened. Although the bridge was only open a matter of a quarter of an hour, the traffic from North Wales to Liverpool and Birkenhead quickly accumulated, and over 200 cars and motorcycles were held up.

A floating grain elevator under tow, 1920s
[J. L. Bennett deposit, FRO D/DM/383/3]

The elevator built to the order of the United Grain Elevator Company, of Liverpool, is adaptable to the discharging of the largest vessels, which enter Liverpool Docks, and is the eighth of its kind built for the firm. It is capable of discharging at the rate of 250 tons an hour, and a feature of the vessel is that the grain is automatically weighed while being discharged.

Large crowds of people lined the banks of the Dee from Saltney to Connah's Quay to witness the elevator's passing and at the Queensferry Bridge the crowd was dense.'[28]

James Crichton died suddenly at his home in Bidston on 15 March 1932 at the age of forty-seven years of age. The week before he was at the shipyard in Saltney and appeared to be in good health. Shipbuilding at Saltney ceased in 1935.

Other Industries

Crichton's had been a large employer of men in the Saltney area and some of these were absorbed by new industries. Some of the well-established manufacturers remained in business in the 1930s. Amongst these were:

The Agricultural Food Products Ltd. This firm traded under the name of Vitamealo, and manufactured cattle food. They employed between 20 and 30 persons.

Clutton's Wonpees. Manufactured wire linings to reinforce concrete.

Rust Proof, Saltney Engineering, took over the site of the Great Western Carriage Works, in the 1930s. They produced metal windows made rust proof by a dipping process. In 1939 the factory was turned over to production for the war effort manufacturing, 'star shells, cartridge catapult cases, ammunition boxes, case magazines, bailey bridge parts, gun turrets, and many smaller items.'[29] After the war they found it difficult to compete in the window market and became the European agent for an American firm, Gehls, manufacturing farm implements. This work was transferred to Corsham whilst the Saltney factory concentrated on machine tools. The factory closed in the 1970s.

The *No-Nail Boxes Company* came from Bootle in 1941 and established a factory at the Dee Oil Works. During the war they were engaged in making fibreboard containers to transport six one-gallon cans of petrol for the air force. After the war the factory was modernised and a variety of cartons and boxes were made. At this time Sir Gerald Nabarro, M.P., was managing director.[30]

H & H. Whitely, Organ Builders, Cathedral Works, Saltney, gained a wide reputation for the quality of their organ building and repair.

The *St David's Manufacturing Company Glass Works.* This factory was directed by Mr and Mrs Greatzer Czechoslovakian refugees. They had a factory in Liverpool and brought to Saltney some of their skilled glass blowers to produce glass balls and tinsel for Christmas decorations, The Saltney works closed in 1970 when the company transferred to Porth in south Wales.[31]

Agriculture, Mr John Roberts, Well House Farm[32]

W. E. Gladstone's career in the House of Commons meant that he was closely involved in agricultural affairs. He was a member of Sir Robert Peel's government of the 1840s, which abolished the Corn Laws, and as President of the Board of Trade and later Chancellor of the Exchequer, his financial policy was based on free trade, the abolition of duties entering the country, and cheap food for the working classes. His close concern with the Hawarden estate, after the Oak Farm debacle in 1847, gave him a working knowledge of farming. Gladstone was chosen to propose the toast to the Agricultural Society of England when it held its meeting in Chester in 1858. He was a frequent speaker at the Hawarden Estate audit dinner held every January. Gladstone obtained his knowledge from reading, observation, and first hand experience. It is not surprising to find the entry in his diary for 12 September 1873: 'I put myself under my friend J. Roberts guidance.'

John Roberts was the tenant of three farms on the Hawarden Estate, which lay close together on land reclaimed at the time of the enclosure of Saltney Marsh in the late eighteenth century. The chief of these was Well House Farm, which received its name from the artesian well, bored to a depth of 72 feet. We learn about John Roberts from accounts given from time to time of the prize farms of the Manchester and Liverpool Agricultural Society of which he was a winner on at least two occasions, in 1877 and 1887.

Gladstone basked in the success of his friend and did everything to help him and, 'as a token of his appreciation of the energy and skill of his tenant, presented him with a model of a plough, which polished bright as silver, was hung up in Mr Roberts kitchen.'[33]

The report of John Roberts' prize farm of 1877 acknowledged the partnership of landlord and tenant.

'There are some model cottages newly erected by Mr Gladstone, with a garden allotment attached, near the Well House. Mr Roberts pays a moderate interest upon the outlay, and his landlord takes a great interest in the comfortable housing of the labourers on his estate.'[34]

The Roberts–Gladstone co-operation was an opportunity for the statesman to put into practice his views on what was known as high farming, 'designed to produce heavier crops through drainage, new fertilisers and higher standards of cultivation, the adoption of superior breeds of livestock, and the integration of arable and pasture to diversify output and take advantage of market trends.'[35]

The 1877 and 1887 reports show how important these elements were in winning prizes for John Roberts. The size of the land entered for competition in both years was similar. 404 acres in 1877 and 412 acres in 1887. The ground was described as 'formerly marshy, flat, laid out generally in fields from 2 to 20 acres, surrounded by fences neatly trimmed, with much of the land deep sandy loam which after steam cultivation in the autumn, and a moderate amount of spring tillage, is in an admirable state for growing roots'. About 70 acres was kept in permanent turf, the greater proportion of which was liable to flood, especially in winter from water backing up the dykes. The drainage of the land was by means of pipe-drains, which emptied into these dykes.

The dressing of the land by dung and fertiliser was an integral part of Roberts's success. In the 1870s he made and carted 1,200 tons of dung spread at the rate of 12 to 15 tons per acre. He was a successful competitor for the premiums of the Saltney based Proctor and Rylands agricultural chemists. Roberts used six hundred weights per acre of their special bone manure. In 1874 he won a prize of fifteen guineas for the best crop of five acres of swede, in the northwest counties of England and Wales with the weight per acre of over 32 tons.[36]

Generally he practised the four-course rotation of crops, and of the 404 acres, rather more than half, was given over to corn and green crops, mangles, swede, late potatoes, and the rest to grasses and seeds. John Roberts used seven well-bred horses worked in pairs by his champion ploughman. Machinery was hired for the steam cultivation of the wheat and bean stubble. He possessed a six horsepower engine to cut the straw.

He reared and fattened a large number of beasts, which were sold by auction in May. For breeding there was a herd of 12 to 15 good shorthorn cows serviced by a shorthorn bull. The sheep stock of 150 Shropshire ewes produced 233 lambs, most of which were sold fat, and 60 ewe lambs were kept for the flock.

In 1887 the payment of labour of the three farms, 652 acres, came to about £1,000, but the paid work and wages was reduced by the extensive employment of steam ploughing and steam cultivation. Irishmen were employed in the summer at 15s. per week, and £2 extra for the harvest. Regular men received 18s per week and a cottage to live in, with an extra bonus for harvest. Expenditure on steam cultivation in 1877 was £70, and the purchase of thirty tons of Proctor and Rylands special bone manure £225. Over the period, 1877–87, the major source of income was the sale of stock. In 1887 £3,000 worth of beef and £800 worth of mutton and lamb were sold.

Religion and Education

The social priorities for new communities in the nineteenth century were threefold. First, religious; working class populations must have the opportunity to worship God, new parishes created and churches and chapels built. Second, education; the three Rs of elementary education, reading, writing and arithmetic must be provided, at first by the voluntary sector, usually the established church, and later by the state. Third, leisure; which must be spent in improvement and in the avoidance of the temptations of the beer house. These three priorities created a community in Saltney between the years 1850 and 1880, at a time when the strategies of evangelism, education and self-help were available.

The Church of the Holy Epiphany, 1855

Religious provision came first. The Reverend W. H. Massey of St Mary's, Chester, established a temporary church in February 1851 with the co-operation of Sir Stephen Glynne and his brother Henry Glynne rector of Hawarden. A meeting of subscribers met at the beginning of September at the City Arms when it was announced that a site had been selected central to the Lache and Saltney. Mr James Harrison of Chester was appointed architect. It was decided that a school should be commenced forthwith to accommodate about 140 children. The management of the Shrewsbury and Chester Railway Company, 'liberally offered to convey the building materials along their lines free of charge.'[37] In the meantime a school had begun nearby on a site given by E. Bennett, with almost a hundred children in attendance. It was described as being, 'entirely of white stone and a good model for a room intended to be used for Divine Service. A fund is in the meantime being raised by public subscription for the speedy commencement of the church.'[38] The foundation stone was laid in October 1853. The site given by the Marquess of Westminster was in the corner of a field the hedges of which marked the boundary between England and Wales. The press noted that, 'since the railway had been constructed and the new works built the population had become so large, their spiritual state had become a serious consideration and had rendered necessary the building of a church.'[39]

The church was consecrated as a chapel of ease, with the dedication, 'The Holy Epiphany', on 9 January 1855, by the Bishop of Chester. It was to serve a consolidated district, taken out of the two adjoining parishes of Hawarden and St Mary's Chester. Tithes to the annual amount of £50 a year were promised in the proportion of two-thirds from Hawarden and one-third form St Mary's. A description of the church read:

> The edifice is of an unpretending character, though solid, holding about 230, but easily capable of enlargement hereafter to three times its present size at least, arches and pillars being built into the walls, for the addition of aisles, transepts, belfries &c, as means and occasion are presented. The general style chosen by Mr James Harrison, the architect, appears to be of the thirteenth century. The east window consists of five narrow lights; slightly cusped and pointed, set within what will eventually be the chancel arch. There are in it small medallions of stained glass by Powell, containing emblems of the four evangelists, and a half figure of the Saviour in the centre light. The pulpit, prayer desk, lectern *etc.* are of oak and all moveable, as simple in design as possible. The font is given by Mr and Mrs W. Wood, the silver flagon and chalice by Mrs Mainwaring; the paten of the same material by the Rev. H. Temple; and the work promoted by a long list of subscribers headed by Sir Edward Walker.[40]

On 24 September 1855, by Order in Council, the chapelry of Lache-cum-Saltney became a parish under an incumbent with the right of presentation and nomination belonging to the Bishop of Chester.

The Wesleyan Church, 1856

The Wesleyan Methodists were established in Saltney in the middle of the nineteenth century and an account of the opening of a new chapel is reported in the press in 1856.

> About six months ago the Wesleyan Body commenced the erection of a chapel, which was opened for public preaching on the 29 June. The cost of the building was about £700, giving accommodation to 300 hearers, and the neat appearance of the place reflects great credit on Mr Penson, the architect, and Mr Hitchen the builder. Various efforts had been made to liquidate the cost of the chapel, and on Tuesday last a tea party was held for the purpose of celebrating the opening and also for reducing the debt. The use of the railway carriage shed at Saltney was courteously granted for the occasion, and a fine display of flags and evergreens gave a most pleasing appearance to the room. At six o'clock about 800 persons had assembled, and tea commenced. The provisions were plentiful and good, but the tea might have been a little stronger without seriously affecting the nerves of the drinkers. After tea, the chair was taken by J. Townsworth, Esq. of Liverpool, who congratulated the meeting in obtaining a place of worship, which he was glad to say would that evening be freed from debt. The Rev. Mr West, of Liverpool, next delivered a lecture on 'Woman'. The lecture occupied about two hours, and had it been shortened one half, it would have been more appropriate to the occasion, more acceptable to the audience, and would have enabled other gentlemen to have a say.[41]

It has been said that the Saltney Methodist Society started in 1844 with the first meetings taking place in numbers 177 and 179 High Street. In 1856 the chapel was built opposite where St Mark's Church now stands on a site given by E. G. Salisbury, M.P. for Flintshire. In 1894 the Wesleyans moved to their present site with the Church of Christ taking over the 1856 chapel.

The Primitive Methodist Church, 1900

The Primitive Methodist Church congregation moved from Stone Bridge to High Street in 1900. A newspaper described the background to this move.

> The primitive Methodists of Saltney are a small but progressive community. They have outgrown the accommodation afforded by the old chapel at Stone Bridge, and taken in hand a scheme for providing a new and

Saltney Methodist Church, High Street
[Saltney & Saltney Ferry publication]

Saltney Methodist Church, High Street
[Saltney & Saltney Ferry publication]

commodious chapel and a new Sunday school. The latter part of the undertaking being the most urgent has been already completed, and until the accomplishment of the other part of the scheme the new school, which is situate rather nearer to the population of Saltney than the old premises, will serve as a chapel. It has cost £750, exclusive of the site, and has been erected at the rear of the plot of ground so as to leave space in the frontage of the projected chapel. The builder who has carried out the contract is Mr James Challinor of Saltney. The opening of the new building took place on Wednesday afternoon, the ceremony of the unlocking of the doors being performed by Mr S. Moss and Mrs John Kendrick. A sermon was preached by the Rev. H. J. Taylor.[42]

The strength of church membership in 1905 was 7 elders, 72 communicants, 150 adherents, 26 Sunday school teachers, and 82 pupils under 15 years of age, 36 over 15 years of age. In 1962 a new Methodist church was built on the vacant plot of ground in front of the school chapel. The previous year Hough Green and High Street Methodist churches united. The partners brought with them an organ associated with George Frederick Handel used by the composer in St Peter's Church, Chester, when he rehearsed his choir in 1741 for the first performance of Messiah, to take place in Dublin. When a new organ was put into St Peter's church by the firm of Charles Whitely in 1888 they received the organ in part payment and installed it in Hough Green Methodist church.[43]

The Roman Catholic School Chapel of St Anthony, 1878

The conversion of Viscount Fielding, later eighth Earl of Denbigh, and his new bride Louisa Pennant, to Roman Catholicism in 1850, coincided with the building of a church at Pantasaph, Flintshire, as a thank offering for their marriage. Instead of giving it to the Anglicans they transferred it to their new spiritual fathers and added a Franciscan friary. Members of the Capuchin community established a mission in Chester, in Grosvenor Street, with their pastoral responsibilities extending to Saltney. The establishment of Board schools by the 1870 Education Act threatened the education of children along denominational lines. Henry Manning, Archbishop of Westminster warned the church of this danger urging that, 'Catholic Schools for Catholic children' must be their motto, a message that was heeded both by the Roman bishops and influential laymen, amongst whom was the Earl of Denbigh. This is the background to the building of the school-chapel at Saltney dedicated to St Anthony of Padua.

There existed a mean mission place for Catholics in Saltney under the care of the Capuchin friars, as revealed by the Earl of Denbigh, when he laid the foundation stone of the new school-chapel, on St Patrick's Day 1878. For twelve years, he said, Mass had been offered up in a garret over a pigsty approachable by a ladder, which was dangerous for old age and youth, and most difficult of access for anybody. The mission to the poor in Saltney was carried out through the energy of the Capuchin fathers, who had worthily and devotedly seconded the desires of the bishop in seeing after the souls of two or three hundred Irishmen who had come to work in those large public works which they saw around them, and it was owing to their energy that they now saw that their labours were about to be crowned with success. The Duke of Westminster to whom the property belonged had given them the fine site.[44]

St. Patrick's Day fell on a Sunday in 1878 and the laying of the foundation stone at Saltney had as its prelude a procession from St Francis Church, Grosvenor Street, Chester, to the site in High Street Saltney. It was reported that several thousand people waited along the route:

The vanguard of the procession was a number of men of the 96th. Regiment garrisoned at the castle, and of the 1st Royal Cheshire Militia. Following these came several hundreds of Catholic laity, the Young Men's Association, and the school children, the rear being brought up by the clergy, chief of whom was the Reverend Father Pacificus, who walked by the side of the Earl of Denbigh. The procession, the appearance of which was made very striking by a number of banners and flags bearing religious emblems, and the many coloured rosettes the processionists wore, consisted of certainly not much less than 2,000 people. It proceeded slowly and reached the place where a second crowd had already gathered, and halted in front of the site of the chapel, which is in the Flintshire part of Saltney, and adjacent to the building familiar to many of our readers, the County Constabulary. P.C. McBride did his very best to keep the crowd in order, and the procession in a very decent fashion. Presently the clergy, the Reverend Fathers Pacificus, Nicholas, Angelus and Louis, in their canonicals, appeared, accompanied by the acolytes, and the ceremony of the laying of the foundation stone was proceeded with. The laying of the first stone, for the school alone, was performed by a pretty little maiden, Miss Hilda Topham, four years of age, the daughter of one of the principal patrons of the cause of Roman Catholicism in Chester. [This was Joseph Topham, clerk of the racecourse, first at Chester and then at Aintree] Before the laying of the stone, both it and the cavity were sprinkled with holy water, and Miss Topham was presented with a silver trowel. The earl of Denbigh laid the stone of the church section of the building and made the speech referred to above. The architect was Mr O'Brien of Liverpool and the builders Messrs Francis and Price of Birkenhead. The estimated cost was between £800 and £1,000.

The school-chapel was opened the same year at All Saints tide with considerable energy. The building was described as being 'of a very plain character, in the Gothic order of architecture, and the material used of red brick with stone facings and slated roof. The church was lighted by eight large windows and the altar of massive stonework. The stone altar and the statue of St Anthony of Padua was the gift of Mr Hanley of Chester. On the front of the tabernacle was a carving of a pelican and its young, a symbol of the Blessed Sacrament. At eleven o'clock the ceremony of consecrating the building took place and was followed by solemn high Mass for the Feast of All Saints. In the congregation were the Countess of Denbigh and her two daughters, Lady Clare and Lady Edith Fielding. The Countess had given Father Pacificus to understand that she would take under her maternal care and protection the poor children of Saltney.

The school-chapel was replaced in 1924 by the building of a new church in the High Street Saltney. The parish priest was Father Austin Pozi.

The activities of other religious groups in Saltney in the nineteenth century were mentioned from time to time in the *Chester Chronicle*. The following are three examples:

1876 July 8. The Sunday school children, teachers, and friends of the Gospel Hall, Saltney, to the number of 150, had their annual excursion to Llangollen, accompanied by the band of the Saltney Lodge of the Good Templars which played a few hymns and other tunes for the enjoyment of the party.

1881 January 22. The new Baptist mission, an offshoot from the Grosvenor Park Baptist Chapel, has been in existence some three months. Special services were held last Sunday afternoon and evening, followed on Monday by a public tea and entertainment. These meetings are held in the Lecture Hall, Saltney. The Sunday school has already an attendance of some hundred scholars.

1887 April 2. The Mission Sunday School opened on 16 January 1887 at the Wood Memorial Schools, Saltney. It is an interdenominational activity with Bible classes arranged for young men and women. The promoters were W. Coltart and W. C. Deeley.

Schools

Holy Epiphany School

W. E. Gladstone considered the situation of Holy Epiphany church and school to be a mistake because of its inconvenience. Nevertheless it was the only school available in Saltney for elementary education until the opening of the Wood Memorial schools in 1874. The numbers attending the school when it was opened in 1853 was about a hundred. When the children held their annual treat in September 1870, two hundred children were there, of these 154 attended the school, which had accommodation for 188. The treat 'was provided by the liberality of the gentry and parishioners. At two o'clock the children marched in procession from the vicarage through the parish to the schoolroom, where they were provided with an ample tea. Afterwards they amused themselves at a variety of games, in a field by the school.'[45]

As the school population increased, two brick-built classrooms were added, connected to the main building through a doorway in the north wall. The first headmaster was Richard Johnson, who married his assistant teacher, Eliza Turner. The last headmaster, Thomas Ellis was appointed in 1882 and after he died in 1909, the school, in disrepair, was demolished.

In December 1872 a public meeting was held in the Lecture Hall, Saltney to consider the necessity of providing

Holy Epiphany School, c.1890
[FRO 58/59]

more school accommodation and 'to devise some means by which the children now running about the streets in an almost wild state might be educated.' Mr E. G. Salisbury informed the meeting that, 'when Mr Wood spoke of erecting schools, he gave him to understand that they were to be altogether unsectarian, open to all, Churchmen and Dissenters, Protestants and Roman Catholics.'

The Wood Memorial Schools

Henry Wood, who brought the Anchor Works to Saltney, died in March 1871. The month before 'he had most generously announced his intention of building a British School at Saltney at an expense of £1,000, if the Corporation would grant him the land necessary for the purpose.' His family respected his wishes and built a two-storey school in High Street, which was opened in July 1874. The *Chester Chronicle* stated that, 'the large number of children who attended on the day of opening, go to prove that the residents of Saltney are fully alive to the importance of, and the benefits to be derived from the education of their children.' The management of the schools was entrusted to the Chester British Schools Association, 'and they have engaged the services of Mr Geo Steel as headmaster with two school mistresses, for carrying on the work in the girls and infants schools. Out of the 232 children who had come there that day, more than 100 had not been to school within the last twelve months.'[46] The Logbook of the boy's school, 1930–57, reveals a little of school life.[47]

> September 15, 1939. 27 evacuees were taken on the register as from today.
>
> November 21, 1939. Up to the present we had air-raid warning practice and gone to the allotted places along the riverbank. Now the Royal Engineers are along there and trenches, *etc.* have been dug, which makes this portion unsafe for children.
>
> November 29, 1939. Air raid sirens tested at noon today. If there is the least noise they will not be heard. Not many people in Saltney heard it.
>
> January, 1940. evacuees and staff of Laird Street Junior Mixed School Birkenhead planned to return home but the instructions were cancelled. They went home for Whitsuntide and stayed there.
>
> January 12, 1942. commencing from today we opened our afternoon session at 1.15*p.m.* and closed at 3.45*p.m.* too many boys came late when we opened at 1*p.m.* They have to take their fathers dinner, and in some cases even get their own, as mother is working, so an hour was not long enough.

A new Council Infants' school was opened in Cable Row in 1909. In 1966 it was realised that one school building was inadequate and it was closed. Instead the premises of Saltney Council School were extended and received the name Saltney Wood Memorial School.

St Anthony's School

For an account of the opening of this school see the opening of the church in 1878. The school and church were in the one building until 1914. Roman Catholic parish boundaries in this area were revised in 1960 when the parish of St Anthony was designated entirely on the Welsh side of the border in the diocese of Menevia, now Wrexham, and a new church and parish of St Clare, was centred on the Lache, in England. A new St Anthony's school was opened in 1969. Some extracts from the school logbook show the difficulties encountered at the beginning of school life here in Saltney.[48]

1880, 9 February. Attendance of 70 children most of whom are in a disorganised state at present.

1880, 11 February. School visited by the Rev. Father Angelo and the Right Reverend Dr Knight, Vicar General of Wrexham.

1880, 12 April. Mrs Cornwallis West, Capt. Wild and Capt. Salisbury visited the school and gave the children a tea party.

1881. Summary of the Inspectors report. This new school has drawn a sufficient number of children to justify its existence and in many respects the work is promising.

1913. Inspectors report. The numbers in this school have grown rapidly. There are now 161 pupils. The tone and discipline are admirable. The head teacher governs a rather rough class of scholars with great kindness and conspicuous efficiency. The strain of having three teachers doing oral work at the same time in a large resonant room is detrimental to the best interests of teachers and taught.

1914, 25 May. His lordship the bishop visited the school. The foundation stone of the new church was laid yesterday.

1914, 16 November. Yesterday Holy Mass was offered up in this school for the last time. The new church was opened.

1914, 4 December. During the week the children have brought potatoes to school and today a good sack full has been sent to Chester for the wounded soldiers.

1953, 21 January. St Bede's Modern Secondary School Chester opened today. All the senior children, 48 in number were transferred. St Anthony's will now be classed as Infants and Primary, number on roll 109.

1953, October. Of its 110 pupils, 65 come from Flintshire, 44 from Chester and 1 from Denbighshire.

Mutual Improvement

Alongside the religious buildings and schools established in Saltney from the 1850s onwards new organisations came into being which gave the working man an opportunity to spend his leisure hours outside the public house. E. L. Roberts wrote in 1905, 'the curse of this part of the country is alcoholism, for every 148 of the population there is a licensed premise.'

The word used to describe the way in which a working man in the nineteenth century might make up for the lack of education was improvement. For this reading rooms were established where local and national newspapers, a lending library and games room, was available. Improvement was very much a social exercise. It was a respectable law abiding process, which involved reasonable discussion, an awareness of the main political issues of the day and a comfortable centre in which to meet.

The Saltney Reading room was established in March 1854. It had a library and reading room. Lectures were given. The first lecture was by the future vicar of Holy Epiphany, the Reverend R. Temple, on the war with Russia and the countries concerned in it. 'The attendance was good and interest displayed by the audience very great.'[49]

In March 1862 it was reported:

There has recently been established at Saltney, amongst the workingmen, a Literary and Reading Society. Although it has been in existence only about nine weeks, it has already registered on the books very nearly five hundred attendances in the week. The Mayor of Chester, John Trevor, Esq., paid a visit and was received by Mr Ford, manager of the Great Western Saltney Works, Mr Thompson, manager of Messrs. Wood Bros., and a considerable body of the members. The Mayor mentioned the eminent services of Lord Brougham, Dr Birbeck and others, who persevered in prosecuting the cause of public education, in the establishing of Mechanics' Institute, and Literary and Reading Societies.[50]

Sometimes improvement was seen as a mixture of popular culture as when a series of Penny Readings was held in the new lecture hall in the spring of 1869. 'There was a numerous attendance, the room being crowded and many persons unable to gain admission.' There were songs, the Reverend F. Whitehouse read a piece on logic, a solo on the violin, and *March of the Men of Harlech* with variations, executed by Edward Catherall, accompanied on the concertina by Mr Basford.[51]

An example of the paternalism behind improvement is a report of a political meeting of the workingmen of Saltney during the 1868 election campaign. The Liberal party were successful and W. E. Gladstone became prime minister for the first time. The meeting was held in the lecture hall:

There was a good attendance of respectable mechanics and workmen, the proceedings being orderly throughout. Mr Briggs was voted to the chair by acclamation, and in opening the meeting congratulated the working men of Saltney on being free to vote for whom they pleased without injury to their own interests, owing to the handsome manner in which Mr Henry Wood had acted in saying that the men employed by him could vote as they liked. The railway authorities, Messrs. Proctor and Rylands, and Mr Salisbury in behalf of the oil works, had done the same. The object of the meeting was that the working classes should come together, and that this should be an open meeting and that the candidates, through the press, might be able to know the political estimation in which they were held by the workingmen of Saltney. After hearing the various speeches he would take the sense of the meeting by a show of hands in front of each of the candidates, Earl Grosvenor, Mr Raikes, Mr Hoare, and Mr Salisbury.

There were a number of speakers. 'Mr. William Dodd harangued his auditory in terms similar to those he employed in the circus the other evening. Evidently he had great faith in Mr Salisbury, who was to hasten the grand political millennium of the ballot, the equalisation of taxation, and the disestablishment of the Irish Church'. Mr. Lewis Davies of Chester said, 'the artisan of the present day was far in advance of the ordinary tradesman of 30 years ago, and far better able than them to form opinions on great political subjects. The dissemination of sound information on every public question by means of the cheap press, had so enlightened men and changed the current of thought, that they seldom heard now of chartists or extreme opinions'. The chairman then took the vote of the meeting for each candidate separately. There was but one hand held up for earl Grosvenor, none for Raikes or Hoare, and the whole for Salisbury.' E. G. Salisbury, eventually Liberal M.P. for Flintshire was a local employer at the oil works.[52]

There were many religious groups most concerned with improvement. In 1873 Mr Charles Drinkwater, a city missionary of Chester came to Saltney and held weekly religious services in the lecture hall with the support of the managers at the G.W.R. Carriage Works and the Anchor Works, whom he thanked 'for their great help to him, in enabling him to get among the men.'[53]

The Saltney Total Abstinence Society and Band of Hope held public meetings at the lecture hall. In September 1876 Mr Loraine of Saltney, a Wesleyan missionary, was chairman of a meeting where, 'several Moody and Sankey hymns were sung and several pledges taken.' When the Sunday Closing Act for Wales came into operation in 1881, publicans on the Welsh side of Saltney were fined for their refusal to recognise it.

Mrs. Coltart, wife of the managing partner of the Dee Iron Works, used the Wood's Memorial schools to inaugurate mothers' weekly meetings and a clothing club. At the annual meeting there was a social gathering for the women and their husbands, tea was served, and the addresses given on temperance and moral and religious welfare, followed by a choir singing hymns and songs.

There emerged gradations of mutual improvement, Pooterish and Wellsian in their seriousness, as may be seen in a report of the Saltney Mutual Improvement Society:

The Literary Institute
[Saltney & Saltney Ferry
publication]

As applied to a meeting of this body the word 'social' is peculiarly appropriate for the chief object the members have in view is to promote good feeling and mental improvement amongst the people of the village and neighbourhood. For four years past their efforts have been directed to this object, and have borne excellent fruit. By instructive lectures information has been imparted and curiosity roused; by earnest discussions minds have been trained and ability developed; and by agreeable intercourse and conversation friendship has been established and strengthened. Such a result has not been attained without patient exertions by the officers of the society who have spared neither time nor trouble in furthering the interests of the society, and diffusing a taste for the culture of those qualities which specially distinguish a gentleman of refinement, and their endeavours have been warmly seconded. The progress of the association has accordingly been very satisfactory, and at present some seventy names are enrolled on the list of membership, in addition to those of the honorary members.[54]

The climax to the movement for improvement in Saltney was reached with the opening of the new library and reading rooms at Saltney in connection with the Literary Institute by W. E. Gladstone on 26 October 1889. It was a two-storied building in Hope Street built to accommodate a lending library of upwards of 4,000 volumes, some of which were presented by Mr Gladstone. Available in the reading room were eight daily, eleven weekly, and seven monthly newspapers and periodicals. For recreation there was a billiard table and games of draughts and chess. The lecture hall and committee rooms were for use mainly in the winter months for concerts, entertainments and lectures.

To welcome W. E. Gladstone flags, were displayed from almost every house in the main thoroughfare. Gladstone was approaching his 80th birthday but he was still able to enthral his listeners and produced on this occasion a discourse on the workman and his opportunities.[55] He spoke about the building being 'a reading room, a place of recreation, a place of study, and a place of improvement for our fellow citizens who belong to the class that we call the working men of the country.' He used his old technique of reminiscence 'to point out to you what remarkable alleviations and improvement have come to the mass of our working men.' These were the lessening of the severity of labour, the progress of machine tools, the cheapness and convenience of railway travel, the value of the press for information, the benefits of cheap postage, and 'a livelier, more active, and more practical sense of benevolence amongst the upper classes than there has existed in past times. All these circumstances which are very pleasing to review, and they bring me back to the purpose for which we have met today, when the various blessings which the population have received are crowned by this important blessing of greater means of mental improvement. This is the crown of them all.' He spoke of the importance of the study of history, recommending a study of the lessons of the French Revolution, the parliamentary institutions of Ireland and the American Revolution. He concluded by saying, 'the purpose for which a man lives is the improvement of the man himself, so that he may go out of this world having, in his great sphere or his small one, done some little good to his fellow creatures. Let me express the fervent hope that this Literary Institute may thrive, and may largely and continuously contribute to the prosperity of Saltney and the happiness of its people.'

Saltney Ferry

Saltney Ferry has had two names. It was first named Higher Ferry, a crossing of the Dee established by Act of Parliament in 1743, which ordered that from 25 May 1744 two free ferry boats should be kept, one at Lower Ferry (later Queensferry), and the other at Higher Ferry (Saltney), to be provided and maintained by the River Dee Company. Thomas Telford recommended in the early 1800s that two boats be used at Higher Ferry, a horse boat, and a smaller one for passengers. Higher Ferry was in constant use, taking children to school, workers to the industrial development at Saltney and the aircraft factory at Broughton, until it was replaced in 1968 by a footbridge.

In 1790 William Manifold, son of a Mersey fisherman, was appointed, and it was his great-grandson Robert, who gave up the job after forty years' service in 1968. For twenty-five years he had to row his boat (later he had an outboard motor), and he calculated that he had rowed right round the world in his time — often against a six-knot tide. Working hours were from 5a.m. to 9p.m., seven days a week, and as many as fifty crossings a day might be made'.[56]

Census returns record 1871 John Kendrick aged 52 boatman; 1881 James Gibson, 58, ferry boatman, Peter Manifold, 51, joiner; 1891 James Gibson, 68, boatman. A footbridge replaced the Ferry in 1968.

The other name for the community was Mold Junction, because it was chosen as a junction by the newly formed Shrewsbury & Chester Railway opened in 1846 to convey minerals to Saltney wharf. It provided a junction with the Chester Mold Railway (later extended to Denbigh) from 1849, and with the Chester & Holyhead Railway opened in 1848. It developed sidings on both sides of the Chester and Holyhead main line, later widened from two tracks to four. The junction was equipped with an engine shed, turntable and coaling tower, and the junction with the Mold Railway eventually formed a triangle, allowing traffic to run directly up the North Wales coast as well as towards Chester. For more than 120 years this was the main sorting and storage yards for North Wales traffic.[57] At its peak the engine shed stationed 42 locomotives. The marshalling yards accommodated 856 wagons, and another 335 wagons in the separate slate sidings. The slate sidings were equipped with special wharves for sorting out slates. In 1852 another 8 acres of land was purchased from the Hawarden estate to store 80,000 tons of slate. The community was developed by L.N.W.R. to house its workers. In 1891 Saltney Ferry Station was opened on the Mold–Denbigh line.

One of the largest buildings in the village was the three-storied Railway Staff Hostel commonly known as the L.M.S. Barracks,[58] although it was built as a lodging house for railway men far from home, by the L.N.W.R. in 1890. On the ground floor there was a mess room, reading room and games room. The reading room served the local community in many ways. In the early days it was used for religious services, scout group meetings, and as a place to collect the tontine or club money for payment whilst sick. On the first floor there was a dormitory area divided into nineteen cubicles, and on the second floor another dormitory area divided into 20 cubicles formed by timber-boarded partitioning. The men cooked their own food. The staff of the hostel consisted of a matron and two female assistants. From 6p.m. to 10p.m. young men from the railway sheds were employed as 'knockers up' until the night attendant came on duty at 10p.m. The hostel was sold in 1966 and is now called Ferry Lodge. Another railway connection, although obscure, was the railway coach used by Field Marshall Sir Douglas Haig, Commander-in-Chief, British Forces, 1916–8, that stood at the end of Saltney Ferry Lane. An old railway guard bought it from Manchester to retire in and his wife had part of it as a sweet shop.

Other shops in Saltney Ferry were a Co-operative stores, bakery, coal merchants, an off licence, Peter Bradshaw's sweets and tobacconist, and Jack Ball's shoe shop in Saltney Ferry Lane. In 1895 there were 104 houses with a population of about 530.

Mold Junction school was built by the L.N.W.R. Company probably in 1891. It was controlled by the Railway Company who made the decisions about the use of the buildings, sometimes contrary to the wishes of the local community as in 1892 when:

The Reverend Dimond Hogg had an interview at Chester with Mr Whale, assistant superintendent of the L.N.W. Rlwy. Mr Whale informed Mr Hogg that the new room which is attached to the school which was understood to be for an Infant Room is for recreation purposes only, and that the idea of providing infant accommodation is not entertained at all by the Railway Company.

The local community supported by the school inspectors persisted in their demands, and the Company co-operated in appointing a certificated teacher for the infants. In April 1903 the Company offered to transfer the

Saltney Ferry, c.1908
[FRO 58/1]

Right: Bob Manifold, ferryman
[FRO 58/30]

Below left: The new footbridge at Saltney Ferry, 1968
[FRO 58/5]

Company's Schools to the Flintshire County Council, the use of the school buildings being reserved by the Company for Sundays and certain other days'. This probably did not take place until April 1910 when the name of the school was changed to East Saltney, Mold Junction Council School. The school remained open until the summer of 1955 when it moved to new premises. Two of the teachers had exceptionally long service at the school, Mrs Chatterton retired in October 1950 after 44 years teaching service of which 35 years were spent at the school, and in 1953 Miss M. M. Price retired after over 45 years service.

The school logbook begins in October 1891 when the school numbers were 138. It was difficult to get children to school.

> Some parents will not send their children regularly to school; in fact a few say they have a perfect right to keep their children at home when they think fit … a few parents keep their children at home to nurse and do other domestic work.[59]

The school was influenced by its locality with the river and the railway. These feature in the logbook entries. The river from time to time claimed the lives of pupils who were drowned whilst bathing. It was also unpredictable, as in November 1935 when 'several families 'over the river' have been surrounded in their bungalows by the flood water'. This affected their attendance, and in February 1936 the headmaster and the attendance officer 'went across the river to see the conditions under which some of the children were living. The conditions are deplorable'. The river was frozen over in January 1940 when the ferryboat was inactive, and in

Railwaymen and locomotive at Mold Junction, c.1930
[FRO 58/21]

April 1943 the ferryboat was prevented from working by stormy weather. The railway paid a major part in children's lives. Four children left the school in 1905 when their father was killed on the line. During the strike of 1910 'Sergt. Williams cautioned several boys who have been caught stealing turnips from Mr Lee's field. Two of these boys complained of being hungry, having had neither dinner nor tea on the day in question'. A more

The slate wharves at Mold Junction, c.1915
[FRO 58/21]

The L.M.S. Railway Barracks
[Saltney & Saltney Ferry publication]

pleasant adventure occurred in June 1919 when:

The teachers and the children of the school went to see the Irish Mail passing through the Mold Junction Station. Among the passengers were Captain Alcock and Lieutenant Brown, the first persons to make a direct flight across the Atlantic Ocean. The train slowly passed through and hearty cheers were given the brave airmen by the children and by the crowd that had gathered together.

Many of the boys began their working lives as cleaners on the railway. In May 1926 the headmaster gave a special warning 'to all the children regarding the throwing of stones at trains or doing anything which would cause friction between the strikers and the legal representatives of the Country.'

In 1954 the headmaster reported to the education authorities a 'complaint received by him of the smoke nuisance caused by the nearness of the locomotive sheds. The complaint is not a frivolous one, but one that very little or nothing can be done about it'.

In November 1918 the influenza 'had developed to a marked extent that a great many children were affected. Several deaths have taken place and many children are ill'.

There were occasions when the headteacher proudly commented on the success of pupils both past and present. In May 1928: 'Mr C. Lewis has gone with Arnold Davies to Belfast. Arnold is to be capped for Wales in the match against Ireland'. In September 1936 a much longer explanation was given to the success of old boy Frank Chilton:

He gained a scholarship for Hawarden County School in 1927 but after starting at that school did not remain there owing to the fact he could not receive the type of beginning which he longed for. He was re-admitted into this school where he remained until he was 16. In school he showed signs of being a boy beyond the average

Ewart Street, Saltney Ferry, looking west. On the left are the CP School and the Co-Op
[FRO 58/3]

Right:English Presbyterian Church, Saltney Ferry
[Saltney & Saltney Ferry publication]

intelligence. He studied languages by the help of gramophone and wireless and became proficient in French, German and Esperanto. He made a camera while in a low standard in school, from a chalk box, and it worked. He was at that time able to do his own developing.

In the logbook is a newspaper cutting announcing that Frank Chilton, aged twenty, a Chester photographer, had been chosen as chief scientific officer of the British Empire Photographic Expedition which leaves England in Scott's famous research ship *Discovery* at the end of the month to undertake aerial survey work of islands in the Pacific, and to collect data for planning new Empire routes in Antarctica.

On the outbreak of the Second World War in September 1939 the school received evacuees from Birkenhead. In 1940 an air raid shelter was provided 'to accommodate about 70 children who cannot reach home within a few minutes', and the school was closed because a high explosive delayed action bomb had been dropped near the school 'and its time had not yet expired'.

Saltney Ferry English Presbyterian Church[60] was established as a result of the missionary activities of the City Road Church Chester under the leadership of the Reverend John Williams. Their first services were held in a reading room in the village, which the worshippers shared, with the Methodist New Connexion. In November 1893 the church was incorporated into the Cheshire Presbytery under the oversight of the Reverend Richard Jones of Mancot, and the church was opened in May 1896. The Reverend E. L. Roberts was elected pastor in 1901 and served this church as well as the Welsh Presbyterian in Saltney Ferry until his death at the age of 54 in 1929. Those succeeding him as Pastor were the Reverend H. Llewelyn Hughes (1930–2), the Reverend G. Whitfield Jones (1934–40), and the Reverend J. Kenneth Bufton (1943–5).

Saltney Ferry Welsh Presbyterian Church[61] was opened in 1900 to serve the Welsh-speaking families of the railway men who had settled here. An example of the life of the congregation is the report of a concert held in January 1908, which describes the evening's entertainment as long and interesting with all the items in Welsh. Miss Jones from Llandrindod was the star, accompanied by six local women, and nine men, with children taking part in action songs. Miss Rowlands presided at the organ and the ladies of the church took charge of the refreshments. With reduction in the railway services and decline in freight traffic, people sought work elsewhere, membership dwindled and the church closed at the end of 1987.

St. Matthew's Church Saltney Ferry. The architect John Douglas prepared a design for a new church at Saltney Ferry in 1905, and in December 1906 The *Chester Chronicle* announced:

> By the gift of a piece of ground for the site of the proposed church, Mr William Gladstone, the young squire of Hawarden, has given the scheme both timely and valuable help. The value of the ground situate on the Saltney Ferry side of the railway bridge, is

Right: Welsh Presbyterian Church, Saltney Ferry
[Saltney & Saltney Ferry publication]

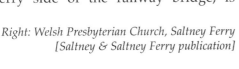

[]

Below: St. Matthews Church, Saltney Ferry
[Saltney & Saltney Ferry publication]

estimated at upwards of £180. It goes without saying that the church people are exceedingly pleased at the receipt of such a generous Christmas gift.[62]

The church was opened near St Matthew's Day in September 1911, and as part of the parish of Saltney it is in the diocese of Chester.

14. Shotton

Old Shotton was a township, which was chiefly made up of a small number of farms in Higher Shotton, and a group of dwellings called Nine Houses, near Wepre brook. Even by the 1881 census, the number of inhabited houses in Shotton Township was only 89, with a total population of 393. There was little industry. The Eleanor Colliery, 1868–78, had closed. A small brickyard provided an unspectacular livelihood for a few men. Any employment was in agriculture, work on the railway, or associated with seafaring and the nearby port of Connah's Quay. All this was dramatically changed in the course of less than ten years with the opening of the Hawarden Bridge in 1889, and the iron works of John Summers and Sons in 1896. For a while it seemed that the name of the rapidly growing community would be changed to Rivertown.

The cottage that stood near the church in Shotton Lane
[FRO 62/63]

Hawarden Bridge

It was long recognised that there should be a railway connection between North Wales and England. Nine applications were made to Parliament between 1861 and 1884 for this purpose. Sir Edward Watkin, Bart. proprietor of the Manchester, Sheffield and Lincolnshire Railway Company, succeeded in getting permission, and on August 20 1887, he invited his friend W. E. Gladstone, to perform the ceremony of laying the first cylinder of the Hawarden Bridge, to cross the river at Shotton. For the ceremony a spacious, covered, grandstand projecting on piles, some distance into the river on the Shotton side, was erected, with a special dais for Mr Gladstone to give the signal for the lowering of the first cylinder.

Sir Edward Watkin, a proponent of the Channel Tunnel, a flamboyant character, brought a touch of showmanship to the occasion. He presented Mrs. Gladstone with a gold whistle, and Mr Gladstone with a silk pennon, embroidered with the insignia of England and Wales. To give notice to the workmen on the Cheshire shore to lower the cylinder, Mrs. Gladstone blew the whistle, and Mr Gladstone, in dramatic fashion, grasped his pennon with both hands, and waved furiously, whilst the cylinder, 'was seen to descend gently into its destined position, amid the cheers of all assembled.' And then Mr Gladstone spoke of the importance of the Bridge in having brought north Wales into full and free communication with England, to the enormous benefit of all. The value of the railway bridge to the north Wales Coalfield, the Buckley clay manufacturers, the Mersey, the salt districts of Cheshire, in giving access to the markets in the large centres of Lancashire and Yorkshire to cause their further development.[1]

It took just two years to build the bridge. Work was carried on throughout the day and night and on one bank there was an electric lighting installation and on the other large vaporised jet spirit lamps.[2] The designer of the bridge was Mr C. A. Hobson, the contractors, John Cochrane and sons Westminster, sub-contractors for the steel structure, Horsley Bridge Co. Tipton, Staffs, chief engineer, Mr Francis Fox, the cost £71,000.

The bridge consists of two fixed spans, each 120 feet long and a swinging span, 285 feet long, weighing 753 tons, which rotates on a steel ball. The main cylinder foundation consists of a steel caisson filled with concrete and finished in bricks. It weighs 2,300 tons and is sunk to a depth of 48 feet below the riverbed. The hydraulic

Hawarden bridge, 1889
[Illustrated London News, 10 August 1889, FRO PR/F/50]

motive power to open the bridge was in duplicate, and consisted of three vertical boilers, two steam driven pumps, and two hydraulic accumulators, giving a working pressure of 700 lbs per square inch, all housed in the red brick control tower. The pumps were electrically driven in later years. The swinging span of 753 tons is operated by two massive hydraulic rams secured to the top of the main foundation. These rams in turn swivel a 32 foot 6 inch-diameter chain-wheel secured to the underside of the steel structure. This mechanism opens and closes the bridge through an angle of 90 degrees. The swinging span could be opened for shipping in half a minute. In the 1890s the bridge was opened for shipping approximately 50 times per month.[3]

The completed bridge was officially opened and named the Hawarden Bridge by Mrs. Catherine Gladstone on August 3 1889. Sir Edward Watkin presented her with a little memento in the shape of a golden casket; and then she touched the electric appliance, the bridge gradually rotated, and the river at high tide presented a lively spectacle, a large flotilla and the tug *Albert* passing the bridge, while the people lustily cheered from the bank of the river.[4]

The Arrival of John Summers & Sons

'John Summers bought a nail-making machine at the Great Exhibition in 1851. It cost him forty pounds, his entire savings, but it made him an iron master. He was a great Victorian. His seventh son, Henry Hall Summers, took the decision to develop the business on the banks of the Dee, and it made him a great steelmaster.'[5] Summers' Stalybridge works on its twenty-four acres site, with thirteen rolling mills, galvanising pots and finishing equipment, had no room for expansion. On a legendary day, in September 1895, young Bill Butler, working at the boat-yard Connah's Quay, earned half-a-crown (12.5p), for rowing Harry and James Summers on the river, to look at a prospective site on the north side, which was the empty Sealand Marshes near the newly opened Hawarden bridge. The brothers decided on the site, with its railway links and proximity to Liverpool. It was said that they paid one shilling per acre for the marshland they acquired. Eventually they bought many thousands of acres and reclaimed more from the estuary.

The news of the intention of Summers coming to Shotton, 'for the purpose of constructing extensive works for the manufacture of galvanised corrugated iron roofing sheets, steel nail strips and sheets', was announced in a matter of days, together, with an optimistic appraisal of the prospects for the locality.

'As Messrs. Summers expect to employ two or three hundred hands and consume about a thousand tons of coal per week at their Hawarden Bridge works, no doubt both Chester and Connah's Quay will reap some benefit and before long quite a town will spring up.'[6] By February 1896, Summers were reported as contemplating 'the construction of a large new stage on the Dee in close proximity to the works, to provide wharfage accommodation for three ships.'[7] In October 1896 the extensive ironworks were in working order and a large number of houses were in the 'course of erection at Shotton, a little place, which is practically a continuation of Connah's Quay.'[8] The works were in full swing by December. Large quantities of raw materials, chiefly iron ore, were arriving and it was estimated that quite two thousand tons each month would be required. 'This new trade is giving a stimulus to the shipping trade on the river, and the new works in other respects are already proving a great benefit to the village.'[9]

The new site had six steam driven mills, galvanising pots, annealing furnaces and finishing equipment, and by the turn of the century there were thirty rolling mills. At first, most of the steel bars for rolling came from the Carnegie Co. at Pittsburgh, but in 1902, they installed No. 1 steelworks with nine hearth furnaces, each of 50 ton capacity, and a bar mill, came into production. A foundry was opened in 1906 and more rolling mills installed the following year. Large quantities of galvanised sheets were exported through Liverpool to the Argentine. To mark the importance of the Hawarden Bridge Works the General Office was built on the bank of the river in 1907. Which Hubbard describes as, 'unconventional but pompous, symmetrical with castellated central tower. Brick and yellow terracotta. Art nouveau detail.'[10]

The development of Shotton

By 1910, John Summers & Sons Ltd. employed a work force of 3,000 and Shotton had become a small town. The 1901 census recorded an influx of iron galvanisers, rollers, corrugators and labourers: migrants from Stalybridge, Cheshire, Durham, Lancashire, Staffordshire and South Wales. They lived in newly built houses in Eleanor Terrace, Grosvenor Terrace, Hawarden Terrace, Ryeland Terrace, Chester Road, Wellington Avenue, North Street, Salisbury Street, and other property. By 1901 the Company had formed Summers Permanent Benefit Building Society to advance mortgages, repayments being made from wages.

Various estimates for the growth in the population, number of houses, the users of Shotton Station, and the

John Summers & Sons' new steelworks at Hawarden bridge, 1897
[Reproduced with the kind permission of Corus]

number of pedestrians, bicycles and vehicle users, were presented to the Hawarden Licensing Sessions in order to persuade the magistrates to authorise a public house near Shotton Station, between 1897 and 1901. At the application in August 1897, Mr Freme of Wepre Hall informed the Bench, that he had 185 applications for the houses he had built. He was of the opinion that the people of Shotton, 'were not rich enough to have their wine cellars, but sufficiently respectable to send out for their jugs of beer without 'boozing' in public houses.' He proposed building a public house and, 'he had a large area which he proposed to cover with houses. They would be picturesque houses, after the Port Sunlight style, and the hotel would also be in ancient Cheshire style.'[11]

Houses were said to have increased from 170 in 1897 to 260 in 1899. Over the same period the population of Shotton increased from 830 to 1,500. The number of pedestrians on a Saturday in August was 2,240, bicycles 724, and other vehicles 362. These had nearly doubled by August 1901 — 4,409 pedestrians, 1,302 bicycles, and 514 other vehicles.[12] By 1904, it was demanded that,

… the rapid growth of Shotton makes it necessary that the district should be up to date. One reform especially is of urgent importance, the naming of streets and numbering of houses. Long streets of villa residences have come into existence with mushroom growth, and the greatest difficulty is experienced in finding the address of any person that may be required. Indeed in some of the streets the residents themselves have difficulty in locating their own house.[13]

An indication of the growth of Shotton is a report on a demonstration and gala, which took place there on the occasion of the opening of a branch of the Queensferry and District Co-operative Society in August 1904. The Shotton branch joined the large central stores at Pentre Lane, Queensferry, and that of Sandycroft, to swell the membership to eight hundred. The demonstration was headed by the Connah's Quay Silver Band, with a procession of the children of the members, numbering 1,100 in all, 'prettily attired, with the various conveyances of the Co-op gaily decorated.' They marched from Sandycroft to Connah's Quay and then returned to Shotton, where Mr Millar, president of the Society, received a silver key, and declared the new premise open for business, 'during the afternoon tea and sports were held on the Shotton football field, the band being in attendance.[14]

Not all occasions were as pleasant and purposeful as this. Strikes in the steel works and collieries caused great distress between the years 1910–12. In good times drunkenness became a problem. In August 1912, the police raided the drinking dens in Shotton, the Grosvenor Working Men's Club in Nelson Street; the Working Men's Social Club, Chester road; and the Queensferry Union Jack working men's club near Sandycroft. It was reported that the membership of the Grosvenor Club was 363 and that between May and August there were 175 cases of drunkenness on the premises. A former steward of the club said he had opened it as early as 5.30*a.m.* and found men waiting to enter, and he told the magistrates, that on August Bank Holiday, 'the roads were strewn with drunken men from Shotton lane to Wepre bridge.'[15]

The Strike at John Summers & Sons, 1909–10[16]

The Strike brought to a head the dominance of the contract system of labour, and led to its abolition at the steel works. The length and bitterness of the dispute was aggravated by the rivalry of the two trade unions involved, which divided the local community and at times led to violence.

The contract system meant that the responsibility for recruiting and paying the labour force was in the hands of a person who was paid by the management to assume these responsibilities on their behalf. In the steel works each rolling mill needed a crew of ten men. The crew was in the charge of a contractor, or boss man, who was paid directly by the firm, at so much a ton for the finished sheets. He it was who decided the rate of pay for the men in his team, the job allocation, promotion, and the allowance of beer. The contracting system was resented because it was often unfair and led to corruption and abuse.

A decision was made by the Midland Wages Board, with regard to the steel industry 'that in every works connected with the Welsh Committee, the tonnage-rate men must pay the day-wage men the scheduled rate of wages and the bonus', thus fixing a definite relation between the tonnage rate and the earnings of the under-hands. The rejection of this decision by the contract men at Shotton led to the strike.

The contractors and the men at the Staffordshire mills at Shotton were members of the Associated Iron and Steel Workers Union. About a hundred of the day-wage under-hands employed at these mills joined this union, but were refused admission to the branch meeting because the contractors were afraid they would have to implement the recommended rate of wages and the bonus.

The new sheet mills, the Welsh Mills, were organised by the Smelters Union, who were in favour of the recommendation of the Midland Wage Board, and moreover, sought the abolition of the contract system. When the day-wage under-hands of the Staffordshire Mills were refused admission to the branch meetings of the Associated Union, they joined the Smelters' Union. The decision by the contractors supported by the Association Union, not to pay the schedule rate of wages and the bonus, to the under-hands, freed the Smelters' Union, to give notice in November 1909, to the Summers Management, that they would strike unless contracting was abolished. After some deliberation the Summers general manager recommended that the contract system be ended, and reached an agreement with the Smelters Union on a schedule of tonnage rates to all grades of mill workers, who were to be paid directly by the firm, thus ending the influence of the contractor.

This resulted in a strike by the contractors and other members of the Associated Iron and Steel Workers Union. Summers attempted to keep the mills working with the under-hands and other members of the Smelters Union, and labour brought in from Stalybridge and elsewhere. This was a declaration of war between the two unions and the beginning of a bitter conflict, some of which was fought on the streets of Shotton. The headlines of the *County Herald* for Friday, 25 March 1910, summarised the situation. Steel Smelters' War at Shotton — the Station besieged — desperate fighting — trains and workmen stoned — women in the conflict. The major disturbance reported, occurred on Thursday and Friday evenings, of a week of 'threats, violent language and menaces.' For nearly a fortnight previously, a contingent of the Flintshire Constabulary had been housed in improvised barracks near the main entrance to the steel works. The first incident took place on Thursday evening. Pickets were set up on behalf of the 'Rollers Society' at Queensferry, Shotton, and Connah's Quay Railway Stations, to molest imported steel workers, particularly the large batch of imported day workers from Flint. The strikers were prohibited from assembling on the platforms at Shotton Station. Not to be put out they walked to Queensferry and caught a train to Shotton, arriving there before the day shift. It was reported that 'the police were in force on the platform, but they were powerless amongst the indiscriminate attacks. The combatants, who fought on the edge of the platform, rolled over on to the track. 'The Black Maria', which is the familiar designation of the workers' train, arrived, and when it departed for Flint it was evident a serious riot had been averted'.

In the early hours of the next day, about one a.m. strikers were observed stealthily making their way along the Sealand embankment of the river, from the neighbourhood of Queensferry. They were spotted on reaching the confines of the Works. 'The workers were greatly exasperated, and men of several departments seizing cudgels and other weapons, rushed out of the Works. Hundreds of men were in a few minutes on the embankment, and the strikers hastily retreated towards Queensferry. Throughout Friday there were declarations that 'blood would be spilt' in the evening. The Railway Companies brought in constables to protect their interests. The Flintshire Constabulary, on duty at the Steel Works, was augmented, and just before five o'clock, there was a small army of constables promenading the platform. Excitement was growing intense as a gang of strikers put in an appearance at the station gates, clamouring for admission, Meanwhile men were approaching from the Great Central Railway

Picket line at John Summers & Sons during the strike of 1910
[FRO 62/65]

Station; and shortly, a crowd assembled outside the station, and on the path leading to the bottom of King Edward Street.

The strikers and crowd were awaiting the in-coming 'Black Maria' conveying the Flint workers for the night shift. They carried 'life preservers', bludgeons, iron bars, and other ugly weapons, whilst one possessed what is known as a 'hanker', which is used for clipping pieces of metal off the sheets. It was a formidable and dangerous looking article, resembling the proportions of a huge knife or sword.

As soon as the train was discerned, the strikers swaying on the station gates, made desperate attempts to break through the police cordon. There were loud cries, 'Here comes the Black Maria.' In alighting from the train, the Flint workers shouldering their weapons marched over the covered bridge to the platform. There was immediately a brisk skirmish. One man, who was said to be strike leader, was met and received a rough handling. When this was being administered, there was uproar from the platform. Men in an adjoining field below the Great Central Station hurled stones at the Flint workers. The police were rendered almost helpless in their duties. At half past five o'clock, when the day men left their work, hundreds of them, furnished with bludgeons of various sizes, marched in military fashion from the works. It was an impressive sight as they passed over the railway bridge and entered Jubilee Street. They were in battle array and ready for anything. The strikers, gathered at the station, realised they were vulnerable from the rear, and near the Station Hotel they were mercilessly set upon. The Flint contingent, in warrior like manner, had practically cut off the retreat of the strikers, and as they arrived at the bottom of King Edward Street, in their onward march to the station, stones were hurled at them. This was the signal for them to attack, and the men from Flint retaliated with fury. The strikers armed with sticks, improvised life-preservers manufactured of piping filled with lead, pockets full of stones and pieces of brick, were caught like rats in a trap, and were impelled to defend themselves. The fighting zone was principally confined to the open space at the end of King Edward Street. The workmen drove the strikers towards the narrow passage running parallel with the gable ends of the houses and the railway. In the general melée, bludgeons were used freely and several of the combatants amongst the strikers fell, stunned and helpless, with wounds to the head.

The police eventually persuaded the workmen to proceed to the station. Whilst they were accomplishing this, the strikers, aided by women and children, picked up stones from the newly macadamised street, and carried out a perfect fusillade. The police were pelted by the scattered mob and forced to retreat from the station. The workmen returned cheering to the station platform, where the 'Black Maria' was standing ready to convey them to Flint. As the train left the station it was stoned by the strikers, assisted by the women, and departed with smashed windows, but luckily none of the men were injured.

On Saturday morning, a special conference was held at the head office of the works, attended by representatives of the Associated Iron and Steel Workers Union, the Steel Smelters' Union, the Police, and the Parliamentary Committee of the Trades Union Congress Conference. It was decided that a truce should take place immediately, all the pickets should be withdrawn, and the workmen employed in the Mills should be permitted to proceed to and from the works unimpeded.

The *County Herald* produced figures to show that earnings under the Smelters' agreement were higher, by a considerable percentage, than earnings under the contractor. The day men operated under such names as 'bar dragger', 'breaker down', 'catcher', 'doubler', 'pryler', 'marker' and 'scrap lad'. The breaker down earned £3 3s. 7d. as compared with £2 5s. 4d. under the contractor and the scrap lad, 18s. 8d. as compared with 16s. 6d. under the contractor.

The strike dragged on, the community was disturbed and divided. At the end of May, religious services were especially arranged, and attended by the men on strike. Although most of the steel mills were kept working it was despite the fact that most of the skilled workers were on strike. The quality and quantity of the steel was affected, Summers lost orders, at an estimated £1,500 a week. Some agreement was reached at the end of October, when G. R. Askwith, of the Board of Trade, presented proposals, which later formed the basis of the final settlement. These were turned down by the Smelters' Union, who churlishly objected to the Associated Union being consulted. The Smelters' came out on strike, the Associated returned to work, and the firm imported workers from Liverpool, then everyone went on strike. This led Harry Summers to address the workers and appeal to their loyalty and commonsense. By 29 December 1910, a new agreement was accepted which laid down the important principles:

1. Piecework as the basis of wages.
2. Employment and payment of wages by the firm direct.
3. Direct representation in respect of all matters affecting their wages and conditions of employment.

With peace and confidence restored between workers and management there was further growth at the Steel works. The site was expanded to 250 acres, with the erection of the marsh mills in 1911, where two steam engines drove twelve mills, a number later increased to nineteen. They were the most up to date mills in the country. A further four hundred men were taken on to the workforce, now totalling 3,400 men. Production reached 4,500 tons.

But there was a dark cloud in the sky, the Coal Strike of 1912. In March it was reported that, 'numerous families were on the verge of starvation, and thousands of men unemployed, many of whom devoted their time to picking coal off the Queensferry Colliery tip. W. G. C. Gladstone, J. R Freme of Wepre, and Harry Summers gave relief. The children were fed in school, receiving a breakfast and a 'soup dinner'. A hunger march of iron workers went to the Workhouse at Broughton, a distance of five or six miles, to inform the Guardians that their wives and children were in dire distress. Here they waited outside, from 10.30*a.m.* until 2*p.m.*, when they were called into the dining hall and served with bread, cheese, and a pint of tea. But they had made their point.

The next day, Saturday, the Workhouse Union officials came to Shotton, and from 11.30*a.m.* until 9*p.m.*, distributed relief tickets at the two local schools. Altogether, about 300 families were relieved, a total of about 1,200 women and children, although the newspaper remarked 'it is a regrettable fact that many women, on Saturday night, were seen running with jugs of beer.'[17]

By the time war came in 1914, John Summers and Sons were in a strong position to make an invaluable

John Summers & Sons pay office, 1910
[FRO 62/129]

contribution. There was an insatiable demand for black and galvanised sheets. Steel was essential for munitions and trenches, and the forty-nine rolling mills at Shotton were in full production to meet these demands.

Harry Summers was now chairman of the firm, and a prominent figure in the steel world. He saw the need for further supplies of steel to aid the war effort, and persuaded the Department of Trade to help finance the erection of No. 2 steelworks and bar mill. The plant cost £900,000, but assistance was given through tax relief. Within eleven months, the new plant was in operation. Eight open-hearth furnaces of seventy-ton capacity, freed the plant from dependence on imports. Castle Fire Brick Company was purchased to secure supplies of firebricks; and the Wolverhampton Corrugated Iron Company at Ellesmere Port, with its twenty sheet mills, came to Summers in 1917. Both the Steel Works at Shotton and the Munitions Factory at Queensferry, with their joint work force of twelve thousand, made a significant contribution to the allies victory in the First World War.

The New Community

The town of Shotton was developed by the beginning of the First World War. Impetus for the provision of religious and educational institutions came from both old and new communities. The old community was under the leadership of Davisons, Rowleys, Coppacks, Hurlbutts, and above all the Gladstone family. Under the leadership of the Gladstone family a school chapel, St Ethelwold's, was erected in 1875 and a coffee house in the 1880s. They were the magistrates and the officers in the Volunteers, and had significant interests in the coal and clay industries. W. E. Gladstone in the year of his death, 1898, gave a thousand pounds to build a new church, which his son S. E. Gladstone, as rector of Hawarden, was responsible for building the new St Ethelwold's, opened in 1904. W. G. C. Gladstone, when he came of age in 1906, demonstrated both the wisdom and liberality of the Grand Old Man. The new community, under the patriarchy of the Summers family, was made up of a migrant population, brought together by employment in the steel works. They had parallel institutions. They worshipped in Rivertown Congregational Church. The council school was built to educate their children. The picture house, *palais de danse* and working men's clubs provided new forms of amusement, enlivened from time to time by travelling entertainers. The annual carnival, their own football and cricket teams, gave them a sense of communal identity, which integrated both old and new communities by 1914. Political leadership, in the main, came from the strong presence of trade unionism.

Rivertown Congregational Church[18]

The Cheshire and Staffordshire folk who came to Deeside to work at Summers, accepted the friendly Christian welcome which greeted them. The new families, Bell, Collins, Cunningham, Eaves, Hazeldine, Holman, Nock, Marsland, Millar, Scager, Walker, Washbrook, Williams and others, who settled in the first houses built either side of the Chester Road, found a pastor awaiting them. The Reverend Joseph Davies from Buckley was no ordinary man. He was full of energy and sound practical sense. He was a Congregationalist and the ideal person to establish a place of worship in a new town. This particular purpose was his vocation. Unusually for a minister of the Gospel, he was of independent means. He was a missionary evangelist, a musician, and an inspiring leader. His first action was to buy a piece of land in a prime position, within walking distance of future housing development. It was essential that a building be raised quickly, and a congregation drawn into the corrugated iron structure he erected. The simple name given to the chapel was Rivertown, an apt description, for the rapidly growing community on the south side of the Dee. Miss King cared for the new families, and Davies brought others from Buckley, to assist with the weeknight services. The small tin tabernacle to accommodate 140 persons was opened on Wednesday, 26 May 1897, when the Reverend Jonathan Evans, of Buckley, preached, and the Reverend Joseph Davies, the founder, assisted. 'A special feature was the attendance of a section of Mr Thomas Croppers orchestra of Buckley, which had an enlivening effect in the accompaniment of the singing.'[19]

Fourteen months later, on 26 July 1898, Mr Samuel Smith, Liberal M.P. for Flintshire, laid the foundation stone for a new chapel. It was situated, in front of the tin tabernacle, on the main road. The chairman, on this occasion, Mr F. L. Hawkins, alluded to the deep interest the Reverend Joseph Davies took in the affairs of the church. 'He understood that Mr Davies had handed over the corrugated building, together with the land, to the trustees of the new church about to be erected. The gift', he said, 'represented £300. The congregation was steadily increasing, and was numbered over 100. This was a new district, and he thought they were doing an excellent work in providing for the spiritual requirements of the neighbourhood.'[20]

The completed church was opened on 24 June 1899 when 'the Reverend Stanley Rogers, of Liverpool,

Shotton from the railway bridge, c.1911. Rivertown Church can be seen on the far left [FRO 62/8]

preached the first sermon to a crowded congregation. A pleasing feature of the evening was the spirited singing, accompanied by the splendid organ, and three violins played by members of the Buckley Congregational Church Choir.' The newspaper report spoke of the good work of the Reverend Joseph Davies. 'From the very outset the little cause began to grow and prosper, and Mr Davies gathered around him a band of energetic co-workers, who laboured with such success that in a very short time it became palpable that a new and more commodious building was required, so rapidly had the congregation grown. The front of the church is built of buff fancy bricks from the Aston Hall Brick Co. The building from the highway, presents a fine and imposing appearance, being lofty and of great breadth. There is a very fine entrance porch, which leads into the two aisles, one each side of the chapel. The interior presents a very striking appearance. The seats are made of polished pitch pine, and the pulpit is also built of the same material. The seating capacity is about 300. At the end of the chapel two doors lead into spacious vestries. The choir stalls are erected in apposition at the back of the pulpit directly over the vestry, and as far as at present can be judged the arrangement is an admirable one, the choir at all times facing the congregation. The organ, which presents a fine appearance and beautifies the new church to a considerable extent, is placed in proximity to the choir. It is a fine instrument, with a smooth, mellow tone, and should prove of great assistance in the rendering of the musical portions of the services. The friends in Rivertown have certainly got a very beautiful and convenient church, and it is hoped that it will play a prominent part in elevating and raising the standard of social and spiritual life of the population of the district.'[21]

Between 1897 and 1918, there were five ministers, the longest staying six years. Each of them made a positive contribution. But the strength of the church was the leadership of the deacons and trustees and the work of Sunday school teachers, secretaries, treasurers, organists, and choirmasters. By 1905 the church was well established with 60 communicants, 200 adherents, 7 class leaders, 19 teachers, 150 Sunday school scholars under 15 years of age, and 50 over. Later, the Christian Endeavour Society numbered 30, and the Band of Hope 60 or more children. The church was well represented at the annual procession of witness of the Sunday Schools of the neighbourhood on August Bank holiday. The Reverend Illtyd James (1907–10) founded the Literary Society, a feature of which was lectures, debates, readings from Shakespeare, *etc*. It eventually reached a membership of 140. From this society grew the library, opened in June 1912, with a gathering of 300. Among those present were Mr Henry Summers, the donor of 200 volumes, and Mrs. J. W. Summers, who performed the ceremony, after a recital on the organ by Mr Tom Roberts of Buckley. Enthusiasm like this, and growing numbers, encouraged the trustees and deacons to think in terms of a larger chapel, in the optimistic days on the eve of the First World War. In December 1915, Sir Arthur Hayworth, Bart, opened a sale of work to augment the new school fund, which reached the sum of £1,000. But it was impossible and inappropriate for anything to be done in the unsettled circumstances and uncertainty of wartime.

St. Ethelwold's School Chapel

S. E. Gladstone, on becoming rector of Hawarden in 1872 was faced with either allowing School Boards to erect non-sectarian schools in the parish for elementary education, or, provide them himself. He chose to build them in the outposts of the parish at Sandycroft, Ewloe, and Shotton, and give them the dual purpose of a school and worship centre. The rector announced in April 1874 that 'an entirely new school is to be built on the Flint road, for boys, girls, and infants. It is intended that services shall be occasionally held there.'

The school, dedicated to St Ethelwold, was formally opened on 12 February 1875, when the rector asked the congregation, 'to pray for a blessing upon the school as a place of education, and also as a house of prayer and praise.' James Adkins, a young schoolmaster trained at Battersea, was appointed head, with Miss Mary Piercy as assistant. Adkins spent the rest of his career teaching at Shotton and Hawarden, and as a lay reader in the church. The families of the Davisons, Hurlbutts, Fox, and the managers of the Eleanor Colliery, Messrs. Thompson and Gilderoy supported the school.

Eighty-three children enrolled on Monday 15 February and eighty-six attended Sunday school. The first service at St Ethelwold's school chapel was held on 18 October, as a Harvest Thanksgiving, and ' before seven o'clock the room was more than filled. Several could not get in.' In 1876 the workmen at the Eleanor Colliery subscribed £1. 16s. towards the purchase of an altar. By 1877 a regular pattern of Sunday services was established. 10.30 a.m. Morning Service, for children, taken by a layman, and 6.30 p.m. Evensong, conducted by a clergyman. The Holy Communion was celebrated on the second Sunday of each month at 8 a.m. A new font was acquired, and a children's Sunday school library provided, at a cost of £5. By December 1877, 'new seats were wanted to go round the walls for the increasing congregation'.

In 1878, Mr S. Wright contracted to build a large room to hold 100 children, with three dormers in the roof, a new porch, a new set of doors for the chancel, and a fireplace instead of a stove, at a cost of £3,350. The new room was formally opened on 15 & 16 November, with the St Ethelwold's choir carrying the new school banner, a celebration of the Holy Communion on the Saturday morning, and a public tea in the afternoon for 200. To enliven the proceedings, Mrs Rowley lent a piano, which was played in turns by Mrs Gladstone, the Misses Rowley, and the Misses Hurlbutt.

The school relied for support on the local gentry, and concerts were the usual means of raising funds. During Christmas week 1881, a dramatic entertainment was given in the boys' school by the Rowley family and friends, with the proceeds of £20 shared between the school building debt and the coffee house. After Christmas a concert was given in the school by the Hawarden cricket club. The newspaper reported, 'perhaps the most remarkable, certainly the most novel feature of the entertainment was the wonderful whistling of Mr Richard Gladstone, whilst he accompanied himself on the piano'. On Monday and Saturday in Christmas week, a dance was given in the girls' schoolroom, to friends and customers of the coffee house.[22]

Mrs Catherine Gladstone opened the coffee house at the beginning of January 1882. It was situated near the Eleanor colliery and was sponsored by the local gentry to provide non-alcoholic refreshments and a games and reading room for working men. The driving force behind it was Mr Hurlbutt, who usually provided the venue for the annual Sunday school treat at Dee Cottage. In 1890 the children, 'about 200 in number, assembled at the school, and marched singing, and headed by their banner through the village. Here they were joined by the boys from Mrs Gladstone's Orphanage and a number of children from Liverpool, sent by the Country Holiday Fund, to cottages in the neighbourhood'.[23]

The New Church of St Ethelwold's

In October 1897, a circular was issued to the congregation of St Ethelwold's school church, inviting them to attend a meeting to discuss proposals for a new church, and present a memorial to the rector, expressing their desire,

St Ethelwold's School, 1895
[S. E. Gladstone]

that 'a church should be erected at Shotton to more fully meet the spiritual wants of this growing district, and signifying their willingness to work for its advancement.'[24] Parishioners from 200 houses petitioned the rector, and he replied in March, 1898, in the Hawarden Parish Magazine, saying,

'When matters had come to this state, it was a timely moment to announce, that Mr W. E. Gladstone had five months before, entrusted him with a promise of £1,000 for this object, a church for the hearts of the people, on certain conditions, *viz.* that the church should be a beautiful building; that it should be free and open to all parishioners dwelling about it; that the people of the locality proved their earnestness by their own offerings. On the same conditions, the rector has also been glad to offer £500 from himself.'

Things moved quickly. A site was chosen on the Chester Road, at the corner of Watery Lane. The rector after inspecting some new churches, several built by John Douglas, received an engraving of the proposed building at Shotton from the architect, and announced, 'it is proposed to build a nave with clerestory, a chancel and apse, a north aisle and porch; and to leave the tower and south aisle for others hereafter to complete. We shall need £3,500 at the least.'[25] the architects engaged, were Messrs Douglas and Minshull of Chester, and Messrs. J. Ward and Sons, Uttoxeter, and were chosen as contractors. The estimated cost, at this stage, was £5,000.

The foundation stone was laid on 14 September 1898, by the Hon. Mrs W. H. Gladstone, 'in the presence of two or three thousand people, and a gay flutter of flags and streamers gave the scene a festive colouring. The sun shone brilliantly and with almost overpowering heat. Around the platform circled the children from St Ethelwold's school with their banner, the Sandycroft Fire Brigade, Shepherds in regalia from Connah's Quay and Hawarden. Everyone sang a hymn, the Bishop of St Asaph, A. G. Edwards and Archdeacon Wynne Jones, said prayers, the choir sang Psalm 122, 'I was glad when they said unto me, let us go to the house of the Lord.' The Hon. Mrs Gladstone then declared the foundation stone well and truly laid. A public tea was afterwards held in a marquee on the ground.[26]

It took almost four years to complete the building of the church. In the meantime a women worker, Miss Stoker, a member of the Parochial Women's Mission Society, was appointed to visit families and, as the rector remarked, to 'be looked on as a friend by all in the district, for Shotton has grown to be a great place; and there is every need of her sympathetic assistance.' Shortly before the consecration of the church, the Reverend Charles Gamlen, a former curate of Hawarden, conducted a seven-day mission. The rector was determined that the church was not to be opened, 'until all is paid and clear', and in November 1901 he offered, together with his wife, to be responsible for raising the outstanding £700, if Shotton district made itself responsible for the organ. A word of praise came from the architect, John Douglas, who said that all the time the building operations were going on, 'not a single act of damage has been done, although the building was not guarded, and was often left open.'

The new church was consecrated on 7 August 1902. An account appeared in the *Chester Chronicle*:

The church has cost over £7,000 and no debts have been contracted. The church has accommodation for six hundred persons. It is built of mottled Hollington stone, and the interior carving being finely chiselled, and consists of a large nave with piers and arches dividing it from north and south aisles, a roomy porch on the north aisle, a chancel with apse and a chapel on the north side of the chancel, which will be used as vestries until the tower is built, the ground floor of which will contain the vestries with the organ chamber over. There is a gallery at the west end, approached by stairs

Douglas & Minshull's (architects) drawing of St Ethelwold's Church, opened 1902. The tower and spire were never built [FRO PR/A/14]

The chancel, St Ethelwold's Church, designed by Douglas & Minshull, architects
[FRO 62/11]

leading from the porch. The nave and sides have open timbered roofs, and the one over the chancel has a panelled and ribbed ceiling in oak. All the roofs are covered with dark Westmoreland slates. The floors of nave, aisles and choir are laid with wood blocks, the chancel with small black and dove coloured tiles, the steps and floor in the sacrarium and under the altar table is in marble, the gift of Messrs Williams and Clay of Warrington. The windows are glazed with cathedral glass, the three lights in the lower part of the west end are filled with stained glass, the gift of the children of the Dean of Lincoln, Mr and Mrs W. E. Gladstone's grandchildren.

The chancel windows have also painted glass, the three centre lights being the gift of the Byron Society; the two side windows the gift of the Hurlbutt family as a memorial to the late Miss Davison. All the painted glass is by Mr Edward Frampton of London. The pulpit and font are carved out in stone, the former having an arcading and *carve patrae*, the later being in Helsby stone, with carved emblems and appropriate inscriptions, and is the gift of local subscribers, the results of the efforts of the children of the parish. The nave and aisles are seated throughout with chairs, the chancel having oak choir fronts and prayer desks; the altar table is of oak, and has been carved by Mr Frank Hurlbutt, whose gift it is; the reredos above is of wood, carved, painted and decorated, and contains subject panels of our Lord in majesty, and adoring angels.

The church is lighted throughout by suspended oil lamps supplied by Messrs Singers of Frome; Messrs J. King & Co., Liverpool, is responsible for the heating. For the equipment and embellishment of the church a number of gifts were received, including the following: Mr and Mrs Rowley, altar rails; Mr J. Douglas and a friend, the handsome altar piece; bell, Major Gibson; shrubs, Mr MacHattie; the altar, Miss Davison and Mr Hurlbutt; south aisle, Mr Gladstone's family, chiefly Mrs Wickham, (the eldest child, Agnes); font by the children of Hawarden parish; altar chair and carpets, Miss Agnes Wilson; font ewer, Mrs Hilda Hancock; vases, Miss Hurlbutt; altar floor marble, by Messrs Williams; books, by Mr G. Spencer, S.P.C.K.; and Hymns Ancient and Modern, by the proprietors; lectern eagle, Misses E. & C. Gladstone and Mr W. G. C. Gladstone; altar cross, the rectory children; porch notice case, Messrs Bailey; Mrs Marks, Litany desk.

The church was consecrated on Thursday by the Bishop of St Asaph, and Master William Gladstone presented the petition of consecration for the bishop to sign. After the service, luncheon was provided for the subscribers, and friends from a distance.

A three-day event, a Japanese Fair and Sale of Work, was held in January 1903, to raise money for the organ fund. The first half of the organ, built under the direction of Dr J. C. Bridges of Chester Cathedral, was opened a year later, and in 1907, Mrs Drew gave £200, to complete the fund. George Wright & Sons, Hawarden, built a clergy house, the present vicarage, at a cost of £1,800, in 1910. The same year, Miss Helen Gladstone, spoke at the opening of the enlarged Church Hall made up of two portions of W. E. Gladstone's iron building, which formed the original St Deiniol's Library. Before declaring the hall open, she gave an account of its early history. She told the people that,

The smaller portion of it was originally given, in the time of rector Gladstone, by Mrs Drew, for use in Mancot, and for years it was of great service there. When Mr Drew became rector, he judged it best to move the building to Shotton, where it has already been of much use. The large portion was specially connected with Mr Gladstone, composed as it was of two large rooms; it was the early form of his long planned gift of a library for the promotion of Divine learning. It now remains for the men and women of Shotton, to make a full and excellent use of it, worthy of its great associations.

The first priest in charge of the new church was W. H. Parkes, 1902–9, followed by R. Wynter, 1909–11, and J. J. Robinson, 1911–33. The fruits of good leadership, strong fellowship and dedicated service, was seen in a number of parochial activities. The Mothers' Meeting came together weekly, and were supported, after the departure of Miss Stoker, by Miss Barton and Miss Hadow. There was a girls' club and young women's Bible class, and the choir of men and boys. In the summer of 1910, the parish magazine reported,

The St Ethelwold's brotherhood, celebrated their foundation, by going in a party of forty, to New Brighton. Most of the party made their way at once to the Tower. Some of us were content with the milder excitements of the figure eight and railway, or of the genuine thrill of the flying aeroplanes. On Sunday, July 3rd, for the first time, the Amalgamated Society of Railway Servants, accompanied by members of the Trade Unions, held their annual church parade in our church. The weather was very bad, rain falling continuously throughout their march from Connah's Quay to Sandycroft. Notwithstanding there were about 130 men in Church.

The church members gave relief during the 1912 Coal Strike by sending parcels of grocery to the most necessitous homes.

Some gifts that have been added since the opening include stained glass windows:

South aisle: in memory of Rosa Harris, given by her husband and three sons, 1914. Subject, Dorcas.
South aisle: in memory of James Vivian Harris, given by his three sons, 1939. Subject, St Christopher.
North aisle: in memory of Leslie Ashcroft, 14 February 1976. Subject, I am the Resurrection and the Life.
North aisle: Arthur Stubbs d. 1978 churchman and craftsman, Hilda Mary Stubbs d. 1979. Subject: St Joseph.
North aisle: Redvers Donald Glendenning 1901–66. Albert Alexander Glendenning 1895–1915, who fell at Gallipoli. The gift of Francis the wife of Redvers, the sisters Alma and Violet and their niece, Millie, 1971: subject St George.

Amongst modern gifts to the church are the following: altar candles, Mrs Brereton, 1972; wooden lectern stand, inscribed Edward Davies, 1876–1967; Book of Remembrance, the gift of Alfred and Elsie Lewis, 1991; lectern Bible to the memory of Grace Thomas, 1981; organ screen, In memory of M. Irene Foulkes; sanctuary chair in memory of Arthur James Robinson 1937; font cover in memory of Philip Parry 1938; frontal chest Grenville Pryce Morris, Verger (died on 27 August 27, aged 57 years); marble plaque in memory of John Thomas (died 1931).

The Baptist Church, Ash Grove

A Baptist church was established in Shotton by 1908 as the following report indicates:

On Sunday afternoon, a special service was held at the Mission Room, Ash Grove, Shotton, when thirty-three members were received into communion. Thus the new cause at Shotton has very bright and promising prospects. There are several others waiting to be baptised, and several more to bring in their transfers. We expect to see in the very near future, when all arrangements are completed, a church numbering from 40 to 50, to commence the new work. The mission room is situated between Shotton Station and the church on the left-hand side of the main road. Services will be held every Sunday at 10.30*a.m.* and 6*p.m.*, Sunday school at 2.30*p.m.* The congregation numbers each Sunday from 85 to 100.[27]

The Church was an iron structure, on a piece of ground at the top of Ashgrove. Eventually it became too small to accommodate its members and in 1928 it was decided to inaugurate a building fund.[28]

St. Ethelwold's School

Accommodation for growing school numbers was a problem, which increased. The inspectors remarked, at the end of 1904,

… the school is conducted with vigour and is doing creditably under trying circumstances.

The highest standard of efficiency cannot be attained under the present condition of overcrowding and inadequate staffing.

School numbers were up to 354, crowded into an extremely limited area, and the employment of two additional uncertificated teachers was recommended. Improvements, costing £1,500, were made to the school before the beginning of a new school year in September 1909. An indication of the growth in population is the number of children: 1,226 up to the age of 14 years, of which 740, were aged 5 to 14 years, and 196 betwen 3 and 5 years. To meet this 'baby boom', the Flintshire Education Committee built a temporary infants' school, and rented additional accommodation in the Rivertown schoolroom. These two buildings, recognised for 295 children, accommodated 359.

In July 1910, St Ethelwold's was recognised by the Education Committee as providing accommodation for 235 children. The St Ethelwold's inspection report of March 1908 spoke well of the school,

The pressure on the accommodation has been relieved by the exclusion of the first standard scholars, who are instructed in the Rivertown Temporary School. The School continues to be most energetically conducted by the experienced head teacher. Mr Haswell attaches much importance to the cultivation of a patriotic spirit amongst the scholars. The playground is furnished with an excellent flagstaff, upon which the Union Jack is hoisted to mark national anniversaries. The practice of encouraging the scholars to make simple meteorological observations of their own is to be greatly commended, as this work, together with the carefully prepared chemical experiments, performed by the teachers in the upper division of the school, will develop in the pupils the power of intelligent and accurate observation. The discipline is excellent, and the children move smartly and assemble and disperse in a most orderly manner.[29]

Shotton Council School

The traditional policy of the rector of Hawarden of building church schools in the various districts of the parish was no longer viable. The new communities at Shotton and Garden City were made of increased nonconformist numbers, who did not want their children to receive the religious education offered by the church schools. The position became clear by the reaction of the Welsh County Councils to the Education Act of 1902, when church schools, in the diocese of St Asaph, were threatened with being taken over by the local authorities. The situation was further aggravated in 1905, when the Flintshire Education Committee acquired an acre of land next to St Ethelwold's school upon which to build a rival council school. Canon Harry Drew, rector of Hawarden, and a county councillor, regarded it as a threat, and said so, to no avail! In September 1908, a tender of George Wright and Sons, Hawarden, was accepted, and the school opened on 10 January 1910. The rector pointedly asked in the local press, that, 'Church parents who valued for their children the religious teaching which their school was allowed to give, to support the Reverend Mr Wynter and Mr Haswell's staff, to stand by the school which had borne the burden and heat of the day for the past thirty years.'[30]

But it was too late the school was built, and its opening was reported in the press:

The newly erected and palatial Council schools were duly opened on Monday morning. The school, which is the largest in the county at the present time, was built under the direct supervision of the county surveyor. The work of erection has been a stupendous task occupying many months. All the modern requirements are provided for. There is accommodation for 480 scholars, and on Monday morning the attendance was 402; and it was expected that the number would be considerably increased when it became generally known in the district that the school was opened. The headmaster is Mr W. M. James and his assistant, Mr William Parry. The certificated female teachers are Miss Lewis and Miss Davison; uncertificated, Miss Roberts, Miss Lewis, Miss Davies, Miss Williams, Miss Jones and Miss Hughes, and supplementary teachers. We understand that the two old school buildings adjoining the grounds will be retained and utilised if necessary, for technical and manual instruction.[31]

Two years later, in 1912, it was stated that,

These buildings, formerly, the temporary council infants school, were opened on 15 March to teach cookery and laundry courses to senior girls in the area. A bedroom and sitting room have been furnished. The classes have made the household linen, curtains, *etc*. A banana case has been made into a child's sleeping cot. Special instruction is given in the cooking of dinner. Most of the girls have shown a keen interest in this work. Several scholars are already engaged in domestic service out of school hours, and are making practical use of the knowledge gained.[32]

The 1912 coal strike seriously affected the health of school children. In August 1912, in the area between Connah's Quay and Sandycroft, 273 children, 'were stated to be unable, by reason of lack of food, to take full advantage of the education provided for them, and the total number of meals provided for this area for the first fortnight in September, was 2,971, whilst the steel works were lying idle.'[33]

Political Activities
The Shotton Liberal Association was formed in September 1908, when Mr W. G. C. Gladstone presided; the chief speaker was Mr Herbert Lewis, whose subject was the unemployment question. The Conservative Unionist party van made a visit to North Wales and came to Shotton in October 1908, where they attracted a crowded meeting at which Mr Hurlbutt presided.

By 1911 they had built their own club in Shotton on land given by their president Mr J. R. Freme, of Wepre Hall. It contained a spacious reading room, billiard room, and several anterooms. In the same year, the members of the Dock, Wharf, Riverside and General Workers' Union, erected their local branch headquarters in Chester Road, with a hall to accommodate 770 people, at an estimated cost of £2,000. The Union's General Secretary was Mr Ben Tillet, M.P. The steel workers were becoming an important element in local parliamentary electoral strategy and in the emergence of the Labour Party.

Social Activities
In 1902 John Summers & Sons provided an Institute, and grounds for outdoor summer amusements, for the benefit of their workpeople and residents of Shotton. In the first decade of the twentieth century, a *palais de danse* was established at the Shotton Picture Palace, with J. Seager as proprietor.

The Shotton and Queen's Ferry Nursing Association was formed in November 1905 to provide the services of a district nurse. Nurse Shepherd was appointed in April 1906, and during her first year paid 2,776 visits and attended 127 patients. Of these 89 were restored to health, 6 relieved, 4 sent to hospital, 13 died, and 15 remained on her books. The association depended on contributions and subscriptions. Messrs Summers gave £25 a year and 134 subscribers provided a modest sum. The Shotton and Connah's Quay cycle parade, a jumble sale and concert raised £90.

An example of the cohesiveness and strength of the community was the success of the carnival, organised to raise funds for the Association. The local schools were deeply involved, both in the organisation of the carnival and the various events: tableaux, morris dancing, cyclists in costume and the great parade. 'Numerous residents entered into the zest of the Gala by decorating their

Sister Halliwell, church worker
[David Pryce Morris]

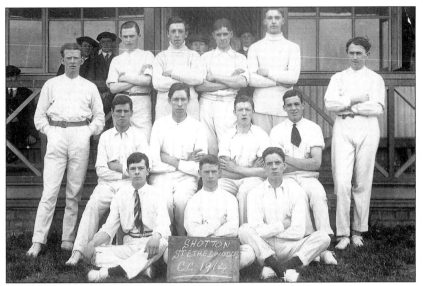

St Ethelwold's Cricket Club XI, 1914
[David Pryce Morris]

business establishments and houses on the main thoroughfare, and the whole locality was *en fete* for the occasion.' The carnival was held on a field adjoining the cricket ground in Shotton Lane. Here a visiting fun fair had erected their numerous side shows and allowed the carnival committee to use the field and charge for admission up to *7p.m.* The newspaper reported:

At the hour of three o'clock some thousands of spectators arrived [to witness the first event] the picturesque ceremony of crowning the Rose Queen, pretty Miss Edith Pagdin attended by her two pages, and nine maids in waiting. Miss Maud Summers, daughter of Henry Summers, crowned the Rose Queen, and the Reverend J. J. Robinson, curate of Shotton, proposed a vote of thanks. The grandeur of the occasion was heightened by the presence of local brass bands and the Queensferry fire brigade. The great carnival parade was a smaller version of the Lord Mayor's with a number of beautiful adorned lorries as tableaux display by local tradesmen, proudly accompanied by members of the Imperial Yeomanry, boy scouts, girl guides, maypole and morris dancers. The procession wound its way from the fair ground to the fountain in Connah's Quay and thence returned via Queensferry, a journey of two hours, with huge crowds along the route. During the afternoon a crowd collected on the field near the Council school to enjoy the ' Derby Stakes'. In the early evening they awaited in vain the arrival of Vivian Hewitt, the pioneer aviator from Rhyl. A telegram was received at 8.25*p.m.* regretting that it was too windy to fly. The day's prizes were presented by Alderman Henry Summers. A masquerade and fancy dress ball held in the council school attended by two hundred people completed the day. Dancing was to the music of Messrs Butterworth and Armstrong. From the day's activities, £100 was raised towards the funds of the Nursing Association.

The First World War

By the end of September 1914 the Shotton recruiting district had sent 600 men to swell the ranks, a decision made more attractive to the volunteers by the announcement that Summers generously promised to grant the wife of every man serving with the Forces, 10s. per week, and 1s. for each child. Amongst those who had enlisted were four Bunnel brothers; a fifth, although under age, had volunteered to join as a bugler. A month later a recruiting meeting at the Picture Palace was attended by two refugee Belgian families, to be regaled by Miss Ada Jones who sang 'Your Country Needs You.'

On the Home Front, as the war progressed, food became scarce. Local butchers shops announced in 1915 that they would be closed on Monday, Tuesday and Wednesday, until further notice. In May 1917, children over the age of eleven attended the Picture Palace to hear addresses on food economy by Miss Sandars of the Ministry of Munitions. The local education authority granted a week's holiday to enable the children to assist in potato picking. The burden of issuing rationing cards fell upon the school staff. They were closed on two occasions in 1918 to enable families to collect them. At the end of the war, news came through that a Shotton man had won the Victoria Cross. Lance Corporal Henry Weale of the 14th Bn. Royal Welsh Fusiliers was born in Nine Houses. The family later moved to 33 Brook Road. As a boy he attended school at Custom Lane, Connah's Quay, and St Ethelwold's, Shotton. Harry Weale enlisted in 1913. During the war he served in France, and was wounded in December 1914, October 1915, and August 1918, and gassed in January 1915. He was awarded the VC for action at Bazentin-le-Grand, France, on 26 August, 1918. The citation read,

For most conspicuous bravery. The adjacent battalion having been held up by enemy machine guns, Lance Corporal Weale was ordered to deal with the hostile posts. When his Lewis gun failed him, on his own initiative, he rushed the nearest posts and killed the crew, then went for the others, the crews of which fled on his approach, this gallant non-commissioned officer pursuing them. His very dashing deed cleared the way for the advance, inspired his comrades, and resulted in the capture of all the machine guns.

He was decorated with the VC by King George V at Buckingham Palace on 1 March 1919.[34] Returning home,

> … he was met at the station by a local band, and blue jackets and soldiers on leave lined the approaches. After a hearty welcome Sergeant Weale was escorted to a waggonette, the horses were unyoked, and the hero, his father, and one of his soldier brothers, were drawn to a square adjoining the hero's old school, St Ethelwold's. Mr T. H. Haswell, secretary of the committee, welcomed him and expressed the pride of Shotton at the great honour he had won. Mr Gardiner, on behalf of Messrs Summers, presented him with a gold watch and chain, and said that at a later date the committee intended to present him with a gift on behalf of the public. Sergeant Weale, VC, in response, thanked them very sincerely for all they had done for him and for their kind welcome.[35]

Harry Weale, VC
[W. Alister Williams Collection]

War Memorials

The Connah's Quay and Shotton War Memorial were unveiled at the beginning of May 1927. The War Memorial stands set well back from the coast road on the border of the two communities at Wepre. The occasion was described.

'Mounted on a pedestal of dulled silver stone a cross rears itself above everything else; telling, if need be, its own story of sacrifice in a war to which most people is rapidly fading from memory.' At the ceremony, 'were soldiers and airmen, girl guides and VAD nurses, uniformed bands from Shotton, Connah's Quay and the Salvation Army. An exceptionally large number of ex-service men paraded under Major Hughes and Sergeant Major Swinnerton. The Reverend J. Griffith Jones announced the opening hymn and the Reverend Owen Owen, the Welsh CM Minister, read the lesson. Colonel T. H. Parry of Mold performed the unveiling of the memorial. The War Memorial was fashioned out of Scotch granite. In the granite, which supports the cross, are bronze plates bearing the names of the fallen. It bears the inscription 'Flanders, Macedonia, Gallipoli, Palestine, Mesopotamia and the High Seas; to keep in memory the men who gave up their lives in the Great War and as a thank offering for those who by God's grace survived its perils. This memorial is raised by the people of Connah's Quay and Shotton.' Underneath on the base are the arresting words of the prophet of old, 'Is it nothing to you, all ye that pass by.'[36]

The members of St Ethelwold's Church decided that their war memorial should take the form of a side chapel. The work was carried out and the names of the fallen carved on an oak screen on the right-hand side of the Lady Chapel forming the division of the choir stalls and the chapel. The Lady Chapel was placed in the former organ chamber on the north side, and the base of an intended tower was built to be used as a vestry and organ chamber. The total cost was £3,200. The Archbishop of Wales, A. G. Edwards, dedicated this extension to the church on Sunday, 2 October 1924.[37]

John Summers & Sons, 1918–39

As workers returned from military service at the end of the First World War, they shared in the boom in the iron and steel industry, with steel prices reaching £54 a ton. At Shotton the work force increased to 5,800 and production was the second largest in the country. The export market was the biggest outlet, and eighty per cent of production was sent abroad. To make them self-sufficient in supplies of pig iron and coal, the Shelton Iron, Steel and Coal Co, Stoke on Trent, was bought in 1920. The boom was not to last long. The slump began in October 1920 and production fell rapidly until the end of 1922. Big imports of sheet bars had their effect on the trade. The General Strike in 1926 interrupted production and disturbed labour relations.

Henry Summers tried to guide the company through this period of strong European competition, and the dumping of inferior steel by exploring new techniques of producing higher grade and more malleable steel sheets

St Ethelwold's School yard, c.1920. Note the First World War artillery piece and the flagpole used on Trafalgar Day [David Pryce Morris]

for the growing market of the motor manufacturer and steel furniture maker. He looked to the United States where the continuous rolling of steel strip and the production of high-grade sheets was achieved in 1925. A collaboration was arranged in 1928 with the American Rolling Mill Company, ARMCO, for experiments and improvements of hand-mill techniques. Changes were made in the open-hearth practice and, electric motors were installed instead of steam engines to drive the mills, and a department for the production of special motor-body sheets opened.

Henry Summers' efforts to maintain production and employment were made impossible by foreign competition and the lack of protection for home markets. By January 1931 there was only 30% of the British Steel Industry working and imports exceeded exports. It was the worst year for steel production since 1904. On 24 April 1931, Black Friday, the steel making plant at Shotton was shut down and notice of dismissal given to more than four thousand men out of a labour force of six thousand men, although the sheet mill remained active with a reduced output. Henry Summers explained the dismissals in a letter to the local paper.

> Until twelve or fifteen years ago we were able to keep the greater part of our plant at work, and find employment for about 6,000 persons, and our weekly payroll was £26,000, this has now fallen to an average of less than £6,000 weekly. In the past, 90% of our product has been exported; it is now little more than 25% of what it was in normal times. At the present time, the surplus-make of steel on the continent is being dumped into this country at prices with which it is impossible to compete. We cannot believe that the world has permanently decided that it can do without the very cheap and useful commodity that we produce, but we are very greatly concerned as to what our position will be when a revival in trade does take place.[38]

H. T. Edwards remembered, when he was appointed organiser of the Transport & General Workers Union at Shotton in August 1932, 25% to 30% of the insured population were out of work and the bulk of our membership at Summers' worked an average of one week in four. Transport Hall was made available for the unemployed and it fell to my lot to give two lectures every week to them on subjects ranging from Workmen's' Compensation to a classless society.[39]

Shotton was in reality a one-horse town. If the steel works were slack whole families suffered, and every assistance was needed to help them. In the aftermath of the General Strike, and with stoppages in the coal industry in the summer of 1926, approximately 3,000

John Summers & Sons. The staff recreation ground situated behind the east block canteen [Reproduced with the kind permission of Corus]

Shotton Grosvenor Working Mens' Club, snooker team, 1920. E. W. Bunnell secretary [FRO 62/98]

men at Shotton were signing on at the Labour Exchange. The proprietors of the Queen's Ferry Cinema made the generous offer in June to give 'the gross proceeds taken at the pictures this week towards the alleviation of distress in the parish of West Saltney and the Garden City ward, through the issue of vouchers for shop keepers.'[40] Every effort was made through the depression years to give the children a normal Christmas. From 1922 onwards, members of Toc H entertained some 150 children to dinner on Christmas Day in the Rivertown Congregational schoolroom. In 1928, 'the afternoon was one of great glee and merriment, Professor John Evans and his dolls entertained the little ones in a grand ventriloquical turn, and before leaving for home each child received a large bag of nuts, sweets, oranges, *etc.* Some 300 children of the members of the Deeside Working Men's Club and Institute were entertained to tea and given a toy each off the gigantic Christmas Tree.' In the summer of 1931, a horticultural show was held by the Shotton Conservatives as part of their Sunshine Guild effort, 'the object being to raise funds to enable them to give local children who were in ill health a short time to recuperate at a Rhyl convalescent home'. Since its inauguration in 1929, the Guild had been able to adopt every suitable case brought to its notice; and no fewer than 38 children were sent to the home, 19 from Connah's Quay, 15 from Shotton and 2 each from Garden City and Mancot.[41]

Edward Prince of Wales, as patron of the National Council of Social Service, made the first royal visit to Shotton on 18 May 1934. He had asked the nation to accept the challenge of unemployment as a national opportunity for voluntary service. The Prince was coming to see the '33 Club, once a derelict brickyard, and now adapted as a centre for social service on behalf of the unemployed. The *County Herald* gave a somewhat critical report:

> The premises looked better than they had ever done. Newly painted woodwork, old buildings renovated and made tidy, footpaths levelled and defined, all helped to impress the Prince, but the wet weather did not brighten an atmosphere of neglect, which surrounds the premises, nor did it make such an important occasion comfortable. Uniformed ambulance men, VAD Nurses, policemen were to be seen everywhere. A.A. and R.A.C. men were present to control traffic that did not come; a tall wireless mast flew the flag of the '33 Club, and on it was fixed a set of amplifiers, which were never used, for community singing. The Connah's Quay and Shotton Bands were there, and also a platform set aside for the Deeside Male Voice Choir and the Shotton Welsh Glee Party, but the rain made all these arrangements impotent, and as soon as the Prince departed, the people rapidly deserted the Club and its environs.
>
> The Prince arrived at Shotton a few minutes before his time, which was 4.45 *p.m.*, and he was away again in about 12 minutes. Outside the '33 Club was drawn up a guard of honour of ex-service men and British Legion members, and the Prince briefly inspected them. Once inside the Club grounds, the Prince was piloted by Mr Spencer Summers. He was shown the grocery office. Here was set out in rows the groceries supplied to Club members at cost price. The Prince was then taken to see the converted brick drying sheds, one of which is now a gymnasium. In it is a boxing ring, and as the Prince walked in two young boxers, Doug Arnold and Stephen Jones, were engaged in a two-minute bout. Fred Fullwood was doing some weight lifting, and the Prince watched him

John Summers & Sons. The main office block, c.1930
[FRO 62/182]

break a six-inch nail. On leaving for Queensferry, the Prince accepted from George Hotchkiss a blue velvet bound booklet setting forth the aims and objects of the Shotton '33 Club. Hotchkiss asked the Prince to accept it from the unemployed as a small token of their appreciation of his continued loyalty and sympathetic consideration for the welfare of the unemployed, and in commemoration of his visit to Shotton.

The steelworks very gradually came out of recession. The Ottawa conference in 1932 imposed a new system of tariffs on imports of steel. Unexpectedly the Argentine Government ordered 22,700 tons of galvanised sheets, to be sent immediately, to protect the nation's crops from a plague of locusts. More pressed steel sheets were needed for the motorcar industry, farm machinery and domestic appliances. The major difference was made by the emergence of a strong managerial team to back Henry Summers, who reached the age of seventy years in January 1935. In hindsight the important decisions made by Henry Summers, Richard Summers, Neville Rollason, Keith Gray and Keith Younghusband, was to modernise Summers between 1935–39, and make it an essential part of the Second World War effort.

There were two major innovations. The first was the Sendzimir process introduced to produce uniformly thin, flat, and flexible steel sheets for which a cold reduction process was necessary. In 1936, with the help of Mr Sendzimir from Poland, a mill was installed for cold rolling strip up to 40 inches wide. To this was added in 1937, a hot dipped galvanising line, installed to produce coated steel, marketed as Galvanite, especially useful in the manufacture of buckets, dustbins, and wheelbarrows. The second major innovation was the introduction of a continuous hot and cold strip mill. Henry Summers wanted the latest technology for Shotton in order to compete

successfully with any rival and with this end in view he sent Neville Rollason and Richard Summers to the United States in March 1937. Arriving in Pittsburgh, they met Lorenz Iverson, President of the Mesta Machine Company. Their mission was to investigate the introduction of a continuous hot and cold strip mill. Iverson came to London to discuss the matter, and at a meeting in the Savoy Hotel, a rough estimate for the cost of

John Summers & Sons. ARMCO finishing bay, 1938
[FRO 62/102, BSC 6047 Album 3. Reproduced with the kind permission of Corus]

introducing the hot strip mill with a tandem cold reduction plant and other finishing units, was worked out to cost 10 million dollars, the equivalent of £4 million. Richard Summers as chairman was responsible for raising this immense sum, which he did with the Bank of England exercising a supervisory role for the next ten years

The new mills were built on 276 acres of marshland reclaimed from the estuary. The development took just over two years. The first slab rolled through on 9 November 1939. 'The installation of a hot strip mill and related developments including a 40-inch slabbing mill and three-stand 56-inch cold reduction mill, represented on of the most momentous decisions in the works' history. The mill was designed to roll 10,000 tons a week, but achieved 17,000 tons before further development.'[42]

Other plans for the building of blast furnace plant and the extension of steel melting were postponed until after the war.

Shotton Between the Wars, 1918–39

Shotton between the wars was self-sufficient. Nearly everything could be obtained there, and if not you could go by bus or train to Chester or Liverpool. The number of shops, professional services (accountant, architect, banks, dentists, doctors, solicitor), and places of entertainment, are seen in Bennett's Business Directory for 1936, with 140 entries, an increase of 43 entries from 1922. In spite of the depression small shops had increased in number, new schools opened, and religious buildings were extended.

Entertainment

Mr. John Jones, the Shotton cinema tycoon, came from the Potteries in 1907, and built the Picture Palace in Victoria Street. In 1923 Mr Jones turned it into a Market Hall, and on its opening 'crowds of people invaded the building and were confronted with a store of surprises and expressions of astonishment were created by the cheapness of the hundred and one articles on view.'[43]

Jones was a great publicist and when the Alhambra was opened on the afternoon of Christmas Day, 1922, it was reported that,

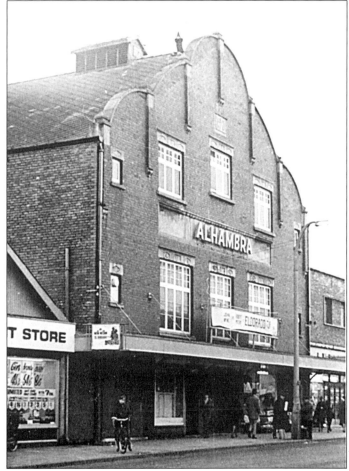

> Scenes hitherto unknown and undreamt of in the short but rapid history of Shotton were witnessed. Queues of a remarkable length formed up on each side of the swinging doors. Once admission began the spacious hall was rapidly filled and many patrons had to be turned away. It is estimated that close on 1,500 attended the first performance.[44]

The Alhambra became the centre not only for the showing of films, but for live entertainment and local pantomimes and concerts. Animals were often involved, and on one occasion two monkeys escaped on to the roof of the building and performed their tricks to an audience of children in the neighbouring school. A list of some of the performances for the beginning of 1925 shows the versatility of Mr Jones the impresario. In February there was skating on real ice with the star performer Phil Taylor, the skating instructor to the Queen of Spain. Films were also shown, and cheap excursion tickets were issued to bring in the crowds. In March there was a performance of Elgar's King Olaf by the Connah's Quay and Shotton Choral Society. In April, clowns, trick cyclists, jugglers, dogs, horses, jockeys and

The Alhambra
[FRO 62/175]

Bennett's Business Directory.

SHOTTON, a village and ecclesiastic parish, is in Flintshire, 5 miles from Flint and 7 miles from Chester. Population 4,304. It has a post, money order, telegraph and telephone call office under Chester. There are two stations in the parish, one on the L. & N.E., and the other on the main line (Chester and Holyhead) of the L.M. & S.R.

Early Closing Day, Wednesday.

Alhambra Picture House—J Jones, propr

Alfred, tailor, Chester rd

Ames H, bootmaker, Nelson st

Ashton's, drapers, Chester rd

Astbury Katie, ladies' hairdresser, 35 Chester rd

Ballance G W, baker, Station Cafe

Banks S, joiner and cabinet maker, Nelson st. French polishing. General repairs

Barker P, fancy goods dealer, Chester rd

Bentley J, fried fish saloon, King George st

Bevan M E, milliner, Chester rd

British Legion Club, off Bridge st

Bryant E, jeweller, 50A Chester rd

Buckley H, newsagent, Chester rd

Bull & Bennett, high-class confectioners & caterers, King's Cafe. Luncheon and tea rooms. Private parties catered for

Butler M D, electrical engineer, High st

Castle Inn, Brook rd

Central Hotel—H Darbyshire

Chantler Mrs, Clogger

Chester Confectionery Co, High st and Chester rd

Chester, Wrexham & District Savings Bank, St Ethelwold's School

Clarke A B, baker, High st

Conservative Club—H Williams, sec

Coppack R, motor car propr, Chester rd

Crofts J R general stores, King Edward st

Darbyshire Brick Works

Davies I, The Ideal Billiard Hall

Davies J, newsagent, 22 Chester rd

Davies W Pryce, stationer, tobacconist and dealer in china, hardware, etc, etc, 26 Chester rd

Davis H R, accountant, Chester rd

Dawson G, high-class confectioner, grocer and tobacconist, Chester rd. Our specialities : Bacon and Cheshire cheese

Deeside Central School. Headmaster, S J G Morris

District Bank Ltd, Chester rd

Dodd E, florist, 45 Chester rd

Dodd T J, grocer, Chester rd

Edwards E, ladies' outfitter, Chester rd

Ellames, outfitters, Chester rd

Ellis & Co, cash grocers, tea dealers and provision merchants, Post Office Stores

Ellsum W, butcher, Chester rd

Fenn H B, dentist, 66 High st

Freeman Edward H, dentist, Chester rd

Frisbys Boot Stores, Chester rd

Garrett S H, architect and surveyor, 68 High st

Glazier M, draper, Chester rd

Grant B & Co, Ltd, wine & spirit mchts, Chester rd

Griffiths D, draper, Bon Marche

Griffiths (Grocers) Ltd, The Moorings, High st

Grosvenor Working Men's Club and Institute

Hague W W, draper, Chester rd

Harris E A, solicitor, Chester rd

Harris Miss, confectioner, 102 Chester rd

Hartwell H, haulage contractor, Nelson st

Hazledine Mrs M, supper bar, Chester rd

Heywood J, fruiterer, Chester rd

Hewitt T J, confectioner, Chester rd

Hobson H, dairyman, Shotton lane

Holden L, confectioner, 74 Chester rd

Holman W J, bootmaker, Chester rd

Hughes H B, grocer & baker, 13 Chester rd. Pies and custards, cakes and pastry in great variety. Home-made bread, noted shop for Bara Brith. Quality and purity of all our goods guaranteed

Hughes W, butcher, Chester rd

Humphreys & Roberts, drapers and milliners

Hunters Ltd, The Teamen, grocers, Chester rd

Isaac Dr B, surgeon, Shotton lane

Jacks C P, hairdresser, Ideal buildings

Jackson S, painter, 35 Chester rd W.—see advt

Jackson W, radio engineer, Chester rd

James R W, boot repairers, Chester rd

Jefferies W & L, grocers, Jubilee st

Johnsons Ltd, dyers, Chester rd

Jones F, grocer, Brook rd

Jones G E, newsagent, stationer, confectioner, tobacconist and glass & china dealer, 11 Chester rd

Jones Miss G, violin teacher, Glanrhyd, King George st

Jones J G, grocer, 26 Chester rd

Jones M & J, fish friers, 7 Chester rd

Jones Miss M, The Quest, Chester rd, for superior quality of sweets, chocolates & cigarettes

Kane's Ltd, hardware dealers, Chester rd

King E, milliner, 40 Chester rd

Knowles W, dining rooms, Chester rd

Lamb Miss, confectioner, 85 Chester rd

Law H, confectioner, Chester rd

Lewis Dan, M P S, F S M C, F I O, F N A O, M I C O, qualified sight testing optician & chemist, 35 Chester rd. Tel 137

Lidbury W, printer, Chester rd

Lloyds Bank Ltd, Chester rd

Lodwicks, grocers, 33 Chester rd

Mayfair (The), ladies' hairdressing saloon, Madame Hannah, proprietress

Maypole Dairy Co, Chester rd

McKie, J J, dentist, Chester rd

Melia Ltd, grocers, Chester rd

Midland Bank Ltd, Chester rd

Millington T J, fruiterer & game dealer, Chester rd

Ministry of Labour Employment Exch'ge, Chester rd

Moore H A, M D, surgeon, Chester rd

Morris Jeane, milliner, Chester rd

Mulliner & Sons, joiner, Chester rd

National Provincial Bank Ltd, Chester rd

Nichol W, draper, Compton House, Chester rd

Owen Mrs, fruiterer, 95 Chester rd

Oxton W, confectioner, 35 Chester rd

Palais de Danse—J Seager, propr

Patten T, beer retailer, Chester rd

Peters M E, builder, Chester rd

Phillips, bootmakers, Chester rd

Phillips & Sons, boot repairers, King Edward st

Pipe Miss, milliner, 91 Chester rd

Price T & H, butchers, Chester rd

Prince E, tobacconist, Chester rd

Prince J & Co, chemists, Chester rd

Queens Ferry Co-operative Society, Salisbury st

Redfern T H, hairdresser, Chester rd

Roberts, butcher, Chester rd

Salter A, plumber, Shotton Lane

Satterthwaite J, painter, Brook rd—see advt

Scholey F, confectioner, 20 Chester rd

Scott J, butcher, Chester rd

Scott Mrs, milliner, 25 Beaconsfield rd

Seager J C, Motor Garage, Ash Grove

Shepherd W, draper, Dee House

Shotton Church of England Schools—Headmaster, T Roberts

Shotton Council School—Headmaster, Ll Williams

Shotton Engineering Co, motor and general engineers, 85 Chester rd. Oxy-acetylene welding. Any make of car supplied. To 130 Connahs Quay. Proprs.: T A Potter and G L Hall

Shotton Hotel—G H Lowry

Shotton Institute. Sec: H J Page, 31 Salisbury st

Shotton Lane Working Men's Club. Sec, J Maybury

Shotton Laundry, Chester rd

Shotton R.C. School. Headmaster, M Larkin

Stenmer J, hairdresser, Chester rd

Stonehouse J, fried fish saloon, Shotton lane

Summers & Sons, Ltd, Hawarden Bridge Ironworks

Sutton & Davies, bakers, Ryeland st

Swinnerton M, grocer and confectioner, 22 Nelson st, Chester road. Home-cured bacon, brawn and sausages a speciality

Taylor W, dentist, 76 High st

Thomas D, butcher, Chester rd

Thomas F G, baker, Byeland st

Thomas J, baker, Chester rd

Tower Billiard Hall, Chester rd

Transport & General Workers' Union. President, H Kershaw. Gen. Secretary, E Bevin. Financial Secretary, Stanley Hirst. Trade Group Secretary, H T Edwards, Chester rd, Shotton. Tel. 38 Connahs Quay

Tudor S, grocer, 30 Ash Grove

Underhill S, plumber, 50 King Edward st—see advt

Vaughan Hall, Victoria rd

Wall F J, hairdresser, Chester rd

Wepre Hall Brickworks

Whitehouse J, bootmaker, Brook rd

Whittle Bros, coal merchants, Salisbury st

Williams E, coal merchant, Shotton lane

Williams, G, ladies' outfitter, Chester rd

Williams J, wholesale fruit merchant, Shotton Lane

Williams Miss, milliner, Chester rd

Williams T I, ironmonger, Chester rd

Withnell Ernest S, motor body builder, Chester rd—see advt

Wood N, butcher, Chester rd

Wright G H, builders' merchant

X.L. Co, dyers and cleaners, 28 Chester rd

Yates Miss, ladies' hairdresser, Ideal buildings

Bennett's Business Directory, 1936

cowboys made their appearance. The Alhambra was a place to escape to, and by the 1930s the cinema became, in the words of A. J. P. Taylor, 'the essential habit of the age.' Going out was the norm, just as staying in was, in the television age.

The pantomime in the new year gave an opportunity for a large group of enthusiastic amateurs of all ages to come together, have fun, and raise money for charity. In January 1939 the Jack Evans amateur pantomime company celebrated their tenth birthday with the production of the 'Queen of Hearts' at the Alhambra. The show ran for nine days in Shotton, and was then taken on tour to Rhyl, Holywell, Mostyn, Ellesmere Port, Neston, and Hoylake. The cast was composed of shop girls, steelworkers and school children, and numbered over sixty, with three sections of dancers, cabaret, chorus, and dancing mites. The wardrobe mistresses Mrs Noakes, Miss Noakes, and their assistants provided over 400 costumes. The Noakes family were deeply involved. Les Noakes was stage manager and publicity officer; Mrs Jack Evans, nee Winnie Noakes was principal boy; Ena Noakes, ballet mistress; Alex Noakes, effects man, and Arthur Noakes, call boy.

The main stay of the company was Jack Evans who wrote and produced the pantomime and contributed his usual good performance as a ventriloquist. Bill Jones was cast in bloodthirsty parts, Horace Ellames had considerable experience as the old dame, and Don Ashton was regarded, as the Buster Keaton of Deeside, Wilmot and Iorwerth Jones were brother acrobats. Wee Gwilym Roberts was billed as the 'King of Comedy', and as 'Deeside's own comedian'. He was a great little man and a great asset to the company.[45]

The carnival was as popular between the wars as it had been before the First War. It acted as a kind of social control, useful as a means of drilling children, and appealing to the creative gifts of the adults. Dressing up meant entering a fantasy world, as much a means of escape as the pantomime was. The members of St Ethelwold's church organised an annual carnival to raise money for the church extension and other purposes. At the end of June 1929, Helen Grace Thomas was crowned Rose Queen, amidst reported 'scenes of great splendour and pageantry'. Shotton was en fete, and the triumphal procession of the six queens was greeted with a profuse

Queen Margaret Parry and her retinue, 1925
[David Pryce Morris]

Helen Grace Thomas, Rose Queen, 1929
[David Pryce Morris]

Shotton Welsh Glee Party, 1960s.
Conductor Mr Hayes
[Leslie George]

display of flags and buntings, and the people of the surrounding localities flocked to give Helen Thomas and her retinue a cordial welcome. The parents of the children had gone to infinite trouble and expense to stage a good show; the children did splendidly. Up to 9 p.m. on the previous evening rehearsals were being held. Promptly at 3.30 p.m. Mrs Cunningham, of Shotwick Aerodrome, accompanied by Mrs Summers, and escorted by the vicar and Mrs Robinson, Mr J. H. Pagdin and Mr J. V. Harris, moved across the enclosure and proceeded to the throne of the Queen-elect.

The crowning ceremony ended with a dance to the music of 'Do you ken John Peel.' In the evening the carnival paraded the streets of Connah's Quay and Shotton. 'During this time boxing matches had been staged on Dee Park by Squadron Leader Tillings. A good fight was fought between Paddy Jones, Shotton, and A. C. Jones, R.A.F. Sealand, Paddy Jones being the victor.'[46]

Another annual event between the wars was the horticultural show held at the side of the Shotton Conservative Assembly Hall. The purpose of the event was to support the Sunshine Guild, established to send ailing children to convalesce in the healthy environment of Rhyl. A feature of the 1931 show were the Morris Dancers who gave exhibitions in the streets, amongst whom were the Shotton Merrymakers, the Dee Park Morris Dancers, and the Shotton Steam Laundry Morris Dancers.[47]

The Shotton Welsh Glee Party received national recognition. They celebrated their coming of age in March 1935 at the Vaughan Dance Salon. They were hailed as

… an organisation which has brought fame to a district already rich in musical tradition. Few choirs in the Principality can equal their record. The choir was founded by Mr D. R. Conway and under the conductorship of Mr R. S. Roberts, now in Canada, won triple honours at the Barry National Eisteddfod, a feat that has never been equalled. Their conductor is now Mr Fred Roberts. The choir enjoy a wide reputation for madrigal singing and they have already been honoured by the BBC, being granted several broadcasts.[48]

Shotton Cricket Club

Shotton Cricket and Tennis Club were founded in 1897. The club's first matches were played on the marsh and later on the old football ground, before moving to the ground in Shotton Lane. Before the First World War they raised money by holding the cricket club sports, with entrants from north Wales and the north-west of England. The competitions were open handicap races of various distances either on foot or bicycle.[49]

The 1929 AGM, presided over by Mr T. H. Haswell, declared that, 'From the playing point of view, the 1928 season was probably the best in the history of the club, the first eleven going the season without a defeat. The averages for batting and bowling were easily in front of any previous year. They have now a ground equal to any in north Wales and the class of cricket played will compare more than favourably with any club'.

Bowling averages

	runs	*wickets*	*average*
W. Roberts	52	9	5.57
B. Williams	517	54	9.57
W. A. Hall	545	44	12.38

Batting averages

	innings	not out	highest score	runs	average
E. Higham	16	2	153	603	43.09
J. Taylor	13	6	68	253	36.14
W. A. Hall	18	2	105	572	35.75

Mr. Parry also gave an interesting account of their cricket tour in Northern Ireland last summer, which he described as one of the best, both in play and hospitality. During four years £1,000 had been spent in labour on their ground.[50]

Cricket came back at the end of the Second World War with the Victory Tests against the Australians. Shotton was delighted to entertain Test cricketers of England, Australia and the West Indies on their ground in August 1945. The first match was between Arthur Hughes's XI and a Shotton XI the teams composed of a mixture of Australian, West Indian, Lancashire, Yorkshire and Cheshire players. Hughes's XI batted first and scored 249 for 4 declared. Lindsay Hassett, a future Australian captain, scored 45, but the innings was dominated by a partnership of 127 runs in 55 minutes between Cecil Pepper, 47, and Keith Miller, who scored 104 not out, his century coming in 70 minutes, with seven 6s and six 4s. The Shotton XI could only muster 150 in reply. In the

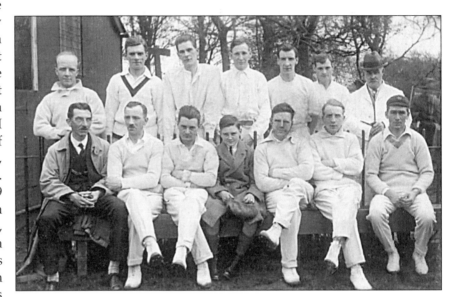

Shotton Cricket Club XI, 1922
[FRO 62/15]

next match a few days later, George Duckworth's XI played a Leary Constantine XI. Washbrook 51, and Paynter 64, opened in aggressive style with Washbrook hitting four successive balls from Constantine out of the ground. Constantine's XI scored 236 for 8, winning by 4 runs. The matches were played in aid of the Deeside Welcome Home Association.

The Rivertown Sunday School

The prudence and foresight of the deacons of the Rivertown Congregational Church enabled them in 1931 to spend over £3,000 on building a new Sunday school. This had been their intention since 1907 when a plot of land was purchased at the rear of the church. Mr J. W. Summers had given £100 towards the cost of the land, the remaining £100 being raised by the Sunday school scholars. In 1915 a sale of work raised £350, which was invested for the Sunday school. Captain Fred Webster became secretary to the new school building committee in 1921, 'and devoted much time to drawing up a scheme which involved the disposal of the corrugated iron structure, which had housed the first church, and building on the same site, a two-storey building incorporating the church vestries, and the organ chamber as part of the school premises. This necessitated the building of a balcony to accommodate the choir and organ.' The new building consisted of five classrooms on the ground floor over which was an upper room large enough to accommodate 280 people.

The opening by Mrs J. W. Summers took place at the beginning of March 1931. Mr T. E. Hibbert of Buckley, the builder, presented the key to Mrs Summers, 'and in doing so expressed the hope that the opening of the door of the new Sunday school would open the hearts and minds of those who would worship there.'[51]

Soon after the opening, the depression tightened its grip and the church was without a minister from 1932–6, then the Reverend A. Thackray accepted the pastorate and remained in Shotton until 1944. Through his enthusiasm youth work flourished, and a Boys Brigade and Girls' Guildry were established.

1st Shotton Boys Brigade, Rivertown
[Mary Moore]

The Girls Guildry, Rivertown
[Mary Moore]

The Baptist Church, Wellington Street

The Baptist Church continued to hold their services in the corrugated iron buildings on the corner of Rowley's Drive. After 1935 the services were held in the English language. In 1937 the membership was over thirty, and the number of scholars attending Sunday school between thirty-five and forty. Land was acquired in Wellington Street for the building of a new church, but this did not take place until 1954, when Mrs R. F. Summers of Neston opened a brick building.

The Shotton Brotherhood

We noticed the formation of the Brotherhood at St Ethelwold's church before the First World War. After the war the Brotherhood was non-sectarian. The Shotton club played a leading part in the Chester and North Wales Federation of Brotherhoods, which promoted Christian Fellowship, temperance, and the ideals of social service. The Shotton club met weekly, opening with religious worship, followed by an address by a local dignitary or local government officer.

The Roman Catholic School

At the end of March 1927, the Bishop of Menevia, the Right Reverend Dr F. J. Vaughan, laid the foundation stone of the first Roman Catholic school to be built in north Wales since the passing of the Education Act in 1902. Priests accompanied the bishop from Buckley, Flint, Connah's Quay, Saltney and Mold. The Director of Education, Mr J Bevans Evans, was present, together with local church members, headteachers, and the architect, Mr Alfred Gilbertson of Liverpool.

The bishop returned in April 1928, to bless the school. Mr Michael Larkin was appointed the first headteacher. The school was in Charmleys Lane. The children numbered 114 and were gathered from the local community.

The Deeside Central School

Shotton was chosen as the first Flintshire school to benefit from the latest educational theory put forward by Sir

Henry Hadow, the leading influence in British education between the wars. His report, the Education of the Adolescent, published in 1926, recommended the division of education into the primary stage, 5–11 years, and secondary education for all after the age of 11 years. Secondary education was to be organised on a selective basis, with a division into grammar and secondary modern school entry. Central schools were to be the first pioneers of this proposal. The Flintshire Education Committee took up these ideas, and Sir Henry Hadow was invited to open the school, which took place on 12 November 1929.

The opening ceremony was brief, and was performed in the presence of a large gathering, by Sir Henry, who was presented by the County Surveyor, with a golden key as a memento, Sir Henry said that he had pleasure in opening the first Central school in Flintshire and in wishing success and prosperity to the school, and to all who had anything to do with it.

The new school occupied a site of three and a half acres, including a playing field of one and a half acres. The contract figure was £21,456, and the contractors were Messrs W. F. Humphreys, of Acrefair, Wrexham. The site was part of the Dee Hall estate. It was designed by Mr R. G. Whitley, the County Architect, who went to endless trouble with the plans, and the building comprised all the latest improvements based on the experience on central schools in other parts of the country. The school is constructed of rustic brick walls with artificial stone facing. The roof is covered with mottled Ruabon tiles and is surmounted by an ornamental dome ventilator, and the whole building presents a very handsome appearance. The main building comprises: assembly hall, ten classrooms, workshop, laboratory, art room, and a sitting room and bedroom, to be used for domestic subjects; dining room, separate kitchen, pantry and larder, for the provision of meals for those pupils who come from a distance. A feature of the school is that all rooms are fitted with the latest apparatus. The windows are fitted with the new Vita glass, which has valuable health properties, and are so arranged that sunshine falls in every room during some portion of the day.

The school was opened to pupils in October, the first headteacher being Mr S. H. Morris. The school is built to accommodate 480 pupils, but at present there are about 250 in attendance as a result of the first entrance examination. Attached to the school, in a separate building adjoining, is a Mining Subjects Training Centre or Institute, which was erected at a cost of £1,500. A grant towards this cost was made from the Miner's Welfare Fund at Wrexham. This building consists of a laboratory and a dark room for use in connection with gas testing training.

The Second World War

Shotton prepared for war. The steel works went into full production to supply a huge government order for steel air raid shelters of a pattern selected by Sir John Anderson. A preliminary order was for 120,000 tons of steel for 400,000 shelters. The shelter, when buried in the ground and banked up with sand bags, was said to bear a steady weight of 20 tons.

In the last fortnight of April 1939, an additional film was provide in all cinema programmes, *The Warning*, an authentic representation of the air menace that threatened all Britain. It dealt with every aspect of aerial warfare and depicted with great realism the consequences of an air raid. At the end of every performance there was a short speech on different aspects of national service.

Anderson Shelter manufactured at Shotton Steel Works loaded with 75 tons of pig iron to demonstrate its strength [FRO BSC 6047 Album 2. Reproduced with the kind permission of Corus]

HM King George VI inspecting the John Summers & Sons Home Guard [Reproduced with the kind permission of Corus]

To inaugurate this programme, the Lord Lieutenant of Flintshire, Rear Admiral Rowley Conwy, came to the Alhambra, preceded by a parade headed by the band of St John's Ambulance and the Boy Scouts.

Shotton Council School was selected as a first aid and decontaminating centre. Its first call to duty began on 1 September 1939, when the school was closed and turned into a reception centre for evacuees from Birkenhead. The Rivertown church became an indispensable centre for servicemen stationed on Deeside. It was estimated that the canteen served 59,943 cups of tea and 57,254 meals by 1942. A voluntary staff did this. The men on the home front were not to be outdone. They joined the Home Guard under the command of Lieutenant R. F. Summers. In July 1943 they gave a demonstration of their progress. The newspaper reported:

> The third anniversary of the formation of the 19th Battalion Flintshire Home Guard, John Summers Battalion, was celebrated by a garden party and display at Messrs Summers. The displays by the Home Guard illustrated the immense strides made in efficiency and training during the past three years. A dramatic sequence was given in three stages showing the development of the Home Guard: stage 1 — the LVD in 1940, was an excellent comic turn out; a small party of men came on dressed in a variety of civilian clothes. They were supposed to be new recruits, and rather noisily learning to become soldiers. The men and their sergeant major, acted their parts with humour and understanding and their portrayal of the awkward squad was greeted with applause and much laughter. The second stage — the Home Guard in 1941, and finally the Home Guard today, showed them to be keen and alert, having the stamp of regular guardsmen and ready to meet any Germans.[53]

Figures were given in the *Chester Chronicle* in June 1945, which demonstrated the huge contribution, which John Summers and Sons had made to the war effort. They produced a total of 3.35 million tons of steel ingots,

> … from this tonnage a vast variety of weapons and equipment was manufactured, including incendiary bombs, army vehicles, bailey bridges, jettison tanks for aircraft, and Morrison air raid shelters. Perhaps the most outstanding contribution was the supply of sheets sufficient to make over 60 million shell and ammunition boxes, over 40 million jerry cans, and 16 million drums for petrol and oil. These and innumerable other articles absorbed almost the whole of the 2.22 million tons of sheet which we have made.

The policy of improvement and modernisation on the eve of war was an indispensable contribution to the war effort and its consequent victory.

Shotton Steel Works

The Summers management team entered the post-war years with an expansion programme, which covered six years, and involved the erection of coke ovens, blast furnaces, new open hearth steel plant, and power station. The new plant was erected on new land, a 280-acre plateau reclaimed from the Dee Estuary by Dutch engineers.

Shotton Steel Works aerial view, c.1965
[FRO 62/188]

These plans were not interrupted by the Government nationalisation of the steel industry when John Summers and Sons were transferred to the Iron and Steel Corporation. On 29 April 1953, the Duke of Edinburgh officially opened the new steelmaking plant and power station. 'Shotton was for the first time a fully integrated steelworks carrying out all the processes for transforming iron ore into sheet steel, mainly for galvanising'.[53]

Expansion continued in the late 1950s and early 1960s with the opening of four furnaces of the open hearth type, 'the hot mill was extended, to accommodate new slab reheating furnaces, two additional stands in the finishing train, making seven, and new downcoilers at the exit end of the mill to produce 13 ton coils instead of five ton. A coil temper mill to skin pass up to 4,000 tons of hot rolled strip a week, a 56in four high cold reduction reversing mill and new annealing furnaces were also installed'.[54]

The production of steel in 1965 was 1,542,607 tons, supplying steel to the car and domestic appliance industries, with one fifth of the annual output coated, with six coating processes in use — hot dip galvanising, electro galvanising, paint spraying, p.v.c. lamination, nickel plating and aluminium powder coating.[55]

With the return of a Labour Government in 1966, the ownership of John Summers & Sons, together with thirteen other companies, was transferred to the new British Steel Corporation on 28 July 1967 and Sir Richard Summers and Reith Gray retired the following year. In the early 1970s the expansion policy was devoted to the production of coated steels and the introduction of computerised controls. In 1972 the Government announced a ten-year modernisation and expansion programme for the steel industry. To make steel on a large scale economically, it had to be produced by the basic oxygen process near to deep water ports, and so all open hearth steelmaking would cease by the end of the decade.[56] This would mean the loss of 6,500 jobs. In January 1973 more than 2,000 employees staged a protest march in London when the Government strategy for steel was debated in Parliament. Flintshire County Council hired an international business consultancy firm to investigate the viability of the plant and to suggest alternatives to the B.S.C.'s plans.

In 1974 B.S.C. undertook to conduct a feasibility study on developing part of the land it owned in assisting the provision of alternative jobs when redundancies occurred to create a total of 12,500 jobs on a 600 acre site. This included the establishment of a petro-chemical plant. In February 1975 the government decided to review the B.S.C. closure programme. The corporation stated that it would honour its pledge to maintain steelmaking at Shotton for 2–4 years and 'would devote strong efforts to providing alternative employment for displaced workers'. In July 1976 the government asked the corporation to re appraise its ideas on steelmaking in Wales. The Corporation responded in March 1977 by replying that the plan to end steelmaking at Shotton was to be dropped, and that the closure would not be reviewed until 1982. However, in the next two years these plans were affected drastically by the increasing world-wide over capacity for steel, which made the older inefficient plants like Shotton increasingly uneconomic to run. It took eight hours to produce 250 tonnes of steel in open hearth, compared with 350 tonnes in 40 minutes from a basic oxygen furnace. A fuel crisis increased the cost of production.

The return of a Conservative government at the General Election in 1979, refused to continue to give massive support to loss-making industries. The reaction of the B.S.C. was to announce at the end of June 1979 that steelmaking at Shotton would be phased out between December 1979 and March 1980 with the loss of 6,400 jobs, leaving 4,200 in the cold mill and coatings. This was the end of open-hearth steelmaking, not only in Shotton but also throughout Britain.

The Amalgamated Union of Engineering Workers (A.U.E.W.), under its district secretary, Mr Rowley Bull, opposed the closure. They had recognised in the 1970s that the plant was outdated and that the workforce should be reduced by some 2,000, but argued that employment for surplus steelworkers would be found in the Deeside Industrial Park where it was anticipated that job creation schemes would provide work for 3,500 by 1981, the date initially set for closure. In this way there would be no redundancies until alternative employment was available. The A. U. E. W. felt that they were able to put forward a valid alternative plan to retain steelmaking in Shotton by using the Czechoslovakian production system of tandem furnaces (basically oxygen assisted open hearth furnaces), to speed production and increase efficiency. B.S.C. refused to review the situation. It was the failure

Facing: Top: Brtish Steel Works Shotton, coatings department
[FRO 62/183]

Bottom: No. 2 Color coat line, commissioned in 1990
[Reproduced with the kind permission of Corus]

to create alternative sources of employment to coincide with the closure of steelmaking when land was available to do so which exacerbated the problem of dealing with 6,400 redundancies in a community which had been built on steelmaking for seventy-five years. Fortunately the undoubted hardship, which occurred, was reduced to some extent by redundancy arrangements by which each employee received fifty weeks pay. In the meantime agencies to find employment for the redundant were set up, which included a job centre, a counselling and advisory service, and training facilities under the Training Opportunities Scheme, which offered 500 courses nationwide. The training schemes received financial assistance from the European Economic Commission and in respect of training programmes, from the Manpower Services Commission. [57]

The closure of steelmaking and the massive 60% loss of jobs in the community meant that the future of the majority of the working population in Shotton lay outside the works, created seventy-five years previously by John Summers. The forty per cent of the work force retained were engaged in the cold strip mill and coatings departments. Shotton was ahead in the galvanising field and boasted the widest range of coating equipment on a single site in the world. In 1990 Shotton 'became the first works in Europe capable of coating 1,000,000 tonnes of strip steel a year, with four lines for applying zinc or zinc alloy coatings by either hot dipping or electro plating, and two lines for the application of a range of organic paints. The metallic coatings protect the steel from corrosion and the addition of paint gives a colourful finish as well as further extending product life.'[58]

Brickworks[59]

Shotton Lane Brickworks was situated between the railway and Shotton Lane, some six hundred yards south of Shotton Station. Mr Harry Rowley of Dee Banks founded the business about 1898, with Mr Tom Rugman as manager. It was closed down about 1922. The site is now covered with dwelling houses and the clay pit was filled to make playing fields.

Wepre Hall Brick Co was situated some seven hundred yards south of Shotton station and immediately west of the railway, on land that was purchased from the Wepre Hall estate. It was opened in 1901 by Messrs Hampson and Darbyshire of Hawarden, and closed down about 1947. There were five beehive kilns. The manager was the late James Hampson, son of the founder, followed by his brother, the late John Hampson. The clay pit produced blue clay.

15. Sealand and Garden City

Sealand in the Manor and Parish of Hawarden lies between the north bank of the new cut of the river Dee and the boundaries between Chester on the east, Cheshire on the north, and the steelwork site to the northwest. Sealand came into existence as a settlement in 1737 and was developed by the River Dee Company from 1741 to 1906. The company reclaimed agricultural land by means of embankments. About half the area, over three thousand acres, had been won from the marsh by the time of the survey of Hawarden Parish, made in 1815,[1] which listed 283 allotments in Sealand. Many of them were large holdings occupied by tenants of the River Dee Company. The largest were Mr Thos. Gorst 438 acres, John Lloyd 249 acres, and Thos. Baxter, 218 acres, with nine other tenants renting over 100 acres. The population in 1851 was 291 with 47 houses inhabited, in 1871 the population was 508 with 81 houses inhabited, and in 1891 there were 89 houses and a population of 485. The population was to increase significantly when Garden City was developed at the beginning of the twentieth century.

An example of the productiveness of farming land at Sealand at the end of the nineteenth century is given in the judge's report for the prizes awarded by the Manchester and Liverpool Agricultural Society in the jubilee year of 1897. The judge Mr J. Chalmers Morton, was particularly impressed 'by the immense areas of extraordinary productiveness, especially of wheat, barley and Swedish turnips, and by the quiet, but most efficient management of both land and labour which is there exhibited.' Of particular notice was Mr Podmore's farm, which received the following review:

Mr R. Podmore, of Deeside House Farm, Sealand, occupies two contiguous farms, each with its homestead, together 640 acres, or a square mile in extent. I feel bound to award the prize in this class to Mr Podmore, for I don't believe that at the time of my inspection there was greater actual or promised abundance of food for man and beast on any other square mile of agricultural and in the country. There is by far the greatest crop of wheat I have anywhere seen, whether spring sown or autumn sown (152 acres); also 52 acres of a magnificent crop of barley, 40 acres of fair oats, 15 acres of good beans, 12 acres of good potatoes, 90 acres of swedes — as good and promising and clean, over a great 50 acre stretch of the crop, as over any ten or twelve acre piece I have seen elsewhere — 20 acres of good mangold worzel, 90 acres of one year old seeds, and 152 acres of pasture carrying a flock of 240 ewes and their produce, and some twenty-five young beasts for subsequent feeding. The whole is managed by a double set of steam-ploughing tackle, fourteen farm horses, and £960 worth of labour. The rent is £2 an acre; the purchase of manures about £130 a year, and of cake and Indian corn about £170 a year. All homegrown oats and the waste of wheat and barley are consumed. Some 130 or more cattle are bought every autumn, at an average price of £10 or £11 apiece. The receipts are derived from annual sales of beef and mutton and lamb, of wheat and beans, and of surplus hay and straw (sometimes as much as £500 or £600 a year). The flock of 240 ewes (kept up by drafting about forty in and out each year) produced this year 390 lambs, fifty of these being sold (at nine weeks old) at the annual sale at an average of £2 each, the remainder being kept to put on turnips, and sold at the sale next spring.

There is a capital house and two homesteads, with a covered yard at one of them. The farm is dependent almost wholly on marketing for the cattle, which converts its swede and oats into beef. For the mutton and lamb sold it is dependent on a constant ewe flock, as already stated. For the maintenance of its fertility it is dependent on the 1,500 tons of farm dung, made from well-fed cattle during winter in its yards (applied to green crops and to clover root) — also on a certain amount of sheep fold possible on its lighter soil, on the comparatively small purchases of food and manure which I have named, and on nearly £4,000 worth of well and quietly directed, and well-housed labour.[2]

The 1881 census reveals that at Mr Podmore's Bank Farm of 408 acres there was a work force of 16 men.

The River Dee Company

The River Dee Company formed in 1741 was wound up in 1902. In 1889 it was renamed the Dee Land Company and as such retained its extensive estate and its right to reclaim land from the sea. In 1897 this new company offered 425,000 £1 shares in a new Dee Estates Company. Its prospectus declared that the company was formed:

> For the purpose of acquiring and developing the Dee Estates, comprising upwards of 3,000 acres of cultivated land between the City of Chester and Queensferry; more than 1,200 acres of marsh land having a frontage to the River Dee and the Estuary; and Reclamation Rights over the Estuary of the Dee and Mostyn Marshes, an area estimated at about 19,000 acres, excepting so much as constitutes the bed and banks of the river vested in the Dee Conservancy Board; as well as the Shipbuilding Yard, Stone Quarries, and Rocks at Connah's Quay and the Mostyn Docks.

The prospectus spoke

> Of the 1,260 acres of what are known as the Marsh Lands, having a mile frontage to the Dee, 43 acres were recently sold to Messrs. Summers & Sons, Corrugated Iron Manufacturers, who have established extensive works thereon … A site has been laid out on the Estate near the Golf Links and Works whereon to build a village. Twenty houses belonging to the Company have been already erected and are well let. As there is an increasing demand it is intended to proceed immediately with the erection of a considerable number of additional houses, the rents of which will yield an increasing income to the Company.

The Dee Estates Company failed in 1902 and did not realise its ambitious schemes to reclaim the east and west estuaries of the Dee and Mostyn marshes. The 1897 prospectus described the land in Sealand as being 'exceedingly rich and fertile, capable of producing magnificent crops of all kinds within the first year of cultivation'. and added, 'there are at present on the Estate a large number of Farms, having excellent Homesteads and Farm buildings, and well let to a responsible Tenantry, for the most part of long standing.'

The Dee Estates sale on 24 November 1906 provides a list of the farms owned by the Company and their tenants:

> Bank Farm, 184 acres, William Milligan, tenant
> Volunteers Rifle Range, 67 acres, Arthur Hassall, tenant
> Yew Tree Farm, 171 acres, Arthur Hassall, tenant
> Elms Farm, 122 acres, John Francis Norden, tenant
> Sealand Farm, 77 acres, Charles Vincent Norden, tenant
> Church Farm, 138 acres, William Caunce, tenant
> Green Lane Farm, 86 acres, Frederick William Howard, tenant
> The Willows Farm, 160 acres, Jane Williams, tenant
> Marsh Farm, 420 acres, Oliver Ellwood, tenant
> Pasture land, 400 acres, George Ledson, tenant

A group of cottages, Nine Houses, opposite Sealand Church, were described as all having good gardens and a large yard in common with a plentiful supply of water from a good well. Four of the cottages had a pigsty and a closet.

Adjoining the Steel Works and the grounds of the Chester Golf Club were: 1,156 acres of enclosed cultivated fertile lands, and 1,072 acres of marsh land 'which is now an excellent sheep pasture, continually being silted up, which will in a few years be ripe for enclosure'.

Other lots were the East Estuary district, 6,353 acres; the West Estuary district, 14,065 acres; Mostyn Marches, 2,566 acres.

The response at the auction was poor, less than 500 acres of land out of a total of 27,300 was sold. The map of the sale shows that Co-operative Bees Ltd. was established at Wood Farm, 202 acres.

The Valuation Returns of 1911 add to the list of Sealand Farms.

> Ferry Bank Farm, 175 acres, owner W. Henry Fox
> Deeside Farm, 340 acres, owner J. & S. Podmore
> Manor Farm, 311 acres, owner J. & S. Podmore
> Waterloo Farm, 105 acres, Mrs Booker

Chester Corporation owned Mill Farm, 112 acres; Ferry Lane Farm, 77 acres; Fir Tree Farm, 76 acres; Bumpers Lane Farm 32 acres. John Summers & Sons owned New Marsh Farm, 932 acres, and a further 472 acres.

The Welsh Land Settlement

Fifty years later an extensive area of land was used as an experimental scheme to place Welsh miners on the land. In April 1937 the *Chester Chronicle* reported:

New Settlement for Sealand. Work on the land for unemployed men. Eighty houses for a new garden village. Three of the largest farms in the district, including a total of 742 acres, have been acquired by the society, for the purpose of establishing a Co-operative Farm Settlement for unemployed men and their families. The farms include Bank Farm, which was owned by Mr William Milligan; Yew Tree Farm owned by Mr William Caunce; and Sealand Manor Farm, owned by Mr Podmore. The unemployed men and their families to be drafted to the Settlement will be from the special areas of South Wales and Monmouthshire.

The Welsh Settlement Society is going to build eighty houses in the form of a garden village. During the period of development, which may last a year, the 'settlers' will be trained in the cultivation of the land and the raising of market garden produce, under supervision. At the end of the development period, when the land will be ready for intensive cultivation, a co-operators' society will be formed for the purpose of carrying on the enterprise. In addition to the regular agricultural wage, all members will be entitled to a share of the profits.

Considerable activities are taking place on the Settlement in preparation for next years cropping. Thirty members have commenced work and live in Sealand Manor Farm house, which has been converted into a hostel. The average period of unemployment the men have experienced is a about fours years. Unemployed married men between the ages of 35 and 50 who have successfully cultivated an allotment, cottage garden, or group holding, and are special desirous of making a fresh start in life, with their families, are invited to apply. When the houses are ready the men's families from South Wales will join them.

The chairman of the Welsh Land Settlement Society is Captain Geoffrey Crayshaw. The society is run on a strictly non-political basis; Mr Thomas Griffiths is the director and Mr E. B. Harris the secretary. Members of the Council of Management include the Right Honourable David Lloyd George.[3]

Eighty houses were built and concrete roads connected the farms with the main roads. By the spring of 1938 over seventy families had joined the Settlement and over a hundred ex-miners were employed by the autumn of 1942. The success of the work of the Welsh Land Settlement was reported in January 1943.

' Producing for the food front. The cultivation of 920 acres' was the headline when the *Chester Chronicle* reporter described his visit to the Settlement.

I saw how bumper crops are being raised. Most of the co-operators are ex-miners and over fifty per cent of the original party are still engaged. For their trim cottages they pay 3s. a week rent. There are 43 co-operators; each holds a one-pound share in the Settlement, which entitles him to a share in the profits. Dividends have only been paid during the past two years. A committee of management elected by the co-operators runs the Settlement. The fertility of the soil has been improved and it responded by yielding bumper crops. Produce is sent direct to the wholesale markets. The Settlement is not allowed to do any retailing. No flowers are cultivated. Generally activities are confined to vegetables although in these days certain acreage is given to wheat. Some 120 acres are used for the growing of Brussels sprouts; similar acreage is given to the growing of cauliflowers. The Settlement generally sells vegetables at current wholesale market prices but usually these are below fifty per cent of the price, which the public has to pay. Tomatoes have always been an important line and in recent years 110 tons have been produced annually. These are grown in two and three quarter acres of greenhouses, but this year more tomatoes will be grown outside.[4]

Sealand Windmill

There used to be a windmill on the sands. It is shown on Greenwood's map of 1819, and Bryant's of 1831 about the site of Mill Farm, a quarter of a mile E.S.E. of Higher Ferry. E. L. Roberts, in 1905 remembers seeing an old stone belonging to the mill on the ground next to the house. He stated that it was used for grinding corn and was last used in the 1860s when a Mr Saddler was the miller.

Garden City

The number of workmen employed by John Summers and Sons Ltd. was increasing rapidly in the 1900s to reach

3,400 in 1911. It was rumoured in the local press in March 1907 that the firm have ' a scheme in contemplation for the building of a new colony on the Sealand side of the River Dee, which will house a large proportion of their workmen and their families who at the present time cannot get cottages in the immediate vicinity of the works. As yet the idea has not yet developed into a practical scheme. The aim of the promoters is not to build in rigid conformity with the architectural style of 'model villages', but we are informed that the cottages will in general design resemble the picturesque garden village of Port Sunlight.'[5] It wasn't until another three years later that a garden suburb was to be built under the auspices of the co-partnership tenants movement. The Sealand Tenants Limited purchased ten acres of land with an option for a further thirty acres. On this site it was proposed to erect 470 houses at a cost of £80,000. The land had been laid out under the supervision of Raymond Unwin, the garden city expert. It was reported in the Liverpool *Daily Post*:

This is the first attempt to erect a garden suburb on co-partnership lines on a site adjacent to a centre of industry. The organisers of the scheme are strongly of opinion that workmen living at a garden suburb situated close to the scene of their labour, and able, therefore to spend their dinner hour in their own homes will prove more industrious and more sober as they be better housed and better fed than those workmen whose dwellings are far removed from their workshops. The rents will run from 5s. 6d. to 8s. per week inclusive of rates and taxes. No tenant will be able to own his house. Every provision is being made for open spaces in which games such as football, cricket, quoits, tennis, &c. may be played.[6]

The roads will be so arranged that each house will have a garden, and that about one tenth of the estate will be available for recreation, allotments, *etc*. To one acre of ground there will not be allowed on an average more than ten or twelve houses, and through the centre of the estate will run a broad main avenue planted with trees, and leading to a club-house or institute around which will gather the social life of the community. The houses will be

Above: Welsh Road, Garden City
[FRO 51/127]

Left: Sandy Lane, Garden City
[FRO 51/149]

of the two-storey cottage type in pairs and in groups. Various artistic designs have been prepared for different sizes of houses.[7]

Building work took place between 1910 and 1913 and again after the war, between 1920 and 1925. But only the southwest half was laid out in accordance with the original plan. Altogether 283 houses and three shops were built on the estate.

When the steel industry was nationalised in 1967, ownership of the estate was transferred to the British Steel Corporation and by 1979, 87 of the 283 homes had been sold privately, mainly to the tenants. The remaining 196 properties acquired by the Manchester-based Collingwood Housing Association in 1979. Another 20 homes were sold to tenants and buyers in the years that followed and the Rhyl based Clwyd-Alyn Housing Association now rents out the remaining 176 properties.[8]

Some idea of the condition of facilities for housing before the garden suburb is seen in a letter from the inhabitants of Queensferry Cottages who informed the Sealand Parish Council in July 1895, 'we earnestly request your kind attention to the want of water. We are obliged to drink the river water, which is now full of young fish, & which is really not fit for using purposes'.[9]

Religious Provision
St. Bartholomew's Church
The Glynne family, lords of the manor were not slow to erect churches throughout the scattered parish, at Buckley in 1822, Broughton 1823, and Pentrobin in 1843. It was planned to add another at Sealand in the 1840s, but this was vigorously resisted by the population of the district who expressed their opposition to the proposal in the form of a petition to the Lord of the Manor, Sir Stephen Glynne, Bart. and his brother, Henry Glynne, the rector. In 1844 the petitioners courteously addressed the squire and the parson, 'with due acknowledgement for the interest you have so considerably shown for our spiritual welfare by your exertions to promote the erection of a church, amongst us, 'but rejecting the building of a church, on the grounds of the annual expense to the squire and his brother, the wide dispersal of the population, and their accessibility to other places 'where Divine Service is performed twice a day.'[10]

In time these obstacles were overcome, and on the last day of August 1865 the foundation stone of a new church at Sealand was laid by Sir Stephen Glynne, 'in the presence of a large concourse of spectators'. The local newspaper explained the circumstances. 'The want of a sacred edifice a little beyond midway from Chester to Queen's Ferry has long been felt and the River Dee Company have come forward in the most generous manner by not only giving the ground but rearing the structure at their own expense. Mr Douglas is the architect, and Mr Bellis also of Chester the builder.'[11]

On 15 October 1867 the Bishop of St Asaph, Thomas Vowler Short, consecrated the church, dedicated to St Bartholomew, and celebrated the Eucharist together with the rector Henry Glynne and his assistant clergy. The Dean of Chester preached the sermon. 'After the morning service, a select company adjourned to an adjoining building where they were entertained at a splendid luncheon given by the River Dee Company.'[12]

The company generously contributed £1,250 to the cost of the church and another £2,300 was raised by subscriptions. At the harvest festival service two years later it was noticed, 'the change that has taken

St Bartholemews Church, 1895
[S. E. Gladstone]

place in the neighbourhood since the opening of the church is most marked, and the great good that has resulted must be very gratifying to the worthy rector and to those gentlemen to whose generous aid the erection of the edifice and the support of a clergyman is owing.'[13] Harvest thanksgiving was beginning to establish its traditions in the agricultural community, and at Sealand,

> … in the afternoon Mrs H. Maddocks and Mrs Humble entertained the members of the choir at St Bartholomew's, the scholars connected with the Sunday school, and a number of the labourers and their wives with an excellent tea, after which, the children were permitted to enjoy themselves with a variety of sports in a field in the occupation of Mr Humble. Mrs Roberts, with her usual generosity, provided a large quantity of toys. Evening service began at seven o'clock when the church was densely crowded, the farmers having kindly allowed their men to finish work at an earlier hour than usual, in order that they might take part in the service.[14]

St Bartholomew's church is designed in the early Gothic style. It is constructed of stone from the Helsby quarries, the interior being finished with chiselled ashlar.' The plan comprises chancel with north organ chamber, and nave with south porch, vaulted in stone, and at the junction of nave and chancel, on the south side, a tower surmounted by a spire, with a vestry in the base from which a door gives access to the pulpit. The whole of the roof timbers and doors are of oak. The spaces between the timbers of the chancel roof are decorated with designs in black and gold on a blue ground. The chancel has sedilia, divided by a detached shaft; the choir seats are of oak, with pierced panels. The east window, the gift of Mr Douglas, the architect, represents the Crucifixion, and is by Hardman & Co. The west window representing our Lord in glory, with the twelve apostles below, is by Kempe, and was presented in 1880 by Anne Maddocks, in memory of her husband and children. The seats of the nave are open, except at the west end, which is furnished with chairs. The pulpit, of Talacre stone, has a sculptured panel to represent our Lord teaching; and the font, which is octagonal and supported on marble pillars, has panels filled with emblems of the passion, the gift of Sir Stephen Glynne, Bart. The organ, by Prosser, bought by subscription, at a cost of £130, was renovated in 1908. A mural tablet commemorates the virtues of 'Thomas Wedge, of Sealand, for more than sixty years the Resident Agent of the River Dee Company', 1853; another, Thomas Edward Hassall and his son, who were drowned off Port Erin, Isle of Man, Oct. 21 1899; and a brass in the name of Robert Podmore, J.P. of Sealand, in whose memory the clock in the tower, by J. Smith & Sons, Derby, was given in 1906. The bell of eight and a half hundredweight was the gift of the rector, Henry Glynne.[15]

St Andrew's Church

On 24 February 1912 the bishop of St Asaph, A. G. Edwards, licensed St Andrew's church hall for divine worship. The building, half of W. F. Gladstone's iron library was erected by the rector of Hawarden F. S. M. Bennett on a site given by John Summers and Sons, on the corner just beyond the Queen's Ferry Jubilee Bridge on the Garden City side.

St Andrews Church interior, 1963
[David Pryce Morris]

The foundation stone of a new church was laid on 27 October 1962 by Sir Richard Summers in the presence of Dr D. D. Bartlett, Bishop of St Asaph, who consecrated the new church dedicated to St Andrew on 27 July 1963, assisted by the Archdeacon of Wrexham, the Venerable B. P. Jones Perrott, the Vicar of Shotton, the Reverend Oliver Hill, the Reverend R. E. Smart, Curate of Shotton and Mr H. Williams and Mr L. Ashcroft, churchwardens of Shotton, Mr R. M. Barrow and Mr G. S. Jacks, churchwardens of St Andrew's. The church was built at a cost of £17,500 and replaced a former church, which stood on the riverbank near the Dee Bridge. The old church was part of the iron library of W. E. Gladstone. The site of the new church was given by Messrs John Summers and Sons, together with the sum of £2,000 towards the building fund. A description of the new church was given in the *Liverpool Daily Post*:

'The new church is of brick and concrete, and has a light and airy appearance inside, with white walls and a sky blue ceiling. Many of the features and furniture have been given by the parishioners, and some of the metal and woodwork including the lectern were made by members of the staff of John Summers and Sons. Mr John L. Jones, of L. W. Barnard and Partners of Cheltenham, was the architect, and Messrs Alun Edwards of Cefnybedd were the builders'.

Nearly eighty gifts to provide church furniture and vestments were generously given by individuals and organisations within the parish of Shotton.

The Marsh Mission Church, 1904
The Marsh Mission Church was established in 1904 by four members of the Rivertown Congregational Church, Shotton, E. Milliard, Joseph Walton, Joseph Parker and J. Graham, who, recognizing the need of a mission room on the Sealand Marsh for Sunday school work and public worship, with the help of a few farmers erected a small mission church. After a time they appealed to Flintshire Education Committee for the opening of a day school.[16]

A Temporary Place of Worship, 1911
In November 1911 the Congregationalists began to hold religious services in the Institute. There were fifty-two attendants at the Sunday school, and the evening service was crowded. Thirty-five expressed their desire to become members and were enrolled.[17]

The New Congregational Church, 1916
A new Congregational church was formerly opened by Mrs. Edith Summers, of Emral Hall in January 1916. It was constructed to serve the double purpose of church and school. 'Mrs Summers, who was the recipient of a presentation key by Mr F. G. Smith, formally opened the door, and a short dedicatory service was then held, conducted by the Reverend Joseph Davies and Mr C. Dodd'.[18]

Schools
Sealand Temporary School
A temporary school was opened in Sealand on 23 April 1906 to relieve the overcrowding at Queensferry school. An inspection report of 3 March 1908 is favourable. 'The school is attended by 37 scholars all of whom were present when it was visited. The capable head teacher has done excellent work since she has been in charge.'

Sealand Council School
An inspection report of 16 February 1912 points out the limitations of the school.

The accommodation in the Infant's room is sorely taxed and the teaching is thereby severely handicapped. The nature of the building and its exposed site renders it to extremes of cold and heat at different seasons, much to the discomfort of the scholars.

The head teacher has unaided, to teach a large class of children of grades varying from Standard I to Standard VII. When allowance is made for this and the inconvenience of the building, the attainment of the children must be pronounced very satisfactory and the devotion and efficiency of the teacher deserving of great praise. She exercises a humanising and refining influence over pupils and aims at inspiring her upper class with a taste for wholesome literature.[19]

Plans for a New School — Sealand Council School
In May 1912 Mr J. W. Summers, M.P. offered to give another site for a school. It was of one and a half acres adjoining the Sealand Tenants estate.

In July 1912 it was reported that 120 houses had been built at the Garden Suburb and it was intended to erect another 150 houses almost immediately. It was decided to build a school 'to provide accommodation for 320 children, in six class rooms, two of which should accommodate 60 children each, and the remaining four, 50 children each. The cost of the erection of the school was five thousand pounds. The builder was Mr Price Williams of Bangor on Dee.[20] It was reported, 'this school was opened on 23 August 1914, and there are now 261 children in attendance. A good scheme of work has been commenced, and the school, upon several occasions, when visits without notice have been paid to it, has been found to be under admirable control in every respect.'[21]

Bees Nurseries

Bees Nurseries were established as Co-operative Bees Limited in 1906. By 1936 in a review of industry in Flintshire it had grown to be a considerable enterprise and was described thus:

'Amongst other industries to be noted are the nurseries of Bees' Ltd. at Sealand. This firm has 900 acres of land upon which it employs about 500 persons. Mass production is the keyword, and mechanization has been introduced wherever possible. Over a million rose-trees are produced each year, and millions of plants, trees, shrubs and fruit trees. Recently glasshouses covering three acres, and a modern bulb warehouse have been erected; bulbs are now grown on a large scale. During the cut-flower season as many as a thousand cases are sent off to the markets each day. These cases will contain a quarter of a million flowers and weigh about six tons. These nurseries are open to visitors for inspection at any and all times during the hours of daylight'

By the 1970s it was announced that:

Messrs Bees have 1,000 acres of farm and gardens with 3 acres of greenhouses; a wide variety of fruit, vegetables, flowers and plants are grown and the show garden is open to the public from April to October.

RAF Sealand[22]

Aircraft were first developed at Sealand by T. Murthwaite Dutton who received his training as an engineer at Sandycroft Foundry. He later opened his own mechanical and electrical engineering business and set himself up as a motor garage proprietor at the Queensferry crossroads. To develop his interest in aircraft he started a flying school nearby on a strip of grassland, which later became part of the south camp of R.A.F. Sealand. He left his own account of these beginnings:

I started on the preparations for my flying school in 1916 and built my own machines of the Caudron Warped Wing type in a hanger on the aerodrome. The timber was obtained locally, and, as lining to cover the wings was in short supply owing to Government demand for their own aeroplanes, our machines had to be covered with a material known as 'Holland', which we bought in rolls of 70 yards from Chester. The engines used were second-hand and reconditioned by our mechanics. Up to 1917 a large percentage of pilots for the Royal Flying Corps were trained in civilian schools, but the advent of the Avro as a trainer took the place of earlier types of machines. My aerodrome was inspected by officers of the Royal Flying Corps early in 1917 and later in the year decided to take it over.

The R.A.F. saw great potential in the area and on 5 September 1917 requisitioned 224 acres of land farmed by George Ledson on both sides of the railway at Old and New Marsh Farm. The area to the north of the railway was known as Shotwick, after the name of the nearest village, and that to the south, Queensferry. Robert McAlpine and Sons were brought in as the main

Thomas Murthwaite Dutton's Flying School, Sealand [FRO 61/2]

contractors and developed both the north and south sites at a cost of £335,000. This included living accommodation for an establishment of 839 including 293 women. Six aeroplane sheds, an aeroplane repair shed and a landing area, which needed careful treatment were reclaimed from the estuary. The south site, Queensferry, was developed as an AAP (Aeroplane Acceptance Park), with three sets of hangars. It was not completed until August 1918.

The progress at the North Camp Shotwick was much quicker, and in October 1917 three squadrons of the Royal Flying Corps became resident. They were No. 90 Squadron, formed at Shrewsbury; No. 95 Squadron, formed at Tern Hill; and No. 96 Squadron from South Carlton. They were fighter squadrons operating with Sopwith Pups, Dolphins, Martinsydes, Salamanders, Avro J's and Camels.

Shotwick was designated solely for training. On 1 April 1918 No. 67 Training Squadron was moved from Shawbury, and Shotwick became No. 51 Training Depôt Station on 15 July 1918, flying mainly Avro 504s. In July 1918, Nos. 95 and 96 Squadrons were disbanded and No. 90 Squadron was posted away. When the war ended Shotwick became a base for the demobilisation of units arriving from France. After the war the land had to be reacquired and this was not completed until 1923.

Between the wars, 1919–39, R.A.F. Sealand, as it was renamed in 1924, became active as a Flying School and a Packing Unit. In April 1920 No. 51 T.D.S. was absorbed into No. 5 F.T.S. (Flying Training School). The first of the six monthly courses passed out on 15 August 1922. During the inter-war years a number of famous pilots were trained at Sealand and in 1940 Air Vice Marshal Johnnie Johnson was a cadet officer before going on to become the highest scoring RAF pilot in World War Two. The R.A.F. Packing Depôt arrived from Ascot on 23 May 1929. Its work was the crating of all aircraft to be sent abroad. This work was expanded on the formation of No. 3 A.S.U. (Aircraft Storage Unit), on 2 December 1935, and with the development and growth of maintenance units it was renamed No. 36 Maintenance Unit on 6 October 1938.

With the growth of Sealand new buildings were necessary to replace those of the First World War and to house extra staff. In 1927 new buildings replaced those of timber. An officer's mess was built on the south side and a sergeant's mess and five barrack blocks on the north side, providing two storey accommodation for airmen. In August 1937 construction began in east camp to house No. 30 M.U. This was completed in July 1938 at a cost of £775,000. In this preparation for war barrack blocks were built to three storeys, instead of the usual two. The guardroom, sergeant's mess, airmen's mess, sick quarters and station headquarters, were built to a standard R.A.F. design.

On the eve of the Second World War the buildings to house No. 30 Maintenance Unit were not complete but work continued to house equipment necessary for the repair of engines, instruments, armament, wireless telegraphy *etc.* Such was the importance of this unit that in December 1940 No. 5 S.F.T.S. (Service Flying Training School), moved to Tern Hill to allow No. 30 M.U. to expand. Many American volunteer pilots had passed through Sealand going on to form the nucleus of the Eagle Squadrons.

R.A.F. Sealand was attacked on 14 August 1940 by two Heinkel 111s. Damage was caused, particularly to the airmen's block, Arras. A warrant officer was killed in the mess and twelve personnel injured. One of the enemy aircraft was chased and intercepted by Spitfires from Hawarden and brought down near Chester.

The packing depot had become 36 M.U. and finally 47 M.U. It was an essential part of the war effort when, for example in February 1941 700 aircraft were crated and despatched overseas and in 1944 the average was sixty a week. Between March 1941 and December 1943 Sealand was the home No. 6 A.A.C.U. (Anti Aircraft Co-operation Unit). It was transferred to Castle Bromwich to form a new squadron.

The training of pilots continued from January 1941 virtually non-stop until March 1945. For the whole of 1941, 19 E.F.T.S. (Elementary Flying School), was based at Sealand, with the task of training flyers from scratch and 740 pupils were trained during this year. No. 24 E.F.T.S. followed in February 1942 to train Royal Naval pilots before they joined the Fleet Air Arm. This personnel was trained until August 1943 when their attention was turned to R.A.F. trainees and providing refresher courses for pilots until March 1945 when the school left for Rochester.

The assistance of Polish personnel during the war was invaluable for 30 M.U. They were distributed amongst all the sections particularly in repairing crashed aircraft and making new inspections, and as attached to 47 M.U. when it was established at the end of 1943, to repair Mosquitos, Wellingtons and Halifax. In 1946 the Polish Squadron was disbanded. A plaque was presented by Group Captain D. S. Brookes, Station Commander from June 1944 to March 1946, commemorating the valuable contribution made by the Polish officers, airmen and airwomen at Sealand.

RAF Sealand, c.1926
[Mike Grant]

By the end of the war the only flights at Sealand were deliveries to No. 47 M.U. or test flights. Its importance was that it became the home of the only packing unit in the R.A.F.

After the war the United States Air Force took over Sealand, which was linked with Burtonwood. The base played an indispensable part in the Berlin airlift 1948–9 when the Soviet closed the borders and all supplies had to be brought in by air. Its usefulness was as a supply depot and Sealand became the 7558th Air Depôt Group undertaking the function of supply, storage and distribution to the U.S. Army and the Royal Canadian Air Force in the United Kingdom of subsistence and medical supplies. It was the 3rd Motor Transport Squadron, which distributed petrol, frozen food, medical supplies and spare parts, on a weekly basis to Strategic Air Command Stations. Another unit at Sealand was the Aeronautical Chart and Information Office U.K., a valuable resource to flyers. By contrast it became the home of 7502nd Retaining Squadron, which turned part of the site into an open prison for offenders on discipline, drink, drugs or similar charges. During the American occupation the standard of most buildings improved and central heating was installed in all R.A.F. married quarters. The U.S.A.F. left the base in 1959 and it returned to British control.

No. 30 M.U. was reformed at Sealand after an absence of eight years. It included No. 2 Wireless Squadron, No. 1 Radar Squadron. In March 1959, No. 48 M.U. came from Hawarden to be responsible for the storage and packing of aircraft. In March 1963, No. 631 Gliding School moved from Hawarden to Sealand to be operated by air cadets. In 1966 west camp was sold off to be developed as Deeside Industrial Park. No. 2 M.U. was disbanded in 1969, their site being taken over by No. 7 M.U. which was a storage unit for aircraft parts.

Sealand became the centre of repair and replacement service for the whole of the R.A.F. for the repair and modification of electronic systems, which meant the considerable enlargement of No. 30 M.U. The workforce began to change with the replacement of service personnel by civilians. In 1978 Sealand employed 1,200 civilians and 650 service men on a 250 acre site with No. 30 M.U. split into four wings: Radio, Electrical, Instrument and Supply & Administrative.

Sealand being a flying school in the First and Second World Wars and between the wars, meant that there were a number of flying accidents. The dead were buried at either Shotwick or Hawarden. Burials at Shotwick Church 1918, 8 R.A.F. personnel. Burials between the two wars at Hawarden churchyard 6 R.A.F. personnel. Burials at Hawarden churchyard 1939–45, 23 R.A.F. personnel, 7 Canadian Air Force personnel, 1 Australian, 2 New Zealand. Burials at Hawarden churchyard after 1945, 8 R.A.F. personnel. Burials at Hawarden Cemetery during 1939–45, 12 R.A.F. personnel, 7 Polish, 7 Canadian, 2 Australian.

Endnotes

C.C. — *Chester Chronicle*
C.H — *County Herald*

1: Beginnings

1. This depends much on *The place-names of East Flintshire*, Hywel Wyn Owen UWP, Cardiff, 1994 and *A Pocket Guide to the place-names of Wales*, Hywel Wyn Owen, UWP / The Western Mail, 1998.
2. ibid., p.63.
3. ibid., p.21.
4. ibid., p.31.
5. ibid., p.41.
6. ibid., p.85.
7. ibid., p.92–3.
8. ibid., p.98.
9. ibid.,.p.103.
10. ibid., p.132.
11. ibid., p.168.
12. The entries for Domesday Book are taken from *The Victorian History of the County of Chester*, vol 1. p.366 f. University of London Institute of Historical Research, OUP, 1987.
13. Quoted in *Conquest, Coexistence and Change Wales 1063–1415*, R. R. Davies, Clarendon Oxford UWP, 1987, p.89.
14. *Brut y Tywysogyon* or The Chronicle of the Princes Thomas Jones, 1952, p.59.
15. Messham, J. E., 'Ewloe in the Middle Ages, part 2, The origins of the Manor and Township of Ewloe'. *Buckley Society Magazine*, No. 13 (1988) p.36f.
16. *Cheshire Sheaf* xvi (3760), May 1919.
17. For Ewloe Castle see *The Buildings of Wales: Clwyd*, Edward Hubbard, Penguin Books, UWP, 1986, p.344-5, and *Ewloe Castle*, Department of the Environment, 1972, HMSO.
18. *Military Institutions on the Welsh Marches, Shropshire, AD 1066–1300*, Frederick C. Suppe.
19. *Flintshire Historical Society Publication*, No. 8, p.42.
20. *The Welsh Castles of Edward I*, Arnold Taylor, The Hambledon Press, 1986, see also Hubbard op cit,
21. W. Bell Jones, *A History of the Parish of Hawarden*, (4 vols typescript FRO 143-5). (hence) WBJ. vol. 3, p 93.
22. *Calendar of Ancient Petitions Relating to Wales*, ed. W. Rees (Cardiff, 1975), No. 125, p.209.
23. ibid p.216 and K. Lloyd Gruffydd, 'Ewloe and its Castle', *Buckley Society Magazine*, vol.8 p.44.
24. *Cheshire Sheaf*, June 1912 (1935),
25. Messham, op cit p.33.
26. WBJ op cit vol.3, p.89.
27. *The Stanleys. Lords Stanley and Earls of Derby, 1385-1672*, Barry Coward, Chetham Society, 1983 p.2.
28. *Cheshire Sheaf* , November 1910, (1763).
29. *A Memoir of Hawarden Parish, Flintshire*, Richard Willett, Chester, 1822, p.3-4. Hence RW.
30. *Cheshire Sheaf*, (10,091), February 1956. (No. 670 William Salt Collections 1924). R. V. H. Burne cites the Great Register of Lichfield Cathedral.
31. For a full list see WBJ, vol.1.

2: The Seventeenth Century.

1. *Learning, Law and Religion. Higher Education and Welsh Society c 1540–1640*, W. P. Griffith, UWP, 1996, p.169
2. For Colonel Whitley see *Royalist Officers of North Wales in the Civil War*, Norman Tucker, Gee & Son, Denbigh,1961, p.64.
3. Much of this information is derived from the Ravenscroft entry in *The Dictionary of Welsh Biography*, Hon. Society of Cymmrodorion, London, 1959.
4. R. Morris, 'The siege of Chester', *Journal of the Chester and North Wales Architectural, Archaeological and Historic Society*, vol. xxv, p.43.

5. quoted from Sir E. W. Gladstone *Hawarden Old Castle.*

6. ibid.

7. *Civil War in Wales and the Marches*, J. Roland Phillips, Longmans Green, 1874, vol.ii, p.114.

8. Gladstone op cit.

9. Phillips op cit.

10. See *North Wales in the Civil War*, Norman Tucker, Bridge Books, Wrexham, 1992, p.93 and more particularly, *My Firelocks use not to parley — Hawarden Castle in the English Civil War*, Peter Francis-Wemyss, Jacobus Publications, Newtown, pp. 11–12.

11. Cowan op cit. p.70.

12. *The Place Names of East Wales*, Hywel Wyn Owen, p.64 and p.67.

13. ibid., p.65.

14. WBJ, ii, p.311.

15. WBJ, ii, p.301

16. E.C. R. Brinkworth, ed. R. K.Gilkes, *'The 'Bawdy Court' of Banbury: the Act Book of the Peculiar Court of Banbury 1625-1638*, The Banbury Historical Society, vol 26(1997), p.16–17.

17. Some are in the National Library of Wales, Aberystwyth, others in the Flintshire Record Office, Hawarden.

18. Dorothy Sylvester, 'Settlement patterns in rural Flintshire', *Flintshire Historical Society Publications*, vol. 15, 1954–55.

19. ibid., p.24.

20. ibid., p.26.

21. W. Bell Jones, Moore Deeds, 1089: 1464, a Rental. 1091 a Compotus Roll, 1474, *Flintshire Historical Society Publications*, vol. 7p. 26f.

22. ibid.

23. 'The Account Roll of Thomas Stanley, Earl of Derby, 1477', FRO D/DM/426.

24. *Exchequer Proceedings concerning Wales in temp. James I*, ed. T. I. J. Jones (Cardiff, 1955) p.204.

3: The Eighteenth Century

1. W. Bell Jones, 'Hawarden in the past', *Cheshire Sheaf*, March 1925, vol. xxii (5186).

2. *The Journeys of Celia Fiennes*, ed. Christopher Morris, London Cressett Press, 1947, p.179

3. *A Journey to Edinburgh in Scotland*, Joseph Taylor of the Inner Temple, 1705. Published 1905. FRO P/28/1/231.

4. quoted WBJ p.127.

5. P. G. D. Thomas, 'Sir George Wynne and the Flint Borough Elections of 1727 to 1741', *Flintshire Historical Society Transactions*, vol. 20 p.51.

6. *Politics in eighteenth-century Wales*, P. G. D. Thomas, UWP, 1998, p. 6.

7. W. B. Whittaker, *The Glynnes of Hawarden*, printed for the Chester and North Wales Architectural, Archaeological and Historic Society, 1906, p.24-5.

8. WBJ p.119.

9. John Cornforth, 'Hawarden Castle Flintshire, *Country Life*, June 15, 22 and 29, 1967. 22 June, p.1609.

10. ibid. 15 June 1967 pp.1518–19.

11. Whittaker op cit. p 27.

12. Clwyd Powys Archaeological Trust Regional Sites & Monuments Record 22956. Hawarden Castle, garden.

13. Quoted by Whittaker op cit. p. 28 from the Neville MS.

14. *Country Life*, June 29, 1967, p.1676.

15. A detailed account of the interior of Hawarden Castle is given in the *Country Life* articles and in Hubbard op cit.

16. CADW listed building report ref. no. 11/A/113 (13).

17. See Calendar of Deeds and Documents, vol.iii, The Hawarden Deeds,(1306), Aberystwyth, 1931.

18. CADW listed building report ref. no. 11/A/9 (17).

19. Bryn Ellis, Quarter Sessions Records for Hawarden and Mold, 1747–1799, *Buckley Society Magazine*, vol.21 p.15.

20. ibid. p.20.

21. K. Lloyd Gruffydd, 'Take food for the famine of your household', *Buckley Society Magazine*, vol.15.

22. op cit. p.57.

23. E. R. Harries, 'Two Hawarden Documents of 1746-7', *Flintshire Historical Society Publications*, vol.15 p.64–68.

24. K. Lloyd Gruffydd, 'Crime and punishment in the parish of Hawarden during the eighteenth century', *Buckley Society Magazine*, vol.25.

25. George Crabbe, Works, edn. 1834 vol.11, pp.83–4.

4: Coalmining

1. This section relies on K. Lloyd Gruffydd 'Medieval Coalmining in Flintshire', *Buckley Society Magazine*, no.1 1970 and 'The development of the Coal Industry in Flintshire to 1740', by K. Lloyd Gruffydd M.A. thesis 1980.
2. See R. Rees Rawson, 'The Coal-Mining Industry of the Hawarden District on the eve of the Industrial Revolution'. *Archaeologia Cambrensis*, xcvi, pt.ii, 1941.
3. Hawarden Deeds, nos. 1214, 1289.
4. Hawarden Deeds, no. 1314, and RW p.10.
5. Rawson p.124.
6. Rawson p.124.
7. *The History of the Parishes of Whiteford and Holywell*, Thomas Pennant, London, 1796, p.189
8. For railways and tramways in the parish of Hawarden see, *The Wrexham, Mold & Connah's Quay Railway*, James I. C. Boyd, Oakwood Press, 1991, passim.
9. ibid. p. 15.
10. RW p. 105.
11. Boyd p. 18.
12. Boyd p. 22.
13. C.C. 28 June 1862.
14. C.C. 6 December 1856.
15. FRO D/HA/973
16. FRO D/HA/980
17. C.C. 30 July 1870.
18. *The Gladstone Diaries* 23/10/1869, edts. M. R. D. Foot, H. C. G. Matthew, Clarendon Press, Oxford, 14. vols 1968 - 1994.
19. The Hawarden Events Book 1909. FRO NT 823.
20. ibid. 1926
21. FRO D/HA/1128.
22. *Mining Journal*, 2 December 1871.
23. C.C. 17 August 1872.
24. Boyd, p.335.
25. C.C. 14 February 1874.
26. See *Gladstone Diaries* 9/6/1874, C.C. 13 June 1874 and *The Denbighshire Historical Society Transactions*, xix, p.201.
27. C.C. 27 October 1894.
28. C.C. 25 February 1910.
29. C.C.27 October 1906.
30. See Shotton chapter.
31. C.C. 8 September 1888.
32. C.C. 22 October 1892.
33. C.C 7 1873.
34. C.C. 11 July 1863.
35. C.C. 31 May 1890.
36. Hawarden Events Book FRO NT 823.
37. C.C. 6 Jan. 1872.
38. See Sandycroft chapter.
39. C.H. 29 July 1887.
40. FRO D/DM/973.
41. C.H. 29 August 1890.
42. C.H. 4 November 1887

5: Hawarden Village

1. J. B. Lewis, 'The Honourable the Very Reverend George Neville Grenville (1789–1854), *Buckley Society Magazine*, vol.19 p.30.
2. RW p.124.
3. *The English School. Its Architecture and Organisation, 1370–1870*. Malcolm Seaborne, RKP, London 1971, p.139.
4. FRO D/DM/1079.
5. FRO D/BJ/445.
6. FRO D/BJ/G44. Benjamin Gummow, architect, Ruabon, worked at Wynnstay, Eaton Hall, Nerquis Hall, Chirk Castle, St. Asaph Cathedral, etc.

7. FRO D/BJ/445.

8. FRO D/BJ/G44.

9. ibid.

10. FRO D/BJ/445.

11. ibid.

12. ibid.

13. RW p.124f.

14. See under Broughton.

15. Hubbard op cit.p.369.

16. WBJ, p.20.

17. FRO D/BJ/445.

18 Gladstone Diaries 25/7/1839.

19. Glynne/Gladstone MS. 2002, Hawarden Castle Events Book.

20. A. G. Veysey, Sir Stephen Glynne, 1807–4, *Flintshire Historical Society Journal*, vol.30, p.161.

21. *Hawarden Parish Magazine,* 1873.

22. *Gladstone Diaries*, Jan. 1848.

23. ibid. 4/10/1850.

24. *The Dairy of Lady Frederick Cavendish,* ed. John Bailey, London, 1927, 2 vols, vol.1, p.58.

25. C.C. 19/7/1856.

26. *Hawarden Parish Magazine,* 1872.

27. Hawarden Events Book, FRO G/G 2002.

28. C.C. 26/3/1892.

29. C.C. 16/6/1900.

30. C.C. 8/4/1905.

31. *Pigot's Directory,* 1828.

32. FRO D/BJ/495.

33. Hywel Wyn Owen, op cit., p.34.

34. ibid., p.68.

35. C.C. 22/1/1881.

36. C.C. 19/9/1908.

37. C.H. 31/8/1888.

38. C.H. 27/4/1888.

39. C.C. 18/9/1875.

40. C.C. 11/8/1877.

41. C.C. 22/9/1877.

42. C.C. 4/5/1878.

43. See account of under Shotton.

44. *Manchester Guardian,* 5/8/1889.

45. C.C. 26 May and 2 June 1888.

46. *Mary Gladstone (Mrs Drew) Her Diaries and Letters edt Lucy Masterman* , 1930 p. 419. For the Institute see A. G. Veysey, 'Hawarden Institute', *Annual Report County Archivist,* 1986, Clwyd County Council.

47. C.C. 27/5/1893.

48. C.C. 1/8/1893.

49. For a detailed history see A. G. Veysey, 'The History of Hawarden Institute', 1993.

50. See under Queensferry.

51. Mr and Mrs Gladstone an intimate biography, Joyce Marlow, London 1977, p.289.

52. The Hawarden Events Book FRO G/G 2002.

53. Based on the report in *The Graphic,* 4/6/1898, p.690.

54. *Catherine Gladstone,* Mary Drew, London 1919, p.287–8.

55. June 17 1898.

56. *Edward Burne-Jones,* Penelope Fitzgerald, London, 1975, p.278.

57 Some Hawarden Letters 1878–1913 written to Mrs Drew chosen and arranged by Lisle March-Phillipps and Bertram Christian, London, 1917, p.298.

58 Hubbard, op cit. p.366.

59 *William G. C. Gladstone. A Memoir.* Viscount Gladstone, 1918, p.31.

60. C.H. 23/4/1915.

61. For a full account see T. W. Pritchard, 'The Reverend S. E. Gladstone (1844-1920)', *Flintshire Historical Society Journal*, vol 35 1999.

62. For an account of F. S. M. Bennett see *The Cathedral 'Open and Free' Dean Bennett of Chester*, Alex Bruce, Liverpool Univ. Press, 2000.
63. C.C. 7/6/1902.
64. C.C. 17/6/1903.
65. See W. Bell Jones, 'The Hawarden Grammar School', *Flintshire Historical Society Publications*, vol.9. and *A concise description of the endowed grammar schools of England and Wales*, Nicholas Carlisle, vol.ii, London, 1818. p.928–31.
66. *Calendar of Wynn Papers*, The National Library of Wales, 1926, no.642 (1613/14) Feb.16.
67. See Carlisle, p.930.
68. *Cheshire Sheaf* ,October 1934 (6492), quotation from Gores General Advertiser (Liverpool) 5/1/1815.
69. Report of the Commissioners of Inquiry into the State of Education in Wales, pt .iii, 1847,p.91.
70.Report of the Charity Commissioners, Flintshire, 1893.
71. C.C. 20/5/1899.
72. Education Commissioners Report. op cit. p.93.
73. C.H. 20/9/1912.
74. C.C. 11/4/1863.
75. C.H. 28/9/1888.
76. Hawarden Events Book FRO NT 823.
77. C.H. 14/2/1919.
78. C.H. 25/1/1918.
79. Hawarden Events Book FRO NT 823.
80. ibid.
81. C.H. 23/1/1920.
82. C.H. 2/6/1922.
83. *Mold Deeside & Buckley Leader*, 8/5/1925.
84. John Jones, 'A History of Tŷ Mam Duw', FRO NT 1626.
85. C.H. 22/8/1930.
86. C.H. 27/5/1932.
87. See *The Story of the Ordination Test School, 1918–41*, R. V. H. Burne, SPCK, 1960.
88. C.C. 7/7/1900.
89. C.H. 27/11/1927.
90. C.C. 11/9/1909.
91. The Hawarden Events Book FRO NT 823.
92. C.H. 11/2/1927.
93. C.H. 14/10/1927.
94. Hawarden Events Book FRO NT 823.
95. C.H. 18/7/1930.
96. See *Hawarden Cricket Club Centenary Souvenir*, 1966, box 2a, FRO.
97. C.C. 9/4/1870.
98. C.C. 13/8/1870.
99. C.H. 13/7 1934 & 23/7/1937.
100. ibid.

6: Modern Broughton and Bretton.

1. Hywel Wyn Owen op cit. p.44.
2. FRO D/LA/2, 5, 8.
3. Copies of the award were lodged with the churchwardens of the parish of Hawarden (to be deposited in the parish chest), and with the Clerk of the Peace for the County of Flint.
4. See under John Oates in *A Biographical Dictionary of British Architects 1600–1840*, 3rd ed. Howard Colvin, Yale, 1995.
5. W. F .J. Timbrell, 'The mediaeval bedposts in Broughton Church', *Transactions of the Historic Society of Lancashire and Cheshire*, vol.66, 1914.
6. See *Church Plate of the St.Asaph Diocese*, Maurice H. Ridgway, Gee & Son, Denbigh, 1997, under Broughton.
7. C.C. 23/6/1877.
8. FRO NT/598.
9. FRO N/31/15.
10. C.C. 11/6/1887.
11. C.C. 3/1/1903.

12. Quoted in *St. Mary's Church Broughton and Bretton. The first 175 years*, Vic Roberts, 1999 p.59.
13. FRO NT 1933.
14. C.C. 9/2/1935.
15. C.C. 10/4/1937.
16. See FRO D/DM/856/3.
17. See *Action Stations 3. Military Airfields of Wales and the North West* (Hawarden p. 85f.) David J.Smith, Patrick Stephens Ltd., 1981.
18. See *Broughton from Wellington to Airbus*, Norman Barfield, Tempus, 2001, p.75.

7: Modern Ewloe

1. *Primitive Methodist* magazine 1863.
2. C.C. 11/5/1895.
3. FRO N/59/1.
4. FRO N/59/2.
5. See C.C. 20/3/1937 & 17/9/1938.
6. See 'Castle Hill Brewery Ewloe', Paul Mason, Clwyd County Council, *Annual Report of the County Archivist*, p.16–20.

8: Modern Mancot

1. *The Deeside Regional Planning Scheme. Chester and Flintshire.* P. Abercrombie, Sydney Kelly and Theodore Fyffe, Univ. Press Liverpool, 1923.
2. Report of the Commissioners Inquiring into the State of Education in Wales,1847, pp.95–6.
3. C.H. 18/4/1913.
4. *Mold Deeside & Buckley Leader*, 14/12/1923.
5. C.H. 12/7/1929.
6. Hubbard op cit. p.420.
7. I am grateful to Mrs Sylvia Roberts for allowing me to see her work on Mancott Presbyterian Church.
8. C.H. 5/9/1924.
9. See FRO D/DM/306 'History of Mancot', compiled by the W. I., editor. I. Beck.
10. ibid.
11. Hywel Wyn Owen op cit. p.86–7.
12. *Hawarden Parish Magazine*, Sept. 1883.
13. ibid. Dec. 1894.

9: Pentrobin

1.FRO N/31/4.
2. C.C 18/4/1874.
3. C.C. 23/3/1878.
4. See booklet for Mount Tabor Chapel Penymynydd, J. Malcolm Brown and Leslie Piercy, 'Upon this Rock. A history of Methodism in Penymynydd from 1824 to 1974'. FRO N/62/49.
5. FRO N/81/2.
6. For this discussion I am indebted to D. R. Thomas, W. Bell Jones and E. Hubbard.
7. For further information see *Church Plate of the St. Asaph Diocese*, Maurice H. Ridgway, Gee & Son, Denbigh 1997.

10: The Making of the River Settlements

1. *England's Improvements by Sea and Land*, Andrew Yarranton, 1677.
2. George Lloyd, 'The Canalization of the River Dee', *Flintshire Historical Society Publications*, vol.23, p.36.
3. P. M. Cohen, 'History of Water Management on the Welsh River Dee', Phd. thesis, Univ. Manchester Faculty of Technology, 1968, p.61.
4. Thos. Boydell, Surveyor, map of lands & premises belonging to the River Dee Company between Chester and towns of Flint and Parkgate, 1770–1.
5. *History of the Parishes of Whiteford and Holywell*, Thomas Pennant, London, 1795, p.189.
6. CPAT report no. 266.

7. FRO D/P/340.
8. DM/5302.
9. *Cheshire Sheaf*, (7123), xxxi June 1937.
10. General View of the Agriculture and Domestic Economy of North Wales, Walter Davies, 1810, p.259.
11. General View of the Agriculture of Flintshire, G. Kay, 1792.

11: Queensferry

1. Hywel Wyn Owen op cit. p120-1.
2. 14/10/1852.
3. C.C. 15/5/1835.
4. C.C. Sept. 1835.
5. FRO S/1.
6. *The Gladstones. A family biography 1764–1851*, S. G. Checkland, Cambridge UP, 1971, p.315.
7. *The London Illustrated News*, 15 Aug. 1857.
8. C.C. 10/3/1860.
9. C.C. 2/8/1842.
10. C.C. 7/5/1853.
11. C.C. 17/2/1872.
12. C.C. 10/10/1883.
13. C.C. 8/3/1884.
14. C.C. 26/4/1890.
15. C.C. 26/7/1890.
16. C.C. 1/10/1839.
17. C.C. 11/2/1854.
18. C.C. 31/5/1844.
19. *Annual Report of the County Archivist*, 1987, Letters from Benjamin Bithell of Wepre, 1843–6, P. F. Mason, pp. 24–6.
20. FRO D/HA/582.
21. Boyd op cit. p.29.
22. C.C. 4/2/1842.
23. C.C. 27/1/1843.
24. RW p.108 c1822.
25. FRO D/DM/1440/1.
26. FRO D/GL/90.
27. C.C. 5/5/1855.
28. C.C. 20/10/1860.
29. FRO D/DM/1400/1.
30. FRO NC/239.
31. C.C. 5/6/1897.
32. FRO D/GL/221/5.
33. ibid.
34. C.C. 13/2/1904.
35. C.C. 25/5/1901.
36. C.C. 3/1/1903.
37. C.H. 22/2/1924.
38. C.C. 1/9/1906.
39. *Flintshire News*, 1/12/1911.
40. *Flintshire Observer*, 1911.
41. FRO D/DM/1036.
42. C.H. 6/7/1888.
43. C.C. 25/5/1889.
44. C.C. 12/5/1894.
45. C.C. 6/10/1894.
46. C.C. 11/9/1897.
47. C.C. 19/2/1898.
48. C.C. 6/4/1907.
49. C.C. 20/9/1907.

50. See D/DM/1036/1 op cit.
51. C.H. 23/7/1909.
52. *The Flintshire Observer*, 2/6/1911.
53. *Mold Deeside & Buckley Leader*, 6/7/1923.
54. See *Cambrian Coasters*, R. S. Fenton, World Ship Society, Kendal, 1989, p.157.
55. ibid. pp.164–8.
56. See FRO D/GL/4.
57. C.C. 15/12/1900.
58. *Pioneers of Modern Design*, Nikolaus Pevsner, Penguin Books, 1960, p.237.
59. C.C. 14/4/1906.
60. C.H. October 1914.
61. C.H.2/10/1914.
62. FRO D/HA/1336.
63. Mancot Circular, 1918
64. C. S. Robinson, 'Biography of Kenneth Bingham Quinan', The Chemical Engineer, November 1966, p.291 (quoted by George Lloyd D/GL/221/5).
65. Entry in *The Dictionary of National Biography 1951–1960*.
66. C.H. 25/1/1924.
67. C.H. 18/2/1916.
68. The Diary of Miss G. M. West, 20 Dec. 1916 to 5 Jan. 1917, Imperial War Museum, DD 77/156/1.
69. FRO D/HA/540.

12: Sandycroft

1. RW p.106.
2. An advertisement in the *Railway Times*, 10/7/1847.
3. C.C. 9/10/1846.
4. ibid.
5. C.C. 16/4/1847.
6. Most of this account is taken from the *Chester Chronicle*.
7. C.C. 28/7/1855.
8. 'The Launch', passages from the English note-books of Nathaniel Hawthorne, vol.1 , p.280, London, 1870.
9. ibid. pp. 282–3.
10. C.C. 2/9/1856.
11. C.C. 29/10/1859.
12. *Illustrated London News*, 28/1/1860.
13. *Mining Journal*, 2/12/1871.
14. C.C. 24/9/1887.
15. C.C. 2/1/1909.
16. C.C. 5/1/1901.
17. FRO D/HA/1502.
18. C.C. 25/8/1877.
19. C.C. 5/8/1876.
20. C.C. May 1899.
21. C.C. 17/2/1900.
22. FRO P/28/1/254.
23. C.H. 1/11/1912.
24. *Hawarden Parish Magazine*, 1912.
25. C.C. 3/2/1883.
26. C.C. 29/8/1908.

13: Saltney and Saltney Ferry

1. C.C. 2/10/1858.
2. FRO NT 903.
3. c.c. 5/11/1847.
4. C.C. 5/9/1857.

5. C.C. 13/10/1860.
6. C.C. 28/8/1875.
7. ibid.
8. C.C. 2/10/1858.
9. C.C. 26/7/1862.
10. FRO D/DM/434/99. *Oil Shale & Cannel Coal*, Institute of Petroleum, 1938, H. P. Giffard.
11. 'The Flintshire Oil and Cannel Co. Ltd., 1864–72. G. S. O. Rippon, pp.1–5.
12. C.C. 11/11/1865.
13. C.C. 29/11/1874.
14. C.C. 6/4/1895.
15. C.C. 5/7/1884.
16. C.C. 28/2/1891.
17. C.C. 14/4/1894.
18. C.C. 6/2/1897.
19. C.C. 7/7/1894.
20. See F.R.O. D/DM/328/6.
21. *The Times*, Industrial Wales section, 6/12/1924.
22. *Saltney & Saltney Ferry Magazine*, 1988, Brian Clark.
23. *Journal of Commerce*, 29/3/1924.
24. *Journal of Commerce*, 9/8/ and 2/9/1926.
25. *Journal of Commerce* (shipbuilding and engineering supplement), 4/12/1924.
26. *The Shipbuilder*, March 1925.
27. *Journal of Commerce*, 15/7/1924.
28. C.H. 27/9/1929.
29. *Saltney & Saltney Ferry Magazine*, vol. ii, 1989, Ted Edwards.
30. ibid. D. Cartwright.
31. ibid. Helen Whitmore.
32. See C.C 21/7/1877 and 3/9/1887.
33. ibid. 1877.
34. ibid. 1877.
35. *Land and Society in England, 1750-1980*, G. E. M. Mingay, London, 1994, p.197.
36. C.C. 28/11/1874.
37. C.C. 6/9/1851.
38. C.C. 2/10/1852.
39. C.C. 8/10/1853.
40. C.C. 6/1/1855.
41. C.C. 12/7/1856.
42. C.C. 17/11/1900.
43. *Saltney & Saltney Ferry Magazine*, 1989, J. H. Reece and K. Roberts.
44. See C.C. 23/3/ and 9/11/1878.
45. C.C. 10/9/1870.
46. C.C. 25/7/1874.
47. FRO E/LB/58//4.
48. FRO E/LB/58/8.
49. C.C. 25/3/1854.
50. C.C. 8/3/1862.
51. C.C. 13/3/1869.
52. C.C. 17/10/1868.
53. C.C. 15/2/1873.
54. C.C. 21/1/1882.
55. Printed and published for gratuitous circulation.
56. C. J. Williams, 'The Dee Bridges and Ferries', *Clwyd County Council Annual Report County Archivist*, 1985.
57. 'Industrial Railways and Tramways of Flintshire' J. R. Thomas and M. Griffiths, pt.1, The Mold Railway, Archive No. 14 June 1997 p.36.
58. Information provided by Mr. J. Lowe.
59. FRO E/LB/58/12 1891-1955.
60. *Saltney & Saltney Ferry Magazine*, 1989, John Heady.

61. ibid. Mena Booth.
62. ibid. N. Shallcross.

14: Shotton

1. C.C. 13/8/1887 and C.H. 19/8/1887.
2. George Lloyd, *Cheshire Sheaf* (no.11, 121), 15/11/1963.
3. FRO D/GL/104.
4. C.H. 9/8/1889.
5. On the sleeve of *The Summers of Shotton*, Brian Redhead & Sheila Goodie, London 1987.
6. C.C. 5/10/1895.
7. C.C. February, 1896.
8. C.C. 3/10/1896.
9. C.C. 12/12/1896.
10 Hubbard, op cit, p.421.
11. C.C 28/8/1897.
12. C.C. 24/8/1901.
13. C.C. 15/10/1904.
14. C.C. 3/9/1904.
15. C.H. 23/8 and 11/10/1912.
16. For the Strike see *A History of the British Trade Unions since 1889,* vol.1, H. A. Clegg, Alan Fox, A. F. Thompson, Oxford, 1964 pp.446–8. *History of the British Steel Industry*, J. C. Carr and W. Taplin, Havard 1962 pp.282–4, and newspaper reports.
17. C. H. 22 and 29 March 1910.
18. See *History of Rivertown Congregational Church 1897–1947*.
19. C.C. 5/6/1897.
20. C.C. 30/7/1898.
21. C.H. 30/6/1899.
22. C.C. 21/1/1882.
23. C.C. 2/8/1890.
24. C.C. 16/10/1897.
25. *Hawarden Parish Magazine*, June 1898.
26. C. C. 17/9/1898.
27. C.H. 29/5/1908.
28. C.H. 26/10/1928.
29. FRO FC/2/10 inspection 6 March 1908.
30. C.H. 7/1/1910.
31. C.H. 10/1/1910
32. FRO FC/2/13, 31/7/1912.
33. FRO FC/2/15, 16/9/1912.
34. *The V.C.s of Wales and the Welsh Regiments*, W. Alister Williams, Bridge Books, Wrexham, 1984, p.88–9.
35. C.H. 10/1/1919.
36. *Mold, Deeside and Buckley Leader*, 6/5/1927.
37. See *Mold Deeside & Buckley Leader*, 2/10/1924.
38. C. H. 1/5/1931
39. *It was my privilege*, Huw T. Edwards, Gee & Son Denbigh, 1957.
40. *Mold, Deeside & Buckley Leader*, 18 & 25 June 1926.
41. C.H. 28/8/1931.
42. See *A Century of Shotton Steel (1896–1996)*, Gordon Smith, British Steel Strip Products.
43. *Mold, Deeside and Buckley Leader*,7/9/1923.
44. ibid. 29/12/1922.
45. C.C. 7/1/1939.
46. C.H. 5/7/1929.
47. C.H. 28/8/1931.
48. C.C. 2/3/1935.
49. C.H. 30/7/1909.
50. C.H. 1/3/1929.

51. C.H. 13/3/1931.
52. C.C. 10/7/1943.
53. op. cit.
54. ibid. p.50.
55. ibid. p.51.
56. ibid. p.55.
57. See 'Facing up to redundancy — a case study on Shotton', S. C. Newton, MBA degree-thesis, 1981 (seen at FRO).
58. Gordon Smith, op cit., p.71.
59. These notes were written in 1959 by George Lloyd, see FRO D/GL/110.

15: Sealand and Garden City

1. FRO D/BJ/345.
2. C.C. 3/9/1887.
3. C.C. 17/4/1937.
4. C.C. 30/1/1943.
5. C.H. 8/3/1907.
6. Quoted in the C.H. 22/7/1910.
7. C.H. 30/9/1910.
8. C.C. 27/3/1987.
9. FRO PC/61/1.
10. FRO D/BJ/390.
11. C.C. 2/9/1865.
12. C.C. 19/10/1867.
13. C.C. 25/9/1869.
14. ibid.
15. See also *The History of the Diocese of St. Asaph*, D. R. Thomas, Oswestry, 1908 (under Hawarden), and Hubbard, op cit. (under Sealand).
16. *Mold, Deeside and Buckley Leader*, 24/6/1927.
17. *Flintshire Observer*, 24/11/1911.
18. C.H. 21/1/1916.
19. FRO FC/2/12.
20. FRO/FC/13.
21. FRO FC/2/16.
22. This section depends on *A History of Royal Air Force Sealand*, Aldon P. Ferguson, Merseyside Aviation Society Ltd, 1978; *Action Stations 3*, David J. Smith, Patrick Stephens Ltd, 1981; *Wings Across the Border — a history of avaition in North Wales and the northern Marches*, Vols. 1 & 2, Derrick Pratt and Mike Grant, Bridge Books, Wrexham, 1998 & 2002.

Sources

1. Manuscript collections
    Flintshire Record Office
    Census returns
    Education records
    Nonconformist records
    Shipping records
    Bell Jones MSS
    Hawarden estate MSS
    Ordnance Survey records

2. Principal Journals
    Annual Reports County Archivist
    Archaeologia Cambrensis
    Buckley Society Magazine
    Cheshire Sheaf
    Journal of the Chester and North Wales Architectural, Archaeological and Historic Society
    Denbighshire Historical Society Transactions
    Flintshire Historical Society Publications (Journal from 1977-8)
    Transactions of the Historic Society of Lancashire and Cheshire
    The Mining Journal

3. Official publications
    Report of the Commissioners of Inquiry into the State of Education in Wales, 1847
    Report of the Commissioners concerning Charities County of Flint, 1890
    Endowed Charities (County of Flint), 1897 and 1899
    CADW listed buildings
    Clwyd Powys Archaeological Trust sites and monuments record

4. Books
    These are given in the text notes

5. Newspapers
    Chester Chronicle
    County Herald
    Flintshire News
    Flintshire Observer
    Illustrated London News
    Mold Deeside & Buckley Leader

6. Photographic collections
    Clwyd Powys Archaeological Trust
    Flintshire Record Office
    The Right Honourable William Ewart Gladstone and Hawarden Castle and Village. A series of original photographs taken between 1889 and 1898, Robert Banks, Manchester & London, 1898